THE IRISH HEDGE SCHOOL AND ITS BOOKS

To Kenneth, Sharon and Lauren

The Irish Hedge School
and Its Books,
1695–1831

ANTONIA McMANUS

FOUR COURTS PRESS

Set in 10.5 on 12.5 point Ehrhardt for
FOUR COURTS PRESS LTD
7 Malpas Street, Dublin 8, Ireland
http://www.fourcourtspress.ie
and in North America
FOUR COURTS PRESS
c/o ISBS, 920 N.E. 58th Avenue, Suite 300, Portland, OR 97213.

First published 2002
First paperback edition 2004; reprinted 2006; 2011

A catalogue record for this title
is available from the British Library.

ISBN 978-1-85182-812-8 pbk

Printed in Great Britain
by Antony Rowe Ltd, Chippenham, Wilts.

Contents

Illustrations

Acknowledgments

I wish to express my thanks and appreciation to a number of individuals and institutions who assisted me throughout the course of my research, and in the preparation of this book. Firstly, I would like to acknowledge the advice and guidance given by Ms S.M. Parkes of the Education Department, Trinity College, Dublin and the support of Professor J.V. Rice of the Department of Higher Education and Research, Trinity College, Dublin and that of Professor Aine Hyland of University College, Cork.

As a number of colleges and libraries have facilitated this research, I would like to thank the library staff in the following: Trinity College; the National Library of Ireland; the Royal Irish Academy; Marsh's Library; the Royal Dublin Society Library; the National Archives; the Russell Library; Carlow County Library; Church of Ireland College of Education; Queen's University, Belfast; the Ulster Folk & Transport Museum; and Belfast City Library. As most of my research was carried out in the National Library of Ireland I wish to express my sincere gratitude for the efficient and courteous service rendered to me during this time.

I value greatly the generous assistance I have received from the following historical and archaeological societies: the Meath Archaeological & Historical Society; North Mayo Archaeological & Historical Society; the Old Dublin Society; Old Bray Society; Wicklow Historical Society; Roscommon Historical & Archaeological Society; Kildare Archaeological Society; Laois Heritage Society; Old Athlone Society; Armagh Historical Society; Belfast Historical Society, West; and the Mid-Antrim Historical Group.

I wish to acknowledge the courteous assistance of Michael Adams and the staff at Four Courts Press, and of Ms Liane Donnelly who typed this work. I would like to acknowledge the invaluable support and enthusiasm of my family for this work and in particular that of my son Kenneth. Finally, I wish to thank my husband Ken, to whom this book is dedicated.

Introduction

This book follows in the footsteps of P.J. Dowling's scholarly work, *The hedge schools of Ireland.*[1] Dowling was clearly influenced by his teacher Timothy J. Corcoran, professor of theory and practice of education in University College Dublin. It was he who gave the first two glowing accounts of hedge schools in his publications of 1916[2] and 1928.[3] However, Dowling avoided the worst excesses of his mentor, as he showed a willingness to acknowledge the contribution to Irish education of the leading Protestant voluntary education society of the nineteenth century. This was the Society for promoting the Education of the Poor of Ireland, otherwise known as the Kildare Place Society. Corcoran, on the other hand complained long and bitterly of the Society's worst excesses in the *Irish Monthly*, from December 1931 to November 1932.

Dowling's account is impressive for his encyclopaedic knowledge of educational history, his grasp of pertinent historical detail and his appreciation of Irish and Anglo-Irish culture. The main weakness in his work is his non-critical view of the hedge schoolmasters. This is apparent from his understating of the role played by some masters in the secret oath-bound society of Whiteboys (1760-80). This was an agrarian movement involved in rural violence, mainly perpetrated against tithe proctors and landlords.[4] It is evident also from his failure to refer to the fact that one of the first leaders of the sectarian revolutionary movement of Defenders (1790s) to be hanged in September 1795 was a hedge schoolmaster called Lawrence O'Connor from Gallow, Summerhill, Co. Meath.[5] The known involvement of several high-profile masters in the Society of United Irishmen and in the 1798 rebellion was also passed over in Dowling's account. He was also too ready to dismiss the genuine concerns of conservative members of society, such as the commissioners of education of 1806 and 1825, bible society members and contemporary writers who were horrified by the reading books on robbers,

1 Dublin, 1932.   2 T. Corcoran, *State policy in Irish education, 1513–1816, exemplified in documents* (Dublin, 1916).   3 T. Corcoran, *Education systems in Ireland from the close of the middle ages* (Dublin, 1928).   4 J.S. Donnelly, 'The Whiteboy movement 1761–5' in *Irish Historical Studies*, 22: 81 (March, 1978), p. 40.

highwaymen and prostitutes which were allegedly supplied by parents to their
children who attended the hedge schools.

Other postgraduate students who came under Corcoran's spell were the
future Maynooth professor of education, the Reverend Martin Brenan whose
Schools of Kildare and Leighlin AD 1775–1835[6] appeared in 1935 and Philip
O'Connell, later principal of the Central Technical School in Clonmel, Co.
Tipperary who published *The schools and scholars of Breiffne*[7] in 1942. Brenan
reproduced important primary source material in the form of parochial returns
for the seven counties, many of which comprised the diocese of Kildare and
Leighlin.[8] These were distributed nationwide in 1824 to Protestant and
Catholic clergymen, at the request of the commissioners of education. The
returns required the clergymen to specify the numbers and types of schools
in their respective parishes and to list the books used in those schools. On reading these returns one might well wonder, what all the consternation was about,
regarding inappropriate books in hedge schools, as a vast range of literary and
academic books was listed, not to mention a staggering number on religion and
related matters. The main flaw in Brenan's work was his partisan outlook. He
made no attempt whatsoever to disguise his antipathy to all educational institutions and societies which competed with the indigenous schools.

O'Connell gave a most interesting account of the hedge schools which
stretched from Donegal bay to Cavan, north-west Leitrim and a small section of counties Meath, Fermanagh and Sligo. Like his predecessors O'Connell held fast to the belief that the native schools and their masters were
beyond reproach. He condemned unequivocally and vociferously those he
considered to be their enemies – establishment figures such as 'tyrannical
landlords and fanatical parsons'.[9] The one-sided nature of his account is obvious from his failure to acknowledge the humanitarian efforts of 'improving'
landlords, members of the Dublin Society, and of a number of Protestant
bishops and clergymen who worked tirelessly for the poor.[10] It is clear also
that he had little tolerance of his opponents' viewpoints. Anthony R. Blake,
one of the commissioners of education of 1825, discovered this to his cost
when O'Connell described him memorably as 'a contemptible specimen of a
Castle Catholic', a 'weak-kneed and cringing sycophant and a consistent opponent of the claims of the Catholic schools'.[11]

In more recent times, regional studies have been conducted of hedge
schools in the northern counties of Tyrone and Monaghan, and the western
county of Roscommon. Both I.D. Johnston's 'Hedge schools of Tyrone and

5 Rev. J. Brady, 'Lawrence O'Connor, a Meath schoolmaster' in *Irish Ecclesiastical Record*, 49,
(Jan–June, 1957), p. 286.   6 Dublin, 1935.   7 Dublin, 1942.   8 Op. cit. Counties Carlow, Offaly,
Laois, Kildare, Kilkenny, Wicklow and Wexford constituted the diocese of Kildare and Leighlin.
9 O'Connell, *The schools and scholars*, pp 358–9.   10 C. Maxwell, *Country and town in Ireland
under the Georges* (Dundalk, 1949).   11 Op. cit., pp 358–9.

Monaghan' (1969)[12] and James Hoban's 'The survival of the hedge schools –
a local study' (1983)[13] have informed this research. The present study outlines
elementary education provision in Ireland from the late-seventeenth to the
mid-nineteenth centuries and draws on the most recent educational research.
Much has been written on the historical and social setting for this period by
contemporary writers and historians and the writer draws extensively from this
rich source also.[14] The primary source for this work consists of the original
textbooks and reading books used in Ireland's hedge schools for over a century. An exact readership figure for any of these books cannot be ascertained nor
can it be stated that every hedge school contained a set of standard textbooks
or reading books. Nonetheless the widespread use of textbooks can be shown
for the hedge schools in the diocese of Kildare and Leighlin, from an examination of the parochial returns. The returns show also that the books were an
eclectic mix of the popular literature of the eighteenth century, and they reflect
the diverse literary tastes of the Irish at this time.

By far the most popular books were the chapbooks. These were crudely
produced works, printed on coarse durable paper, containing between eight to
thirty pages, usually illustrated from rough woodcuts. They were termed
'chapbooks' from 1824. Previous to this they were called 'Burton books' after
the name of a printer or bookseller who supplied them.[15] Their original cost
was a mere halfpenny, but eventually they became more expensive and came to
be called 'sixpenny books'.[16] Such was the demand for the chapbooks that four
Dublin booksellers were engaged in printing them exclusively in 1825. One
bookseller had four presses in operation, publishing some 50,000 books annually. Other presses were located in Cork, Limerick, Belfast and Galway. From
all these sources, it was estimated that the circulation of chapbooks grew to
about 300,000 per annum.[17] Irish chapbooks were mostly pirated versions of
English originals. They owed their existence to a thriving reprint industry
which had developed in this country between the years 1740 and 1800, due to
an oversight in the Copyright Act of 1709, which excluded Ireland from its
provisions.[18]

The commissioners of education in 1825 reported that the 'books which
were easily and cheaply to be procured were those naturally preferred by the
children and their parents'.[19] They also supplied a list of all the books found

12 *Clogher Record* (1969), pp 34–55.   13 *Irish Educational Studies*, 3:2 (1983), pp 21–34.   14 The
social history of the period is largely drawn from twenty three statistical surveys (1801–33), travellers' accounts (1764–1846), contemporary Irish poetry and modern research by social and economic historians. For details see Antonia McManus, 'The groves of Academus: a study of hedge
schools and their reading books'. PhD thesis, Trinity College, Dublin, 2000.   15 Biblio., 'Irish
chap books' in *Irish Book Lover*, 2 (Feb. 1911), p. 110.   16 J. Warburton, J. Whitelaw and Robert
Walsh, *History of the city of Dublin* (London, 1818), p. 1814.   17 Op. cit.,   18 R.C. Cole, *Irish
booksellers and English writers, 1840-1800* (London, 1986).   19 First report of the commission-

in 'the common schools', drawn up from the parochial returns for four counties, representing each of the four provinces – Donegal, Kildare, Galway and
Kerry, to serve as a specimen of the whole. Ninety two books were classified
under the heading *Religious* and two hundred and ninety nine under the heading *Works of entertainment, histories, tales etc.* Of the total number of three
hundred and ninety-one books listed,[20] only a dozen came in for repeated criticism by education commissioners, evangelicals and conservative groups in
Irish society.

This study provides a critical appraisal of a selection of these controversial
books to include books of criminal biographies such as *The life and adventures
of James Freney, commonly called Captain Freney*[21] and *Irish rogues and rapparees,*[22] works of entertainment such as *Fair Rosamond, mistress to Henry II and
Jane Shore concubine of Edward IV,*[23] and the perennially popular chivalric
romance *The seven champions of Christendom*[24]. Many of these books were
wrongly ascribed to a juvenile readership when in fact they were never intended for children, while others were clearly unsuitable for young readers but
were hardly likely to have led them to a life of 'lawless and profligate adventure, to cherish superstition, or to lead to dissension and disloyalty'[25] as successive commissioners of education had predicted.

Concern for the moral well being of the young reader was behind the three
attempts in the late eighteenth and nineteenth centuries to either supplant or
suppress the 'offensive' chapbooks. The first to undertake such a task was a
bible society suitably named the Association for discountenancing vice and
promoting the knowledge and practice of the Christian religion (1792), which
published the 'excellent tracts of Hannah More' (1745–1833). It was hoped
that they would serve as an antidote to the chapbooks which the association
believed 'were of the most immoral kind and inculcated principles the most
pernicious'.[26] They did not however, supplant the chapbooks but they did
complement them. A selective sample of More's tracts[27] is scrutinized in this
study to highlight the fact that moral tales also formed part of the reading
material of children at elementary level, a fact never acknowledged or possibly even recognized by critics of hedge schools.

The book subcommittee of the Kildare Place Society made a more daring
bid to supplant the chapbooks by purchasing thirty seven of the offending

ers of Irish education inquiry 1825 (xii), p. 44.   20 First report of the commissioners of 1825,
App No. 221, pp 553–9.   21 Dublin, 1754.   22 J. Cosgrave, *A genuine history of the lives and
actions of the most notorious Irish highwaymen, tories and rapparees* (Belfast, 1776).   23 *The unfortunate concubines or the history of fair Rosamond, mistress to Henry II and Jane Shore, concubine of
Edward IV* (Dublin 177–).   24 R. Johnson, London, n.d..   25 Commissioners of Irish education inquiry 1806–12. Fourteenth report, p. 94. First report of the commissioners, 1825, p. 38.
26 Warburton et al., *History of the city of Dublin*, pp 888–91.   27 Rev. H. Thompson, *The life of
Hannah More* (Edinburgh, 1838). See D. Raftery, *Women and learning in English writing 1600–
1900* (Dublin, 1997), pp 74–86.

books[28] with a view to modelling their own replacement readers on them. From a brief analysis of these readers, it will become clear just why they couldn't possibly have hoped to compete with their more exciting rivals. In fact, the successful removal of chapbooks from elementary schools was achieved after a sustained effort over six years and then only after extreme measures were adopted by the commissioners of national education of 1831. They issued free sets of their lesson books to all national schools and reserved the right of refusal of any books they considered unsuitable. Compulsion was exercised by making teachers' promotion conditional upon their passing an examination on the contents of their lesson books.[29] A cursory look at a broad sample of the lesson books will be enough to show that had they been forced to compete in the open market place with the popular chapbooks, it is almost certain that they too would have suffered a similar fate to the Kildare Place readers, upon which they were so closely modelled in both form and content.

The hedge schools of Ireland provided education for students intended for the priesthood,[30] for service in the foreign armies, for trading on the continent or for employment at home. English reading books at a more advanced level than the chapbooks were therefore required. Once again it was parents who supplied the novels, manuals and periodicals to their sons and daughters and once again this was facilitated by the reprint industry which allowed enterprising Irish publishers to produce expensive English novels at affordable prices. A sample of these books is examined in this study.

From this selection, it would appear that the Irish had an appreciation of widely contrasting styles of writing, from the self-improving manuals of etiquette in courtship to the formal letter writing manuals, from the realistic novels of Daniel Defoe and the polished Augustan prose of Jonathan Swift, Joseph Addison and Robert Steele to the romances of intrigue of Aphra Behn (1640–89) and the decorous novels of Penelope Aubin (1707–39). However, it was the innovative novels of the four major contemporary novelists Samuel Richardson, Henry Fielding, Tobias Smollett and Laurence Sterne, which dominated the sixth decade of the eighteenth century.[31] These novels reached high literary standards and would have provided pupils in the hedge schools with challenging and interesting reading material.

In the third quarter of the century, the revolutionary climate in Ireland, as in many other European countries, let to the popularity of a type of literature which completely overturned the accepted literary conventions. This was the

28 List of Burton books dated 15 April 1819, KPS 11/23/31 in research area, C.I.C.E. Dublin. 29 Report from the commissioners of primary education (Irl.), 1870, Powis, p. 119. 30 Student priests, hopeful of gaining entry to one of the Irish Colleges on the continent, relied on the hedge schools for instruction in the classics. The first Irish seminaries were founded in 1793 in St Kieran's College, Kilkenny and St Patrick's College, Carlow. 31 E.A. Baker, *The history of the English novel* (London, 1929–35).

literature of terror or Gothic literature, which allowed for the portrayal of violent emotion and sadistic aberrant behaviour, as exemplified in the novels of Ann Radcliffe (1754–1823) and Matthew Gregory Lewis (1775–1818).[32] Radcliffe's novels in particular would have necessitated a highly advanced standard of reading and comprehension from pupils, as she quoted extensively from Shakespeare and Milton. It is questionable whether many pupils or indeed their parents, could possibly have overcome such obstacles to reading.

32 D. Punter, *The literature of terror* (London, 1996).

The historical and educational context, 1695–1831

Hedge school education, 'a kind of guerilla war'

The hedge schools of Ireland had their nascent period during the common-wealth when Oliver Cromwell (1619–58) was lord protector, and when, according to Cromwellian records of 19 March 1655

> *severall popish schoolmasters doe reside in severall parts of the Counties* of Meath and Lowth, and teach the Irish youth, trayning them up in superstition, idolatory and the evill customs of this Nacion.[1]

The hedge schools really only took root at the beginning of the eighteenth century, due to the strictures of the penal laws, which forced Catholic teachers to work underground. It was in the aftermath of the Williamite wars (1689–91), that the penal laws were considered necessary by the Irish parliament. Even though the Jacobites lost the war Protestants still felt vulnerable, being a minority group in Irish society. Their fears were heightened by the terms of the treaty of Limerick (1691) which concluded the wars, and which left Catholics in a stronger position than they had expected.[2] The Catholic landed interest had been left largely intact by the treaty and as land lay at the base of all political power, the harshest of the penal enactments were directed against Catholic property.[3]

Among the first of the penal laws to be enacted in 1695, during the reign of King William (1689–1702) were those against Catholic education. The title of the measure was 'An act to restrain foreign education'. No doubt the purpose of this act was to limit contact between Irish Catholics and their continental allies. There was also a domestic provision added on, forbidding any 'person whatsoever of the popish religion to publicly teach school or instruct youth in learning'.

1 Commonwealth Records, P.R.O. Ireland, A. 5.99, Dublin, March 19, 1655 in Corcoran, *Education systems of Ireland* (Dublin, 1928), p. 27. 2 D. Keogh, *Edmund Rice* (Dublin, 1996), p. 11. 3 P. J. Corish, *The Catholic community in the seventeenth and eighteenth centuries* (Dublin, 1981), p. 74.

Queen Anne's reign saw the continuation of the Williamite tradition of suppression of Catholics' education. In 1703, an act entitled 'An act to prevent the further growth of popery' (2 Anne c.6) stated;

> ... and if any person or persons being a papist, or professing the popish religion ... willingly suffer to be sent or conveyed, any child under the age of one and twenty years ... into France or any other parts beyond the seas ... shall incur the pains, penalties and forfeitures mentioned in an act made in the seventh year of his late majesty, King William, entitled An act to restrain foreign education.[4]

It would appear that Protestant schoolmasters colluded with their Catholic counterparts by allowing them to take up positions as ushers, under-masters and assistants in Protestant schools so that in 1709, during the eight year of the reign of Queen Anne, a further act was introduced called 'An act for explaining and emending an act entitled An act to prevent the further growth of popery' (8 Anne c.3) which warned

> Whatsoever person of the popish religion shall publicly teach school, or shall instruct youth in learning in any private house within this realm, or shall be entertained to instruct youth in learning as usher, under-master, or assistant by any Protestant schoolmaster, he shall be esteemed and taken to be a popish regular clergyman, and to be prosecuted as such.[5]

The purpose of these acts was not so much to reduce Catholics to a state of ignorance and servitude, as claimed by the nineteenth-century historian W.E.H. Lecky and by Edmund Burke but rather to force their children to avail themselves of the Protestant education already on offer, an education guaranteed to train them up to be loyal Protestant subjects. This didn't happen, because the initiative was seized by Catholic masters who ignored the law by conducting what Dowling, in his pioneering work on hedge schools described as 'a kind of guerilla war' in education, where the teacher was constantly evading the law officers.[6] Teaching was done surreptitiously and schools were hidden away from public gaze. The safest area was considered to be beneath the sunny side of a hedge, and it was from this location they derived their name. A pupil was usually placed on sentry duty to warn the master if a suspicious-looking stranger was approaching. Appropriate arrangements were then made to reconvene at another location on the fol-

4 H. Hislop, 'Voluntary effort and official enquiry 1791–1831' in Á. Hyland and K. Milne (eds), *Irish educational documents I* (Dublin, 1987), p. 48.   5 Ibid., p. 49.   6 Dowling, *The hedge schools of Ireland*, p. 48.

lowing day. During the winter months or periods of inclement weather, the master knew he could rely on the hospitality of the people, as he moved from one location to the next 'earning a little perhaps by turning his hand to farm work, or, when he dared, by teaching the children of his host'.[7]

The masters taught at considerable risk to their own personal liberty as there is ample evidence to show that prosecutions were brought against them, particularly during politically sensitive periods, such as the Jacobite scare of 1714.[8] Corcoran in his study of the penal era, listed nineteen indictments against popish schoolmasters brought before the Limerick grand jury alone, between 1711 and 1722. A schoolmaster who contravened the penal laws was liable to three months' imprisonment and a fine of twenty pounds. He could be banished to the Barbadoes, and if he returned to Ireland, the death penalty awaited him. A ten pound reward was offered for his arrest and a reward of ten pounds for information against anyone harbouring him.[9]

When the Irish parliament introduced the penal laws, it did so with the limited powers of a colonial parliament. It was hampered by the old Poynings' Law of 1494 which required that all proposed bills should be submitted to the British parliament at Westminster before a licence to summon parliament was issued. It was hampered also by an act of 1720, known as the sixth of George the first (6 George I c.5) which gave Westminster the right to legislate for Ireland.[10] The British parliament could therefore exercise the power to repeal these laws, when they wished, irrespective of the wishes of the Irish parliament. Corruption and bribery were common practices in both parliaments and through a crude system of pensions, preferments and political jobbery Westminster's lord lieutenant in Ireland, could force through any act in the Irish parliament.[11] However, the lord lieutenant spent only one winter in every two years in this country until 1767. During his long periods of absence the Irish parliament was ruled by two or three lord justices, one of whom represented the British interest, by a disreputable system of management, whereby votes were bought from the great Irish borough owners, known as 'undertakers', who, in return for a large share of the patronage of the crown 'undertook to carry the king's business through parliament'. The formidable ascendancy figure Hugh Boulter, archbishop of Armagh, 'a pure bred Englishman', was lord justice of Ireland thirteen times between 1724 and 1742,[12] while Ireland was ruled by English-born prelates up to 1764.

The Established Church occupied a privileged position in Irish society in the eighteenth century. It was 'a handmaid of the state' as the higher posi-

7 Ibid., p. 46.   8 W.P. Burke, *The Irish priests in the penal times 1600–1700* (1914; reprinted Shannon, 1969), p. 387.   9 P.J. Dowling, 'Patrick Lynch, schoolmaster 1754–1818', in *Studies* 20 (1931), p. 461.   10 J.C. Beckett, *The making of modern Ireland 1603–1923* (London, 1981), p. 51.   11 J. Kelly, 'The government of Ireland 1692–1785', in Sean Duffy (ed.), *Atlas of Irish history* (Dublin, 1997), p. 80.

tions in the church 'were reserved for the members of such families as the government wished particularly to reward'. Both the British government and Irish parliament regarded the Church of Ireland as a prime source of government patronage. It has been calculated that of the 340 episcopal appointments and translations during the eighteenth century, 239 went to Englishmen and 101 went to Irishmen thus lowering the morale and commitment of Irish bishops. While the purpose of the penal laws as they related to religion in particular, was supposedly the elimination of Catholicism and the conversion of the Catholic population to Protestantism, few historians to-day would agree that clergymen of the Church of Ireland, at the time, were in a position to engage in such a campaign of mass conversion or indeed that they even wished to. This was due to the status of the Church of Ireland, being the state church of a colony, its first duty was to secure British political ends and as Thomas Bartlett observed in *The fall and rise of the Irish nation*, the 'history of the Church of Ireland during the early eighteenth century is studded with glaring examples of non-residence, pluralities, ... Churches were in an acute state of disrepair, glebe houses lacking and tithe collection irregular'.[13] Besides lay Protestants didn't support their clergymen, a fact the bishops openly acknowledged. Bishop Woodward of Cloyne wrote that many Protestants 'discountenanced all religion by entirely neglecting public worship'. Archbishop King of Dublin admitted that Protestants didn't want mass conversion of Catholics:

> It is plain to me by the methods which have been taken since the Reformation, and which are yet pursued by both the civil and ecclesiastical powers, that there never was or is any design that all should be Catholics.[14]

Just as the Protestant laity had no desire for mass conversions, neither had the Protestant propertied or professional class; as Maureen Wall remarked 'few of the Protestant propertied or professional class in Ireland wished to see the masses of the people converted to Protestantism, since it was to the material advantage of the ruling class to keep the privileged circle small'.[15]

It was the clergymen of the Established Church who had a legal responsibility for education provision in Ireland in the eighteenth century and they fulfilled their legal obligations through a network of parish, diocesan and royal schools. These had been created in peacemeal fashion by successive parliamentary measures spanning the Tudor and Stuart eras. Like the penal laws, their aim was primarily one of conversion of Catholics to Protestantism. The

12 E. Curtis, *A history of Ireland* (London, 1968), pp 294 and 299.   13 Dublin, 1992, p. 27.   14 P. J. Corish, *The Irish Catholic experience. A historical survey* (Dublin, 1985), p. 125.   15 'The age of the penal laws (1691–1778)' in T.W. Moody and F.X. Martin (eds.), *The course of Irish history*, 3rd edn (Dublin, 1994), p. 226.

parish schools which were initiated during the reformation, in the reign of Henry VIII, were intended to provide mass elementary education, supervised by the Established Church clergymen. In an act of 1537 entitled 'An act for the English order, habit and language' they were required, on appointment to a benefice to take an oath that they would 'keepe or cause to be kept within the Place, Terratorie, or Paroch where he shall have Rule, Benefice or Promotion, a Schoole for to learne English'. The expected conversions as envisaged in the Tudor legislation didn't take place.[16] The extent of their failure is well illustrated in an investigation carried out in the 1780s, which revealed that there were only 361 operative parish schools teaching 11,000 children from a population of some four million.[17]

Next followed the diocesan schools which were introduced in the reign of Elizabeth I (12 Elizabeth c. 1), by an act passed in 1570 directing that a 'Free School' should be set up in every diocese. 'The Schoolmaster' was to be 'an Englishman, or of the English birth of this realm'. These were grammar schools intended to provide education for the middle classes, just as the parish schools were to have catered for 'the lower classes'[18]. The diocesan schools made little progress despite specific legislation passed in 1725 and 1755, aimed at encouraging the Church of Ireland clergymen and the grand juries to improve the system. By the late 1780s there were only 18 schools for 34 dioceses, catering for as few as 324 pupils. The third category consisted of the Free schools of royal foundation, set up during the reign of the Stuart kings James I (1603–25) and subsequently that of his son Charles I (1625–49), in order to anglicise the plantation counties of Ulster and elsewhere. James introduced them in Tyrone, Derry, Fermanagh, Cavan, Armagh and Donegal, while Charles introduced them in Banagher, King's County, Carysfort, Co. Wicklow as well as Clogher, Co. Tyrone. By the 1780s they had no more than 211 pupils. Their influence was therefore hardly felt.

In 1731 a house of lords committee was appointed under Archbishop Hugh Boulter, a man who was strongly committed to the idea of conversion, in order to inquire into 'The present state of popery'[19]. He was to be greatly disheartened by the findings of this report which revealed that the number of illegal schools or hedge schools was as high as 549, with as many as 45 in Dublin alone.[20] Wexford was unusual in that there was no 'popish schoolmaster' in or near the town, whereas the Protestant bishop of Killala stated in the report that in his diocese 'the popish schools are so numerous, that a Protestant schoolmaster cannot get bread'.[21] Returns from Armagh showed that

16 Hislop, 'The Kildare Place Society 1811–1831', p. 14.   17 Report from the commissioners of the board of education in Ireland: eleventh report, parish schools, p. 273, quoted in Akenson, *The Irish education experiment*, p. 24.   18 Dowling, *The hedge schools of Ireland*, p. 32.   19 Keogh, *Edmund Rice*, p. 36.   20 M.G. Jones, *The charity school movement* (Cambridge, 1938), p. 232. 21 E. Cahill, 'The native schools of Ireland in the penal era' in *Irish Ecclesiastical Record* 55

there were 157 Catholic schools in existence, which must have caused some surprise, coming from 'that part of Ireland which is best planted with Protestants and where popery is thought to be in the most languishing condition'[22]. The mayor of Cork, in his reply said that he failed to ascertain the number of Catholic hedge schools or popish schoolmasters because there was such an abundance of them. When Boulter submitted his own report, he stated that from Clonfert there was a hedge school in every parish. The report drew attention to the fact that there were more Catholic schools in operation but they proved impossible to identify as they were illegal.

Boulter's response to the alarming success of the hedge schools, despite being proscribed by law, was to mobilize support among the leading members of the ascendancy, both lay and clerical, to petition the British government to set up a suitable education system in Ireland, to instruct 'the children of the Irish Natives ... in the English tongue and the Fundamental Principles of the true Religion'.[23] Dorset, the lord lieutenant forwarded the petition to King George II (1727–60). In February 1733 the charter was granted and the Incorporated Society in Dublin for promoting English schools in Ireland came into existence, later to be known simply as the charter schools. The charter was signed by many powerful and influential ascendancy figures such as the lord primate, the lord chancellor, the archbishops of Dublin, Cashel and Tuam, six earls, five viscounts, twelve bishops, six barons and by over a hundred gentlemen and beneficed clergy.[24]

This marked the last serious attempt by the Protestant hierarchy at conversion. The society aimed to train the children in a Protestant environment to be thrifty and hard working by giving them a practical and religious education. By so doing they expected to 'rescue the souls of thousands of popish children from the dangers of superstition and idolatry and their bodies from the miseries of idleness and begging'.[25] The children were set to do manual labour in the charter schools, 'the boys in husbandry and agriculture ... and the girls in knitting, spinning, dairying and domestic work. In both cases they were to be put out to apprenticeship or service with a Protestant master or mistress at the society's expense';[26] but the greatest emphasis was placed on religious instruction and inducements were offered to deter Catholics from lapsing back into the 'errors of popery', for instance 'from 1748 a premium of £5 was given to those who completed apprenticeships and married a Protestant'. Eventually the conversion policy was taken to extreme lengths when a decision was taken to adopt a system of transplanting Catholic children to

(1940), p. 121.   **22** D. Kennedy, 'Popular education and Gaelic tradition in north east Ulster' in *Studies* 30 (1941), p. 274.   **23** Report made by his grace, the lord primate to the house of lords committee, pp 226–7, quoted in Jones, *The charity school movement.*   **24** Jones. *The charity school movement*, p. 235.   **25** op. cit.,   **26** K. Milne, 'The Irish charter schools: The grand design in principle and practice' in *Irish educational studies* 4:1 (1984), p. 42.

schools many miles from their homes, in order to eliminate parental influence and temptation.[27] This policy continued for over a century and caused deep resentment among Catholics. The charter schools were doomed to failure mainly due to a complex and inefficient administrative structure and lack of supervision. A litany of abuses was documented by eminent visitors to the schools, people such as John Wesley (1703–91) the founder of Methodism, and John Howard the philanthropist, who found the children in the hedge schools 'much forwarder than those of the same age in the charter schools'[28]. Sir Jeremiah Fitzpatrick, inspector-general of prisons visited twenty-eight charter schools in the year 1786–7, and he too recorded that children were under-nourished, poorly-clad, unhealthy and their instruction very much neglected.[29]

Throughout the second half of the eighteenth century the charter schools were practically deserted by Catholics. In 1776 the society maintained that its schools were responsible for 1935 children and its provincial nurseries for 400 more. In 1786 the number cited was 1710, but when a parliamentary authorized investigation was carried out two years later, the society's claim that it was responsible for 2100 pupils proved unsustainable.[30] According to the figures published by the commissioners of education for the years 1806–12 and 1824–7, the charter schools lost pupils to the hedge schools in very large numbers. One example would be the charter school at Newport, which was built to accommodate forty children, but which by 1824, contained only twelve pupils, as parents sent their children to the local hedge school, despite the fact that it was overcrowded. There were ninety-six children attending this hedge school, thirty eight of whom were Protestants.[31] Some thirty four schools were in operation by the Incorporated Society in 1824, enrolling over 2150 children but numbers continued to plummet so that by 1825 this number had fallen to 1099 and by 1830 was as low as 834.[32]

In contrast to the charter schools, the numbers in the hedge schools rose at an impressive rate. In his diocesan report of 1790 Bishop Patrick Plunkett of Meath noted 240 hedge schools in his diocese. This was a number which was not far short of what the general survey conducted in 1824 revealed, namely an average of six schools in each rural parish, with far more in the towns.[33] Likewise, in 1807, Dr Coppinger, bishop of Cloyne and Ross, drew up a list of 316 hedge schools in his diocese, which catered for 21,892 children, and this also came to an average of six schools in each parish.[34]

Nineteenth century historians were harshly critical of the charter schools. Lecky contended that they left a legacy of 'bitterness hardly equalled by any

27 Ibid., pp 44–5. 28 Dowling, *The hedge schools of Ireland*, pp 36–7. 29 First report of the commissioners, 1825, p. 25. 30 Ibid., p. 6. 31 Commissioners of Irish education inquiry 1806–12, p. 342. 32 Akenson, *The Irish educational experiment*, p. 36. 33 Corish, *The Irish Catholic experience*, p. 164. 34 I. Murphy, 'Primary education' in P.J. Corish (ed.), *A history of*

portion of the penal code'[35], while Froude called them 'a conspicuous and monstrous failure'[36]. Modern historians such as Akenson described the elaborate central administration of the charter schools as 'a Taj Mahal built on quicksand'[37] whereas Milne concluded that 'the charter schools were never intended to be places of horror, the prototypes of Dotheboy's Hall, that they so frequently became' but that it happened because the society was 'insufficiently aware of the existence within its own system of those very phenomena central to its purpose: the frailty of human nature and the prevalence of Original Sin'.[38]

Despite damning statistical data first gathered against the charter schools in 1787–8, the Irish parliament failed to hold the Church of Ireland responsible for their failure to supply mass elementary education and the parliament continued to provide state aid to the Incorporated Society from 1733 to 1831, to the tune of 'over one million and a quarter sterling in public parliamentary grants'[39]. It would take a powerful pressure group in the nineteenth century to change the status quo and force parliamentary change in Irish education, and the main contributors to it would be the Catholic hierarchy, a body set to grow in strength and influence throughout the eighteenth century despite being proscribed by the penal laws for most of the century.

The Catholic church, the penal laws and Catholic parish schools

The only penal laws which were rigorously enforced were those against Catholic land ownership. Penal measures against the Catholic clergy were contained in the Banishment Act of 1697 (9 William III, c.2), the 1704 act 'to prevent the further growth of popery' and the Registration Act of the same year (2 Anne c. 7).[40] The Banishment Act ordered all regular clergy and all clergy exercising jurisdiction to leave Ireland by 1 May 1698. The great majority went and the few who remained found protection in the provisions of the Registration Act. This act ordered all diocesan clergy to register with the civil authorities, to indicate the parish or parishes where they ministered and to provide two sureties of fifty pounds each for their continuing good behaviour. This had the effect of granting legal recognition to the Catholic diocesan clergy, and far from leading to the extinction of the church actually facilitated its re-emergence. Many regulars – members of religious orders registered as diocesan clergy and bishops as parish priests. The thriving state of

Irish Catholicism. The church since emancipation 5 (Dublin, 1971), p. 2.   35 *History of Ireland in the eighteenth century*, i (London, 1913), p. 234.   36 J.A. Froude, *The English in Ireland in the eighteenth century*, ii (London, 1872–4), p. 492.   37 Akenson, *The Irish education experiment*, p. 33.   38 K. Milne, *The Irish charter schools 1730–1830* (Dublin, 1997).   39 Brenan, *Schools of Kildare and Leighlin*, pp 111–12.   40 Corish, *The Irish Catholic experience*, p. 125.

the Catholic church was clear from the returns made in the 1731 *Report on the state of popery* which showed that almost every diocese had a bishop, clerical numbers had risen and mass houses continued to be built.[41]

The Catholic church had a keen interest in education, not just because of the conversion ambitions of the Established Church but because it was controlled mainly by hedge schoolmasters who operated private pay schools. The clergy kept a careful watch over what was happening in the indigenous schools, while at the same time attempting to establish their own system of Catholic parish schools. As early as 1730 the Roman Catholic diocesan statutes of Dublin required every parish priest to have a schoolmaster in his parish to teach Catholic doctrine.[42] However, it was only when the charter schools were established that the clergy really began to systematise their schooling. In 1742, John Kent in his *Report on the state of the Irish mission* recommended the establishment of a fund from which a sum could be paid annually to each bishop for the purpose of Catholic education. This suggestion was quickly acted upon by Rome and by the second half of the century, there was an effective parish school system over much of the country, controlled by the Catholic clergy.[43]

Detailed accounts of the diocesan visitations for Cashel in the 1750s show that in that town there were at least 73 schoolmasters teaching catechism. Records also show that in 1775 Cloyne had 117 parish schools and in 1787 Dublin had 40 with 1770 pupils, while Ferns in 1796 had schools in each parish, under the direction of the parish priest.[44] The episcopal visitations in Archbishop Butler's reports on Cashel show clearly the priority given to the school and the important role the schoolmaster played in parish life. In three instances it was stated that the school was held in the mass-house, showing the close co-operation between the priest and the master. In any event the archbishop regarded the 'schoolmaster as an object of his visitation equally with the priest. He was expected to teach the Catechism' and as P.J. Corish has observed, 'If he did not he was carpeted; if he could not he was instructed'.[45] With regard to hedge schoolmasters, the ecclesiastical regulations for Cashel (1810) and Dublin (1831) clearly stipulated that the parish priest had a general duty of supervision, with the right to visit the school, to see that the children knew the catechism and that the teachers taught it. He also had the right to ensure that the master was a man of good moral life.[46] Hedge schoolmasters needed the approval of the parish priest if they expected to survive in a competitive market; as Corish remarks, 'The private schoolmaster may not have needed his permission to open, but his disapproval might well have closed

41 Keogh, *Edmund Rice*, p. 13.   42 J.L. McCracken, 'The ecclesiastical structure, 1714–1760' in T.W. Moody and W.E. Vaughan (eds.), *A new history of Ireland. Eighteenth-century Ireland 1691–1800*, iv (Oxford, 1986), p. 95.   43 Keogh, *Edmund Rice*, p. 36.   44 Corish, *The Catholic community*, p. 102.   45 Ibid., p. 103.   46 Corish, *The Irish Catholic experience*, p. 164.

him down.'[47] Brenan, who conducted research on the schools of Kildare and Leighlin (1775–1835) based on an examination of the parochial returns compiled for this diocese in 1824, established 'that the teachers either were appointed directly by the priests – sometimes in conjunction with the parishioners – or where they set up schools of their own accord, they taught with the sanction and approbation of the priests, who visited the schools and superintended the instruction of the children'.[48] The returns show clearly that of a total of 657 schools mentioned, some 161 were subject to some degree of patronage or control at the hands of the local clergy, and in virtually all cases the school was a pay school.[49]

The Catholic church had little option but to avail of the professional services of the hedge schoolmasters because of the shortage of priests at this time, a situation which was exacerbated by a rapid increase in population. The population had risen by 80% between 1731 and 1800, but the number of priests only rose by 12%. There were 1587 Catholics to every one priest in 1731, compared to 2627 Catholics at the end of the century.[50] With every single Protestant school hoping to win over converts, and with so many lax practices in the Catholic church, following the penal laws, catechesis became the church's main priority.[51] Their main allies in this missionary work were the hedge schoolmasters who placed special emphasis on the teaching of religion in their schools. According to the parochial returns submitted to the education commissioners of 1825 by the various church clergymen, there were sixteen catechisms in all, used in the hedge schools of Counties Kildare, Donegal, Galway, and Kerry.[52] The parochial returns for the diocese of Kildare and Leighlin alone showed that there were twenty-five different religion books in use as well as twenty-six doctrinal and devotional books.[53]

The masters also played an important role in the Catholic revival movement known as the Confraternity of Christian Doctrine, which had its origin in the sixteenth century but which was re-established in most dioceses in the eighteenth century. Its members were expected to attend chapel every Sunday to instruct the children in catechism. Evidence was given before the education commissioners in 1825 that

> Several Roman Catholic schoolmasters are frequently employed for this purpose, under the direction of the Roman Catholic clergymen. The instruction is exclusively catechetical ... In the city of Limerick

47 Ibid., p. 165.   48 Brenan, *Schools of Kildare and Leighlin*, p. 62.   49 Daly, 'The development of the national school system, 1831–1840', p. 152.   50 S.J. Connolly, *Priests and people in pre-famine Ireland 1780-1845* (Dublin, 1982), pp 32–3; reissued in a new edition, Dublin, 2001.   51 Keogh, *Edmund Rice*, p. 15.   52 First report of the commissioners, 1825. App No. 221, p. 553. The parochial returns resulted from a nationwide survey of school provision in Ireland in 1824, ordered by the commissioners.   53 Brenan, *Schools of Kildare and Leighlin*, pp 67–8.

it occurred to one of the commissioners to witness on one Sunday upwards of 4,000 children collected in four chapels for this purpose, and in several parishes similar instruction is given on Saturdays as well as on Sundays.[54]

Dr Kelly, the archbishop of Tuam testified that such Sunday schools were widespread in Connaught, and Dr Doyle, the bishop of Kildare and Leighlin, proudly boasted, 'I am sure that there is no part of Ireland in which Sunday schools are more diligently attended to than in my diocese'. The parochial returns for his diocese would certainly bear this out, as well as the fact that hedge schoolmasters were members of the confraternity who gave of their services gratuitously, possibly in an effort to stay on friendly terms with the parish priest.[55]

Catholic bishops and native schoolmasters – the loyal and the disloyal

The two main players in the field of Catholic education were the Catholic church and the hedge schoolmasters, but they adopted very different political stances in the eighteenth century. The church decided to win favour with the government of the day and to remain consistently loyal to the English crown by working covertly with Dublin Castle, the seat of parliamentary power in Ireland. Some hedge schoolmasters, on the other hand, found loyalty to the government at variance with their nationalist views and their sense of grievance at perceived inequities in the law, and opted therefore for a more combative approach and later a subversive one.

A number of hedge schoolmasters had convictions for being active members of the Whiteboy agrarian movement. This secret oath bound society originated in Co. Tipperary in 1761, in protest against the enclosure of common land. The Whiteboys or Levellers as they were sometimes called, from the practice they engaged in of levelling fences, spread throughout much of Munster and south Leinster, where they opposed high rates of rent, evictions, and above all the hated tithes paid to the Established Church.[56] The defining characteristic of the society was a predilection for oaths binding their members to secrecy. According to J.S. Donnelly in 'country schoolmasters were prominent as organisers and penmen of secret societies'.[57] Although reliable evidence is scarce for the early part of the century one execution of a hedge schoolmaster was reported in *Faulkner's Dublin Journal* in 1763 for a Whiteboy crime committed by 'James Fogarty, alias Captain Fearnot' who was 'exe-

54 First report of the commissioners, 1825, p. 88.   55 Brenan, *Schools of Kildare and Leighlin*, pp 43–5.   56 Keogh, *Edmund Rice*, p. 24.   57 J.S. Donnelly, 'The Whiteboy movement, 1761–1765' in *Irish Historical Studies*, 21: 81 (March 1978), p. 40.

cuted at Clonmel in June 1763 for levelling the deerpark wall of the Tipperary squire John Chardin'[58]. The second wave of Whiteboy activity lasted from 1769 to 1776. In late March 1770, John Quin who kept a school near Kilkenny city was executed for engaging in acts of violence and for seriously wounding Patrick and William Shee of Thomastown. Another schoolmaster, William O'Neill of Borris 'was committed to gaol in November 1771 and charged with being a notorious Whiteboy'.[59]

The Catholic church, of which most Whiteboys were members, cast a very unfavourable eye on their activities. As Wall observed, 'Frequent excommunications of Whiteboys and members of other secret societies' served as 'proof of their sincerity'.[60] The bishops of Munster denounced the Whiteboys in a series of pastorals in the 1760s. In 1764 Bishop Burke of Ossory ordered his clergy to read on three successive Sundays and to explain in Irish, an instruction which, among other things counselled the Whiteboys

> If they think themselves grieved in any respect, they might be redressed by lawful ways and means. They ought to be amenable to the laws of the nation, and not provoke the government, which is mild beyond expression.[61]

This temperate admonition was in contrast to Bishop Troy of Ossory's 'Gothic excommunication of Whiteboys' in 1775, in which he condemned them to:

> Everlasting Hell … When they shall be judged, may they be condemned … may their posterity be cut off in one generation. Let their children be carried about as vagabonds and beg and let them be cast out of their dwellings. May the usurers search all their substance and let strangers plunder their labours. May there be none to help them, nor none to pity their fatherless offspring. May their names be blotted out … and let their memory perish from the earth. Let all the congregation say Amen, Amen, Amen.[62]

The Catholic church's political policy was occasionally guided as much by pragmatism as by diplomacy. This was evident in the decision taken by Archbishop O'Reilly of Armagh and six other bishops to address a letter to the Catholic clergy in 1759 asking them to pray for the king and royal family at every mass, and on the first Sunday of every quarter to read a declaration

58 Ibid.   59 James S. Donnelly, 'Irish agrarian rebellion: the Whiteboys of 1769–1776' in *Proceedings of the Royal Irish Academy* 83:12 (1983), p. 316.   60 M. Wall, *The penal laws 1691–1760* (Dundalk, 1967), p. 67.   61 Corish, *The Irish Catholic experience*, p. 140.   62 Keogh, *Edmund Rice*, p. 24.

denying the pope's deposing power and certain other 'odious tenets' imputed to Catholics. The prelates were hoping to ward off strict enforcement of the penal code because of the vulnerability of the British government, following the outbreak of the seven years' war between England and France (1756–63). Bishop Troy of Ossory became archbishop of Dublin in 1786 and he was set to become the church's representative in the political life of the country, a task he conducted with considerable skill and success. He took his place on the newly formed Catholic Committee (1760) along with the Irish gentry Lords Kenmare and Fingall to campaign for repeal of the penal laws.[63] For the first twenty years of its existence the Committee confined itself to making repeated declarations of loyalty to the British crown. However, in private discussions, held in the early 1770s Troy was perfectly capable of negotiating with Luke Gardiner (1745–98) for repeal of certain ecclesiastical and religious sections of the penal laws. Troy swore the papal nuncio to secrecy regarding these negotiations, on the grounds that he 'would not wish anyone to suspect that they treated of such things with a Catholic bishop'.[64] By the end of the century Catholic bishops, and Troy in particular, were to have regular contact with Dublin Castle and were to become accustomed to being consulted by the government.[65]

Repeal of the penal laws and the rise of the Catholic church

The penal laws against Catholic education were repealed by Gardiner's second relief act of 1782 in spite of the wishes of the Irish parliament. It was done because England was approaching the end of a war with France, Ireland's traditional ally, in an effort to discourage Catholics from finding common cause with the Volunteers.[66] This was an armed force set up in 1778 for the defence of the country and now politically active, championing reforms that included Catholic relief.[67] The Catholic education relief act was entitled 'An act to allow persons professing the popish religion to teach school in this kingdom, and for regulating the education of papists, and also to repeal parts of certain laws relative to the guardianship of their children' (21 and 22 Geo. III, c. 62).[68] In it came an admission of the failure of the penal laws:

63 Wall, 'The age of the penal laws', p. 227.   64 Bartlett, *The fall and rise*, p. 98. Luke Gardiner was an MP for Co. Dublin, 1773–89, who introduced measures for Catholic relief into the Irish house of commons, 1778 and 1782, which were partly carried.   65 T. Bartlett, 'The origins and progress of the Catholic question in Ireland' in T.P. Power and Kevin Whelan (eds.) *Endurance and emergence* (Dublin, 1990), p. 8.   66 Keogh, *Edmund Rice*, p. 19.   67 Corish, *The Irish Catholic experience*, pp 157–158.   68 Hislop, 'Voluntary effort and official enquiry', p. 60.

> Whereas several of the laws made in this kingdom, relative to the education of papists, or persons professing the popish religion are considered as too severe and have not answered the desired effect.

It allowed the establishment of Catholic schools, on receipt of a licence from the Protestant ordinary, but endowment of such schools was forbidden.[69] As Dowling observed, 'This was not a charter of liberty to teach. The schoolmaster was free to educate, but only on certain conditions,[70] while Akenson called it 'a new penal educational element' because 'no popish university or college' could be endowed and neither could Catholic schools.[71] However, Troy's secret negotiations with Gardiner now bore fruit under this act, as all secular clergy were allowed to perform ecclesiastical functions, though they were still prohibited from assuming ecclesiastical rank or titles, or to minister in a church with a steeple or bell. The Catholic church was now a legal body.

Further relief measures would not be introduced for another eleven years, when English domestic politics would make it expedient and necessary to do so. In the meantime the French revolution of 1789 had a profound effect on the political situation in Ireland. Reform movements north and south took inspiration from it. In July 1790 the Volunteers revived, and marched to celebrate the fall of the Bastille and in Belfast 'there was much talk of new clubs and alliances. The lord lieutenant, Westmorland, was aware that an alliance was being proposed between Catholics and dissenters in Belfast and this was confirmed for him by events which took place in the summer of 1791. The first phase of the alliance was brought about after the Belfast Volunteers' Bastille Day celebrations of 14 July 1791 when three resolutions were put forward by Wolfe Tone (1763–98), a young Protestant barrister and whig pamphleteer from Co. Kildare. The third one of Tone's resolutions called for the inclusion of Catholics in the political life of the country and while it was rejected at the time, the setback was only temporary.[72] Tone then published his 'masterpiece of journalistic propaganda'[73] a pamphlet entitled *An argument on behalf of the Catholics of Ireland*, in which he pointed out that it was only through a reform of parliament that England's stranglehold on Irish affairs could be broken, and that this parliamentary reform could only be won if Irish Catholics and Protestant dissenters united to bring about a reform programme that included Catholic emancipation. These views won wide acceptance among the Presbyterians and the radical thinkers of Belfast and Dublin, where numerous debating societies flourished. As a result Tone was invited to Belfast where in October 1791 he, along with Rowan Hamilton, founded the Society of United Irishmen. A month later the Dublin Society of the Unit-

---

69 Keogh, *Edmund Rice*, p. 19.   70 Dowling, *The hedge schools of Ireland*, p. 26.   71 Akenson, *The Irish education experiment*, p. 45.   72 J. Smyth, *The men of no property*, 1st ed. 1992 (Dublin, 1998), p. 56.

ed Irishmen came into existence. The aims of the movement reflected the influence of the French revolutionary principles of *liberté, egalité, fraternité*, only the United Irishmen hoped to achieve their aims by peaceful means and by uniting all Irishmen in a just cause, which was 'to abolish all unnatural religious distinctions and to unite all Irishmen against the unjust influence of Great Britain and to secure their just representation in a national parliament'.[74]

It wasn't long before members of the Catholic Committee had dual membership with the newly established radical Society of United Irishmen, much to the alarm of the conservative wing of the Committee. Lord Kenmare and Archbishop Troy were prompted to secede from the Committee on 17 December 1791, thus leaving the merchant class members of Keogh, McCormick and Byrne free to take a more forward line with the government, for the repeal of the remaining penal laws. It was widely believed at this time that the prime minister, William Pitt, and his colleagues in government were willing to make concessions to Catholics, partly because of the pope's persecution by the French revolutionaries and the Catholic church's strong condemnation of them. The British government also wished to lessen the 'prospect of the Catholics and the dissenters making common cause together', especially as war with France was a distinct possibility in 1792.[75] Westmorland was opposed to the granting of concessions to Catholics and he was supported by other members of the Dublin Castle administration such as John Foster, the speaker in the house of commons, and John Fitzgibbon, the Irish lord chancellor.[76] Pitt responded by granting the relief act of 1792, which allowed minor concessions to Catholics, but which were a far cry from the Catholic emancipation which they had expected. The act dealt mainly with the admission of Catholics to the legal profession but from the educational perspective it removed the 'obsolete act against foreign education, and the equally obsolete clause of the act of 1782, which made the licence of the ordinary necessary for Catholic schools.[77]

The Catholic Committee was insulted by these paltry concessions and responded quickly to the offensive remarks made by members of the Irish parliament that they were not representative of the Catholic body as a whole. They put plans in place to convene a 'Catholic convention' (an ominous title in which the French influence was clearly evident), in order to pressurise the British government to secure more relief. Westmorland and his allies were staunchly opposed to any such concessions but Pitt could hardly refuse a Catholic petition as England and France nudged closer to war – a war which was eventually declared in February 1793. In order to present a united front,

73 M. Elliott, *Partners in revolution* (New Haven and London, 1982), p. 22.   74 Curtis, *A history of Ireland*, p. 330.   75 Bartlett, *The fall and rise*, p. 132.   76 Bartlett, 'The origins and progress of the Catholic question in Ireland', p. 13.   77 Lecky, *History of Ireland*, p. 242.

when the committee would send its delegation to London, a reconciliation was brought about with the disaffected members of the committee, Lords Kenmare, Fingall and Archbishop Troy.

By November 1792 some twenty-five counties along with the main Irish towns and cities returned 233 delegates to the Catholic convention which was held from 3 to 8 December 1792, when it was decided to bypass Dublin Castle by sending five delegates, led by Tone, who was the assistant secretary of the Committee, to present a petition to King George III. The petition was presented to the king in January 1793 and Hobart's relief act followed. Hobart proposed to give Catholics the franchise both in town and in country on exactly the same terms as Protestants and to 'repeal the laws ... to authorise them to endow colleges, universities, and schools, and to obtain degrees in Dublin university'. This did not give the Catholic Committee or the United Irishmen what they were really looking for which was Catholic emancipation, that would have allowed Catholics to take seats in parliament.[78] Had that happened perhaps the rebellion of 1798 would never have occurred.

However, with regard to Irish Catholic education the future looked more promising. The Catholic church could now set about building its diocesan schools and seminaries. One year after the passing of the relief act of 1782, the first Catholic diocesan school was opened at St Kieran's College, Kilkenny. By 1793 the college assumed the responsibility of educating candidates for the priesthood for all the dioceses of Ireland. Similarly at Carlow, where St Patrick's College was founded as a secondary school in 1793, it too opened a seminary department soon afterwards. The growing confidence of the Catholic church was obvious from its foundation of schools for the upper classes as well as for the poor. Apart from the institutions of Carlow and Kilkenny the church could boast of ten further foundations before Catholic emancipation was conceded.[79] Catholic educational endeavours continued to expand rapidly, and by 1796 there were at least fifteen Catholic charity schools in Dublin. In 1797 the bishop of Waterford, Dr Hussey maintained a free school in each of the principal towns of his diocese.[80] The closing years of the eighteenth century saw the Presentation sisters, founded by Nano Nagle in Cork in 1791, open a school in Killarney in 1793, and in 1794 they began their work in George's Hill, Dublin and in Waterford in 1798. Brother Edmund Ignatius Rice and his congregation of Christian Brothers founded their first school in Waterford in 1802 and by 1820 the Christian Brothers had ten separate establishments in five dioceses. In 1825 the nuns had forty-six schools in the towns and the brothers had twenty-four.[81] Yet for the vast majority of

78 Lecky, *History of Ireland*, p. 252. Robert Hobart, afterwards fourth earl of Buckinghamshire was chief secretary for Ireland.   79 N. Atkinson, *Irish education* (Dublin, 1969), p. 58.   80 Murphy, 'Primary education', p. 1.   81 Corish, *The Irish Catholic experience*, p. 164.

Catholic children the fee-paying hedge school continued to be the main source of their education, a situation which was set to continue well into the nineteenth century. By 1824 an official commission calculated that there were 9000 'pay' schools in Ireland, which catered for almost 400,000 children, and most of these schools were hedge schools.[82]

The Catholic church was now facing an acute manpower shortage following the closure of the French seminaries, during the French revolution.[83] In November 1793 Troy met Hobart at Dublin Castle to urge the necessity 'of domestic education' for Catholic priests. He requested also that it should be 'subject only to their own ecclesiastical superiors'. The following month an address of loyalty was delivered to the lord lieutenant from the hierarchy, extolling the merits of 'the best of constitutions' under which they lived, and giving thanks for the relief act of 1793. Clearly this was not the position adopted by the Catholic Committee but this was a risk Troy was prepared to take. Political circumstances favoured the hierarchy on this occasion, as the war against France led to the formation of a coalition government in England in July 1794. It consisted of Pitt and his tory party and Lord Portland and the whigs. Westmorland was replaced by the whig Earl Fitzwilliam, who was known to favour Catholic emancipation. Catholic expectations ran high but unfortunately Fitzwilliam exceeded his instructions when he arrived in Ireland by unseating John Beresford (1760-1805) the commissioner of the revenue and Pitt's adviser. This reckless action resulted in his swift recall in late February 1795.

Following Fitzwilliam's departure tension mounted as rural disturbances escalated. The United Irishmen, banned since May 1794, sought French assistance and were now organising themselves along military lines. Under such trying circumstances and in defiance of Pitt's instructions to avoid giving concessions to Catholics, the new lord lieutenant Earl Camden decided to make a major gesture to the bishops by agreeing to the establishment of a Catholic seminary at Maynooth in 1795. Troy was well pleased and declared that he would 'very easily be able to negotiate' with the new administration. The proposed seminary was seen in London and Dublin as an acceptable substitute for emancipation, but few Catholics saw it that way.

The situation was now so volatile that within the space of three years it led to a bloody civil war. Camden now required the moral support of the Catholic hierarchy as he had to implement harsh law and order policies. A very appreciative clergy had no difficulty giving Camden the support he expected. Troy gave the lead by issuing a pastoral advising Catholics to maintain 'a peaceable demeanour and respectful obedience to the laws'.[84]

---

82 Graham Balfour, *The educational system of Great Britain and Ireland* (Oxford, 1903), p. 79.
83 Bartlett, *The fall and rise*, p. 192.   84 Ibid.

'Ministers of treason': the hedge schoolmasters

Involvement of hedge schoolmasters in the Whiteboys was clear for all to see by the number of convictions obtained against a small number of them. It would be reasonable to assume that they participated in other such secret societies in the eighteenth century, ones that closely resembled the Whiteboys with regard to aims and tactics employed. Take for instance the Hearts of Steel or Steelboys, who were active from 1769 to 1772, and whose activities were primarily aimed at the great south Antrim estate of the fifth earl of Donegall, they too agitated against rents, the demand for renewal of fines and local cess. Between 1770 and 1772 large areas of rural Ulster were rendered ungovernable by the activites of the Steelboys.[85] The parallels between the southern Whiteboys and the Steelboys were obvious, both employed threatening letters and nocturnal raids to pursue their objectives.[86] But the movement in which hedge schoolmasters were most likely to have been involved was the well organised, and confident Rightboy movement which originated in Cork in 1785 and which spread throughout Munster and south Leinster over a three year period. Their grievances were not new – tithes, cess, hearth tax, high rents, Catholic church fees and priests' dues, but the manner in which they laid down what they considered an acceptable schedule of tithes, rates and rents was new, so too was the assertive manner in which they challenged the Catholic church and their bishops.

The movement was unique also insofar as it had the support of some of the Protestant gentry, who were resentful of the payment of tithes to the Protestant clergymen. It was the practice for the Rightboys to seek public support for their schedule of rates by placing tables 'at the chapel doors with books laid on them' and 'to swear all the mass-goers' to adopt a publicly displayed schedule of tithes and priests' dues.[87] There was one bishop however who outwitted the Rightboys, this was the redoubtable Bishop of Troy, who on hearing that the Rightboys intended to administer their oaths in the chapels of the country, immediately ordered all the chapels of his diocese to be closed, thus leaving the population of Kilkenny without mass.[88] Eventually the Rightboys reached a compromise settlement with the clergy. Only educated men with organisational ability and good communication skills could have brought this about. It would therefore seem highly probable that hedge schoolmasters had an input into the Rightboy movement. Apart from the gentry, the precise social status of leading members was 'almost never mentioned in newspapers accounts of their committal'.[89]

85 W.A. Maguire, 'Lord Donegall and the hearts of steel' in *Irish Historical Studies* 28:84 (September, 1979), p. 351.   86 J.S. Donnelly, Jr., 'Hearts of oak, hearts of steel' in *Studia Hibernica* 21 (1981), p. 72.   87 Ibid.   88 Keogh, *Edmund Rice*, p. 25.   89 Donnelly, 'The Whiteboy movement', p. 149.

The level of violence used by these movements was limited and in the case of the Whiteboys, historians generally agree that the movement was 'unpolitical and unsectarian'.[90] The same could not be said of the Defender movement of the 1790s, in which hedge schoolmasters were known to have played a role. The Defenders had originated in Armagh in the 1780s as a non-denominational movement, formed to defend Catholics from attacks by militant Protestant groups such as the Nappach Fleet and the Peep O'Day Boys, who were in competition with them for land.[91] In 1792 this competition became acute because of the trade slump and Protestant attacks were revived in Armagh. However, it was as a sectarian Catholic body that Defenderism spread through fourteen different counties between the years 1792 and 1794. Most worrying for the authorities was the fact that as early as 1792, it was widely believed that the Defenders had made contact with French agents in London, with the intention of seeking help for a rebellion. They had also adopted a crude version of republican ideology independent of and antedating that of the United Irishmen movement.[92]

Camden was so alarmed by these events that he had a digest of material drawn up on their activities. It contained a list of Dublin Defenders, who were mainly tradesmen. For other parts of the country, the Defenders were described as 'poor, ignorant labouring men' and in many places it was noticeable that 'papist country schoolmasters' were prominent among them. They were characterised by a militant Catholicism or aggressive anti-Protestantism and a distinct anti-English and anti-settler ethos.[93] In Camden's digest it was recorded that the Defenders swore to 'quell all nations, dethrone all kings, and plant all true religion that was lost since the Reformation'. The digest also revealed their strong millenarian beliefs because their oaths and catechisms were filled with messianic and millenial hopes.[94]

The Defenders were also capable of acts of great savagery such as the one recorded of eleven revenue commissioners in Leitrim being cut to pieces by the local Defenders as they fled from a barn which was subsequently set ablaze. The government reacted by implementing counter-terror measures such as the show trials of 1794–5. It was no coincidence that a well-known leader of the Defenders, Lawrence O'Connor was apprehended on 12 July 1795. O'Connor was a hedge schoolmaster and on 1 September 1795 he was tried by Justice Finucane and found guilty of treason. He was then sentenced to be 'hanged, disembowelled, drawn and quartered'. On Camden's orders his head was cut off and impaled on an iron spike in front of Naas prison.[95] Camden's decision was no doubt prompted by the information supplied to

90 Smyth, *The men of no property*, p. 35.   91 Elliott, *Partners in revolution*, p. 40. The Peep O'Day Boys (1785) owed their title to their custom of visiting the houses of Catholics at daybreak in search of arms.   92 R.F. Foster, *Modern Ireland 1600-1972* (London, 1989), p. 272. 93 Bartlett, *The fall and rise*, pp 211–12.   94 Ibid., p. 212.

him by imprisoned Defenders and government agents such as Leonard McNally.[96] The Catholic church didn't voice any objections. In fact as early as December 1793 when Troy and the hierarchy submitted their address of loyalty to Westmorland, they 'expressed approval of the manner in which Defenderism had been suppressed'.[97] Now the ever vigilant Troy was well aware that O'Connor had filled the role of parish clerk in a Co. Meath village, and he therefore took it upon himself to write to the bishop of Meath Dr Plunkett to express his concern that the church should be seen to be associated with such a traitor and he advised Plunkett that 'by more caution in future on the part of the priests, the like surmises may be prevented'.[98] The show trials proved to be counter-productive and Camden was forced to admit that 'the speedy execution of offenders' and exemplary punishments made 'little impression on the multitudes'. Certainly O'Connor's execution had not the desired intimidatory effect judging from McNally's report that 'O'Connor's sufferings are considered a martyrdom'.[99]

A number of hedge schoolmasters were arrested during disturbances in Connaught in 1795 and were suspected by the authorities of acting as 'the principal Defender-makers'.[100] Meantime a west Ulster regional organiser of the Defenders earned something of a national reputation for himself in 1795. This was Arthur Donnelly, known as 'Switcher Donnelly', a dancing teacher from Tyrone, who was a Defender commander at the battle of the Diamond,[101] a battle which took place on 21 September 1795, at the crossroads near Loughgall, Co. Armagh, when the Peep O'Day Boys and others killed some thirty Defenders and afterwards formed themselves into the Orange Society.[102] According to a report in the *Dublin Evening Post* for 7 November 1795, Donnelly was capable of circulating like 'quicksilver' through the northern counties of Donegal, Tyrone, Antrim and Derry.[103]

The Catholic hierarchy both before and during the rebellion had been unremitting in their condemnation of the United Irishmen and the Defenders. Bishops Lanigan of Ossory, Dillon of Kilmacduagh and Moylan of Cork issued pastorals and addresses warning their flocks against insurrection and enjoining them to obey the laws of the land. In fact Portland was so impressed with Moylan's pastoral instructions that he recommended that they be translated into Irish and disseminated widely. Archbishop Troy had no hesitation in excommunicating all Catholics who took part in the rebellion. He also expelled nineteen seminarians from Maynooth College whose loyalty to the state was in doubt.

95 Bartlett, 'Select documents', p. 377.   96 Bartlett, *The fall and rise*, p. 226.   97 Ibid., p. 192.
98 Brady, 'Lawrence O'Connor', p. 282.   99 Bartlett, *The fall and rise*, p. 214.   100 Smyth, *The men of no property*, p. 115.   101 Ibid., p. 116.   102 Bartlett, *The fall and rise*, p. 216.   103 Smyth, *The men of no property*, p. 115.

The loyalty of some hedge schoolmasters to the state was equally doubtful. Many contemporary writers including T. Crofton Croker, the antiquarian and folklorist, Edward Wakefield, and William Shaw Mason were of this opinion. This view was shared by Judge Robert Day, who claimed that the United Irishman's 'army of advocates' included 'neglected apprentices, needy journeymen, seditious masters hoping to rule in the whirlwind' who 'familiarly discoursed on rebellion as the sacred birthright of the people'.[104] An anonymous pamphleteer, writing in 1799 referred to the disguise employed by some masters to spread the principles of the United Irishmen, or simply to pass on information. He claimed that rebellion 'was planted and cherished by means of active, artful emissaries dispersed thoughout the land, who worked in disguise and spread their doctrines in darkness and secrecy'.[105] There is more than a grain of truth in this claim, as the Cork scribe and hedge schoolmaster Micheál Óg Ó Longáin (1766–1839), who joined the United Irishmen in Cork in 1797, assumed the disguise of a poor scholar or student teacher, travelling Ireland with his satchel of books under his arm, when he acted as a courier for the United Irishmen.[106]

Contemporary writers such as Whitley Stokes were critical of the pernicious effects of the popular literature read in the hedge schools, for example chapbooks that romanticised the exploits of highwaymen and robbers, which Stokes alleged had a subversive sub-text.[107] Robert Bell, writing in 1806, considered the effect of 'rapparee literature' extremely dangerous, because he believed that 'the transition from theory to practice was but short'[108] but the popularity of the genre was merely a symptom rather than a cause of the lawlessness of the time. These books had been read in hedge schools for over twenty years prior to the 1798 rebellion, and the fact that they were still popular might well suggest the prevalence of attitudes favourable to Whiteboys, Defenders or United Irishmen.

A notable feature of the hedge schoolmasters who were involved in the United Irishmen was the calibre of master who enlisted. Without exception they were highly respected in the teaching profession. Richard MacElligott (1756–1818)[109] was an eminent Celtic scholar from Limerick who was arrested in 1798. The Belmullet, Co. Mayo poet, linguist and hedge schoolmaster Riocárd Báiréad (1739–1819),[110] was imprisoned for his membership of the United Irishmen and James Baggott (1771–1806),[111] called James O'Baggott as

104 Whelan, *The tree of liberty*, p. 77.   105 Ibid., p. 83.   106 T. Ó Donnchadha, 'Micheál Óg Ó Longáin', in *Journal of the Ivernian Society* 1 (July 1908–June 1909), pp 223–33.   107 Whelan, *The tree of liberty*, p. 82. Whitley Stokes (1763–1845) was a close friend of Wolfe Tone and an early United Irishman. He was a fellow of Trinity College who wrote a didactic critique of Paine's *The age of reason*.   108 Smyth, *The men of no property*, p. 41.   109 R. Herbert, 'Four Limerick hedge schoolmasters' in *Irish Monthly* (1944), pp 48–53.   110 T.F. O'Reilly, 'A song by Richard Barret' in *Gadelica* 1 (1912–3), pp 112–26.   111 Op. cit., pp 55–7. Baggott was a

a mark of respect for his considerable ability as a mathematician, was a Limerick hedge schoolmaster who was actively involved in the United Irishmen at the highest level. Other masters who offered the benefits of their learning and organisational skills to the movement were happy to remain anonymous to avoid the risk of being hanged, excommunicated or banished from their parishes.

The main reason why so many hedge schoolmasters became involved in radical political organisations was firstly because they were sufficiently well educated to understand the radical writings of Thomas Paine (1737–1809), Jean Jacques Rousseau (1712–78) and William Godwin (1756–1836), and their relevance to the Irish political situation. According to McNally the works of Paine were in the hands of 'almost every schoolmaster'.[112] This would correspond with the evidence given by the Presbyterian moderator, Henry Cooke before the 1825 commissioners of education that 'the works of Tom Paine and such writers were extensively put into the hands of the people. Paine's *Rights of man*, a political work, and *Age of reason*, a 'deistical' one, were 'industriously circulated'. He added, 'I am also inclined to believe that not a few of the schoolmasters were men of bad principles, who preferred any book to the Bible'.[113]

Secondly, hedge schoolmasters were independent of state control and to a certain extent of church control. While both bodies strongly disapproved of revolutionary activity, they had no authority over the schoolmasters who selected that course of action. It is likely that the masters were motivated to participate in the United Irishmen or the Defenders because of the resentment they felt at perceived inequalities. The resentment was all the greater because they saw themselves as inheritors of a proud cultural tradition, being the descendants of that learned class of poets who lived by the patronage of the old Gaelic chiefs. As Corish has noted, 'Some of the poets had been schoolmasters at an earlier date, when the learned classes still had a measure of patronage',[114] and in fact very many eighteenth and nineteenth century hedge schoolmasters were also Gaelic poets. Another historian Louis Cullen described them as the inheritors of 'the resentments of the leaders of the old Gaelic landed class'.[115] These ancient resentments easily fused with democratic French doctrines, which the United Irishmen had done so much to disseminate.

The United Irishmen were defeated in the 1798 rebellion but there was one area where they could claim victory and that was in the paper propaganda war. They made exceptionally good use of the written word, not only

personal friend of Lord Edward Fitzgerald, one of the leaders of the 1798 Rebellion. He often used Baggott's hedge school during his visits to the revolutionary centres in the area.   112 Smyth, *The men of no property*, p. 115.   113 First report of the commissioners, 1825. Examination of Henry Cooke, 5 January 1825, p. 820.   114 Corish, *The Irish Catholic experience*, p. 165.   115 L.M. Cullen, *The emergence of modern Ireland 1600-1900* (London, 1981), p. 236.

through a vast distribution network of radical literature, pamphlets, handbills and newspapers, but also through the publication of popular ballads. These appeared in such books as *Paddy's resource* and *The Irish harp new strung*. They succeeded in politicising the people or as one member, Thomas Addis Emmet explained, the United Irishmen sought to 'make every man a politician'.[116] However, this would have been impossible unless the people had the levels of literacy required to read such works, the credit for much of which must surely be attributable to the education they received in the hedge schools. Proof of high literacy levels are not scarce for the eighteenth century. In the 1790s there were fifty printers in Dublin alone, thirty-four provincial presses and at least forty newspapers. The strength of the Dublin and country book selling and publishing industry is borne out by the surge[117] in devotional literature in the late eighteenth century, both of which testify to the existence of a substantial literate population. More concrete evidence of literacy is provided by the 1861 census figures which reveal that 54% of Catholics could read and that 35% could both read and write. The age structure of the literate indicates that the percentage of the Catholic population which could read and write in the 1790s was lower – less than 50% but that it was steadily rising.[118]

Irish education in the age of the Enlightenment

After twenty years of agrarian violence in which hedge schoolmasters were known to have been involved, and in the wake of the French revolution which stimulated a rebellion in which hedge schoolmasters were known to have participated, it was to be expected that the question of Irish education provision would be moved close to the top of the political agenda. The question took on an added urgency as Established Church clergymen were failing in their duty to provide an acceptable education for the majority of the population as neither the parish, diocesan, royal or charter schools were attracting Catholic pupils. The first serious attempt to resolve the issue was undertaken by the chief secretary Thomas Orde (1746–1807). But just as he set himself the difficult task of unravelling the complexities of the Anglican school structure in Ireland, a 'massive intellectual movement ... known as the Enlightenment' began to dominate European educational thought.[119] The writings of the revolutionary French philosophers Rousseau and Helvétius and the writing of the English philosopher John Locke (1612–1704) had a major impact on political and social thought in Britain. Like Helvétius, Locke expressed the view in his book *Some thoughts concerning education* (1693), that all social classes were born with a mind that was blank and that they eventually became what edu-

116 Ibid., p. 5.   117 Whelan, *The tree of liberty*, p. 63.   118 Connolly, *Priests and people*, p. 28, p. 77.   119 Atkinson, *Irish education*, p. 64.

cation made them.[120] Education, they maintained should be open to all because educational advancement was essential to the attainment of social ideals. This liberal philosophy fitted well with the laissez-faire economics of Adam Smith (1723–90) and the utilitarian philosophy of Jeremy Bentham (1748–1832). The social philosophy of Smith and Bentham held that a more just and orderly society was best achieved by the interplay of free forces and they demanded education for all, to make them useful members of society. Such a philosophy was anathema to conservative evangelicals such as Hannah More and Sarah Trimmer (1741–1810) who were involved in the establishment and running of Sunday schools in England. They had no wish to change the class structure of society and they believed that libertarian doctrines would threaten social stability. Both the liberal and conservative philosophies would have a significant effect on official education policy in Ireland from 1787 to 1812, when elementary education provision would be put under close scrutiny through a succession of education inquiries.

Orde was the first chief secretary in Ireland to instigate an official investigation into educational provision, and he did so in 1786. He was fortunate to have the assistance of John Hely-Hutchinson, the provost of Trinity College, a man with a deep interest in educational matters. Hely-Hutchinson did a great deal of preparatory work in 1785 and presented Orde with a very important assessment of the deficiencies in the existing educational system. He informed Orde that the royal and diocesan schools required financial assistance, the charter schools needed 'looking into' and the parochial system could be greatly promoted by 'obliging every parish clergyman to keep such a school pursuant to ... statute'.[121]

By 12 April 1787 Orde was ready to present his educational plan to parliament, but before he did so he outlined the underlying philosophy behind his scheme. It was clear from this that he belonged to the conservative school of thought which urged the use of education for the pacification of Ireland. He announced that the education to be provided was to be a 'superior' Protestant education and in a speech which took up to three hours to deliver, he attributed 'all the violent and atrocious acts which had too often disgraced this nation' to a 'want of education'. He saw education as a means of infusing 'the balm of information into the wound of ignorance' and he argued that the voluntary participation of Catholics in such schools would disperse 'the mists of ignorance' and encourage their appreciation 'of the superiority of our own (Protestant) doctrines'.[122] On the positive side Orde viewed the education system as a whole and recommended a much more active role for the state in edu-

120 J. Lawson and H. Silver, A social history of education in England (London, 1973), p. 229.
121 J. Kelly, 'The context and course of Thomas Orde's plan of education of 1787' in Irish Journal of Education 20:2 (1986), p. 10.   122 Akenson, The Irish education experiment, p. 59.

cation provision, as well as an efficient system of inspection. Catholics were to
be given equality of treatment and admitted indiscriminately into the schools
but the schoolmasters would be Protestants. It was expected that in exchange
for the benefits such a system would bring the Established Church, that its
clergymen would now fulfil the educational duties, they had so long neglected.[123] Orde considered the abolition of the charter schools to make funds available for a more satisfactory system.[124] He hoped also to breathe new life into
the parish schools already in existence 'by requiring incumbents to make the
prescribed educational donations'.[125] He wished to create provincial schools
and to introduce new branches of education in the form of provincial and col-
legiate colleges. He proposed doubling the university sector, a suggestion
which was rejected by Hely-Hutchinson on the grounds that Trinity College
was legally 'the sole university of Ireland'. However, he seconded Orde's resolutions and called on parliament to implement them in the 1788 session.

This never happened. The three churches opposed Orde's plan and the
strongest objections came from the Established Church. They objected, not
just because of the burden of cost the church was expected to carry but
because of the proposed abolition of the charter schools, and the more active
role envisaged for the state in education supply. Many clergymen saw this as
an attack on the Established Church's rights in regard to education provision
and control. The Presbyterians objected because they had been campaigning
for some time for a Presbyterian university in Belfast and the Catholic church
objected but didn't comment publicly throughout 1787, as they were 'reluc-
tant to be seen to be critical of a chief secretary, not least one who harboured
suspicions of Catholics'.[126]

Orde's plan was never implemented and the chief secretary left office in
October 1787. The Irish parliament never discussed Orde's proposals possibly because of the regency crisis (1788) which occurred when George 3 suffered from a temporary fit of insanity.[127] Other reasons may have been the
impact of the French revolution, but more importantly the churches strong
opposition to the plan. Orde's successor, Alleyne Fitzherbert, faced with such
strong church opposition appointed a commission of inquiry to examine the
various officially sponsored schools in greater detail. Even though there were
seven commissioners appointed including Fitzherbert himself and John
Hely–Hutchinson, no report was published. A draft was reputedly ready in
late 1788 or early 1789, but no copy has survived. The commission's warrant
was extended until they could complete their work in 1791. This report was
never published either but later education commissioners had access to it.[128]

123 Ibid., p. 67.   124 Atkinson, *Irish education*, p. 65.   125 Akenson, *The Irish education experiment*, p. 65.   126 Kelly, 'The context and course', pp 17–21.   127 Foster, *Modern Ireland 1600-
1972*, pp 256–7.   128 Akenson, *The Irish education experiment*, p. 70.

Unlike Orde's plan, the 1791 report and a third one which issued following an education inquiry in 1799, showed clear signs of liberal enlightenment thought on education. The 1791 report criticised the inefficient way the parish schools were run and their failure to provide for the education of the poor. The commissioners proposed a non-denominational system of education, similar in many respects to the national system of education introduced in 1831. This report recommended, as Orde's did, that all students be admitted indiscriminately to the educational institutions and that the system be treated as a whole. Schools were to be administered by a central board of control made up of a number of commissioners with power to oversee the efficient running of schools. This would include the right to direct the plan of education to be pursued, and the right to obtain progress reports and the right to visit and inspect the schools. The most remarkable proposals made by the commissioners referred to a power sharing approach in education to include members of the Catholic hierarchy and lay Catholics. The governing body of each school was to consist of the local incumbent, churchwardens and four laymen, two Protestants and two Catholics. The incumbent was to share his formerly exclusive control over the parish school with a board of laymen, two of whom were to be Catholics. The radical suggestion was also made that the local Catholic priest was to have the right to visit the schools to instruct the children of his flock on religion, a right heretofore enjoyed by his Protestant counterpart only.[129]

The commissioners were not quite so generously disposed towards hedge schoolmasters. They intended that masters who were involved in violent movements and who taught from chapbooks with an alleged subversive content, be excluded from any new system. They desired that masters would have to undergo examination, receive certificates of morals and ability and be licensed annually. They required also that the books they used would be subject to inspection. The report was never published however and nothing ever came of the scheme. One reason suggested for the suppression of the report was that its findings, especially those in respect of the charter schools, were too damaging to be made public.[130]

Eight years lapsed before the next education inquiry took place, during which time the remaining Catholic education disabilities had been removed in 1792 and 1793. A Catholic seminary at Maynooth had been established in 1795 and from 1796 to 1798 the country was in a state of smothered civil war which eventually exploded into the rebellion of 1798. The government was pre-occupied with its administrative difficulties but the education question was re-opened by Richard Lovell Edgeworth, a known supporter of Rous-

129 Report of the commissioners of Irish education inquiry for the year 1791, published in H.C. 1857–8 (2336–11) 22:3, pp 343–4.   130 Op. cit., p. 71.

seau's liberal philosophy of child-centred education. He did so by attracting
attention to the subject of education by the publication in the autumn of 1798
of the three-volume work entitled *Practical education* and then by requesting
Westmorland, the lord lieutenant, on 8 February 1799, that the 1791 report be
laid before the house of commons. Following on this request, a select committee was appointed, with Edgeworth as chairman. They reported back
expeditiously and he introduced a bill to effect its recommendations on 28
March.[131]

Edgeworth's report didn't add any new thinking on educational structures.
It put forward a system of denominational education but with some favourit-
ism to be shown to the Established Church. It proposed that in schools attended by Protestants only or by Protestants and Catholics, the master would be a
Protestant but where schools consisted entirely of Catholics, a Catholic master would be appointed. This report acknowledged the right of Catholic children to a state aided system of education, which would see state grants for
Catholic schools and Catholic religious education. The bill was given a first
hearing in the house of commons but it didn't proceed any further, probably
due to the politics of the forthcoming Union.[132] The failure to implement any
of the reports was sufficient proof that the government was not quite ready to
accept the consequences of state supplied education which would inevitably
have involved a role for the Catholic church.

Irish education inquiry, 1806–12

From the moment the Act of Union was passed on 1 August 1800 the Irish
administration was fully accountable to the Westminster parliament. The lord
lieutenant, the council and the law courts still remained in Dublin, while the
legislature had been moved to Westminster. From the signing of the Act of
Union all concessions to Catholics ceased. Efforts to address the grievances of
the people were not even contemplated by the government even though social
and economic difficulties had worsened by the early nineteenth century. The
most pressing problem the people faced was the land question. There wasn't
enough land available to provide a living for a rapidly expanding population,
which reached five million in 1800 and rose to over six and a half million in
1821. Competition for land drove up rent prices and in the poorer regions in
the west of Ireland, where the population grew more rapidly, over dependence
on the potato led to the sub-division of holdings. The situation was worsened
by the local famines of 1817 and 1822.[133]

131 Hislop, 'Voluntary effort and official enquiry', pp 62–4.   132 Ibid.   133 D. Bowen, *The
Protestant crusade in Ireland, 1800–70* (Montreal, 1978), p. 178.

This severe hardship led to widespread rural unrest and a corresponding increase in secret societies with intriguing titles such as the Whitefeet, Blackfeet, Threshers, Carders, Caravats, Shanavests and Rockites who asserted the cause of the tenant against the landlord and the tithe proctor.[134] The government responded to every wave of disturbance by introducing a series of coercion acts, in order to suppress crime, a practice which continued for more than twenty years after the Union. The government also had at its disposal the services of 30,000 to 50,000 regular troops, 21,000 militia and numerous bodies of yeomanry, in the tense years following the rebellion; Sir Arthur Wellesley, the chief secretary, summed up the anxious mood of the government about the state of the country when he wrote in 1807, 'We have no strength here but our army. Ireland in a view to military operations must be considered as an enemy's country'.[135]

In the decades following the Union attention was paid to ecclesiastical discipline not just in the Catholic church but also in the Church of Ireland, with the primary abuses in both churches being curbed if not eliminated. In the case of the Church of Ireland, these reforms would be accompanied by an enthusiasm for evangelical work, sparked off by the influence of a Protestant religious revival movement in England. The most serious consequence of the Protestant religious revival or Second Reformation as it was called, was the appearance among British and Irish Protestants of a new enthusiasm for missionary work. Some Protestant denominations took the view that the rebellion merely served as proof of the need for a sustained missionary endeavour among the Irish peasantry. The events of 1798 convinced the Methodists that Catholics were disloyal and violent by nature and that Ireland would never be at peace until a mass conversion to Protestantism was effected. As early as 1799 they sent three Irish speaking missionaries to work among the Catholic population. By 1816 there were twenty one Methodist missionaries operating from fourteen stations in different parts of the country. Some other denominations got involved in missionary work such as the Church of Ireland missionaries who used the Irish language to convert Irish speaking Catholics. They formed societies like the London Hibernian Society (1806), the Baptist Society for promoting the gospel in Ireland (1814) and the Irish Society for promoting the education of the native Irish through the medium

---

134 Foster, *Modern Ireland*, p. 292–6. In Connaught the Thrashers became so formidable that, according to the charge of Chief Justice Bushe in 1806, the king's judges could not move through the country upon a special commission except under a military escort. The Carders got their name from the custom they had of flaying their victims with a wool-card. The Caravets were originally called the Moyle Rangers but when their leader Hanley was hanged with a caravet about his neck, they were since known as Caravets. The Shanavets got their name from wearing old waistcoats. See Alan O'Day and John Stevenson (eds.) *Irish historical documents since 1800* (Dublin, 1992), pp 26–7.   135 Ibid., p. 285.

of their own language (1818). Missionary societies who used the English language to convert formed in Ireland during this time also, the more important of which included the Hibernian Bible Society (1809), the Sunday School Society for Ireland (1809), the Religious Tract and Bible Society (1810) and the Scripture Readers Society (1822).[136]

More worrying from the Catholic church's perspective was the involvement of several of these societies in elementary education. This education was provided free of charge to those who were prepared to accept the scriptural and religious instruction that went with it. The first of these was the Association for Discountenancing Vice and Promoting the Knowledge and Practice of the Christian Religion. By 1800 the Association was incorporated by an act of parliament and between 1800 and 1827 it had received from public funds no less than £102,000.[137] By the 1820s it had become a vigorous proselytising agency. Next was the London Hibernian Society which was formed in London under the name of the Hibernian Society for the diffusion of religious knowledge in Ireland. This was to become possibly the most notorious of the education societies because of its openly aggressive style of proselytising and because of its blatant anti-Catholic principles. It viewed the Catholic church as one of idolatry and superstition and held that

> The great body of the Irish wander like sheep that have no faithful shepherd to lead them. Legendary tales, pilgrimages, penances, superstitious offerings, priestly domination, the notorious habit of reconciling sanctimonious accents and attitudes with abandoned practices, and all that shocks and disgusts in the mummery of the mass house, cannot fail to fix a mournful sentiment in the heart of every enlightened and pious observer.[138]

Of all the education societies, the only one formed on liberal principles, was the Kildare Place Society, as it set out to provide elementary education for the poor of Ireland by adopting what it called its 'leading principle', which was 'to afford the same facilities for education to all classes of professing christians without any attempt to interfere with the peculiar religious opinions of any'. In all schools under its auspices, a strict rule had to be observed that the bible was to be read to the children 'without note or comment' and no other religious instruction was to be allowed.[139] Within eight years of its foundation, just as the religious fervour and zeal of the Second Reformation began to impact on education societies, this Society was destined to suffer from some of its worst effects, which would eventually bring it into disrepute.

136 Keogh, *Edmund Rice*, p. 61.   137 First report of the commissioners, 1825, pp 30–1.   138 Ibid., p. 66.   139 S.M. Parkes, *Kildare Place. The history of the Church of Ireland training college, 1811–1969* (Dublin, 1984), pp 17–18.

In the meantime a great deal of religious rivalry was centred on the education question, especially in view of the fact that with financial assistance from the treasury, some of the education societies set up free schools in poorer counties such as Cavan and Mayo where there was a dearth of hedge schools or Catholic parish schools. This was evident in Co. Clare where the London Hibernian Society had over eighty schools with 1000 Catholic children on their rolls. Bishop O'Shaughnessy of Killaloe and the bishops of Tuam, Ardfert and Galway expressed their concern at this situation and the resultant damage to ecumenical relations.[140] Bishop Thomas Hussey of the diocese of Waterford and Lismore, in his controversial pastoral letter of 1797, favoured a more aggressive stance against his religious rivals. He publicly challenged the proselytising schools and urged his priests to resist their efforts and to remonstrate with parents who sent their children to them. If they refused they were to be denied the eucharist. He issued orders to

> Stand firm against all attempts which may be made under various pretexts to withdraw any of your flocks from the belief and practice of the Catholic religion. Remonstrate with any parent who would be so criminal as to expose his offspring to those places of education where his religious faith or morals are likely to be perverted ... if he will not attend to your remonstrances, refuse him the participation of Christ's Body; if he should continue obstinate, denounce him to the church in order that, according to Christ's Commandment, he be considered as a heathen and a publican.[141]

The commissioners of education of 1806 faced a number of challenges – they would have to decide how to make the Protestant church clergymen more accountable in their role as managers of parish and royal schools and how to eliminate the irregularities in these institutions. They would have to decide whether or not to allow the Catholic hierarchy a role in any new educational system and the best means of safeguarding the religious beliefs of children of different denominations. A decision would have to be taken also with regard to 'seditious masters' and their 'licentious books'.

The Irish education question was indeed a priority for the post-Union parliament of Lord Grenville's 'Ministry of all the talents', which took up office upon the death of William Pitt in 1806. Prime Minister Grenville appointed the duke of Bedford as Irish lord lieutenant, a well known supporter of the English educationalist Joseph Lancaster, but it was Grenville himself who first pressed for an inquiry into Irish education. The inquiry was in fact a revival of the 1788–91 commission. Under the provisions of the act, the lord lieutenant was to appoint up to six commissioners, and commissioners of

140 Keogh, *Edmund Rice*, p. 63.   141 Ibid., pp 38–9.

charitable bequests were to appoint up to five of their own body as commissioners.[142] This provision was made due to the efforts of the primate of the Established Church, the formidable Archbishop William Stuart, who reluctantly agreed to co-operate with the establishment of the new board of education, because, as Hislop in his study noted, 'he wished to limit any potentially damaging investigations into the Established Church's role in education'. He was less than pleased that the government appointees 'were almost entirely of liberal disposition on religious and educational matters'.[143] In fact the commissioners appointed by Bedford formed a link with pre-Union educational thinking. Isaac Corry, MP for Co. Armagh had served on the 1788 commission which recommended power sharing with Catholics in the management of schools, and Edgeworth who was instrumental in bringing about the 1799 commission was well known for his liberal views on education.

The lord lieutenant's other nominees were William Parnell and Henry Grattan two notable liberal politicians, and Robert S. Tighe who had called for educational reform in his pamphlet of 1787. The only conservative appointee was William Disney, a member of the management committee of the Protestant charter schools. The appointees of the commissioners of charitable donations and bequests were the primate, Archbishop William Stuart of Armagh, Charles Agar, earl of Normanton and archbishop of Dublin, James Verschoyle, dean of St Patrick's and later bishop of Killala, George Hall, the provost of Trinity College, and James Whitelaw, minister of St Catherine's, Dublin.[144]

From the beginning of the inquiry on 21 October 1806 the Established Church clergy took a leadership role, with Stuart chairing this meeting and almost all of the subsequent meetings of the board. The commissioners worked for six years and produced fourteen reports. The first thirteen dealt with schools investigated by the three major education inquiries between 1788 and 1799. The fourteenth report dealt with the current educational situation. The core of establishment commissioners successfully ensured that damaging criticism was limited in the report on parish schools and managed to find positive features in the charter schools.[145] They concluded, upon examining thirty nine charter schools 'that they were in a flourishing state, the education in them efficacious and practical and in every respect such as put it beyond the reach of private defamation or public censure'.[146]

This contrasted strongly with their outright condemnation of hedge schools, which they described as 'that ordinary class of country schools, generally known in Ireland by the name of 'hedge schools' which were frequent-

142 Akenson, *The Irish education experiment*, p. 76.   143 H. Hislop, 'The 1806–12 board of education and non-denominational education in Ireland' in *Oideas* 40 (1993), p. 51.   144 Ibid., Tighe's pamphlet was entitled *A letter addressed to Mr Orde upon the education of the people* (Dublin, 1787).   145 Hislop, 'The 1806–12 board of education', p. 52.   146 Commissioners of Irish education inquiry 1806–12, p. 329.

ly of an objectionable character'.[147] The professional ability of the masters was held up to ridicule also as the commissioners claimed that the only instruction given in the hedge schools was in basic literacy and numeracy skills. They stated that 'even this limited instruction the masters are in general very ill-qualified to give, having been themselves taught in schools of a similar description'.[148] They suggested that as the profession was so poorly remuner-ated it held 'out no temptation to a better class to undertake the office of instructors'.[149] As a result of their poverty hedge schoolmasters couldn't afford to purchase 'such books as are fit for children to read', and they were obliged to use chapbooks which the commissioners considered to be very dangerous and a threat to the morals of the children. According to the commissioners it frequently happened 'that instead of being improved by religious and moral instruction, their minds are corrupted by books calculated to incite to lawless and profligate adventure, to cherish superstition, or to lead to dissension or disloyalty'.[150]

A determined effort was to be made to rid all future schools of chapbooks by the suggestion in the report that the new education commissioners were to have control over all texts used in their schools. The commissioners wished to replace the hedge schools and to take some of the power from the hands of the Church of Ireland clergymen, by appointing a permanent body of edu-cation commissioners with responsibility for creating supplementary schools, to be under their control. They recommended a series of training institutions for the proper training of teachers but most importantly, the fourteenth report made a strong case against any form of proselytising taking place in Irish schools. This was an enlightened 'leading principle' and one that was to be 'pivotal in all later Irish educational discussions'.[151] The commissioners out-lined it as follows:

> We conceive this to be of essential importance that in any new estab-lishments for the education of the lower classes in Ireland, and we ven-ture to express our unanimous opinion, that no such plan, however wisely and unexceptionably contrived in other respects, can be carried into effectual execution in this country, unless it be explicitly avowed and clearly understood as its leading principle, that no attempt shall be made to influence or disturb the peculiar religious tenets of any sect or description of christians.[152]

They were also to draw up a volume of sacred extracts to be read during secular instruction, so that all children would have access to the scriptures in the new school system. They may have ruled out proselytism but conversion

147 Ibid., p. 94.   148 Ibid., p. 38.   149 Ibid., p. 331.   150 Ibid.   151 Akenson, *The Irish edu-cation experiment*, p. 77.   152 Commissioners of Irish education inquiry 1806–12, p. 328.

must surely have been behind the ecclesiastical commissioners' thinking in this recommendation. They also accepted the mixed education principle but they rejected the separate religious education of children by their respective pastors. All existing educational institutions were to be left in the hands of the Established Church and, as Hislop pointed out, the Established Church commissioners 'were determined to prevent the supplementary schools from becoming state supported schools under the control of the Catholic church'.[153]

In fact they had no wish to see the supplementary schools established at all, or indeed the formation of a new board of commissioners who would 'have a general control over the whole of the proposed establishments for the instruction of the lower classes'.[154] This became apparent in September 1812 when the newly appointed chief secretary Robert Peel took up his post and attempted to implement the recommendations of the fourteenth report, by establishing the supplementary schools. However 'lobbying from the Irish bench of Bishops in 1813 persuaded him to limit legislative measures to the creation of a board of commissioners to oversee endowed schools'. By March 1814 Peel established exactly how the ecclesiastical commissioners of 1806 felt about the supplementary schools and it transpired that they no longer supported their own report. They rejected it because they would have been obliged to share power in education with the Catholic church.

Peel was placed in a difficult situation but fortunately for him an idea was mooted at the meetings held in 1814, that state aid for education could be channelled through a voluntary society. The government acted on this suggestion and gave grant aid to some of the education societies, one of which at least had a dubious reputation. The one which got the largest grant still had its reputation intact, this was the Kildare Place Society, which had formulated its guiding principles in accordance with the fourteenth report's 'leading principle', which eschewed proselytism in a mixed education system. Consequently the society was awarded a generous grant of £6980 in 1815 which rose to £25,000 in 1828 and reached £30,000 in 1831.[155]

Lay and clerical opposition to the Kildare Place Society, 1819–24

In 1800 William Pitt and his chief secretary Lord Castlereagh had intended that the union of the two parliaments should be accompanied by the admission of Catholics to membership of parliament. When the measure had to be dropped due to the strong anti-concession lobby in England and the hostility of the king, both of them resigned in protest.[156] Irish Catholics renewed

153 Hislop, 'The 1806–1812 board of education', p. 53.   154 Hislop, 'Voluntary effort and official enquiry', p. 67.   155 Coolahan, *Irish education*, p. 11.   156 Beckett, *The making of modern Ireland*, p. 288.

their efforts to pursue emancipation when, in November 1804, under Lord Fingall, they resolved to prepare the first Catholic petition for emancipation since the Act of Union. It was at this stage that Daniel O'Connell (1775–1847), a very successful Catholic barrister decided to become actively involved in politics.

In order to achieve his political ambition it was essential for O'Connell to find a cause which would interest the Catholic clergy and by so doing win their support for Catholic emancipation. In 1820 he found such a cause in the Kildare Place Society's bible reading rule and the nugatory effect he alleged it had on its 'leading principle', matters he had first raised at the Society's annual meeting in 1819.[157] Before the annual meeting of the Kildare Place Society in 1820 he laid the foundations of a carefully planned strategy to win the support of the Catholic hierarchy, by firstly applying to the archbishop of Dublin for some direction regarding the education of Catholic children, bearing in mind no doubt the papal bull of Pius VII of 1818 which 'excludes from Catholic schools the Testament even with note and comment, even though these might be acceptable to Catholics'.[158] Having consulted their parish priests the archbishops framed a resolution which O'Connell read to the meeting on 24 February 1820 which stated that 'The Scriptures, with or without note or comment, are not fit to be used as a school book'.[159] According to the Society's historian H. Kingsmill Moore, the annual meeting proved eventful, as O'Connell was supported by the duke of Leinster, the earl of Fingall and lord Cloncurry and 'Both sides approached the occasion as a test of strength'.[160] O'Connell expressed his approval and admiration of the Society's leading principle of non-interference with the religious beliefs of any sect, but he added that the 'difficulty felt by him and others had been caused by the rule which required that the Scriptures without note or comment should be read'. He suggested that 'This rule had rendered the means employed by the Society inefficient, and the principles of non-interference nugatory.' This insistence on the use of the bible discriminated against Catholics, and to prove his point he cited cases in which Catholics had refused aid from the Society rather than comply with the rule. He referred to the papal bull and to the archbishops' resolution, a gesture which must have appealed to the Catholic hierarchy. A motion that there should not be an inquiry into the possibility of changing the Society's rules to accommodate Catholic difficulties was upheld by eighty votes to nineteen, at which stage O'Connell and his friends withdrew from the Kildare Place Society.[161]

157 H. Kingsmill Moore. *An unwritten chapter in the history of education, being the history of the society for promoting the education of the poor of Ireland, generally known as the Kildare Place Society* (London, 1904), p. 75.   158 Fontana to bishops of Ireland 18 September 1818, quoted in Keogh, *Edmund Rice*, p. 68.   159 McGrath, *Politics*, p. 157.   160 Moore, *An unwritten chapter*, p. 77.   161 McGrath, *Politics*, p. 157.

O'Connell had selected his ground well. He had picked exactly the right issue with which to lure the clergy. It was controversial, provocative and held out the attraction of control of Irish Catholic education.[162] For the next eleven years this power struggle over control of education would prove a battle of wits between members of the government who supported the Kildare Place, members of the Society and the powerful clerical leaders in the Catholic church. As subsequent events unfolded, with O'Connell publishing a letter dated 25 February, 1820 in the *Dublin Weekly Register*, addressed to the Catholic prelates, in which he accused the Society of pretending to afford equal educational opportunities to all, while their real aim was proselytism, the Catholic church couldn't remain outside the world of politics.[163] O'Connell had found an issue which would take them centre stage. The main players would be Dr James Warren Doyle, bishop of Kildare and Leighlin, and to a lesser extent the archbishops of Dublin and Armagh. In his letter O'Connell also advised the bishops to establish a 'National association for education' lest they leave themselves open to charges of hostility to the education of the poor.[164]

The bishops accepted O'Connell's advice and promptly established a society in January 1821 which was intended to be the Catholic equivalent of the Kildare Place, called the Irish National Society for promoting the education of the poor. Both Catholic prelates and influential laymen founded this society in the hope of altering the distribution of the Kildare Place funds to permit Catholic control of funds for the education of Catholic children, or that they might at least obtain a share of the public money accruing to the education societies. The constitution and rules of the new society, even as to phraseology were almost identical to those of the Kildare Place.[165] Six months later the society had only managed to establish one non-denominational school for boys at No. 4 Lower Abbey Street, Dublin, in contrast to the rapidly expanding Kildare Place which had started off with only eight schools in 1816 but had grown to over a thousand schools by 1823, a number which was set to rise in the following years.[166] Without state funding the society couldn't hope to survive and therefore Doyle, who was about to become the leading Catholic church spokesman on education, requested Sir Henry Parnell MP to present a petition to the house of commons from the Catholic archbishops, bishops and laity, for funding for the education of the Irish poor. Catholic hopes were high as the chief secretary Charles Grant was known to favour such a scheme.

Before presenting the petition to parliament on 18 May 1821, Parnell requested a report from Doyle on the state of Catholic education in Ireland.

162 Moore, *An unwritten chapter,* p. 77.   163 *Dublin Weekly Register,* 26 February, 1820.   164 McGrath, *Politics,* p. 158,   165 Brenan, *Schools of Kildare and Leighlin,* p. 156.   166 Akenson, *The Irish education experiment,* p. 87.

This report was most revealing as up to this the parish priests had kept a careful watch over proceedings in the hedge schools.[167] They had engaged the services of the masters for Sunday school teaching and the parochial returns from the diocese of Kildare and Leighlin in 1824 clearly showed that they were happy with the masters they had either sanctioned or appointed. Right through the returns the hedge schoolmasters were described as 'of excellent character', 'of moral character', 'of good character'.[168] Now that Doyle was seeking a grant for Catholic education, it wasn't in the church's best interest for him to paint a picture of hedge schoolmasters as worthy educators, even though he was well aware that the teachers in his own diocese at least, were competent to teach. This was evident from an analysis of the returns, which showed that 168 out of 262 Catholic male teachers or 64% were competent to give further instruction beyond the basic numeracy and literacy skills.[169] Yet Doyle was critical of hedge schoolmasters in his report, stating that 'In the counties of Carlow, Kildare and the Queen's County very nearly all the Roman Catholic children attend schools during the summer and autumn, are taught reading, writing, and arithmetic, but their masters, in many instances, are extremely ignorant.' He added, 'we have not funds to buy forms, books or to pay a master capable of instructing'. To obtain a grant Doyle was prepared to sacrifice the professional reputation of the hedge schoolmaster, the reputation upon which he survived as a teacher. He repeated, 'Of these three counties, I may safely say that nine-tenths of the farmers' children and all those of the better classes, receive education of a very imperfect kind, and imparted in a very defective way, by men, in most instances, incompetent to teach.' The bishops' petition for grant aid for Catholic schools when submitted by Parnell, was rejected, most likely due to the change in administration.[170]

Undaunted by this rejection, Doyle employed a new strategy which was that of pressurising the Kildare Place to modify its rules to suit the requirements of the Catholic bishops and at the same time he continued his policy of discrediting hedge schoolmasters. He did so in the autumn of 1821 by drawing up a manuscript entitled 'Thoughts on the education of the poor in Ireland', which was submitted to the chief secretary, Charles Grant, by Lord Fingall, Archbishop Troy and three other prelates, for the government's consideration. In it he attributed the lack of a sound religious education to the growth in secret oath bound societies in the country, and he took the opportunity to alert the government to the fact that one half at least, of the population, in his estimation, was 'unprovided with any kind of useful instruction in their youth', and those who attended school did not benefit 'owing to the lack of a good system of education, proper schoolhouses and well-educated

167 McGrath, *Politics*, p. 163.   168 Brenan, *Schools of Kildare and Leighlin*, pp 61–2.   169 Ibid., p. 84.   170 McGrath, *Politics*, p. 164.

schoolmasters'. He stressed that Catholics couldn't provide for the education of their children, although he knew that this wasn't true because very many Catholic parents were paying for the education of their children in the hedge schools. He claimed also that Catholics could not benefit from the education provided by the Kildare Place because of the rule which laid down that the bible was to be read 'without note or comment'.[171] This wasn't true either because at this time 'the Kildare Place Society ... came very close to being the basis of a successful national system' as numbers of scholars increased steadily from the years 1816 to 1824, from 557 scholars to 100,000 scholars.[172]

The assertive tone of Doyle's suggestions reflected the new confidence of the Catholic church. From now on the customary address of loyalty to the crown, such as that received by King George IV from the bishops on his arrival in Ireland in 1821,[173] would be supplemented by petitions for civil rights for Catholics in the field of education. Doyle suggested also that the Kildare Place should be made more acceptable to the Catholic church and he envisaged that this could be achieved by the appointment of the two archbishops of Dublin as vice-presidents of the Society and six parish priests in Dublin city, or others, to the committee of the Kildare Place. He wanted the *Evangelical life of Christ* to replace the *New Testament* for Catholic children and he requested that books objected to by the three members of the committee should not be printed. There was a veiled threat also in his statement, that the church would withdraw Catholic children from Kildare Place schools if aid was not forthcoming in the future for Catholic education. For the present the Catholic clergy 'overlooked in many instances what they disapproved of, as no duty could be more painful to them than to withdraw children from one school without being able to receive them in another'.[174]

Doyle also referred to the undemocratic nature of the Lord Lieutenant's Fund for the education of the poor. This was a fund set up in 1819 following an appeal on behalf of Catholics by William Parnell, the spokesman in parliament for Catholic claims, but the funds were largely inaccessible to Catholics because title to the site of an aided school had to be vested in the anglican minister and church wardens of the parish.[175] Finally Doyle suggested that if the Kildare Place could not modify its rules to comply with the demands of the Catholic church then the assistance Catholics required from government might be given through a separate fund to be placed in the hands of the trustees of Maynooth College. The government ignored his *Thoughts on education* but a copy of the submission came into the possession of the Kildare Place, which rejected all the charges made against it as well as the suggestions for power sharing with the Catholic church, the suggested

171 Ibid., pp 165–6.   172 Akenson, *The Irish education experiment*, p. 87.   173 McGrath, *Politics*, pp 8–10.   174 Ibid., p. 166.   175 Akenson, *The Irish education experiment*, p. 84.

modification of the bible reading rule and the proposed replacement for the New Testament.[176]

The Kildare Place Society's 'leading principle' had little hope of success due to the effects of the Second Reformation which peaked in the 1820s, when the Society's managers granted part of their income to proselytising education societies. As well as that their strict rule that the bible was to be read 'without note or comment' was largely abandoned in the early years of the 1820s when 'local Protestant clergy and landlords quite freely violated the Society's rules by providing exposition of the scripture lessons'.[177] Eventually the three fundamental rules of the Society were to be broken, as the 1825 commissioners of education reported:

> The use of the scriptures is frequently a matter of form … Catechisms are taught as freely in many of their schools as in any others merely by the fiction of treating the appointed times as not being school hours; and the selection of masters and mistresses though nominally uninfluenced by religious considerations are truly and practically confined to Roman Catholics, when the patrons are the Roman Catholic clergy, and to Protestants, when the schools are in connection with the Association for discountenancing vice, or the patrons are clergymen of the Established Church…[178]

By the mid 1820s it became apparent to some Catholic leaders and clergymen, that the Kildare Place was another proselytising agency. In February 1820, a young Maynooth priest, John MacHale, later professor of theology in Maynooth College, coadjutor bishop of Killala (1825) and archbishop of Tuam (1834), began issuing a series of letters under the nom de plume 'Hierophilos' warning the clergy of the proselytising intent of the Society. These letters continued for three years and highlighted the monopoly enjoyed by a minority group in the field of education, and warned of the threat this posed to the Catholic church. In somewhat more restrained tones Doyle wrote a series of letters to the *Dublin Evening Post*, using the initials JKL, in which he castigated the proselytising societies especially those engaged in education for the 'wide superstition which, under the name of bible reading or bible distributions, is now disturbing the peace of Ireland and threatening the safety of the state'.

On 9 March 1824, James Grattan, MP for Co. Wicklow, presented a petition of the Irish Catholic bishops on education to the house of commons,

176 McGrath, *Politics*, p. 167.   177 Akenson, *The Irish education experiment*, p. 90.   178 First report of the commissioners, 1825, p. 56. By 1824 there were 57 schools of the Association for discountenancing vice, 340 of the London Hibernian Society, and 30 Baptist Society schools receiving aid from the Kildare Place Society.

which outlined Catholic grievances on education.[179] The bishops contended that the state funds for Irish education of the poor were adequate but that they were misapplied, because 'the manner in which they were distributed was at variance with Catholic religious principles, especially the indiscriminate use of the Bible which was uniformly insisted upon'. The lack of grants to Catholic schools, the activities of the proselytising societies, the rules of the Lord Lieutenant's Fund were all enumerated among their grievances. Both the chief secretary Henry Goulburn and the home secretary Robert Peel were strong supporters of the Established Church and of the Kildare Place Society. Nonetheless, when Sir John Newport moved for a royal commission to investigate the state of Irish education, to include not only the Kildare Place but all schools maintained in any part from public funds, the motion was agreed to on 25 March 1824 and the commission of Irish education inquiry was duly established by the king. This was generally seen as a victory for the Catholic bishops because it was set up in response to their petition, and as a defeat for the Kildare Place, but the battle for the control of Irish education still continued through the 1820s and the early 1830s.[180]

'The country was being convulsed by sectarian zeal.'

The Catholic emancipation campaign was renewed again in 1823 with the formation of the Catholic Association. This was to become a well organised, successful pressure group for Catholic civil rights. A vital element in the success of the renewed campaign was the participation of the clergy and the use O'Connell made of the education question in order to win over the Catholic bishops. From the outset the clergy were ex officio members of the Association. O'Connell promised them that £5000 would be set aside for the education of priests, £5000 for building chapels and presbyters and most significantly £5000 for the use of Catholic schools and the purchase of books. This must surely have appealed to a church threatened by proselytising schools and rising sectarianism.[181]

There can be little doubt that the Association used the education issue to grow closer to the Catholic church. In the house of commons on 29 March 1824, when John Henry North, a founder member of the Kildare Place claimed in his maiden speech that until the establishment of the Society in 1811 'the whole country in regard to education was in a state of thick and palpable darkness' and that 'the Catholic priests never undertook the task of instruction themselves',[182] the Catholic Association invited the clergy to refute

179 Op. cit., pp 91–3.   180 McGrath, *Politics*, p. 170.   181 Keogh, *Edmund Rice*, pp 72–3.   182 W.J. Fitzpatrick, *The life, times and correspondence of the Rt Reverend Dr Doyle*, i (Dublin, 1861), pp 320–1.

North's speech. Letters poured into the Association's Capel Street rooms and the first to respond was the redoubtable Doyle.[183] In his reply Doyle gave the Catholic clergy full credit yet again for keeping the light of education alive during the dark days of the penal laws, which of course would have been an impossible feat for them, considering their size relative to the population. He never gave the hedge schoolmasters the credit which was due to them and consistently overstated the contribution of the Catholic clergy. He boasted that since the repeal of the penal laws against Catholic education in 1782 priests had founded schools in their homes and allowed their churches to be used as schoolhouses. In defending his clergy he wrote that 'This calumniated order of men have proceeded steadily and perseveringly in the discharge of their duty, and without succour or support, have succeeded in this part of the country, in removing "the thick and palpable darkness" created by a flagitious code of law'.

North's speech referred to the immoral and seditious books which were read in the native schools and he held the clergy personally responsible for that, but Doyle refuted this allegation, calling it a 'gross and unfounded calumny'. He stated that the Catholic clergy had taken steps to remove any such books before the Kildare Place was ever founded.[184] This part of Doyle's statement was no doubt true because he testified to it before the 1825 commissioners of education,[185] but when Peel read Doyle's letter, which had been inserted in the minutes of the Catholic Association, he didn't believe his claim on the church's contribution to educational provision. Peel commented 'Dr Doyle is a clever fellow. I have read a letter from him on the education of the Roman Catholics, giving, I dare say, a very inaccurate account of the state of education, but very ably written'.[186]

Sectarianism was emerging as one of the biggest problems in Irish society in the mid-1820s. There were several reasons for this. It occurred not just because of the Second Reformation but also because of the scale of the campaign for Catholic emancipation and the Catholic church's unremitting pursuit for equality in education. It manifested itself in the growth of the deeply sectarian secret society of Ribbonmen, which was a Catholic organisation with a strong connecting link to the revolutionary nationalist societies of the previous century. The earliest mention of this society dates from 1811[187] but, according to the government informer Michael Coffey, they had an insurrection planned for 28 July 1817 and a later one planned for 1820 when they were hoping for French assistance.[188] Ribbonmen inherited Defenderism's anti-

183 McGrath, *Politics*, p. 171.   184 Ibid.   185 First report of the commissioners, 1825, App. p. 778.   186 McGrath, *Politics*, p. 173.   187 T. Garvin, 'Defenders, Ribbonmen and others: underground political networks in pre-famine Ireland' in C.H.E. Philpin (ed.), *Nationalism and popular protest in Ireland* (Cambridge, 1987), p. 220.   188 M.R. Beames, 'The ribbon societies: lower class nationalism in pre-famine Ireland' in *Nationalism and popular protest*, p. 254.

Orange character. The Orange societies were strong throughout the country at this stage and they had their own oaths which Ribbonmen tried to match. The society did much to aggravate Protestant fears, with their sectarian catechisms which contained the refrain 'What are your intentions? – to regain all lost rights and privileges since the Reformation'.[189]

They, like other agrarian societies, active during this period, promoted Pastorini's prophecy, which foretold the extermination of Protestants in the year 1825 when Catholics would reign supreme once more. This prophecy was first published in 1771 in a book entitled *The general history of the Christian church*, and was written by the Catholic bishop of Rama, Charles Walmesley, under the pseudonym Signor Pastorini.[190] It was hardly a coincidence that Pastorini's prophecy first began to acquire a popular following in this country at the end of the Napoleonic wars in 1815 when agrarian disturbances increased as the post-war price slump produced nothing but hardship. By the 1820s the drastic fall in the price of grain had shown little sign of abatement so that many farmers switched from labour intensive tillage to pasturage thus causing untold misery to cottiers, labourers and tenant farmers. A precarious food supply combined with a rapid increase in population ensured that secret societies were never short of recruits.[191] The activities of the Ribbonmen and Pastorini's prophecy spread simultaneously after the bad harvest of the autumn of 1821 when people were on the verge of starvation. Pastorini's prophecy can therefore be seen 'as a response to the desperate social conditions of those years'.[192]

The Catholic church strongly disapproved of the society of Ribbonmen and of Pastorini's prophecy. Doyle directed his pastoral address of 1822 'against the illegal association of Ribbonmen' in which he poured scorn on their professed 'love of religion' and their faith in prophecy, especially that of Pastorini.[193] In 1825 he returned once again to this theme in his pastoral, when he encouraged the people to read the books in their chapel libraries in preference to those 'profane, irreligious books and pretended prophecies, which distract your minds, and corrupt your hearts and disturb your peace'.

The widespread involvement of hedge schoolmasters in the Ribbonmen was alleged by the contemporary novelist and hedge schoolmaster William Carleton (1794–1809) in his autobiography.[194] Doyle revealed in his *Familiar dialogues* that he too suspected hedge schoolmasters of membership of secret societies. He wrote that 'the master counts over the traditions of the country, tells of the battles which were won and lost in the neighbourhood...He retires with the younger branches of the family, sons and servants to some place of

189 Ibid., p. 253.   190 S. Ó Muireadhaigh, 'Na fir ribín' in *Galvia*, 10 (1964–5), p. 19.   191 Beckett, *The making of modern Ireland*, pp 292–3.   192 Connolly, *Priests and people*, pp 82–3.   193 Bowen, *The Protestant crusade*, pp 63–4.   194 W. Carleton, *The autobiography of William Carleton* (London, 1968), pp 77–80.

rest – he inflames their minds anew, and before the rising sun has summoned them to labour, they are perhaps all bound to some mysterious compact by an unlawful oath'.[195] According to Carleton's account, he himself had been sworn into the Ribbonmen movement in 1813, when, as an inebriated nineteen-year-old, the oath had been administered to him, following wedding celebrations. Carleton claimed that there was scarcely a hedge schoolmaster in Ireland who did not 'hold articles', 'that is, who was not a ribbon lodge-master'.[196]

It should of course be remembered that Carleton's own experience was limited to the Ulster borderlands and then only for a limited period around 1813. A more reliable source, for establishing with accuracy the social profile of Ribbonmen would be the list of Dublin Ribbonmen for 1821 contained in the diary of the notorious chief of police for Dublin, Major Sirr. Of the seventy-six names listed in his diary, only one was a hedge schoolmaster and according to another reliable source – the list of Ribbonmen suspects for 1842 in the Public Records Office in London, no hedge schoolmasters were involved.[197] It would seem highly unlikely that there would be widespread membership of masters in this movement particularly as it ran concurrently with the hugely successful campaign of the Catholic Association.

Irish education inquiry, 1824–7. 'A safe body of schoolmasters'

The Catholic hierarchy suspended its campaign of petitioning parliament on the education question while the 1824 commission of inquiry was in progress, although it was no secret that they were dissatisfied with the appointment of a commission rather than a committee of the house of commons. Doyle wrote 'all our hopes were blasted and from that hour to this (September 1826) we looked with doubt and apprehension to whatsoever we have witnessed on the part of this commission and to all that has emanated from it'.[198]

The composition of the board did nothing to raise their level of expectations. The crown appointed Thomas Frankland Lewis. Lewis had been a member of parliament since 1806 and had served on the commissions which inquired into Irish revenue in 1821 and the revenue of Great Britain and Ireland in 1822. Charles Grant was a Scotsman who had been chief secretary of Ireland from 1818 to 1821. James Glassford was a Scottish advocate who toured Ireland three times between 1824 and 1826 and he was a well known supporter of the London Hibernian Society. Leslie Foster's appointment was greeted with dismay by the hierarchy as he had no Catholic sympathies and was an active member of the Kildare Place.[199] The appointment of the first Roman

195 McGrath, *Politics*, p. 165.   196 Op. cit., p. 82.   197 Beames, 'The Ribbon societies', p. 248.
198 Pastoral letter of Dr Doyle, 4 September, 1826, quoted in Brenan, *Schools of Kildare and Leighlin*, p. 6.   199 W.J. Fitzpatrick, *Unpublished essay by Dr Doyle. An essay on education and the*

Catholic in modern times to a commission of inquiry was regarded by prominent Catholic figures as mere tokenism. The person appointed was Anthony
Richard Blake, the treasury remembrancer, one who was already burdened
with onerous duties. Daniel O'Connell criticised Blake's appointment as 'a
mere delusion in order to make a show of great liberality'.[200] As Akenson
remarked Blake's 'presence might have reassured the Catholics as to the commission's integrity were it not that all Catholics who took office were suspect
by their fellow religionists'.[201]

Nonetheless the Catholic clergy were impressed by the impartiality shown
by the commissioners in the collection of their statistical data.[202] In July 1824
when the commissioners conducted a nationwide survey of all schools in Ireland, the parochial returns showed that the hedge schoolmasters were still the
dominant educators in Ireland, a situation that hadn't changed since the
1806–12 education inquiry. There were now 9352 pay schools, which received
no assistance of any kind, and the hedge schools formed the majority of
these.[203] The number of schools in connection with the societies at this time
was 1727 out of a total number of 11,823. The Kildare Place was the largest
education society in the country but it represented only 25% of the total number of schools found in existence in 1825. It should be remembered also that
the majority of the youth population did not attend schools, as revealed by
the 1821 census. Research by the historian Joseph Lee shows that:

> If the figures for the population aged 5–15 years remained constant
> from 1821–1824 (or increased which is more likely), then at best just
> over 32% of this age cohort were found in attendance at schools of any
> sort in 1824, the Kildare Place schools would have accounted for only
> 3% of the total.[204]

The challenge which faced the commissioners of 1825 was precisely the same
as that which faced the commissioners of 1806, namely how to replace 'those
ill-taught and ill-regulated schools'.[205] They acknowledged this fact by quoting verbatim from their report, with regard to the hedge schools, as the situation had altered little since. The only difference now was that the matter had
taken on some degree of urgency due to the rapid growth of the hedge
schools and the well documented evidence of the past involvement of hedge
schoolmasters in agrarian societies and revolutionary movements. This was a
source of considerable disquiet to the Anglican primate of Armagh, Archbishop Beresford, who made a strong representation to the commissioners,

state of Ireland (Dublin, 1880), pp 19–20. 200 Dublin Evening Post, 22 June 1824. 201 Akenson, The Irish education experiment, p. 94. 202 Hislop, 'The Kildare Place Society, 1811–1831',
p. 722. 203 First report of the commissioners, 1825, pp 1–24. 204 Op. cit., pp 738–9. 205
First report of the commissioners, 1825, p. 38.

to look into the question of the 'provision for the training of a safe body of schoolmasters'.[206]

Once again a body of education commissioners found instruction in the hedge schools to be 'extremely limited' and the masters in general to be 'ill-qualified' and the books to be 'an evil which still requires a remedy'.[207] Brenan, writing in 1935 about the hedge schools of the diocese of Kildare and Leighlin, viewed the 1825 commission as inequitable because of the negligible amount of time allotted to discussion of the native and Catholic educational establishments compared to the disproportionate amount given over to the discussion of the schools and societies of the Established Church. He estimated that of a report consisting of 102 folio pages, only 3 were devoted to Catholic educational organisation; and of 881 pages of appendices giving evidence on oath, only 36 were given to Catholic apologists.[208]

Much more serious than this was a fact which emerged some years later, that at least three of the commissioners had shown themselves prejudiced against hedge schools and their masters. Charges they made were based on either superficial evidence or hearsay. One such was Blake who testified before the select committee of the house of lords in 1837, and when asked whether 'pay schools' were synonymous with 'hedge schools' replied:

> I mean pay schools, schools in which the masters receive some small stipend from the children who attend them; schools set up on private speculation; schools that received no aid either from the state or from any society established for the promotion of education. The masters received a 1d. a week or so from the children; sometimes more and sometimes less. The schoolmasters, I thought in these schools were of a very inferior class.[209]

He was asked for his opinion on the character of the hedge schoolmasters, and even though he had never spoken to them personally, he replied that they:

> appeared particularly bad from what I could hear of them, they were described as very mischievous people, they were supposed to be persons, engaged in writing inflammatory letters and notices.

It transpired that his evidence was based on 'Communications with gentlemen as I went through the country'.[210] Glassford was also negatively disposed towards the masters. In his *Letter to rt hon. earl of Roden on the present state of Irish education* (1829) his comments on their professional abilities were quite derogatory. He wrote:

---

206 Corcoran, *Selected texts*, p. 119.   207 Op. cit., p. 44.   208 Brenan, *Schools of Kildare and Leighlin*, p. 8.   209 Report on new plan 1837, First Report, p. 54.   210 Ibid., pp 53–54.

...in that poorest class, formerly called hedge schools, we do not look for an intelligent system of instruction: the teacher is himself too igno-rant, or if naturally endowed, has not the ability to exercise the minds of his pupils.[211]

Later he added 'The common pay schools of the country were kept up on private speculation of the teachers, and these were of the lowest classes of the community'. Grant's negative views on the hedge schoolmasters appear to have been based on his objections to their chapbooks which he considered to be immoral. He informed the select committee of the house of lords in 1837 that he believed

The hedge schools ... were schools in which the lowest possible state of morals was observed, in which the most immoral books were admit-ted, and in which intellectual education was at the lowest possible scale.[212]

Despite the fact that 'The country was being convulsed by sectarian zeal'[213] evidence was given by Robert Daly, the rector of Powerscourt on 15 Decem-ber 1824, that hedge schools provided non-denominational education. Cooke, who gave evidence on 5 January 1825 also testified to the non-denomination-al nature of the hedge school and stated that he himself had been taught the Presbyterian catechism in one of them by a Roman Catholic master.[214] Even Doyle verified that this was so in his testimony before the house of lords com-mittee on the state of Ireland on 21 March 1825. He said that where there was no suspicion of proselytism Catholics and Protestants were educated quite happily together in the hedge schools.[215] The commissioners of educa-tion in their report accepted this evidence and

Declared themselves 'much struck' by the many pay schools (or hedge schools which constituted the vast majority of Irish schools) managed as private speculative ventures, unattached to any particular denomi-nation or society, in which there appeared to be 'perfect harmony' amongst the children of all persuasions. In these schools the masters taught religion to all denominations separately.[216]

211 Glassford, *Letter to rt hon. Earl of Roden*, p. 20.   212 Report of the select committee of the house of lords on the plan of education in Ireland, with minutes of evidence H.C. 1837, 1, p. 560.   213 McGrath, *Politics*, p. 183.   214 First report of the commissioners, 1825, pp 811–2. 215 House of lords committee on the state of Ireland, 1825 (181), 9:1, p. 244.   216 First report of the commissioners, 1825, p. 92.

The hedge schools were successful in attracting pupils because they offered a broad curriculum which the education societies failed to match. Captain Pringle ascribed this reason for the failure of the London Hibernian Society schools.[217] Daly confirmed that parents were not satisfied with mere scripture schools as they also wanted arithmetic taught to their children. He told the commissioners that parents:

> Think a fine arithmetic book, written out, is a sure test of a good school and if a master is not able to put the children through Voster or Joyce, he is considered an ignoramus ... In order to gratify the children's parents, teach them profit and loss, and tare and tret, which will never do them any good whatever.[218]

There was a strong belief held by conservative contemporary writers, political figures and shared by bible societies involved in education, that the poor should not be educated above their station in life. This was the philosophy behind the Lancastrian monitorial plan of education, which was a scheme which had been designed in England by Joseph Lancaster in 1798 and later at his Borough Road premises (1801), to teach a large number of children basic skills using a small teaching force, by using the older children as monitors.[219] This was the plan of education submitted to John Foster in 1805 and applied by the Kildare Place in order 'to make youth more useful, without elevating them, above the situation in life for which they may be designed'.[220] But it was a plan which found little favour with Irish parents in general, as the growth of the hedge schools which supplied individual instruction, bore witness to, and as Cooke testified to. He stated:

> I have observed them in the country; the people look at them there with great prejudice; they think they are useless; they think the master must teach the children himself, and that his inspecting the monitors is not teaching the children; and the prejudice is so strong as almost to render them inefficient.[221]

Parents and masters rejected the utilitarian philosophy. This was evident from the broad curriculum in the hedge schools. It was evident also in their choice of fictional works as reading material, in an age which viewed the imagination and works of fantasy with the deepest suspicion. On the recommendations of the 1806 commissioners of education the Kildare Place attempted

---

217 Ibid., App p. 689. Examination of Captain George Pringle.   218 Ibid., p. 798.   219 Coolahan, *Irish education*, p. 11.   220 Corcoran, *Selected texts*, p. 104.   221 First report of the commissioners, 1825, p. 821.

to supplant the hedge school chapbooks by attempting to replace them with their own published works which they considered 'sufficiently entertaining to enter into fair competition with the hedge school books and at an affordable price'. Even though the Society produced nearly a million of these books within seven years, the chapbooks still remained popular and the 1825 commissioners 'nevertheless found the Traces of their former Abundance'; in the returns made by the respective clergymen.[222]

Two Catholic prelates Dr Kelly, archbishop of Tuam, and Doyle, gave evidence that no such books were in use in the hedge schools in their dioceses. Kelly made the strictest inquiry over two years with respect to the books in use in the schools in his diocese and he 'could not discover that throughout the whole extent of the archdiocese of Tuam there was an immoral or obscene book made use of, except in two instances'. He verified also that it was the parents of the children who provided them with books.[223] Doyle made particular enquiries as to whether there were any immoral books in the hedge schools in his diocese, and from a careful study of all the returns from his clergy, he testified that:

> During the last year I made particular enquiries as to whether there were any immoral books in schools of that description.. and I discovered that there was one, and that in the town of Ballynakill: it was brought to the school in that town, by a child, the son of a Protestant parent who had come to reside in Ballynakill from the diocese of Ossory.[224]

The 1825 education inquiry had the effect of exposing the failure of the Kildare Place to implement non-denominational education. The commissioners concluded that the Society had 'failed in producing universal satisfaction' but they also acknowledged the benefits the Society bestowed on Ireland through:

> The issue of books, the arrangement of the model school, the training of masters and mistresses, their system of rewards, and their directing the public mind so powerfully to education, they have conferred the most extensive and undoubted benefits on Ireland.[225]

The commissioners recommended that the activities of the Kildare Place should be severely limited. It was to cease giving grants to other societies, and following the establishment of a proposed education board, it was to cease adding schools to its connection. The Incorporated society was to have aid with-

222 Ibid., p. 43.   223 Ibid., App p. 777.   224 Ibid., p. 778.   225 Ibid., p. 58.

drawn from it and the Association for discountenancing vice was to limit its activities to printing and distributing books. Like the Kildare Place, its schools were to be transferred to the control of the government education board.

This proposed new board would superintend the management of the 'schools of general instruction' which were to be established in each benefice. Like their predecessors, the commissioners recommended a mixed education system where children would be united for secular instruction and where separate religious instruction would be given on one or two days a week. Religious instruction for Protestant children was to be given by the Protestant clergyman or Presbyterian minister but Catholic children were to be taught by a Catholic lay teacher who had received the bishop's approval.[226] The last recommendation was hardly likely to find favour with the Catholic bishops. The government education board was also to have sweeping powers, including the expenditure of public money on education, it was to have a legal right to the schoolhouse, the right to determine what books should be used in the schools, and the sole right of appointing and dismissing all teachers.[227] Doyle found these proposals totally unacceptable but in general Catholic opinion was much better disposed to the report – the *Dublin Evening Post*, Archbishop Curtis and the Catholic Association approved of it but the latter felt that it would not find acceptance among Catholics as a future system of education unless 'it were very considerably modified'.[228] Ironically it was Doyle, of all the prelates who gave evidence at the commission, who made the biggest impression before the commissioners of 1825. As Ó Cannáin pointed out in his study on the inquiry, it was Doyle's skilful answering of questions on such topics as allegiance to the crown, papal authority, and keeping faith with heretics, which managed to allay Protestant fears and to reassure the government that the Catholic clergy could be trusted.[229] He offered re-assurance that the pope's power was limited to the spiritual domain and he could not, for instance, absolve Catholics from oaths of allegiance.[230] The commission provided a platform for Doyle, on behalf of the Catholic church, to prove conclusively that it was far from being the church of superstition, idolatry and political sedition that many Protestants might have thought. As Ó Cannáin observed:

> The evidence of the Catholic prelates to the commissioners, much of which was concerned with the interpretation of traditional Catholic doctrine rather than education, was a prerequisite to the acceptance by Protestants that Catholics could be full, loyal citizens of a constitutionally Protestant state.[231]

226 Akenson, *The Irish education experiment*, pp 96–7.   227 First report of the commissioners, 1825, p. 99.   228 McGrath, pp 196–7.   229 S. Ó Cannáin, 'The education inquiry 1824–1826 in its social and political context' in *Irish Educational Studies* 3: 2 (1983), p. 8.   230 Ibid., p. 10.   231 S. Ó Cannáin, 'Relations between the Catholic church and the state with regard to educa-

The Catholic church's campaign against the Kildare Place Society, 1826–31

It was Daniel O'Connell who first drew the attention of the Catholic hierarchy in 1820, to what he considered to be the 'nugatory principles' of the Kildare Place. Since the setting up of the short-lived Irish National Society for promoting the education of the poor in January 1821, O'Connell was happy to leave the Catholic education question in the capable hands of the prelates. Following the publication of the first report of the commissioners in 1825, the emancipation campaign was well under way and once again 'O'Connell made the conscious decision to leave educational dealings in the hands of the Irish bishops'.[232]

While the majority of prelates were not as incensed as Doyle with the First Report of the Commissioners, 1825, the Catholic church did adopt a hard-line stance on the education issue, most likely due to the pressure they felt from the challenge posed by the bible society schools. This became apparent when Archbishop Murray forwarded to the commissioners six resolutions, unanimously passed by the Catholic archbishops and bishops. These resolutions called for wide reaching powers for the church in a state aided education system, to include a say by the Catholic church in the appointment of Catholic teachers, male and female Catholic model schools, and the right to select or approve books to be used in the schools. They also expressed their disapproval of the commissioners' recommendation that schools should be vested in the proposed new board. But the government was not prepared to take power away from the Kildare Place and the Established Church just yet, nor was it prepared to agree to a denominational system of education,[233] to suit the Catholic church, in a country torn by sectarian strife.

Parliamentary opposition to the Kildare Place was very much in evidence when the debate took place on the Irish estimates for education in the house of commons, on 20 March 1826. Thomas Spring-Rice, the member for Limerick, produced damaging statistics to show that the Society was not educating the majority of the school going population. He stated that of 408,065 Catholic schoolchildren in Ireland, 377,007 were educated at their own expense. Of 69,186 children in schools supported by public aid only 31,058 were Catholics. Neither the chief secretary Sir Henry Goulburn or the home secretary Robert Peel was swayed by this evidence and the Society was granted £25,000 on 22 March.

Doyle was now spurred into action and in April 1826 he ordered his parish priests and Catholic patrons to sever all connections with the Kildare Place.

Four months later he issued an important pastoral on the education question, in which he outlined the efforts made by the Catholic hierarchy in a bid to secure government aid for Catholic education. Not surprisingly he criticised the rules of Kildare Place which turned it into a bible society and the government's decision to grant it £25,000. He ordered the withdrawal of Catholic children from the Society's schools and suggested that each parish should build a schoolhouse to be funded by the parishioners, although many parishes had already undertaken such a scheme and were providing non-denominational education.

Doyle's efforts at seeking educational reforms received a significant boost when Thomas Spring-Rice became the spokesman in parliament for Catholic interests. In April 1828 he secured a select committee on education in Ireland to examine the reports of the education inquiry 1824–7 and all previous reports. As chairman of the select committee Spring-Rice entered into correspondence with Doyle in the 'strictest confidence' but warned him that secrecy was essential, otherwise his plan of education would be jeopardised. Spring-Rice's plan was the one which would form the blueprint for the national education system. It was to be a non-denominational system, where the principle of non-interference in the religious beliefs of children was to be upheld. A new board of education was to be appointed, with members from all denominations represented on it. It was to have wide ranging powers – it would superintend a model school, edit and print all books for the literary instruction of pupils, and religious books that had been approved by all churches. The board would receive title to all schoolhouses built at public expense and grant aided by the board. Spring-Rice suggested combined moral and literary instruction on four days of the school week, the remaining two days to be set aside for separate religious instruction. The latter was to be under the sole supervision of the respective clergy.[234] Interestingly, the pragmatic Doyle now accepted this arrangement even though in his petition to parliament in 1824 he rejected separate religious instruction out of hand. Ignoring the confidential nature of the plan Doyle wrote to O'Connell giving him the relevant details and urging him to support Spring-Rice's education scheme when it would eventually come into the public domain.

Spring-Rice's report was well received by the Catholic prelates. The authorities of the Established Church and the supporters of the Kildare Place were strongly opposed to it while the government was apathetic to it. Spring-Rice received little assistance from the new Irish chief secretary, Lord Francis Gower, even though he had been an active member of his committee.[235] He next approached Anglesea, the lord lieutenant who frankly admitted that there was little he could do because the Kildare Place had already disposed of

234 *The Irish education experiment*, pp 102–3.   235 McGrath, *Politics*, pp 212–13.

the entire education grant. When the bishops petitioned for the implementation of Spring-Rice's suggested reforms, the Kildare Place countered with a petition of their own for continued grant aid. The Society won on this occasion and the bishops lost.

Wellington's government had much more pressing problems than the Irish education question to cope with in 1828 as the emancipation campaign was nearing its climax. Besides Peel had no great desire to withdraw his support from a Society he had done so much to promote and defend throughout his political life. However, by August 1828 even Peel recognised that the position of the Society was untenable, because the education offered by it was unacceptable to the majority of parents.[236] Doyle didn't allow himself to be distracted by the exciting political events that were unfolding, judging by an entry in the minute book of the meetings of the Irish Catholic hierarchy for 9 February, 1829, when he moved a resolution 'that the prelates in their respective dioceses do issue instructions to their several clergy to prevent by every means in their power the attendance of Catholic children at schools in connexion [sic] with the Kildare Place Society'. The following day he wrote the petition to parliament on education on behalf of the hierarchy, which was submitted to parliament once again by James Grattan.

On 5 February 1830 the bishops presented yet another petition to the lord lieutenant and the chief secretary, but the response was unsatisfactory.[237] Seven months later the luck of the Catholic prelates was about to change with the formation of the whig cabinet in November 1830. Lord Anglesea who had Catholic sympathies and who had been dismissed as lord lieutenant under Wellington was now re-appointed under the new prime minister Lord Grey. Lord Edward Stanley, later earl of Derby, became the Irish chief secretary, and he approached the education question with an open mind. To crown their good fortunes Doyle found a welcome ally in the arrival on to the educational scene of Thomas Wyse, the newly elected MP for Tipperary and former Catholic Association activist and historian.

Wyse informed Doyle on 30 November 1830 that he intended to bring forward a motion on education before the house of commons after the Christmas recess. Wyse was optimistic and had confidence in the new administration that they would solve the Irish education problem. He wrote to Doyle in this vein 'I have every confidence that the new administration, liberal and energetic to a degree we could not have hoped for a few years ago – I might even say a few weeks – since, will direct their immediate attention to the urgent wants of education'. On 9 December 1830 Wyse submitted a detailed plan for national education to the government, in the form of the heads of an education bill. Wyse's plan didn't offer anything new. It was, as Akenson noted

236 McGrath, *Politics*, p. 213.   237 Ibid., pp 214–16.

'merely a rehash of generally accepted educational ideas'. Lord Stanley ignored Wyse's plan at the end of 1830 and for the first half of 1831.[238]

Doyle was not idle, however. In January 1831 he took the initiative to inform the chief secretary of the educational needs of his own diocese to demonstrate what the government would have to consider when dealing with the country as a whole. It was apparent from his communication that his hostility to the Kildare Place was equalled only by his disdain for hedge schoolmasters, as he informed Stanley of the exclusive education provided by the Society and the 'bad system' of education supplied by the hedge schools. Doyle gave full credit to himself and his diocesan clergy for the education of the poor, even though, he had publicly acknowledged as early as 31 January 1820 in his letter to the *Carlow Morning Post*, that the Catholic clergy were 'overwhelmed with other duties of their calling'. Now it suited his purpose to impress upon Stanley the obstacles the church faced when providing education for the poor. It helped his case also to state that they were making little progress but that he took heart from the fact that they had been 'more successful in correcting or removing a bad system of education than in the establishment of a good one'. He qualified this by stating that 'We have within these few years suppressed numberless hedge schools, and united, often within the place of worship the children theretofore dispersed.' Doyle pressed his case that the Catholic church couldn't afford to 'pay respectable masters' nor could they afford to furnish schools or supply them with requisite materials. He then made the radical but practical suggestion to Stanley that as Catholics outnumbered Protestants eight to one, in his diocese alone, and as a large expenditure would be required to maintain 'Catholic' schools, it would be better to devise an education system uniting the children of the different religious persuasions in the same schools.[239]

Doyle's suggestions were favourably received by Stanley who cordially replied 'I am, in Ireland, opposed to all exclusive education, supported by the state … In the attainment of this great national object I feel sensibly how much benefit I may derive from your suggestions'. Doyle was happy to oblige and he advised Stanley along the lines of Spring-Rice's education plan, to educate all children without social distinctions, in a system where religion was left solely to the respective clergymen, and where a board of commissioners acceptable to all denominations, would have power to devise their own rules and regulations. Unlike Spring-Rice's plan, Doyle, for obvious reasons, suggested that the commissioners should be able to extend aid to existing schools without having the titles of the schools vested in themselves.[240]

It could be argued that O'Connell had little direct input into the long running campaign for educational rights for Catholics. Nonetheless he played a pivotal

238 Akenson, *The Irish education experiment*, pp 107–10.   239 McGrath, *Politics*, pp 158–221.
240 Ibid., p. 222.

role by his successful campaign for Catholic emancipation, the achievement of which provided 'a practical demonstration that Catholic demands for fair treatment could not be suppressed any longer'.[241] In March 1831 O'Connell was once again vocal on the education question and his message was the same as in 1820. He stated that 'Catholics might justly claim a share of the public money, without its being made a condition that they must renounce their father's faith'. The battle for the control of Irish education took place in earnest in mid-July when an important two-day debate on the topic took place. The battle lines were clearly drawn between the supporters of the Kildare Place and those who vigorously opposed the Society. O'Connell presented a petition which had been drafted by Doyle and signed by twenty-six Irish prelates seeking the discontinuance of the Kildare Place grant. The education debate was raised again on 26 July and 23 August when pro- and anti-Kildare Place petitions respectively were presented and O'Connell presented yet another petition from the Irish prelates, in their tireless pursuit for a share of the educational grant.

On 9 September 1831 the Catholic church won a major victory when Stanley set out his proposals for the national education system of Ireland in the house of commons. In doing so he referred to the failure of the Kildare Place to provide an education for all, due to its restrictive rule on bible reading, the failure of the government for not taking action when it was obvious that the Society could never become a national one, and for allowing education to fall into 'hands unqualified for that task'.[242] Stanley followed Spring-Rice's educational plan of 1828 almost exactly, even though he never gave him credit for it. A non-denominational board of seven commissioners was to be appointed, which would have 'complete control over the various schools which may be erected under its auspices' and 'the most entire control over all books to be used in the schools', and 'absolute control over the funds which may be annually voted by parliament'.[243] Stanley asked that the commissioners look on joint applications 'with peculiar favour'. Privately, he had admitted to Archbishop Murray that joint applications would not be essential or even likely.[244] Like Spring-Rice he proposed to have united moral and literary instruction and separate religious instruction on different days of the week but Stanley also ordered that denominational instruction should be allowed outside of school hours on other days of the week.[245] It was clear to the keen observer that it would only be a question of time before the proposed non-denominational system of national education would become a denominational one.

O'Connell was well pleased with Stanley's plan. So too was Thomas Wyse. The Catholic prelates had won the education battle and even though Doyle had some reservations, he took particular satisfaction in the proposed scheme

241 Coolahan, *Irish education*, p. 4.   242 McGrath, *Politics*, p. 224.   243 Á. Hyland, 'National education, 1831–1922' in *Irish educational documents*, pp 100-2.   244 Hislop, 'The 1806–1812 board of education', p. 56.   245 Coolahan, *Irish education*, pp 10-11.

for the training of teachers, and he looked forward to the displacement by them of the independent hedge schoolmaster. He wrote: 'The rule which requires that all teachers henceforth to be employed be provided from some model school, with a certificate of their competency, will aid us in a work of great difficulty, to wit, that of suppressing hedge-schools, and placing youth under the direction of competent teachers'.[246]

The uneasy relationship between some of the Catholic clergy and the hedge schoolmasters lived on into the national school system according to the study carried out by Mary Daly on the applications to the commissioners of national education for the years 1831 to 1840 for the counties of Cavan, Mayo, Cork and Kilkenny. She found evidence that many priests hoped that the establishment of a national school would undermine the existence of local private pay schools.[247] James Hoban in his study of the hedge schools in Co. Roscommon found that the hedge schools were still educating the majority of school children in 1841. This was also borne out by the census report for that year. According to the report of the royal commission of inquiry into primary education of 1870 (Powis), 'some hedge schools continued in existence, forty years after the introduction of the national schools'.[248] In the diocese of Kildare and Leighlin none of the hedge schools changed over to the national system in the early years, even though their bishop had struggled so long to bring it about.[249]

However, the hedge schoolmasters' loose, haphazard educational enterprise couldn't possibly hope to compete for long with the new formalised, structured and well financed system of education, which had the support of the Catholic church and eventually of parents. In Roscommon in 1835 there were 189 hedge schools, by 1879, a year after the passing of the Intermediate Act, this number had fallen to 11, and a very small number continued into the latter years of the nineteenth century.[250] The Catholic church had not only won a victory over the government supported Kildare Place Society but it had also won a major victory over 'that sturdy figure, the old independent hedge schoolmaster'.[251]

246 P.J. Dowling, *A history of Irish education* (Cork, 1971), pp 117–18.   247 Daly, 'The development of the national school system, 1831–40', pp 156–7.   248 Hoban, 'The survival of the hedge schools – a local study', pp 25–6.   249 McGrath, *Politics*, p. 237.   250 Op. cit., p. 34.   251 Dowling, *A history of Irish education*, p. 118.

2

The social setting, 1764–1831

'Through Erin's Isle to sport awhile'. 'A seat behind the coachman'

Misery, naked and famishing, that misery, which is vagrant, idle, mendicant,
covers the entire country ... it is the first thing you see when you land on the
Irish coast and from that moment, it ceases not to be present to your view.[1]

Gustave de Beaumont, Ireland, social, political & religious *(1839)*

Throughout the late eighteenth and early nineteenth centuries, a period when
hedge schoolmasters dominated Irish education, poverty among the ordinary
people had reached alarming proportions. Travellers to Ireland were deeply
affected by some of the scenes of hardship and misery they witnessed. As
early as 1764, John Bush noted beggars on 'the high roads ... throughout the
southern and western parts'.[2] In 1775 Richard Twiss, considered Irish beggars to be reasonable in their demands, with 'most of them offering a bad halfpenny, which they call a "rap", and soliciting for a good one in exchange'.[3]
Writing in 1805, Sir John Carr was struck by the number of beggars he witnessed who seemed to him 'to be even more numerous and wretched than
those he had seen in France'.[4] Von Puckler-Muskau, the German prince who
arrived in Ireland on 11 August 1828, was shocked by the dirt, the poverty
and the ragged clothing of the people. Beggar-boys buzzed around him like
flies, so much so that he always kept his pockets full of coppers to throw out
to the beggars 'like corn among the fowl'.[5]

The cabins which the peasants occupied were the source of much comment by many travellers, mainly because of their primitive nature. A typical
cabin was described by Coquebert de Montbret who recognised a strong sim-
ilarity between it and the mud huts built by beggars on the highways in
France. Travelling through Limerick in 1791, he observed:

---

1 London, 1839, p. 264. 2 *Hibernia curiosa* (London, 1979), p. 30. Quoted by Lecky and J.A.
Froude in *The English in Ireland in the eighteenth century* (London, 1872–4). 3 R. Twiss, *A tour
in Ireland in 1775* (London, 1776), p. 73. 4 J. Carr, 'The stranger in Ireland' in Constantia
Maxwell (ed.), *The stranger in Ireland* (London, 1954), p. 225. 5 'Tour in England, Ireland and

> The Irish cabins ... are like the mud huts which beggars build on our
> highways ... very few have windows. In some there are one or two holes
> which are stuffed, at night, with a wisp of straw. Less frequently still,
> have they chimneys and when there is one, it is made of boards or bun-
> dles of sticks. The roofs are often weighted with stones and even with
> pieces of wood as protection against the wind. The entrance is gener-
> ally the dirtiest place on the main road.[6]

De Montbret was well acquainted with scenes of poverty. He had witnessed
them before in France and Germany, yet he was taken aback at the extent of the
poverty in rural Ireland. Three of the eighteenth century travel writers mentioned the hedge schools they observed on their travels. In 1775 Twiss
'observed a dozen bare-legged boys sitting by the side of the road scrawling
on scraps of paper placed on their knees'.[7] Arthur Young (1741–1820) noticed
many hedge schools also but he felt that this was a misnomer for them. He
wrote 'they might as well be termed ditch ones, for I have seen many a ditch
full of scholars'[8] and the French tourist de Latocnaye who walked around Ireland between the years 1796 and 1797 and found 'numerous schools in the
hedges'.[9]

As the penal laws were relaxed after 1782, the hedge schools moved to a
bewildering assortment of buildings, but they still retained the name hedge
schools. Chapels were used regularly as schools, as William Shaw Mason
reported from Limerick in 1814. At Ennistymon, where there was no chapel,
the sessions-house was used for this purpose.[10] The Scottish visitor Christopher Anderson made the unusual discovery of a hedge school being conducted in a graveyard,[11] whereas in Monaghan they used corn kilns, out-offices, a
mill, a wheat store and two rooms at Monaghan race course.[12] Proof of these

France' in Maxwell, *The stranger in Ireland*, p. 266.   6 'A Frenchman's impression of Limerick town and people in 1791' in *North Munster Antiquarian Journal* 5:4 (1948), p. 96. De Montbret was sent as consul to Ireland in 1789. He spent the greater part of his two years service
touring the countryside. He kept a written record of his six tours – his 'carnets de voyages',
which were edited in the mid 20th century by Síle Ní Chinnéide.   7 R. Twiss, 'A tour in Ireland in 1775' in J.P. Harrington (ed), *The English traveller in Ireland* (Dublin, 1991), p. 171.   8
A. Young, 'A Tour in Ireland' in Constantia Maxwell (ed), *A tour in Ireland* (Cambridge, 1925),
p. 202. Young's account was rated highly by Lecky and Maxwell. The Dublin Society commissioned John Wynn Baker to compile an abridged edition of Young's *Tour of England*, for the
benefit of their members.   9 Chevalier de Latocnaye, 'Promenade d'un Français dans l'rlande'
in John Stevenson (ed), *A Frenchman's walk through Ireland* (Belfast, 1917), p. 145.   10 *A statistical account or parochial survey of Ireland*, i (Dublin, 1814), p. 495. The statistical survey writers were mainly members of the establishment and the landed class, and Church of Ireland
clergymen who were employed by the Dublin Society. The Society consisted of patriotic landlords, anxious to improve the social and economic life of Ireland. It received the royal charter
from George II in 1750.   11 *The native Irish and their descendants* (Dublin, 1846), p. 205.   12
Johnston, 'Hedge schools of Tyrone and Monaghan', p. 48.

locations is to be found in the report of the commissioners of education, 1824–7, drawn up from the parochial returns submitted to them by Catholic and Protestant clergymen. From an inspection of the parochial returns it is clear that hedge schoolmasters and Irish parents were living in abject poverty and the conditions in which children were taught were very spartan. Take for example the following extract from the 1824 parochial returns for the hedge schools in Breiffne.

John Rothwell   ...   Income £6 ... a miserable hovel.
Edward Smith   ...   Income about £5 ... a mud cabin
Peter Rogers   ...   Income about £5 ... [Schoolhouse] serves also for
                           a barn and a cowhouse.[13]

The parochial returns for Kildare and Leighlin paint a similar picture of deprivation and discomfort:

Pat Byrne   ...   Income £4 ... Schoolhouse in an old ditch built
                        of sods.[14]
William White   ...   Income £2

Where these children are belongs to a poor farmer where he fothered cows last winter, at this moment I am greatly annoyed by the rain coming down at every side of me: as to its accommodations, there are none, except some stones laid round by the walls on which the children sit – not even a table or form.[15]

In many instances the returns show that parents built hedge schools for the masters 'The most frequently recurring phrase to be met with being "built by the parish"'. These were usually primitive structures, little more than 'a miserable hovel with a clay wall only partially thatched, 15 feet long and 10 feet wide', like the one built for Fanny Moore in 1817 in Kill.[16] The number of female teachers was not nearly so numerous as the men, due to the severity of the lifestyle. Only ninety-six female teachers were mentioned in the parochial returns for Kildare and Leighlin and if we add the findings of the 1824 survey to this, the number comes to one hundred and seventy female teachers in all.[17] The most notable feature of the hedge schools was their lack of windows, a factor which can be explained by the window tax introduced in 1799, which applied to every inhabited house. Another reason why hedge schools were devoid of creature comforts was to avoid confiscation by the landlord.

13 O'Connell, *The schools and scholars of Breiffne*, pp 392–3.   14 Brenan, *Schools of Kildare and Leighlin*, pp 104, , 453, 86.   15 Ibid., p. 417.   16 Ibid., p. 253.   17 Ibid., p. 86.

A typical hedge school was described graphically by Shaw Mason, writing of Maghera, Co. Derry in 1814. His account is almost identical to that recalled by William Carleton of his hedge schoolmaster Pat Frayne's school at Skelgy in Clogher, Co. Tyrone,[16] and that of Humphrey O'Sullivan (1780-1838) recorded in his diary (1827-35) on 14 May 1827 of his father's first hedge school at Callan, built for him at the crossroads in the summer of 1791.[17] Shaw Mason wrote:

> Schoolhouses are in general wretched huts, built of sods in the high-way ditches, from which circumstance they are designated hedge schools. They have neither door, window nor chimney; a large hole in the roof serving to admit light and let out smoke. A low narrow wall of mud, hard baked serves as a seat. A hole cut in the mud wall on the south side affords ingress and egress to its inhabitants.[18]

By 1824 the hedge schools were known in official quarters as 'Catholic pay schools'. The evidence of the Anthony R. Blake given before the select committee of the house of lords in 1837, provides us with the official definition of a hedge school.

> 'Do you mean by Pay Schools what are usually called Hedge Schools?'
> 'They are usually called Hedge Schools.'
> 'Are they called Pay Schools because the Children pay for their own Instruction?'
> 'Yes: they are distinguished as "Pay Schools" in the Reports which we had in 1825 and 1826.'
> 'Will you explain further what you mean by Pay Schools?'
> 'I mean by Pay Schools, schools in which the masters receive some small stipend from "the children who attend them", schools set up on private speculation; schools that receive no Aid, either from the State or from any Society established for the Promotion of Education. The Masters received 1d a week or so from the children; sometimes more and sometimes less.'[19]

Although the hedge schools were little more than 'wretched huts, built of sods in the highway ditches', by 1812, a contemporary writer who visited Ireland could confidently claim that 'the people of Ireland are, I may almost say,

16 Carleton, *The autobiography*, p. 29.   17 T. de Bhaldraithe, *The diary of Humphrey O'Sullivan 1827–1835* (Dublin, 1979), p. 23.   18 Shaw Mason (ed.), *A statistical account*, pp. 19–20.   19 Report of the select committee of the house of lords on the plan of education in Ireland, 1837,

universally educated',[20] while another gave credit for this phenomenon to the parents, who made 'meritorious sacrifice of earnings ... for the education of their children'.[21] Lord Palmerston too acknowledged, the great sacrifices made by his Irish speaking tenants in Co. Sligo, in 1808, to secure a hedge school education for their children

> The thirst for education is so great that there are now three or four schools upon the estate. The people join in engaging some itinerant master: they run him up a miserable mud hut in the roadside, and the boys pay him half-a-crown, or some five shillings a quarter.[22]

Considering that a shilling represented a full days wage for a farm labourer, 'in poorer districts it would have paid three days' wages',[23] the sacrifice made by parents was quite considerable.

A striking illustration of this quest for learning was given in the official recognition of the existence of evening schools run by hedge schoolmasters, for those who had to work on farms or 'for those children whose service during the day their parents could not afford to lose'. The commissioners of education in 1806 mentioned the fact that in one parish alone there were eleven evening schools.[24] Of greater curiosity for the modern reader however would be the two recorded cases of parents who required the services of hedge schoolmasters so desperately that they kidnapped them from other areas. The husband and wife team of Halls who travelled in Ireland, referred to this as common practice, as they recalled

> The people who inhabited a rude district of the Connemara mountains felt the necessity of a teacher for their children ... they took forcible possession of a domine, and conveyed him by might from a distance of several miles to the vicinity of their rude mountain huts.

The teacher was forbidden to travel a mile from his domicile until he had trained a replacement. The imprisonment lasted five years, at the end of which the domine had no desire to leave a people he had become attached to.[25] Carleton also mentioned this practice in his story 'The hedge school', when Mat Kavanagh, the fictional representative for his own teacher Pat Frayne,

p. 54. **20** E. Wakefield, *An account of Ireland, statistical and political* (London, 1812), p. 397. Wakefield spent four years writing this critical account, having been urged to do so by John Foster, later Lord Oriel and former chancellor of the exchequer. **21** S.C. Curwen, *Observations on the state of Ireland* (London, 1818), pp. 388–9. **22** A. Stopford Green, 'Irish national tradition' in *History* (July, 1917) p. 28. **23** Dowling, *The hedge schools of Ireland*, p. 77. **24** Fourteenth report 1806–12, p. 331. **25** Mr and Mrs S.C. Hall, *Ireland, its scenery, character* (London, 1841), p. 260.

was kidnapped by the parents of Findramore, Carleton was at pains to impress upon the reader why kidnapping a schoolmaster was a necessity at the time.

> The country was densely inhabited, the rising population exceedingly numerous ... the old and middle-aged heads of families were actuated by a simple wish, inseparable from Irishmen, to have their children educated; and the young men, by a determination to have a properly qualified person to conduct their night schools.[26]

He stressed the fact that the kidnapping incident he related actually took place.

The 'hidden Ireland'. The underworld of Gaelic poets and hedge schoolmasters

Writing in 1924, Daniel Corkery (1878–1964) explored what he called the 'hidden Ireland' of the eighteenth century. This was the underworld of the Gaelic Munster poets, several of whom were hedge schoolmasters. It was also the underworld of the old Gaelic families of the big houses who had escaped the Williamite confiscations and the subsequent penal laws. He demonstrated from the sentiments expressed by these poets in their verse and song that their racial pride was offended by their poverty. Jonathan Swift was no doubt correct when he said that to his conquerors the peasant was little more than 'a hewer of wood and a drawer of water', but this was not how the poor regarded themselves.

   Their songs and poems continuously reminded them that they were the 'children of kings, the sons of Milesius'.[27] However, the poet/hedge schoolmasters certainly never regarded themselves as poor peasants even though they were indistinguishable from them in dress, manner and speech. They saw themselves as men of learning, what Corkery called 'the residuary legatees of over a thousand years of literary culture', with an aristocratic lineage. Eoghan Rua Ó Súilleabháin (1748–84) introduced himself in one of his poems as 'I that come of the stock of the Gaels of Cashel of the provincial kings'.[28] Their status was confirmed for them by the welcome they received at the big houses. Corkery speculated that the Clare poet/hedge schoolmaster Brian

26 W. Carleton, *Traits and stories of the Irish peasantry* (London, 1979), pp. 287–8.   27 D. Corkery, *The hidden Ireland* (Dublin, 1924), p. 41. This book encourages people to seek their cultural heritage in an exclusively Gaelic past, while his *Synge and Anglo-Irish literature* (1931) dismissed the idea that the writings of Anglo-Irishmen, could be espoused as the national literature. He was professor of English at UCC (1930); senator, 1951–4; member of Irish Arts Council, 1952–6.   28 Ibid., p. 196.

Merriman (1747–1805) 'never a rich man, visited these houses, and perhaps was set to teach the children in some them'. We know that Ó Súilleabháin not only worked for them as a spalpeen or migrant labourer but also as a private tutor. Other hedge schoolmasters who provided private tuition for the children of the gentry were Donnchadh Ruadh Mac Conmara (1715–1810) in Waterford, Riocárd Báiréad in Erris, Co. Mayo and Tomás Rua Ó Súilleabháin in Iveragh, Co. Kerry to name but a few.

Corkery identified two classes in Irish society – the harried, poverty-stricken cottiers of the smoky cabins and the Gaelic speaking cultured landlords of the big houses. But he failed to identify two further groups of wealthy middle class Catholics among the landed classes. There were Catholic middlemen, many of them displaced Irish gentry, who leased lands from absentee English landlords who had received confiscated lands after the Williamite wars. Their leases were 'sometimes for ever, more often for lives extending over forty, fifty, sixty or seventy years'.[29] The other group consisted of strong Catholic farmers, who had emerged just as the middleman system went into decline at the end of the eighteenth century, aided by the Catholic relief bill of 1782 which admitted them into the land market where they were permitted to purchase and dispose of land. They had accumulated capital during the agricultural boom in the last quarter of the century.[30]

Education was quite important to these families so they engaged the professional services of the hedge schoolmasters 'usually by a system of patronage-cum-tutelage' because 'education paved the way for openings in trade, the church or abroad'.[31] The older gentry-derived middlemen families were contemptuous of the rising Catholic families. This contempt was evident in the Irish poetry of the period, which generally reflected the aristocratic aspirations of the middleman class. They were portrayed as upstart gentry, without manners or education. Two northern poets, Art MacCumhaigh and the poet/hedge schoolmaster Peadar Ó Doirnín, satirised the 'arrivistes' or the upstarts with their social pretensions. MacCumhaigh satirised the O'Callaghans of Cullaville in Armagh, when he nicknamed them 'Bodaigh na hEorna' – the churls of the barley because they made money from owning a distillery. Indignation also marked the poem *Tarlach cóir Ó hAmaill* by Peadar Ó Doirnín.[32]

Travellers to Ireland, according to Whelan (1998), who passed 'rapidly through the roadside raggle-taggle of miserable cabins'[33] were so overwhelmed by the images of poverty that greeted them that they failed 'to notice the discreet but comfortable world of the strong farmer insulated from the

29 Lecky, *A history of Ireland*, p. 67.   30 Foster, *Modern Ireland*, p. 201. This occurred as a direct result of Foster's Corn Law of 1784 which favoured landlords and tenants. It gave large bounties on the export of wheat and limited imports by duties.   31 K. Whelan, 'An underground gentry? Catholic middlemen in eighteenth-century Ireland' in *Irish popular culture*, p. 137.   32 B. Ó Buachalla, *Peadar Ó Doirnín: amhráin* (Dublin, 1969), p. 55.   33 Op. cit., pp 139–40.

perimiter of poverty around them', consequently he claimed that 'the seat behind the coachman was ... a biased one in pre-famine Ireland'. It is true that they may not have been aware of the Catholic strong farmers' hidden wealth but de Montbret was forcibly struck by the contrasts presented by the two extremes of opulence and poverty when he met both poor and wealthy Catholics in Kerry, Limerick and Cork.[34] All travellers to Ireland remarked on the prosperity of the north in comparison to the south but great poverty did exist in certain parts of Belfast. Sir Walter Scott recognised the scale of Belfast's poverty when he travelled there in 1825 and noticed 'mountainous packages of old clothes; the cast off raiment of the Scotch beggars on its way to a land where beggary is the staple of life',[35] and yet this city could boast of a chamber of commerce as early as 1783 and of a harbour corporation and a white linen hall in 1785.[36] If the seeming prosperity of Belfast was deceptive so too was the magnificent splendour that formed much of the exterior of Georgian Dublin. The elegance and grandeur of its architectural showpieces was praised by Young (1776), de Latocnaye (1796), Carr (1805) and Curwen (1818) but many of them also referred to the scenes of filth and squalor and the wretchedness of the poor which they witnessed in parts of the city.

Young described in considerable detail a large number of resident land-lords who had devoted their time to 'improving' agriculture and to rooting out the system of middlemen. By 1793 they had achieved some success in this regard, in the more prosperous parts of the country. Many Irish landlords were philanthropic members of the Dublin Society such as its founding mem-ber Dr Madden (1686–1765) who wrote his *Reflections and resolutions proper for the gentlemen of Ireland, as to their conduct for the service of their country* (1738) advocating agricultural improvement and social reform. He established pre-miums for the encouragement of learning at Trinity College, and for the encouragement of Irish agriculture, manufacture and trade under the aus-pices of the Dublin Society.

Absentee landlords made their contributions also, even though most com-mentators, including Young, were critical of them for drawing rental out of the country. It was they, who had the best managed estates and who invested heav-ily in the agriculture of Ireland, throughout the eighteenth century.[37] However, despite the fact that there were so many 'improving' landlords, the majority of them failed to effect any change in the system of agricuture, to bring about a

---

34 C. de Montbret, 'A new view of the eighteenth century life in Kerry' in *Journal of the Kerry Archaeological and Historical Society* 6 (1973), p. 96. He refers to the existence of opulence and poverty in the following two articles also: 'A journey from Cork to Limerick in December 1790' in *Kerry Historical & Archaeological Society* (1971), p. 72 and 'A new view of Cork city in 1790' in *Journal of the Cork Historical and Archaeological Society* 78:227 (Jan-June 1973), p. 1.   35 D. Ó Muirithe, *A seat behind the coachman* (Dublin, 1972), p. 26.   36 Foster, *Modern Ireland*, pp 203–4.   37 Maxwell, *Country and town*, p. 188.

radical improvement in the living conditions of the bulk of the population of
Ireland. As for the Anglo–Irish gentry, they behaved, not as a body of philanthropic gentlemen but rather according to the standards of their time and the
code of conduct expected of their class. As Constantia Maxwell remarked in
Dublin under the Georges, 'they lived up to their incomes'. The employed more
servants than they needed, their dress was extravagant, and their equipages
exceeded their incomes in many instances. In 1799 the duke of Leinster had
an annual income of £20,000, the duke of Ormonde £22,000, Mr Conally of
Castletown £25,000, and in addition, the lowest value of their estates in 1812
was £100,000. It should be noted also that the wealthiest landlords in Ireland
had their incomes supplemented by the rents they received from a half starv-
ing population, living on the verge of famine for much of their lives as the
potato crop, the main staple of their diet, failed on average 'one year in every
two or three'.[38]

Another influential landed class in Irish society – the governing body of
ecclesiastical gentlemen in the Church of Ireland, also failed to make any
appreciable difference to the lives of these cottiers. There were of course some
exemplary, humanitarian archbishops such as 'Bolton, archbishop of Cashel,
who died in 1744, and Hoadly, archbishop of Armagh who died in 1746', who
were credited with having 'done good service to the country by draining bogs,
and improving husbandry'. Other prelates who were noted as ecclesiastical
'improvers' in the late eighteenth century were Archbishop Robinson of
Armagh, Augustus Hervey, bishop of Derry, and Bishop Percy of Dromore,
and the philosopher George Berkeley (1685–1753), bishop of Cloyne (1732).
However, many Irish bishops were absentees, due to the fact that nearly all
the higher posts in the Church of Ireland were filled with Englishmen. Some
resident prelates were also distracted from their pastoral role because they
were closely involved in the politics of the state, when they ruled the country
as lord justices in the absence of the lord lieutenant, in the first half of the
eighteenth century. By the end of the century bishops of the Established
Church were among the richest men in Ireland, due largely to the rise in rents
and tithes. Young recorded that 'the primate was receiving £8000 a year, the
archbishop of Dublin £5000. The bishop of Derry had £7000, that of Cashel
£4000 and that of Cloyne £2,500'. The Edinburgh Review of 1835 made
interesting observations also when it noted that the Established Church population in Ireland 'was less than that found in the diocese of Durham in England, yet it was governed by four archbishops and twenty-two bishops and its
revenues were some £800,000, three-quarters of which came from tithes
mostly paid by the more than 6,000,000 Catholics in Ireland'.

38 C. Ó Gráda, *Ireland before and after the famine* (Manchester, 1988), p. 2.

John Bush was among the earliest writers to reject the unjust system of tithes and the pressing demands for priests' dues. The 'rapacious, insatiable priests' who exacted tithes, were, he regretted to say, 'English persons'. He castigated Catholic priests also for demanding their 'full quota of unremitted offerings'. When de Latocnaye attended mass in the chapel near Tralee, he said the priest 'consigned to all the devils (although in highly proper terms) all those infamous enough not to pay his dues'. While he recognized that many dedicated priests were very poor, he had seen others who appeared to be quite 'comfortable', having between 'one and two hundred a year, besides a tolerable house, and dinners innumerable'. The wealthiest Catholic bishop resided in Co. Cork and according to de Montbret, who visited Cork city in 1790, he earned a modest £1000 per annum, while the income of the parish priest of Carrigaline, was 'almost equal to that of a bishoprick in any other part of Ireland' but their Protestant counterparts were in receipt of incomes five, six, seven and sometimes even eight times these amounts.

Rack rents, tithes and priests dues placed a severe financial strain on the cottier class but in 1758 an even worse calamity befell them. They, along with the day labourers who couldn't afford to rent land, and the migrant workers or 'spalpeens' were reduced to a condition of almost hopeless wretchedness due to the English government's decision to allow Irish landowners to export live cattle into England. The decision was taken because 'a murrain which had broken out in 1739 among the horned cattle of Holstein ... had at length extended to Holland and England'.[39] This had the effect of turning whole baronies into pasture land, resulting in 'numerous evictions'.[40] This produced a situation whereby 'vast herds of Irish bullocks were set upon the roads towards the Irish ports ... the result of all was that herds of dispossessed human beings, as well as the herds of beasts, began to darken the roads'.[41] Charles Topham Bowden writing in 1791 regarded the exportation of Irish cattle to England as 'an evil of the most pernicious tendency'. He had it on good authority that there was 'scarce a port or creek in the south of Ireland, where some thousand head of black cattle were not shipped off'.[42] He was outraged when he saw that 'the whole country was almost appropriated to pasturage, and human beings were banished the soil to make way for sheep and bullocks'. He considered that the situation in which the peasant now found himself, rendered him no 'better than a beast of burden', because he couldn't enjoy or experience 'the necessaries of life or the just rewards of his labour'. De Montbret who travelled from Cork to Limerick in 1790 was also horrified at the sight of so 'many wretched dwellings confined to the roadside to avoid breaking up the pasturage'.[43]

39 Lecky, *A history of Ireland*, 2, p. 1.   40 Lecky, *A history of Ireland*, 1, p. 219.   41 Corkery, *The hidden Ireland*, p. 38.   42 *A tour through Ireland* (London, 1791), p. 161.   43 de Montbret, 'A

The rapid conversion from tillage to pasturage led to enclosures, when landlords withdrew from their tenants 'a right of commonage which had been given them as part of their bargain, when they received their small tenancies, and without which it was impossible that they could pay the rents which were demanded'.[44] It was hardly a coincidence then that the Whiteboy movement should have been activated at the end of 1761 just as the system of enclosing commons was extending throughout the country. Bush who travelled through Ireland three years later, witnessed at first hand the misery which provoked the Whiteboy disturbances, and he wrote with sympathy:

> What dread of justice or punishment can be expected from an Irish peasant in a state of wretchedness and extreme penury, in which if the first man that should meet him were to knock him on the head and give him an everlasting relief from his distressed and penurious life, he might have reason to think it a friendly and meritorious action; and that so many of them bear their distressed abject state with patience is to me a sufficient proof of the natural civility of their disposition.[45]

Before 1770 Whiteboy activity had nearly ceased only to erupt with new vigour in 1775, in Kildare, Kilkenny and the Queen's County. It continued there with partial interruptions until 1785, when it spread once more through Munster. Philip Luckombe who toured Ireland in 1780 displayed little sympathy with the native grievances and even less with the 'lawless ruffians called White-boys'. He proceeded to elaborate:

> These are ignorant peasants, who do not chuse to pay tythes, or taxes, and who in the night-time assemble sometimes to the number of many hundreds, on horseback and on foot, well armed, and with shirts over their clothes, from whence their denomination is derived.[46]

He gave an account of their daily activities, which were acts of the utmost barbarity. He wrote '... they stroll about the country, firing houses and barns, burying people alive in the grounds, cutting their noses and ears off'. Luckombe noted that there was strong Whiteboy activity in the counties of Kilkenny, Waterford, Wexford and Carlow even though rewards of up to fifty pounds were offered for their apprehension and despite the fact that sometimes the 'deluded wretches' were hanged. In spite of acts against the Whiteboys dating from 1765 and in spite of 'admonitions, denunciations and even excommunications ... oathbound secret societies continued to exist, and particularly in times of distress, the people obeyed the local Whiteboy code instead of the

journey from Cork to Limerick', p. 69. **44** Lecky, *A history of Ireland*, 2, p. 11. **45** Bush, *Hibernia curiosa*, p. 33. **46** *A tour through Ireland* (Dublin, 1789), p. 100.

law of the land'.[47] Those instrumental in administering the oath and in for-
mulating the objectives of the Whiteboys, were as Lecky pointed out 'evidently men of some education and of no small organising ability'. It would be
reasonable to conclude that they were the local hedge schoolmasters, educated men who held such sway over the people because of the deferential attitude
of the people towards their learning.

Education and religion

> Their church makes a part of their history. It has shared in all the
> vicissitudes of their good or evil fortune; it has drunk deeply of
> their almost exhaustless cup of bitterness.[48]

A strong bond was forged between the priests and the majority of the Catholic
population in Ireland in penal times as they colluded with one another to
evade the law. As Lecky remarked, 'Priests were an illegal class compelled to
associate with smugglers, robbers, privateers, to whose assistance they were
often obliged to resort in order to escape the ministers of justice'.[49] Priests
carried out their religious obligations by responding bravely and imaginatively
to the challenges that faced them. Mass was celebrated 'in secret rock-clefts,
with sentries posted on the hilltops',[50] and in 'sand-pits, barns, the upper
rooms of public houses ... the ruins of ancient churches'. De Latocnaye came
across such a service being conducted in the ruins of an old abbey in Co.
Leitrim. He was taken aback by the wretched appearance, not only of the
building, but also of the people in attendance. He also observed two or three
priests in the graveyard hearing confessions. They each sat on a stone and
held a piece of cloth in their hands to separate the penitent from the crowd,
so 'that the flock might afterwards truthfully swear, if put to it, that they knew
not who the celebrant was'.[51] Bishops also braved the perils of the time and by
using disguises managed to carry out their episcopal duties. One such was the
bishop of Kilmore, Dr Andrew Campbell, who attended the fairs dressed as
a highlander, carrying his bagpipes under his arm. As children wearing some
distinctive sign advanced, he dutifully administered the sacrament of confirmation to each.[52]

In the 1760s and especially after the relaxation of the penal laws against
religion in 1782, the power of the priest over his flock diminished temporar-
ily. This was mainly due to the church's denunciation of agrarian agitation

---

47 Wall, 'The age of the penal laws', p. 229.   48 T. Reid, *Travels in Ireland in the year 1822*
(London, 1823), p. 116.   49 W.E.H. Lecky, *A history of Ireland in the eighteenth century* (abr.)
(London, 1972), pp 79–80.   50 Corkery, *The hidden Ireland*, p. 40.   51 Op. cit.   52 Maxwell,
Country and town, p. 349.

and its subsequent excommunications of Whiteboys and members of other secret societies. The Catholic bishops recognised that a substantial part of their agitation 'reflected widespread anti-Catholic church sentiment'.[53] The archbishop of Tuam, Oliver Kelly, pinpointed one of the reasons for this, when he gave evidence before the parliamentary committee inquiring into the state of Irish education in 1825, as the resentment people felt at 'the payment of the Catholic clergy'.[54] In fact the people were so resentful of having to pay priests' dues that on occasions they openly rebelled by converting to the Protestant religion en masse. One such incident was recalled by Bowen (1978), in *The Protestant crusade*, of a priest in the Cork area who was forced to seek refuge in the parsonage, due to the wrath of the people at his exaction of dues. Many of them also tried to convert to Protestantism.[55]

Even the hedge schoolmasters, whose livelihoods depended on the approval of the priests, not only supported the secret societies but some were in fact instrumental in setting them up, and in organising many of their activities. According to Crofton Croker, the hedge schoolmaster was

> frequently the promoter of insurrectional tumults; he plans the nocturnal operations of the disaffected; writes their threatening proclamations studiously mis-spelled and pompously signed, Cpt. Moonlight, Lieut. Firebrand, Major Hasher, Col. Dreadnought; and Gen. Rock, night errant, and Grand Commander of the Order of the Shamrock Election.[56]

This assertion can be substantiated by court records, as Foster (1988) in *Modern Ireland 1600-1972*, pointed out, 'the classic picture of hedgeschoolmasters as conduits of subversion' can be 'borne out by court records'.

The Catholic prelates strongly disapproved of the United Irishman's rebellion of 1798, which was based on what they considered to be dangerous French principles. Many of these prelates had been trained in seminaries on the continent and they 'knew well how dangerous revolution could be, and how ineffectual the church usually was when it tried to control social agitation'.[57] The people didn't follow the guidance offered by their spiritual leaders on this occasion either and neither did some of the hedge schoolmasters who had either direct or indirect involvement in the rising. After the 1798 rebellion the priests gained in popularity with the people once more. The reason for this was that the ruling classes grew suspicious of the priests, suspecting some of them of having sympathy with their revolutionary parishioners.

---

53 Bowen, *The Protestant crusade*, p. 3.   54 First report of the commissioners, 1825, pp 259–60.
55 Op. cit., p. 143.   56 Crofton Croker, *Researches in the south of Ireland*, pp 328–9.   57 Bowen, *The Protestant crusade*, p. 3.

Several priests were killed and their houses were attacked by Orangemen and militia. This was sufficient to restore the clergy to their old position of influence and to help them to regain their hold over the people.

Travellers to Ireland in the 1790s commented on priestly power in local communities, the readiness of the priests to excommunicate law breakers and to banish the morally lax. De Latocnaye remarked 'The priests have greater power over their people. They are in fact the judges of the country and settle everything connected with morals and manners. They excommunicate a peasant and oblige him to leave a parish'. Sometimes they were obliged to use their powers against their strongest allies and intellectual equals – the erring poet/hedge schoolmasters. It should be stated however, that the majority of the poets and masters, greatly assisted the clergy in keeping the faith of the people strong, poets such as Séamus Dall MacCuarta (c.1647–1732) who lived most of his life in Omeath, Co. Louth and won fame for the fervour of his religious poems and Tadhg Gaedhealach Ó Súilleabháin (1715–95) from Limerick.[58] Other poets supported the Catholic church by censuring priests and brothers who converted to the Protestant religion. This they did by means of satire: 'the conforming priest was attacked in some very bitter poetry, mockingly bitter if he married, savagely bitter if he exercised orders in the Established Church'.[59] Others still, played a supportive role to the priests by working as coadjutors in the teaching of the catechism and Christian doctrine on Sundays.

English travellers to Ireland in the nineteenth century were exceptionally critical of Catholic clerical influence. George Cooper, a young English law student, who came here on the eve of the Act of Union, was one of the first writers to accuse Catholic priests of being ignorant and bigoted. To Cooper the priest was 'the petty tyrant of each village'. He held him responsible for the degraded character of the Irish, whom he regarded as being indolent, ignorant, impoverished and superstitious.[60] As many of the contemporary writers were either Protestant Englishmen like Cooper or Irish Protestant clergymen, or landlords, one should not be too surprised by the unfavourable comments which many of them reserved for the Catholic clergy. The Reverend James Hall who toured Ireland in 1813 accused them of bigotry and ignorance. He was exasperated by the exceedingly large numbers of Catholics he encountered in the capital. He wondered how their number might be lessened, because he considered that 'the Catholicism established in Ireland, is in many places, of the most bigoted and absurd kind, and when we consider the ignorance of many of its professors, not likely soon to purify itself'.[61] Further

58 R. Ó Foghludha, *Tadhg Gaedhealach Ó Suilleabháin* (Dublin, 1927), p. 13. Ó Suilleabháin wrote exclusively on religious themes, his most famous work being the *Pious miscellany*, which was published some forty times after its first publication in 1802.   59 Corish, *The Catholic community*, p. 110.   60 G. Cooper, *Letters on the Irish nation* (London, 1800), p. 45.   61 Rev. J. Hall,

claims were made against the clergy by Dutton in 1808 and by Glassford in 1824. Dutton accused them of being negligent in their duty regarding the education of the poor. It was the practice at the time to convert Catholic chapels into 'hedge' schools, especially in winter, but Dutton was outraged at the damp, dirty state these chapels were in, considering it to be to 'the disgrace of the priest and his flock'.[62] Glassford for his part, accused the clergy of deliberately adopting a policy of keeping the peasantry ignorant, in order to retain their power over them. He alleged

> there is an evident indifference, on the part of the Roman Catholic clergy, to extend the sphere of intellectual knowledge among their people. This is the natural operation of the religion: for the ignorance of the people is the power of the priest; his temporal policy is therefore obvious.[63]

There is a significant amount of evidence to counter these charges against the clergy. First we have de Montbret who was an objective writer, who made a strong claim for the complete lack of bigotry among the Catholic clergy. In fact he asserted that they compared favourably with their Protestant counterparts, who were ever ready to criticise them:

> Protestant ecclesiastics tell him this and that about the Catholic clergy, but in truth he finds among them 'much regularity in their way of life, together with a great deal more zeal, more enlightenment and less prejudice', than is to be found among their critics.

This claim was further substantiated by Thomas Newenham, a major in the militia and an Irishman who wrote in an objective, balanced way regarding the political, commercial and social conditions of Ireland in 1809. He stated:

> That the lower orders of the Irish are extremely illiterate and ignorant and that the Roman Catholic clergy successfully exert their influence in keeping them so are hasty assertions equally trite and untrue ... it is not evident, either that the Roman Catholic clergy take no pains to keep the lower class of their laity in a state of ignorance, or that their influence does not extend sufficiently for to do so ...[64]

It was to be expected that the Catholic clergy would discourage parents from sending their children to schools whose aims were clearly to convert to

Tour through Ireland (London, 1813), pp 244–5. **62** H. Dutton, *Statistical survey of the county of Clare* (Dublin, 1808), p. 235. **63** J. Glassford, *Notes on three tours in Ireland in 1824 and 1826* (London, 1832), p. 211. **64** T. Newenham, *A view of the natural, political and commercial circumstances of Ireland* (London, 1809), p. 19.

the Protestant faith, especially during a period of intense evangelising. There is evidence to suggest that priests did exercise their clerical influence in this regard. In 1812 Edward Wakefield noted that 'the Catholic clergy have the power of interdicting children from attending Protestant schools',[65] and Glassford's assertion that the Catholic clergy used physical force to keep children away from Protestant schools and abused clerical privilege by denouncing the schools from the altar may well have more than a grain of truth in it. He reported that the Roman Catholic priests in Ballinasloe 'by violent means and actual force, compelled the removal of children, by the parents, who had agreed to place them in Protestant schools'.[66] In Kilchreest the priest denounced the Protestant school from the altar, but despite his opposition, the school thrived and numbers soared, until finally, three quarters of the children who attended, were Roman Catholics.

The clergy dealt just as ruthlessly with indigent hedge schoolmasters who were forced through straitened circumstances to accept jobs, teaching Irish in the bible society schools. The clergy denounced them from the pulpit, thus bringing disgrace upon them and their families in the local community. Two such masters were Peter Gallegan (1792–1860) from Kells, Co. Meath, and Michael Farrelly, an inspector of the Irish Society's schools. The parish priest in this instance was Fr John Halpin of Nobber. Not only did he condemn them from the altar but he also banished Farrelly's parents and brothers from the chapel, on the grounds that he could not possibly read mass in the presence of those related to the 'devil incarnate', the 'Bible-reading rascal, under the Irish Society'.[67] Gallegan was to suffer also as a result of Halpin's action, as parents decided to boycott his hedge school, thereby cutting off one of his main sources of income. The two masters decided to defend their reputations by publishing written replies.

Gallegan put a notice in the paper subsequent to the holding of a large public meeting of the Irish Society in Kingscourt in 1827. In it he stated that poverty had forced him to accept employment with the Irish Society, that he strongly disapproved of their resolutions and that he regretted a mistake he made in supporting them publicly. He then rendered an explanation for this action; and announced his decision to continue in the employment of the Society:

> Declaration of Peter Galligan [sic], of the parish of Moynalty, in the presence of Reverend P. Kiernan, and Peter Cassidy, farmer. States he was master under the Irish Society ... is now resolved to continue being attached to the society as he is rather poor to give up the quarterly gra-

65 An account of Ireland, 2, p. 417.   66 Glassford Notes on three tours, p. 269.   67 S. MacGab-hann. 'Salvaging cultural identity: Peter Gallegan 1792–1860' in Ríocht na Midhe (1994), p. 75.

tuities; is a Roman Catholic; wishes to remain one and is sorry that his poverty forces him to act contrary to Catholic principles; ... was at the meeting at which the resolutions were passed and did not distinctly hear the resolutions read, and consequently did not understand the meaning and import of said resolutions ... he was not aware of the evil tendency of the resolutions; he now regrets that his name should be published as an agent to support the resolutions which he does not approve or sanction.[68]

Farrelly defended himself and his colleagues in the Irish Society in an eight page pamphlet, in which he castigated Halpin in tones which reflected clearly the prevailing tense and bitter atmosphere occasioned by the recent events.

> You first asserted, that they sold their immortal souls for ten pounds per year – that I was the devil incarnate – that they go to mass on Sunday and to the devil on Monday – Roman Catholics to-day and devils to-morrow – that I offered ten pounds to a foolish young boy, in order to convert him from his religion. Your next manly and Christian-like action was to turn my parents and brothers out of the chapel because I was 'a devil incarnate', 'a bible-reading rascal, under the Irish Society'.

Halpin won in the end, as the Irish Society's activities ceased in Co. Meath shortly afterwards.

When Thomas Reid travelled Ireland in 1822, the evangelical societies were very active, especially in the schools they had established. This prompted the comment from him that 'proselytism has ever been the bane of peace and social happiness in Ireland. It has been the end and aim of every school established'.[69] Allowing for a little exaggeration, he did nonetheless capture the spirit of the age, and like some of his fellow writers such as Mason,[70] Weld[71] and Glassford,[72] he singled out the London Hibernian Society for commendation. Most of them however, were eloquent in their condemnation of the charter schools.[73] Even Carr, who as Milne (1997), pointed out was 'by no means unfriendly to the establishment', described the charter schools as 'most infamous jobs ... scarcely productive of any good'.

As leaders in the community the independent hedge schoolmasters were bound to come under sharp scrutiny by contemporary writers. The latter made many unsubstantiated claims against them but they did have some grounds for being sceptical about their allegiance to the government and their

68 C. Dawson, *Peadar Ó Gealacáin: scríobhaí* (1992), p. 22.   69 Reid, *Travels in Ireland*, p. 365. 70 Shaw Mason, *A statistical account*, p. 372.   71 I. Weld, *Statistical survey of the county of Roscommon* (Dublin, 1832), p. 438.   72 Glassford, *Notes on three tours*, pp 272–3.   73 K. Milne, *The Irish charter schools 1730–1830*, p. 303.

loyalty to the crown. Carleton claimed that 'disloyal principles were industriously insinuated'[74] into the minds of the children by the masters. In 1819 Shaw Mason expressed a view shared by many of his fellow writers employed by the Dublin Society, that the government should try to get rid of the hedge school masters because of the security threat they posed and should replace them with 'proper masters'. He wrote:

> It would be the wisdom of the government and the public to take it (ed.) out of the hands of persons ill-qualified to give it a proper direction, and to carry it on under some plan calculated to instil into children principles of moral and civil order.[75]

Their professional competence was called into question most notably by Carr and Glassford, but in reality the masters had to have a considerable level of professional competence, in order to survive in a very competitive academic market. If they hadn't they would simply have had to close down their schools.

Finally, the hedge school masters were widely condemned throughout the nineteenth century for the reading material they permitted in their schools. The education commissioners of 1806–12 and 1824–7, the bible societies, the education societies and of course the contemporary writers Dutton (1808), Wakefield (1812), Shaw Mason (1816) and Glassford (1829) were all outraged that children should be exposed to such dangerous books. It is difficult to accept that the only reason they were so vocal in their disapproval was to discredit the masters in a bid to precipitate their replacement. A much more compelling reason would be the suspicion works of fiction aroused in the minds of many people living in a deeply conservative age and in a country in the grip of the Second Reformation. Even the learned Glassford displayed a narrowness of outlook in these matters one would not have expected. In a letter to the earl of Roden in 1829 he expressed his dismay at the fact that the novels of Fielding and Smollett were being read in the hedge schools, and indeed books which he considered to be even more objectionable. He stated:

> It is not unusual to find the children in these schools reading promiscuously some portions of scripture, along with the romances of Fielding or Smollett, or the works of authors still more objectionable.[76]

---

74 W. Carleton, 'The hedge school' in *Traits and stories of the Irish peasantry* (Dublin, 1843), p. 234.   75 *Survey of Tullaroan, or Grace's parish in the cantred of Grace's country and county of Kilkenny* (Dublin, 1819), p. 148.   76 Glassford, *Letter to rt hon. earl of Roden*, p. 39.

Professional status of the hedge schoolmaster

> The village all declared how much he knew;
> 'Twas certain he could write, and cipher too;
> Lands he could measure, terms and tides presage,
> And e'en the story ran that he could gauge ...
> ... While words of learned length and thundering sound
> Amazed the gazing rustics rang'd around;
> And still they gazed, and still the wonder grew
> That one small head could carry all he knew.[77]

Oliver Goldsmith, The Deserted Village

Next to the ministry of the priesthood, the teaching profession was regarded as a noble and elevated calling in eighteenth-century Ireland. Consequently both student teachers, who were called poor scholars and hedge schoolmasters, were given special treatment in society. But Irish society demanded high academic standards from its educators and in order to meet these demands, poor scholars had to undergo a long and arduous training, under schoolmasters of repute. When the student had learned all that was possible from the local hedge schoolmaster, he issued a challenge to him 'This challenge was generally couched in rhyme, and either sent by the hands of a common friend, or posted upon the chapel-door'. The public viewed these contests with intense interest. If the student was defeated, he continued on in the school of his conqueror, but if he succeeded, he would seek out a more learned teacher. The success of the pupil was not, generally, followed by the expulsion of the master as this was merely the first 'of a series of challenges' which the pupil would have to undertake 'before he eventually settled himself in the exercise of his profession'.[78] During the course of his studies it wasn't unusual for the poor scholar to have to travel considerable distances to hedge schools of repute, especially if he intended to become a priest, in which case he would probably converge on the classical school at Faha in Kerry. As Robert Bell (1804) explained, 'in that Province the classical scholars were always the best and most numerous, their ultimate objective was that of being admitted to the Romish priesthood'.[79]

Fortunately, education was held in such high esteem, that the hospitality of the people, and the professional services of the master were offered gratuitously to him. Carleton was the recipient of such hospitality when as a poor scholar travelling south he soon discovered that 'his satchel of books' was a passport to the hearts of the people. The school at Faha, which was attended

---

77 D. Davie, *The late Augustans* (London, 1977), p. 60.   78 Carleton, 'The hedge school', pp 273–4.   79 *A description of the condition and manners of the peasantry of Ireland between the years 1780 and 1790* (London, 1806), pp 41–2.

by the well-known poet and master, Eoghan Rua Ó Súilleabháin had won for itself a national reputation, as it played host to many a student

> To such a school they were accustomed to come without books, without money, without a way of supporting themselves, to be guests at the hearthstones of these people.[80]

This was a harking back to a happier age when Ireland and her monastic schools served as the university of western Europe and merited the title of 'Oileán na Naomh is na nOllamh'. The poor scholars in the Irish monastic schools were 'the young Anglo-Saxon strangers, who ... were welcomed by the Irish and supplied gratis with lodging, food and books'.[81]

The school at Faha came to be regarded as 'a sort of preparatory school for Salamanca',[82] while Louvain was the goal of many Kerry students because of burses which were founded in some universities, by and for Kerrymen:

> John O'Sullivan, himself, a Kerryman and president of the Irish College, Louvain, founded a burse of 732 florins for his relations of the second degree ... this munificence was imitated by his nephew, Florence O'Sullivan, who was appointed President of the Irish College on his uncle's resignation in 1699. He endowed a scholarship of 1098 florins which, in effect, was also mainly for Kerry students, who wished to study theology, philosophy, law or medicine.[83]

Many poor scholars remained in Ireland and continued their education in the hedge schools. The masters were pleased to extend hospitality to them as they served as advertising agents for their schools, when they returned home to their own provinces.[84] Having a poor scholar in his school enhanced the master's reputation and gave him added status. This was vital in such an insecure profession where a master could easily be deposed at any time, by a new challenger. When a poor scholar was finished his training in one school, it was customary for the schoolmaster to give him a letter of recommendation, to hand to his next tutor. This was called a 'pass'. The 'pass' given to Richard Fitzgerald by the erudite Donnchadh Ruadh Mac Conmara displayed a certain amount of professional snobbery as he instructed that the poor scholar should only be allowed to mix with the learned and the refined. Professional rivalry was also in evidence as he heaped scorn on his fellow professionals and competitors:

80 Corkery, *The hidden Ireland*, p. 187.   81 E. Cahill, 'The native schools of Ireland in the penal era' in *Irish Ecclesiastical Record* (1940), p. 24.   82 S. Atkinson, *Mary Aikenhead: her life, her works, her friends* (Dublin, 1879), p. 47.   83 J. Anthony Gaughan, *Listowel and its vicinity* (Cork, 1973), pp 210-11.   84 Crofton Croker, *Researches in the south of Ireland*, p. 326.

I ordain and command that he be not forced to associate with illiterates, or cowherds, dog-boys, dog fanciers or cold-whistling fellows or with long, chilly, tiresome and talkative schoolmasters without culture, courtesy, or learning such as ... 'Giddyhead O'Hackett', 'Coxcomb O'Boland', and 'Buffoon O'Mahony', 'Tatter O'Flanagan', dirty puffy John O'Mulrooney, Bleary-eyed O'Cullenan and Giggler O'Mulcahy.[85]

As soon as the poor scholar qualified as a hedge schoolmaster his first priority was to establish his own hedge school, build up his reputation and then enter into competition with other hedge schoolmasters. On establishing himself he would write out in his best copperplate handwriting a 'flaming advertisement' detailing the subjects he had mastery of. He would then post it up on the chapel door for all to see. Carleton parodied this practice by claiming that Mat Kavanagh had proficiency in forty nine subjects and assorted works, which included such novelties as 'stereometry, gauging, dialling, astrology, austerity, glorification, physics (by theory only) and ventilation'. When the reckless and wild Irish poet Eoghan Rua Ó Súilleabháin opened his first school at the age of eighteen, at Gneevegiulla in Kerry, he was forced to flee the parish 'with a threatening priest behind him',[86] due to his indiscretions. Undaunted by this clerical rebuff, Eoghan requested the assistance of the Reverend Ned Fitzgerald, some eighteen years later, to advertise 'from the altar that he was about to open a school at Knocknagree'. The request was in the form of a poem entitled 'A shagairt ghil cháidh'.

> Reverend Sir,
> Please to publish from the altar of your holy mass,
> Where, the tender babes will be well off
> For it's there I'll teach them their criss cross;
> For it's there I will teach them how to read and write; ...
> The Catechism I will explain
> To each young nymph and noble swain
> With all young ladies I'll engage
> To forward them with speed and care,
> With book-keeping and mensuration
> Euclid's Elements and Navigation,

85 S. Hayes, 'Donnchadh Ruadh Mac Con-Mara' in *A Slave of Adversity*, pp. 5–6. D. Ruadh Mac Conmara, *Eachtra ghiolla an amaráin or the adventrues of a luckless fellow* (Dublin, 1897), pp 99–104. 'The pass' (1759) was intended to confer the right to pass through the country and to claim hospitality at the best houses. It was written in the form of a legal document which was called a 'barántas' or warrant. Donnchadh is credited with composing a Latin elegy in his nineties, for a fellow Irish poet who died in 1800 – Tadhg Gaelach Ó Súilleabháin.   86 Corkery, *The hidden Ireland*, p. 189.

With Trigonometry and sound gauging,
And English grammar with rhyme and reason
With the grown up youths I'll first agree
To instruct them well in the Rule of Three;
Such of them as are well able,
The cube root of me will learn
Such as are of a tractable genius.
With compass and rule I will teach them
Bill, bonds and informations,
Summons, warrants, supersedes
Judgement tickets good
Leases receipts in full,
and releases, short accounts,
with rhyme and reason
And sweet love letters for the ladies.[87]

Eoghan was prepared to cater for all age groups and to offer a wide curriculum including the writing of love letters. He was qualified to teach the classics also and being a talented Irish poet, he would no doubt have taught these subjects through Irish, but being of a wayfaring nature 'the school did not last long'. When Richard MacElligott (1756–1818) promoted his school at Crosby Row in Limerick city, he advertised in the *Limerick Chronicle* in a similarly boastful style, like the one adopted by the fictitious Mat Kavanagh. One advertisement opened with the line: 'When ponderous polysyllables promulgate professional powers'. In another he claimed that

> Richard MacElligott, observing with regret, the many years devoted to the Greek and Latin languages, and the very inadequate proficiency; and ever ambitious of a distinguished superiority in his pupils, has through much labour these years past, completed a plan which reduces the Greek and Latin languages to the level of the tenderest capacities … Mac Elligott shall, in addition to the above, teach the English grammatically, and so that the entire language can be acquired by any boy of moderate talents and attention, with ease and accuracy in one year.[88]

It was common practice for masters to refer to themselves as 'professors' or 'philomaths' in their advertisements. Mat Kavanagh was a 'philomath and professor of the learned languages'.[89] Philip Fitzgibbon (1711–92) placed an advertisement in *Finn's Leinster Journal* in Kilkenny in an edition dated 8–11 November, 1786, giving his credentials:[90]

87 Ibid., pp 201–2.   88 Herbert, 'Four Limerick hedge-schoolmasters', pp 48–9.   89 Carleton, 'The hedge school', p. 296.   90 S. Ó Casaide, 'Philip Fitzgibbon' in *Journal of the Waterford &*

Philip Fitzgibbon, Kilkenny, Classic Teacher, and Professor of Book-keeping and Mathematics, these sixteen Years past, with the approbation of his Employers, in his private and public Capacity) has opened School in John street. He teaches English Grammer and Geography, the Use of the Globe and Maps, both plain and spherical, and to find the Bearing and Distance of Places by Multiplication and Division of tabular Numbers, of his own Formation, in one Page.

N.B.—He also teaches the Irish Language grammatically, with its Derivatives and Compounds.

The professional status of the hedge schoolmaster was usually determined by his reputation for erudition and of course his success as a teacher. His immediate aim, however, was to achieve a name for wit and learning and to this end he was forced to engage in ludicrous pedantry in order to live up to parental expectations. This he achieved by a timely use of crambos, which he kept stored in his mind 'for accidental encounter', ones 'which would have puzzled Euclid or Sir Isaac Newton himself'.[91] He spoke in words which were 'truly sesquipedalian' and which were 'dark and difficult to understand'. Mat Kavanagh gave this display of his classical learning, in the presence of a parent visiting his school:

Lanty Cassidy, are you gettin' on wid yer stereometry?
Festina, mi discipuli, vocabo homerum, mox atque mox.

Silence, boys. Tace. 'Conticuere omnes intentique ora tenebant.'[92]

It was vital for the master's reputation that he should impress parents, so that they might spread his name. His future rested on this, because, as Edgeworth stated in a letter to the lord primate in the early nineteenth century, 'the best teacher ... soon attracts all the scholars, and the inferior master is soon obliged to give way'.[93] This meant that the hedge schoolmaster lived with a profound sense of insecurity. He never knew when a rival was going to set up in opposition to him. Peadar Ó Doirnín at Forkhill, Co. Armagh, found himself in such a situation and as he did not relish the idea of Muiris Ó Gormáin competing with him he decided to resort to the ancient bardic tradition of satirising the weaknesses of a rival. He did this in a bilingual poem called *Suirí Mhuiris Uí Ghormáin* in which he poked fun at Muiris' poor command of the English language.[94] The humiliation proved too much for Muiris who immediately fled the district.

South-East of Ireland Archaeological Society (January, 1920), p. 50. 91 Carleton, 'The hedge school', p. 275. 92 Ibid., p. 308. 'Festina ...' = Harry, pupils. I shall call Homer quiet. 'They all fell silent and held their concentrated gaze [*Aeneid*, 6k.2, l.1]. 93 Fourteenth report 1806–12, App. No. 3, p. 238. 94 S. de Rís, *Peadar Ó Doirnín* (Dundalk, 1973), p. 29.

Some masters however, adopted a more diplomatic approach in order to stay in business. Peter Daly excelled in this particular art, as the following flattering stanzas will show. He addressed them to the parents of his students at Bohermeen, Navan. In it he made a subtle reference to his rivals, one of whom was probably Gallegan, who were suspected of taking assistance from the bible societies, although there is evidence that he 'himself was something of a religious opportunist'.[95]

> With all the desires that friendship inspires
> I offer my thankful endeavours
> To those who have been my friends in Boarmeen,
> Conferring their generous favours–
>
> In teaching the young our old mother tongue
> At least I may venture to mention
> I'm better than some who greedily thumb
> The Bible-Society-pension.
>
> I'll never forget the moment I met
> Those true born sons of shillaly
> With whom I would fain for ever remain
> Their dutiful friend – Peter Daly.[96]

It was poverty which forced Gallegan to draw 'The bible society pension', a situation he bitterly resented. Over a period of twelve years he had taught at sixteen different locations, and for one third of that time he had no school at all.[97] Micheál Óg Ó Longáin suffered from the same trials and tribulations, in a volatile teaching market.

> He had taken to teaching as a means of existence, and a precarious one it was at the time. In 1810 he was at Glanmire; in 1812–13 at Boherard ... From 1815 to 1819 he taught in the city. In 1820 he went to Na Cloicíní, or Clogheen, at the Kerry Pike.[98]

The rates of payment per subject varied, depending on the extent of the poverty in an area, but the normal rates were:

95 R. Flower, *Catalogue of Irish manuscripts in the British museum* (London, 1926), Egerton 208, p. 139.   96 Dowling, *The hedge schools of Ireland*, pp 95–6.   97 Ms. G. 809. 'Peter Gallegan – collections in English and Irish, entirely written by himself' (16 Jan. 1824), N.L.I., pp 789–90. 98 Ó Donnchadha, 'Micheál Óg Ó Longáin', p. 230.

Literature	1s. 8d.	Reading	2s.
Writing	2s. 3d.	Latin	11s. to 12s.
Maths	4s. or 7s. depending on the master's reputation.		

Poverty was often so acute that the hedge schoolmaster did not get paid and was obliged on occasions 'to have recourse to the magistrate' to recover his 'miserable wages of 1s. 8d. per quarter'.[99] Sometimes he lived with a family or alternatively, travelled from house to house to teach the children 'for his diet'.[100] Carleton's teacher, Pat Frayne, represented by the fictional Mat Kavanagh, was paid in kind, with 'flitches of bacon, dishes of eggs, turf, poteen', and 'crate after crate of turf'.[101] One of the lowest payments recorded was sixpence a quarter or 'rael sa ráithe', which was paid to the poet from Iveragh, Tomás Rua Ó Súilleabháin. Tomás was quite disenchanted with the people of Poll na nGeatairidhe who paid such a derisory sum to him, that he expressed his sense of humiliation in verse

> I bPoll na nGeatairidhe 'seadh fuaireas mo náire,
> Ag múineadh páistidhe ar rael sa ráithe

> In Poll na Geatairidhe I experienced humiliation
> Teaching children for 6d. a quarter.[102]

Mac Conmara complained also that schoolmastering was an empty trade, in a poem called *Eachtra ghiolla an amaráin* or *The adventures of a luckless fellow*.

> Bé múineadh scoile dob' obair dom laethibh,
> 'S rún don phobul gur b'fholamh an cheird sin.[103]
> Teaching school was my daily work, and to
> tell you the truth, it wasn't a paying job.

Complaints such as these were exceptional so that one can only assume that the status enjoyed by the master, and 'the knowledge that a warm welcome awaited him whenever he pushed open the half-door of the humblest dwelling',[104] was adequate compensation for any deprivations he may have suffered.

The good character of the master was on occasions impugned by such writers as Wakefield, who accused him of immorality. The anonymous pamphleteer of 1820 added 'inebriety to his other accomplishments',[105] a claim supported in an official report of 1837, in which the master was described as

99 Shaw Mason, *A statistical account*, p. 374. 100 Wakefield *An account of Ireland*, p. 399. 101 Carleton, 'The hedge school', p. 295. 102 S. Dubh, *Amhráin Tomáis Ruaidh. The songs of Tomás Ruadh O'Sullivan – The Iveragh poet (1785–1848)* (Dublin, 1914), p. 22. 103 Mac Conmara, *Eachtra ghiolla*, p. 36. 104 Dowling, *The hedge schools of Ireland*, p. 152. 105 *Thoughts and sug-*

being 'incompetent, of harmless character, but disposed to tipple'.[106] This charge might well have been made against the entire population. By the end of the eighteenth century 'tippling' had become something of a national hobby, and one which was encouraged by the government, because of the revenue received from the sale of spirits. In 1791 the amount of duty-paid spirits consumed by each member of the population, was over one gallon,[107] and this estimate didn't take into account the many thriving illicit distilling businesses spread throughout the country. It should be noted also that these allegations were never substantiated. A more reliable source would be the parochial returns from the diocese of Kildare and Leighlin, which were filled in by clergymen, all of which vouched for the probity of the master. Right through the returns the teacher was spoken of as 'of excellent character', of 'good character', '... moral men' and 'of quiet, inoffensive habits'.[108]

Many of these men saw teaching as their mission in life. It was their vocation and they devoted their lives to learning and to teaching. For some of them, it was a hereditary profession – for Irish scholars such as Laurence Denn of Waterford and his son Pádraig, or Amhlaoibh Ó Suilleabháin and his father John, who taught together at the crossroads at Callan. They were well equipped to withstand the insults that were hurled at them or the competition that forever challenged them, because they had the privilege of being fêted locally and of having their academic achievements acknowledged. The people displayed their appreciation by conferring honorary titles on their finest poets and scholars, titles such as 'The bright star in mathematical learning',[109] 'The star of Ennistymon', 'The great O'Baggott' and 'The great O'Brien par excellence'. In these circumstances one can understand why the hedge schoolmasters possessed such an inordinate deal of professional pride. Even in retirement, they retained their status by travelling from school to school. Carleton recalled how selective his teacher, 'The great O'Brien' was, about the schools he agreed to visit. He was not prepared to associate with his intellectual inferiors by accepting their invitations 'for he spoke of dunces, with the most dignified contempt, and the general impression was, that he would scorn to avail himself of their hospitality'.[110] He realised that a visit from him was considered an honour and that it would raise the status of the hedge schoolmaster whose school he visited. The Halls met an equally superior minded master in Kerry – the domine Mr Devereaux – 'no domine ever entertained a more exalted opinion of his own learning or held ignoraamuses (as he pronounced the word) in greater contempt than Mr Devereaux'. He

gestions on the education of the peasantry in Ireland (London, 1820), p. 13.   106 Report of the select committee of the house of lords on the plan of education in Ireland 1837, p. 314.   107 Maxwell, Country and town, p. 129.   108 Brenan, Schools of Kildare and Leighlin, pp 61–2.   109 O'Connell, The schools and scholars of Breiffne, pp 275-6.   110 Carleton, 'The hedge school', p. 276.

warned the poor scholar to maintain the highest 'classical' standards when he visited the ladies in the big house. He was to address them in Latin, 'Greek was only to be given on request'. He should be ready to receive such a request, as he had the distinct advantage of being his pupil.[111]

Social status of the hedge schoolmaster

... next to the lord of the manor, the parson and the priest, he is the most important personage in the parish.[112]

The hedge schoolmaster was a central figure in the life of the community and his social status was therefore enormous. According to Carleton, he was 'the master of ceremonies at all wakes and funerals and usually sat among a crowd of the village sages, engaged in exhibiting his own learning and in recounting the number of his religious disputations'.[113] Crofton Croker estimated that his standing in the community was almost on a par with that of the parson and the priest.

In Munster the village master forms a peculiar character; and, next to the lord of the manor, the parson and the priest, he is the most important personage in the parish. His 'academic grove' is a long thatched house, generally the largest in the place, surrendered, when necessary, for the waking of a dead body, or the celebration of mass while the chapel is undergoing repairs; and on Sundays, when not otherwise engaged, it is used as a jig or dancing house.

His status was enhanced by his displays of intellectual superiority:

In an evening, assembly of village statesmen he holds the most distinguished place, from his historical information, pompous eloquence, and classical erudition.[114]

He worked closely with the priest, not only in his capacity as coadjutor and Sunday School teacher but also in his role as self-appointed judge of religious values and morals. If a Catholic converted or taught Irish in a bible society school, the master would reprimand him in verse. The people feared the satire of the poet/hedge schoolmaster just as much as the priest's tirade from the pulpit. When Mr Mahony of Iveragh, 'abandoned the ancient faith', he had to bear many personal insults, but there was one which proved intolerable for

111 Hall, *Ireland, its scenery*, pp 265–6. 112 Crofton Croker, *Researches in the south of Ireland*, p. 326. 113 Carleton, 'The hedge school', p. 322. 114 Op. cit., pp 326–9.

him. 'I could stand them all,' he claimed, 'but oh! to be sung about in the Cahirciveen fair by the villainous Tomás Rua'.[115] The teacher also filled the role of parish clerk, an honorary position which afforded him the patronage of the priest, and consequently greater security of tenure.

The master served his community in a multiplicity of roles, sometimes out of a sense of civic duty but more often still out of economic necessity. He was the village scribe employed by the unlettered. He was also the 'cheap attorney of the neighbourhood',[116] who carried out an immense amount of legal work. Gallegan, Eoghan Rua and a Cork diarist for the year 1793,[117] named John Fitzgerald, were all in a position to carry out legal transactions. An anonymous contemporary observer, with strong racial prejudice, doubted whether these teachers had the integrity to conduct such business honestly. To him the master was little more than 'the fabricator of false leases and surreptitious deeds and conveyances'.[118] We know also that most of the masters were engaged in transcribing the manuscripts while others still were forced to work as part-time labourers 'for a subsistence'.[119] 'In the case of Eoghan Rua, teaching was combined with intermittent bouts of activity as a migrant labourer'.[120] David Manson, the Belfast hedge schoolmaster was also a brewer while Amhlaoibh Ó Súilleabháin had a drapery business. In Co. Kilkenny, teachers with special expertise at accounts, found ready employment as clerks in the collieries.[121] The master was also the village surveyor, a service considered to be vital in the community. Bicheno was bemused by this requirement of the Irish people, considering how little land they themselves had to measure. He contended that the reason why the teaching of arithmetic and geometry was carried to such lengths in the hedge schools was because of 'the practical application of them in measuring land, which is carried to such minuteness, as seems quite ridiculous to those who have been used to see farms of 500 and 1000 acres'.[122]

Creative teachers with a gift for oratory, like the Waterford hedge schoolmaster James Nash (1826–47), who was a friend of Thomas Francis Meagher

115 Dubh, *Amhráin Tomáis Ruaidh*, p. 18. It was in the poet/hedge schoolmaster's interest to support the work of the parish priest as errant masters of poetic bent had been known to have been banished from areas by irate priests, poets such as Eoghan Rua Ó Súilleabháin, A. Mac Craith, D. Ruadh Mac Conmara and P. Ó Doirnín.   116 *Thoughts and suggestions*, p. 12.   117 T.A. Lunham, 'John Fitzgerald's diary' in *Journal of the Cork Historical and Archaeological Society*, 24:118 (April-June 1918), p. 154.   118 Op. cit.   119 Dutton, *Statistical survey*, p. 236.   120 L.M. Cullen, *Life in Ireland* (London, 1968), p. 100.   121 W. Tighe, *Statistical observations relative to the county of Kilkenny* (Dublin, 1802), p. 514. Nine other surveys were carried out in 1802, four by James McParlan of Sligo, Leitrim, Donegal and Mayo. The prolific Sir Charles Coote, responsible for five surveys in total, completed one of Cavan in 1802. The Reverend John Dubourdieu completed one of Cavan, R. Thompson of Meath and H. Dutton produced *Observations on Mr Archer's statistical survey of the county of Dublin*, which was considered to be a second volume to the Dublin survey and Dutton was commended by the society for taking this initiative.   122 J.E. Bicheno, *Ireland and its economy* (London, 1830), p. 285.

(1823–67), added sparkle to the political life of that city for over twenty years.

> During the days of the Catholic rent, he was conspicuous.
> In Stuart's election which broke down the prestige
> and power of the Beresfords he was conspicuous ...
> In 1843 he emerged from his classic seclusion ...
> And appeared once more as a Demosthenes on
> the hill of Ballybricken, the Acropolis of Waterford.[123]

While Nash himself was a pacifist he was fondly remembered by the 1847 revolutionary 'Meagher of the sword' as 'the schoolmaster' who:

> was full of humour, full of poetry, full of gentleness and goodness ... a patriot from the heart and an orator by nature. Uncultivated, luxuriant, wild, his imagination produced in profusion the strangest metaphors, running riot in tropes, allegories, analogies and visions.

Nash's social status was such that he could share a platform at a public meeting with 'The right worshipful the mayor of Waterford and the Rt Reverend Dr Foran',[124] the Catholic bishop of the city. Audiences enjoyed the 'audacity, humour and pedantry'[125] of his speeches, and they always reserved the loudest cheer for him. At one meeting he spoke out passionately against the evils which legislative union with Britain had produced, and against the government's threats of coercion. He defied the government, who were the enemies of his land, to come and fight

> 'Let them come on', he exclaimed, 'let them come on; let them draw the sword; and then woe to the conquered! – every potato field shall be a Marathon, and every boreen a Thermopylae.'

Nash was a confirmed O'Connellite but he understood why the Young Irelanders were frustrated with the Liberator's peaceful policy. In his customary charming style he spoke of the Young Irelander's newspaper *The Nation* in superlatives of praise. 'It was the greatest paper published! Nothing could transcend the sublimity of its teachings! The prose left the dream of Plato in the background, and the poetry eclipsed the Iliad!' With touching humour he made his dying request 'to have the last number of *The Nation* stitched about me as a shroud, so that when I appear hereafter I may have something national about me', but unfortunately, like so many other hedge schoolmasters such

123 T.F. Meagher, 'Meagher of the Sword' in Arthur Griffith (ed.), *Speeches of Thomas Francis Meagher in Ireland, 1846–1848* (Dublin, 1916), p. 281. 124 Ibid., p. 286. 125 Dowling, *The hedge schools of Ireland*, p. 113.

as MacElligott, Eoghan Rua and Seán Ó Coiléan (1754–1817), Nash was destined to die 'in utter poverty'.[126]

The poet/hedge schoolmasters were deep in the affections of the Irish people. Ó Coiléan, the lyrical poet from Cork was known as 'The silver tongue of Munster'. Eoghan Rua was to them, according to Corkery, 'Eoghan an bhéil bhínn', 'Eoghan of the sweet mouth', whose musical verse 'had for them the double gift of the drug: it put pain aside, and it raised vision'. They entertained the people according to their own unique styles. Some of them were endowed with the ability to laugh at themselves and their own foibles. One such poet was Andrias Mac Craith, affectionately referred to as the 'merry pedlar', because of his reputation as 'the wildest of all the bards of that wild time'. He converted to the Protestant religion for social advancement, but the Protestant minister simply 'threw him out', of his church. Andrias was greatly entertained by the occurrence and decided to immortalise the event in verse: 'Since he had ceased to be either Protestant or Papist he must needs become either a Calvinist or an Arian' (Corkery).

There were other innocuous forms that poetry and song took, the favourites being those which made the enemy appear ridiculous or which prompted laughter. Among these were Mac Conmara's bilingual verse in which he used two complimentary lines in English, praising 'noble George', followed by two denunciatory lines in Irish against 'that brute', George, which the enemy could not understand. Like many of the poets he used the Irish language as a 'protecting hedge behind which' he 'could snipe at the English'.

> We'll fear no cannon, nor war's alarms
> While noble George will be our guide,
> *O Christ may I see the Pretender's arms*
> *Safe home from exile – and that brute destroyed.*[127]

Riocard Bairéad the talented song writer from Leam, Belmullet, Co. Mayo, who was reputed to have been able to teach at least four or five languages,[128] penned a poetic satire in the style of Swift, whom he greatly admired. In his mock elegy called *Eoghan cóir* – Owen the honest and humane, he told of the deep sorrow felt by the people because of the death of so lovable a person as Eoghan cóir who was in fact a rapacious landlord, hated by the people. The chief mourners were in reality two bitter enemies of Eoghan, but 'The like of

126 Meagher, 'Meagher of the Sword', pp 287–9. MacElligott died 18 April 1818. He left a large family in a destitute condition, and a public collection was made on their behalf. Eoghan Rua died in poverty aged thirty six, having contracted a fever following a sharp blow to the head sustained in a fight at an ale-house in Killarney in 1784. Seán Ó Coileáin died in miserable poverty in Skibbereen, Co. Cork.   127 V. Mercier, *The Irish comic tradition* (Oxford, 1962), p. 171. 128 T.F. O'Rahilly, 'A song by Richard Barret', in *Gadelica* 1 (1912–13), pp 112–26.

the bawling and keening was never heard in the land before'. Bairéad wasn't at all surprised by this phenomenon, in view of Eoghan's endearing nature. He ended his poem with an ironical sting as he prayed fervently that 'According as' Eoghan 'was to others, may Christ be the same to him' .

There was little malice in their humour. Poetry and song was their palliative against the ills of the day and it was often the masters who taught their children, in the hedge schools, who supplied it.

Cultural survival

> ... and all the time there was a soul under the ribs of this death; that the music which was the life of that soul had strength and beauty in it.[129]

The Irish peasantry were a tenacious people who survived by being enterprising and resilient. They knew that if they were to provide their children with an education, they would have to employ some imaginative strategies for making money. One such strategy, was the provision of a board and lodgings service, from their 'rude habitations'. They advertised by placing a board at the side of the cabin door, which read 'dry lodgings and tobacco'. Sometimes it was just 'good dry lodgings' which were offered, other times it was 'lodgings and snuff'. Some families advertised the sale of a single item, for instance, when they wished to advertise the sale of milk, they hung out a white rag on a stick. Luckombe described these cabins as 'despicable hovels' and he doubted very much whether the guests were ever afforded, what could reasonably be termed 'dry' lodgings. Twiss was equally sceptical. Upon observing a board with the words 'Good dry lodgings' placed over the door or chimney, as the same opening served for both, he decided to continue walking on.

Another business venture entered into by the peasantry was the lucrative if somewhat risky, illicit distilling trade, the profits from which helped to pay the rent, tithes, dues and the master's fees. Between the years 1802 and 1806, no fewer than 13,489 unlicenced stills were seized by the government;[130] therefore great secrecy usually surrounded these activities. Success could only be achieved by involving the trustworthy and by finding a location for the still, which wouldn't draw down the attention of the excise officer. The poor people of Erris, Co. Mayo, approached the most trustworthy person they knew, who was their local priest and sought his permission to use his chapel as a distillery. He co-operated because he saw it as a guarantee that his dues would be paid. He knew also that it would lead to the steady growth of oats and barley, but above all he knew that it would result in a steady cash flow into the pockets of his flock. The distillery was discovered in the chapel by a god-fear-

---

129 Corkery, *The hidden Ireland*, p. 19.   130 Maxwell, *Country and town*, p. 129.

ing excise officer who decided that 'to leave it standing, would be contrary to the fiscal statute' but 'to level it would be sacrilege'.[131]

Though poor in worldly possessions, the peasants had a rich treasury of folk culture, which had been handed down to them by previous generations and which was carefully nurtured for them by their poets and hedge school-masters. On a winter's evening large gatherings of people would assemble around the turf fire in a cabin to hear the contents of what Crofton Croker was pleased to call 'monotonous olios' but which the poor looked upon as 'a treat of the highest order'. De Montbret was quite impressed with the peasants' pre-occupation with cultural pursuits. He hadn't expected to find such an appreciation of poetry among the poor that in one Gaeltacht area he visited in Munster, he met a beggar-woman who appealed for alms in verse. This same reverence for tradition was to be observed also in Dungiven and remote parts of the north. Shaw Mason conducted a small experiment to test the accuracy of the old seanachies while they recited 'poems attributed to Ossian, and other Bardic remains'. He engaged the services of a young mountaineer, named Bernard Mac-Loskie, who was a good Latin scholar and well acquainted 'with the native traditions, customs and language', who wrote down eight Ossianic poems as they were recited. Later on Shaw Mason compared their accuracy, against those published in a volume entitled *Transactions of the Gaelic Society*, 'and strange as it may seem, they were found to agree together word for word', with a few minor exceptions. The reason for 'the accurate preservation of these ancient poems' was the professional approach adopted by the seanachies themselves. They frequently met to recite their traditional stories and if anyone repeated a passage, which appeared to another to be incorrect, he was immediately stopped, the matter was then debated, and the dispute was 'referred to a vote of the meeting. The decision of the majority' then became 'imperative on the subject for the future'. Little wonder then that the oral tradition was so strong and that the written account of it was preserved so accurately.

Love of music and dance contributed in no small measure to the vivacity and cheerfulness of the people. Young considered them to be much more sociable, personable and extrovert than his fellow-countrymen. He wrote:

> the circumstances which struck me most in the common Irish were, vivacity and a great and eloquent volubility of speech ... They are infinitely more cheerful and lively than anything we commonly see in England, having nothing of that incivility of sullen silence with which so many Englishmen seem to wrap themselves up, as if retiring within their own importance.

131 C. Otway, *Sketches in Erris and Tyrawly* (Dublin, 1841), p. 362.

Young couldn't understand how an impoverished people could set such high value on artistic pursuits that they would actually employ dancing masters for their children. It is interesting to note also that the masters didn't confine themselves to the Irish jig, which we are told was danced 'with a luxuriant expression'. On the contrary they taught minuets and country dances, and what's more there was even 'some talk of cotillions coming in'. In the late eighteenth century the masters' creative talents reached new heights when they incorporated quadrilles into the native Irish jig and reel steps, by the adoption of faster rhythms. The Irish style quadrilles which had been introduced into Ireland by the soldiers who had returned home from the Napoleonic wars were to become the most popular dance in the Irish countryside for most of the nineteenth century.[132]

The cultural survival of the people depended to a large extent on the hedge schoolmasters as it was in the hedge schools that the people developed an appreciation of music, song, dance and poetry. It was this love of the arts which raised their spirits and sustained them through very difficult times. Travellers to Ireland were surprised by the spirit of the people and their capacity to rise above their miserable living conditions. Bowden was at a loss to understand how 'Amidst the unspeakable miseries' the peasants could 'enjoy in a very exalted degree poetry and song'. Providence, he felt 'had given them the talent of soothing woe'. Even though he did not understand the Irish language, he found the Irish airs haunting in their beauty. He often 'sat under a hedge and listened to the rustic songs of those peasants, while at labour, with a pleasure that transcended any' he 'had ever felt at Vauxhall'. Carr echoed Bowden's sentiments. He too found the peasantry 'uncommonly attached to their native melodies', some of which Carr felt were 'exquisitely beautiful'.

There were occasions during the 'long peace', which marked the period between the Williamite wars and the 1798 rebellion, when the upper classes in Irish society shared some of the cultural pursuits of the lower classes. Nowhere was this more apparent than in the attendance at the theatre by the lower classes and in the participation in the national game of hurling, by the upper classes. With regard to the theatre, Dublin had 'a vigorous stage' in the eighteenth century. Lucombe mentioned two theatres in Dublin 'The old house in Smock Alley' and 'the new one in Crow Street'. The best known theatrical names at the time were Garrick and Mrs Siddons, Samuel Foote and Tate Wilkinson, John Edwin, George Anne Bellamy, Mrs Abington and the Kembles. It is interesting to note that among the books read in the hedge schools were ones on some of these famous thespians, for instance *Apology for the life of George Anne Bellamy*, *History of Tate Wilkinson*, *Life of Garrick* and a book on the playwright Farquaher entitled *Memoirs of George Farquhar*.

132 B. Breathnach, 'The dancing master'. In *Ceol*, 3 (1970), p. 117.

Attendance by all classes at the theatre certainly didn't denote their equality. Class divisions were highlighted by the social stratification maintained at the theatre by means of prices charged and places allotted. Admission prices were 5*s.* 5*d.* for a box, 3*s.* 3*d.* for the pits, 2*s.* 2*d.* for the gallery and 2d for the upper gallery.

The two cultural worlds interacted through the game of hurling also. An advertisement which appeared in *Finn's Leinster Journal* for 30 July 1768 illustrated gentry involvement in the sport.[133] The poor approached the game with great energy and enthusiasm, so much so that Young 'declared it to be a testimony to the nourishing properties of the potato', but he dismissed the game itself as simply 'the cricket of savages'. De Montbret on the other hand, was fascinated by the sport, and familiarised himself with the Irish terminology for the game 'The coumáne or hurley, is the flat curved stick with which they chase the liarode or balle à jouer'. He attended a match in Kerry in 1790 and in Galway in 1791, and he gave credit to the masters for having taught the skills necessary to play the game. He called them the 'special teachers' who taught 'this cudgel game'.

As the political situation in Ireland became more tense in the years prior to the 1798 rebellion 'the government and individual members of the ruling élite' began to 'look with new suspicion at the amusements and cultural traditions of the common people'.[134] The gentry withdrew their patronage of Irish cultural activities and withdrew from participating in popular games. But it wasn't just because of the volatile political situation that this occurred as it was a development which had already taken place in England and France by the early seventeenth century.

The culture of the ordinary people was to be spurned by yet another powerful group in Irish society in the late eighteenth century – this was the Catholic hierarchy, who were forbidden by a church undergoing reform from attending weddings, banquets, station dinners, horse-races, theatres, public houses, or other places of amusement. The easy familiarity once enjoyed by the poor people with their priests was now gone especially after the priests were directed to adopt a distinctive clerical dress, which as S.J. Connolly remarked 'provided the outward symbol, as well as being an effective guarantor, of the new social distance between the pastor and his flock'.

The tightening of ecclesiastical discipline also meant that the priests were precluded from attending such quasi-religious celebrations as the pattern. This was the festival day of a saint to whom a well or a shrine was dedicated, a day on which thousands of people assembled for religious devotions at a holy site but which sometimes degenerated into a scene of 'dancing, drink-

133 L.P. Ó Caithnia, *Scéal na hIomána* (Dublin, 1981), p. 20.   134 Connolly, 'Ag déanamh commanding', p. 26.

ing, roaring and singing'.[135] Irreverent behaviour at the traditional 'merry wake' was hardly likely to meet with church approval either as the normal amusements of an Irish social gathering were also to be found at the wake-house. There was dancing, story-telling, singing, excessive drinking and match-making. In 1748 Bishop Gallagher of Kildare prohibited 'unchristian diversions of lewd songs, and brutal tricks called fronsy fronsy' which formed part of the 'merry wake', but the people continued with the custom regardless of subsequent edicts of synods of the church or bishops' pastoral letters.[136] By 1800 the archbishop of Cashel and Emly was still warning his flock against shameful practices at wakes, which he maintained were 'growing in strength daily', even though the penalty for such behaviour was excommunication.

There was nothing whatsoever to prohibit the hedge schoolmasters from participating in these quasi-religious festivities because, as an anonymous pamphleteer explained, the hedge schoolmasters were 'imbued with the same prejudices, influenced by the same feelings, subject to the same habits'[137] as the people among whom they lived. This was indeed the case with regard to the 'merry wake' as it was well known that on occasions they even supplied the wake house to poor families who lacked suitable accommodation of their own. According to Crofton Croker, the hedge schoolmaster's 'academic grove' was 'a long thatched house, generally the largest in the place, surrendered when necessary, for the waking of a dead body'. Carleton also declared that the hedge schoolmaster was 'the master of ceremonies at all wakes and funerals'. It was of course in the masters' interest to support the festivities of the poor as they relied heavily on their patronage, but it is also true to say that the hedge schoolmasters for the most part, shared the same cultural outlook at the people, and venerated the same old customs.

The people found many mediums for releasing tension and easing their daily burdens but not all of them met with the approval of the travellers to Ireland in the eighteenth and nineteenth centuries. In the 1770s Young estimated that whiskey was so cheap in Ireland that 'a man might get drunk for fourpence'. Both he and many other travellers, condemned 'the excessive drinking of whiskey as a great national evil, and many petitions were presented to the Irish parliament asking for some restriction on the sale of spirits'. In 1791 the parliament responded by raising the tax on spirits and lowering it on beer, but this was only a temporary measure in view of the fact that the government badly needed all the revenue it could produce, to assist in the war effort against France. In this year also the amount of duty-paid spirits consumed by each member of the population, was over one gallon. By 1811 the quantity of spirits charged with duty in Ireland had practically dou-

---

135 Crofton Croker, *Researches in the south of Ireland*, pp 280-1.   136 S. Ó Súilleabháin, *Irish wake amusements* (Cork, 1967), pp 146–54.   137 *Thoughts and suggestions*, p. 12.

bled since 1791 and by 1828 the consumption of home-made spirits was actually estimated at 11,775,067 gallons.

It would therefore be difficult to expect hedge schoolmasters to isolate themselves from a drink culture that was all pervasive. As already mentioned, wide scale inebriety by hedge schoolmasters certainly seems unlikely but Carleton's masters would appear to have imbibed more regularly than most. St Gregory's Day, 12 March, was traditionally viewed as a holiday to be celebrated in hedge schools, a day when 'pupils generally brought money or food for the Gregory Day repast'.[138] This was how the occasion was marked in the hedge schools of Breiffne but in Tyrone the celebrations tended to be less sedate, if Carleton's account is anything to go by. He reported that 'pupils were at liberty for that day to conduct themselves as they pleased'. The result was that they became generally intoxicated, and were brought home in that state to their parents.

Carleton also made the interesting observation that 'If the children of two opposite parties chanced to be at the same school, they usually had a fight' but if the master 'identified himself with either faction, his residence in the neighbourhood would be short'. Faction fights were an accepted feature of Irish life in the eighteenth century, right up to the first quarter of the nineteenth century. They consisted of a display of ritualised aggression, by members of feuding groups or families and they formed part of most social gatherings in Ireland throughout this period. According to de Montbret, 'a game of hurley' invariably ended 'in a fight' and people arrived at patterns armed with batons. De Latocnaye witnessed 'a vigorous fight' at a funeral in Killarney in 1796 when both sides of the family fought over burial rights and William Reed maintained that this was a regular occurrence at funerals in Ireland.[139] O'Sullivan's diary contained a record of faction fights at Callan, Co. Kilkenny – 'Callan of the ructions'[140] as he was pleased to call it. Faction fights were commonplace events, which were seen as a means of releasing pent-up anger or tension, and as a way of settling old scores. The English traveller Henry D Inglis strongly disapproved of the tradition of faction fighting which he regarded as not only a barbarous practice but also a criminal act. He wrote:

> Regular agreements are made to have a battle; the time agreed upon is generally when a fair takes place; and at these fights, there is regular marshalling and 'wheeling' and as for its being a crime to break a 'boy's head', such an idea never enters the brain of any one.[141]

138 O'Connell, *The schools and scholars*, p. 421.   139 W. Reed, *Rambles in Ireland* (London, 1815), p. 41.   140 H. O'Sullivan, 'The diary of Humphrey O'Sullivan, 1827–1835' in Tomás de Bhaldraithe (ed.), *The diary of Humphrey O'Sullivan*, p. 131.   141 Cooper, 'Letters on the Irish nation', p. 228.

Other escape routes chosen by the poor to withdraw from the cares of daily living were also disapproved of by contemporary observers, among these were gambling and reading 'licentious books'. Cooper in his *Letters on the Irish nation*, written during a visit to Ireland in 1799 observed that

> The public streets of Dublin are filled with lottery offices beyond the conception even of a Londoner ... In these shops are crowds of the most miserable ragged objects (of which Dublin contains more than any other city in Europe) staking their daily bread on the chance of gain. I have often heard of the families of industrious mechanics and manufacturers driven by their frauds into the streets to beg their bread ... but yet these are all trifles when compared with the extent to which the evil of lottery offices is carried on in Ireland.[142]

The lottery draw was held in a hall in Capel Street, Dublin, where the poor gathered 'many of them having sold or pawned all their possessions in order to try their luck'.[143] Not only that but according to Twiss, Irish lottery tickets were even sent to England to be sold 'in open defiance of acts of parliament'. In 1792 the Association for discountenancing vice was formed in Dublin to counteract the spread of dangerous French principles in the wake of the 1789 French revolution, but more especially for the suppression 'of licentious books, consumption of spirituous liquors, betting and gambling'.[144] The Association commissioned William Watson to re-publish the 'excellent tracts of Hannah More', the great evangelical writer of religious tracts in England, in order that they might serve as an antidote to the chapbooks 'which were of the most immoral kind and inculcated principles the most pernicious'.[145] A favourite in the hedge schools was a tract entitled *The wonderful advantages of adventuring in the lottery*,[146] which was a salutary tale recounting the misfortunes of a husband who became addicted to playing the lottery. He brought ruination upon himself and misery to his wife and finally ended up with his head in a noose.

Travellers to Ireland generally adopted a sympathetic attitude to the poor people and were genuinely moved by their generosity. Young was deeply impressed by their hospitality, especially when he considered their own abject state. He said 'their hospitality to all comers, be their own poverty ever so pinching, has too much merit to be forgotten'. De Montbret was convinced that the Catholic religion had this affect on the people 'a religion that encourages politeness and leniency'. He noted also that 'the best place at the fire'

142 Cooper, *Letters on the Irish nation* (London, 1801), pp 33–4.   143 Maxwell, *Dublin under the Georges*, p. 147.   144 Ibid., p. 148.   145 J. Warburton, et al., *History of the city of Dublin*, ii (London, 1818), p. 891.   146 H. More, 'The wonderful advantages of adventuring in the lottery, or the history of John Doyle' in *More tracts* 2 (Dublin, n.d.,), pp 3–22.

was 'reserved for the poor man', a practice which obviated the necessity for poor laws for Ireland until 1838. The poor regarded it as their duty to look after beggars and to fulfil this obligation they would 'sit with their doors open at meal-times as an invitation to those that were passing to partake of their homely fare'.[147]

When S. C. Curwen visited Ireland in 1818 he was somewhat surprised at the high spirits and the warm atmosphere that filled their miserable cabins. Contrary to one's natural expectations, there exuded from these unlikely quarters 'warmth of heart – an overflowing of the kindest domestic affections, and of the purest joys of life'.[148] Like de Montbret, Curwen was struck by the affection they displayed for their families: 'In no country are conjugal and parental affections exceeded more warmly or powerfully felt, or more sincerely and unaffectedly exhibited, than in Ireland'. The travellers reserved their kindly sentiments and complimentary words for the poor. It wasn't to be expected that they would draw from the same lexicon to describe the hedge schoolmasters or their schools.

The social and professional status of the hedge schoolmaster among his own people, was acknowledged by a number of contemporary writers, such as Carleton, Crofton Croker, de Montbret and the Halls. However, the reality of the situation was that the masters were held in such suspicion by the majority of establishment writers, influential commentators and in particular by successive commissioners of education, that insufficient attention was paid to what was actually being taught in the hedge schools. The truth is that in some cases a very broad curriculum was taught, and often to a very high standard, but the government of the day remained blind to this fact. The historian Mary Daly's, assessment of the hedge school curriculum was accurate when she concluded in her study of applications from counties Cavan, Mayo, Cork and Kilkenny to the commissioners of national education, that the 1824 education commissioners were seriously in error when they were dismissive of the hedge schools. She wrote:

> There is little doubt that in dismissing hedge schools as insignificant institutions the commissioners of 1824 seriously erred and that had they taken greater account of their existence and the nature of many of the hedge schools, the 1831 provisions might have been drafted differently and provoked less subsequent conflict.[149]

147 Maxwell, Country and town, p. 152.   148 S.C. Curwen, Observations on the state of Ireland (London, 1818), p. 169.   149 Daly, 'The development of the national schools system, 1831–1840', p. 162.

3

Unique education in the hedge school

'The Groves of Academus – what was Plato himself but a hedge schoolmaster?'[1]

> In the Middle Ages, there were everywhere little groups of persons clustering round some beloved teacher and thus it was that man learned not only the humanities but all the gracious and useful crafts. There were no state art schools, no state technical schools ... It was always the individual inspiring, guiding, fostering other individuals: never the state dispensing education like a universal provider of readymades, aiming at turning out all men and women according to regulation patterns.[2]

William Carleton, a hedge schoolmaster of the nineteenth century, and Patrick Pearse, a schoolmaster of the twentieth century, drew an analogy between the great educator philosopher Plato (*c*.427–347 BC) who favoured a personalized approach to education and the hedge schoolmasters. The comparison was a fair one as they were among the finest exponents of this educational method although modern day educators would scorn its total disregard of the economies of time. But then it should be remembered that the hedge schoolmasters were continuing a tradition that had been passed down to them from early christian times from the monastic schools 'when a Kieran or an Enda or a Colmcille gathered his little group of foster-children (the old word was still used) around him'. In the seventeenth and eighteenth centuries, Irish parents selected the hedge school of their choice, based on the master's reputation for learning, the strength of his personality and his dedication to his calling. This too was part of the Irish tradition: 'Always it was the personality of the teacher that drew them there. And so it was all through Irish history. A great poet or a great scholar had his foster-children who lived at his house or fared with him through the country'.[3] Long after the battle of Kinsale (1601) when Queen Elizabeth's forces defeated the Gaelic chieftains and put an end to the Gaelic way of life, and the patronage which the chieftains had provided for the

1 Carleton, 'The hedge school', p. 318.   2 P. Pearse, *The murder machine* (Cork, 1976), p. 15. 3 Ibid., pp 15–16.

Gaelic poets, 'Munster poets had their little groups of pupils'[4] as many poets became teachers. It should come as little surprise then to note that 'Nearly every Irish poet of the eighteenth century and early nineteenth centuries appears to have been a schoolmaster;'[5] Pearse was therefore correct when he stated that 'the hedge schoolmasters of the nineteenth century were the last repositories of a high tradition'.[6]

As these were fee-paying schools, the master was no doubt anxious to ensure that all his pupils were happy and contented and given the individual attention that parents expected. A wide variety of activities could be taking place in the classroom at any given time because all age groups were catered for in the hedge schools. Brian Friel captured the atmosphere in a hedge school very well in his play *Translations*[7] when he portrayed a typical class-room scene with Jimmy studying his Greek and talking aloud, Bridget prac-tising her headlines, Maire learning her tables and Sarah receiving speech therapy from the master's son Mahon. It would appear that 'enlightened chaos' often ensued where 'The schoolmaster, like the head of any one-room school, had to be ringmaster of myriad varieties of intellectual animals'.[8] Two written accounts of hedge schools bear this out, Carleton's 'The hedge school'[9] and 'An Irish hedge school',[10] written by a constant visitor to the hedge schools of Wexford, spanning a period of over fifty years. Both writers provide a pleasing account of this haphazard but creative approach to class-room management where a happy, industrious climate prevailed. Foreign vis-itors, like the German writer J.G. Kohl, were impressed by what they saw in the hedge schools. Even though there was awful poverty in evidence, Kohl noticed that the children looked very cheerful, smart and bright-eyed in appearance as they poured over their studies. He remarked 'when their pover-ty, their food, their clothing are considered, this may appear surprising, but it is the case with all Irish children and especially those in the open country'.[11] John Howard, the philanthropist, found the children in the hedge schools 'much forwarder than those of the same age in the charter schools'.[12]

In general, discipline wasn't too severe in the hedge schools. Carleton believed that 'a master should be a monarch in his school, but by no means a tyrant'. He had many progressive ideas on education as he advised teachers not to send children 'in quest of knowledge alone, but let him have cheerful companionship on his way'. He recommended greater freedom for children to behave like children, and he warned teachers that they should never treat them like adults:

4 Ibid., p. 16.   5 Dowling, *The hedge schools of Ireland*, p. 118.   6 Pearse, *The murder machine*, p. 16.   7 B. Friel, *Translations* (Dublin, 1981), p. 11.   8 Akenson, *The Irish education experi-ment*, p. 53.   9 Carleton, 'The hedge school'. pp 271–324.   10 A constant visitor, 'An Irish hedge school', in *Dublin University Magazine* (Nov. 1862), pp 600–16.   11 J.G. Kohl, *Travels in Ireland* (London, 1844), p. 125.   12 Dowling, *The hedge schools of Ireland*, pp 36–7.

We shall never forget that they are children: nor should we bind them by a system whose standard is taken from the maturity of human intellect. We may bend our reason to theirs, but we cannot elaborate their capacity to our own.

Carleton expressed his contempt for the monitorial system which was used by rival educational societies. He considered it to be a crude, mechanical system of educating children and he condemned it in the strongest terms:

Bell or Lancaster would not relish the pap or caudle-cup three times a day; neither would an infant on the breast feel comfortable after a gorge of ox beef.

He advised them to 'put a little of the mother's milk of human kindness and consideration into their strait-laced systems'.[13] Irish parents had an aversion to this system also, according to the evidence given by Cooke, on 5 January 1825, before the commissioners of education. He informed them that

the people look at them there with great prejudice; they think they are useless; they think that the master must teach the children himself, and that his inspecting the monitors is not teaching the children; and the prejudice is so strong as almost to render them inefficient.[14]

Ironically, it was the alleged mechanical methods of instruction employed in the hedge schools which were to elicit some of the sharpest censure of contemporary writers. In 1810, the Protestant clergyman Horatio Townsend denounced the mode of instruction called 'rehearsing', or oral repetition, whereby 'all the boys gabble their lessons together, as loud and as fast as they can speak'.[15] Shaw Mason reported on the prevalence of rehearsing in the schools of Kilmanaheen, Co. Clare: 'these are all called public schools, and are on an old established plan, reading aloud or humming together'.[16] Townsend considered that the masters seemed to rate levels of progress by 'the scale of vociferation', as they enforced a greater crescendo in volume, on seeing anyone approaching the school. In Carleton's short story, Mat instructed his pupils to rehearse, in order to impress the passer-by: 'Silence, back from the door, boys, rehearse: everyone of you, rehearse, I say ... till the gentleman goes past'. This process had little to do with teaching method. It was merely showmanship, a form of advertising, to display the spirit of industry that prevailed within their schools. It had the added merit of training students' memories

13 Carleton, 'The hedge school', pp 307–8.   14 First report of the commissioners, 1825, p. 821. Evidence of the Reverend Henry Cooke, 5 January, 1825.   15 *General & statistical survey of the county of Cork* (Cork, 1815), p. 97.   16 Shaw Mason (ed.), *A statistical account*, p. 495.

which helped to compensate for the lack of printed material at this time, especially in the Irish language.

Play was allowed in the classroom while the master was busily engaged with another group of students, a practice Plato and much later Froebel (1782–1852) would certainly have approved of: 'the younger children ... amuse themselves in corners with straws, or pebbles, or slate and cutter games of 'Fox and Geese' and 'Walls of Troy'[17] and 'games of marbles' were sometimes played. Their lunch break lasted for an hour, the time being ascertained by 'a peep at the sundial in the yard, or the shadow of a certain tree, or an angle of the chapel' all of which 'announced to the master the welcome presence of noon', during which the children of Rathnure hedge school in the year 1811, played a variety of games. The girls played Jack-stones (five in number) which was a juggling game with stones. Boys were included in a game called High Gates or Thread the Needle, which necessitated 'catching hands in a circle, and one chasing another in and out under the linked arms of the players'. The boys played Heck-a-beds, which was commonly known as Scotch-hop in Dublin, as well as Pillar the Hat and Hunt the Fox.

Even though senior students aged between nineteen and twenty four years of age attended the same school as young children, the Wexford writer noted with some satisfaction that 'their treatment of the younger folk was most considerate and good natured. They played all sorts of pranks on each other, but a quarrel among them was unknown'. Contemporary progressive educators, as well as future ones, would have approved of many of the practices enacted daily. Dr Maria Montessori (1870–1952)[18] favoured the age mix in classrooms and would have been very edified by what took place in the hedge schools. No doubt children did learn much from observing the older students at work and from listening to the master instructing them. Pestalozzi (1746–1827) wished to re-create the happy loving atmosphere of a home in the classroom. This was precisely what the hedge schools achieved with their homely atmosphere as each day was punctuated by visitors calling to the master. Carleton mentioned many callers from the local priest to Mrs Doran, who wanted Mat to write a letter for her, to the neighbouring gentry and travelling schoolmasters. In Wexford the schools had visits from prospective pupils, parents and a local wit by the name of Dr Kelly. The doctor assumed his medical title, as he was in possession of a cure for ordinary maladies, being the seventh son of a sev-

17 'An Irish hedge school', p. 610.   18 Montessori was the first lady physician in Italy and the foundress of the Montessori teaching method. Her system is based on giving children freedom (to do right, not wrong), in a specially prepared environment, under the guidance of a trained directress. Johann Heinrich Pestalozzi was a Swiss reformer in the field of education. His school at Yverdon became the educational Mecca of his day. He believed in child-centred education and emphasized the value of observation in relation to consciousness, speech and the higher forms of reasoning.

enth son. The purpose of his visits bore no relationship to his special gifts. He simply set a series of mathematical mind teasers for the students, after which he extended a generous invitation to them to visit his orchard.

> Now, master, I must make some amends to these brave boys and girls for keeping them idle so long; so I'll expect to see every son and daughter of them at the orchard gate next Saturday, at one o'clock, to see if they like the taste of the apples this year.

The actual daily routine in the hedge school classroom was well documented by the Wexford visitor in particular and to a lesser extent by Carleton. The first chore the master undertook each morning, after 'hearing the tasks' was to make or mend the pens for the students in the writing class. Very few of them could afford Cumberland lead-pencils, so the master improvised with 'the end of a broken lead spoon, or a piece of the metal run in the shape of an ordinary pencil, being the equivalent'. Bits of soft slates, found anywhere, did duty as pencils. Another favoured writing implement was a quill pen 'many of the quills having been extracted from gander or goose's wing that very morning'. The paper used was ordinary pott in the native length, unruled and stitched in a brown paper cover. The ink was home produced also, being made from the root of the bramble or sorrel. The writing class commenced as the master 'set the headlines, the pupils surrounding him in a ring, and each bearing away his own book with a "Thankee, Sir", as soon as the headline was completed'.[19] Copying headlines was the common practice in hedge schools according to Edmund Grace, a Christian Brother from a hedge school in Callan, Co. Kilkenny, who verified that 'Writing meant copying headlines set by our teacher'.[20] Edmund Ignatius Rice also profited greatly from the instruction given in handwriting in the hedge school at Moate Lane in Callan.

The younger children were taught the alphabet and reading from the *Primer*.[21] *The child's new play-thing*[22] and *Reading made easy*,[23] while the seniors studied reading and grammar from Daniel Fenning's *Universal spelling book*.[24] These textbooks were used in the hedge schools of Wexford, Breiffne and in the seven counties that comprised the diocese of Kildare and Leighlin. In the senior class, the second part of *Reading made easy* was in use. This contained difficult material like the *Principles of politeness*,[25] *Letters written from the earl of Chesterfield to his son*,[26] and the *Economy of human life*, written by an ancient brahmin.[27]

19 'An Irish hedge school', p. 603. 20 A Christian Brother, *Edmund Ignatius Rice and the christian brothers* (Dublin, 1926), p. 97. 21 *The child's new spelling primer or first book for children, to which is added the stories of Cinderilla and Little Red Riding Hood* (Dublin, 1799). 22 Dublin, 1819. 23 *The imperial spelling book or reading made easy* (Dublin, n.d.). 24 Dublin, 1820. 25 P.D. Stanhope, *The accomplished gentleman, or principles of politeness* (Belfast, 1827). 26 P.D. Stanhope, Dublin, 1775. 27 Report from the commissioners of primary education (Irl) 1870,

THE

Child's New Spelling Primer;

O R,

FIRST BOOK for CHILDREN.

To which is added

The STORIES of CINDERILLA, and
The LITTLE RED RIDING HOOD.

DUBLIN: Printed by *T. Wilkinson,* No. 40,
Winetavern Street, 1799.
[Price Two Pence]

(11)

The STORY *of* CINDERILLA; *or, The*
Little Glafs Slipper.

ONCE there was a Gentleman who
married, for his fecond Wife, the
proudeft and moft haughty Woman that
ever was feen. She had, by a former Huf-
band, two Daughters of her own Humour,
who were indeed exactly like her in all
Things. He had likewife, by another
Wife, a young Daughter, but of an un-
paralled goodnefs and fweetnefs of temper,
which fhe took from her mother, who was
the beft creature in the world.

No fooner were the ceremonies of the
wedding over, but the mother-in-law began to fhew herfelf in her colours. She
could not bear the good qualities of this
pretty girl, and the lefs, becaufe fhe made
her own daughters appear the more odious.

1 Title page from *The child's new spelling primer; or, First book for children* (1799)
2 Page from 'The story of Cinderilla; or, The little glass slipper',
from *The child's new spelling primer*

It should be noted that a spelling book in the eighteenth century consisted also of a reader, a grammar and a dictionary. It contained the usual format. The alphabet was followed by lessons in monosyllables, both in spelling columns and reading lessons and the subsequent more difficult lessons were accompanied by word meanings.[28] The spelling book also had a very difficult grammar section which was strongly criticised by the Wexford observer, as follows:

> Our chief objection to it, consists in the steep nature of the stairs allowed to the unfortunate pupils in their ascent from the alphabet, to the highest attainment of knowledge acquirable at school.[29]

Despite its flaws Fenning's *Universal* was one of the best spelling books available at this time. It was in nationwide use in Ireland despite its prohibitive cost of 1s. 1d. It also remained 'one of the popular and widely used early spelling texts' in America, being reprinted many times up to 1810.[30]

Some enterprising Dublin, Cork and Limerick printers assumed responsibility for supplying these textbooks to the hedge schools. Two Dublin printers, Pat Wogan of Merchant's Quay and William Jones of 75 Thomas Street, took a personal interest in educational matters. They were the self-appointed 'educational and miscellaneous Alduses of the day, and considered themselves as lights burning in a dark place for the literary guidance'[31] of their people. The personal commitment was obvious from the frontispiece of some editions of the spelling book which showed a tree of knowledge, laden with fruit, each piece marked with a letter of the alphabet. Beneath the tree they had placed this doggerel inscription:

> The tree of knowledge, here you see,
> the fruit of which is A B C
> But if you neglect it like idle drones,
> you'll not be respected by William Jones.[32]

Jones and Wogan were well aware of the poverty of parents. Out of concern for their obvious needs, they employed some cost-cutting measures when producing the English textbooks. To economise, they printed and bound two of the books as one, and as an alternative, they produced three of the books in one bound edition. It has been explained[33] that 'The "Reading made easy"

Powis, p. 505.   28 Sr E.T. Whelan, 'Primary school readers in Ireland 1800–70'. Unpublished MEd thesis, University College Cork, 1976, pp 46–7.   29 'An Irish hedge school', p. 601.   30 C. Carpenter, *History of America school books* (Philadelphia, 1963), p. 149.   31 J.J.M., 'Irish chap books' in *Irish book lover*, 1: 12 (July, 1910), p. 157.   32 Ibid.   33 'An Irish hedge school', p. 601.

3 Page from 'The story of St George and the dragon', from *The child's new play-thing; or Best amusement*

(pronounced Readamadaisy) included the primer. The "Universal spelling book" included the primer and the "Reading made easy."'

The highlight in the hedge school day was the spelling lesson, which was performed in a ritualistic fashion. All the students who were capable of spelling were put into the 'class', while those not directly involved were free to enjoy their games. Each student had to put down a pin, which the master placed in the spelling book. Then they assumed their places as they formed a circle which almost encircled the whole school.[34] The challenge facing them was quite a daunting one as they were not allowed to read unless they could spell the longest word in the *Universal spelling book*. This book contained many sesquipedalian words such as 'antitrinitarians' and 'coessentially',[35] and it was the students who asked each other spellings. These were usually 'the

34 Carleton, *Autobiography*, p. 33.   35 'An Irish hedge school', p. 603.

most out-of-the-way words he or she could remember from the columns of the 'Universal', or Entick's or Jones' oblong little 'dixhenry'. The rewards were eagerly sought after. They consisted of the honorary royal titles of king, queen and prince respectively, as well as brass pins, which made suitable gifts for a 'mother, sister, aunt or little sweetheart'.

Carleton recalled in his autobiography how he coveted all the pins for himself and how he returned home from school every day with his coat sleeve 'shining with the signals of my triumph from my shoulder to my wrist'. It was a simple, inexpensive reward system that motivated students to learn through play and amusement. 'Great was the triumph of the little boy who won the pins,' wrote the Wexford visitor, and for the others there was always the hope that they would win tomorrow. He considered this a worthwhile exercise as 'no plan devised could have been more effective in making good spellers'. This was a view shared by an anonymous commentator who remarked upon the spelling ability of the 'poorest of this class' whose 'attainments in orthography and perspicuity of style, have frequently, to my knowledge, excited the amazement of strangers'.[36]

In teaching English, the hedge schoolmasters paid close attention to the rules of grammar, as many of them were classical scholars. One such was Carleton, who used a fictional character called Denis O'Shaughnessy, from his short story 'Denis O'Shaughnessy going to Maynooth',[37] to express his own views on the rules of grammar. Denis, according to Carleton was one of those 'grammatically minded preceptors' who held the rules of grammar sacrosanct. He was greatly irritated by the way his father flaunted the rules of English grammar.

> Father, I condimnate you at once – I condimnate you as being a most ungrammatical ould man, an' not fit to argue wid any one that knows Murray's English grammar an' more espaciously the three concords of Lilly's Latin, one – that is the cognation between the nominative case and the verb, the consanguinity between substantive case and the adjective and the blood-relationship that irritates between the relative and the antecedent.

An illustrious past pupil of a hedge school, John Tyndall, who was born in Carlow in 1820 and was elected Fellow of the Royal Society in 1855, declared in later life that he had received an invaluable education in the study of English

36 T. Corcoran, 'Kildare Place Schools' in *Irish Monthly* 60:705 (March, 1932), p. 165. Corcoran was quoting an anonymous writer of *An essay on the population of Ireland. By a member of the last Irish parliament* (London, 1803) in Halilday coll., p. 838.   37 T. Flanagan, *The Irish novelists 1800-1850* (Westport, Conn., 1976), pp 286-7.

grammar. He gave credit for this to the hedge schoolmaster John Conwill of Ballinabranagh. Addressing students of University College, London, he stated:

> The piercing through the involved and inverted sentences of Paradise lost, the linking of the verb to its often distant nominative, of the relative to its transitive verb of the preposition to the noun or pronoun which it governed, the study of variations in mood or tense, the transpositions often necessary to bring out the true grammatical structure of a sentence, all this was to my young mind a discipline of the highest value and a source of unflagging delight.[38]

Two shining examples of how highly English grammar was rated as a subject in the hedge schools, are Patrick Lynch (1754–1818) and Peter Gallegan. Lynch was an eminent past pupil of the Irish speaking hedge schoolmaster Donnchadh an Chorráin (Denis of the Heap) O'Mahony, affectionately known as 'The star of Ennistymon',[39] from Ennis, Co. Clare. He was taught Greek, Latin and Hebrew so well by Donnchadh that he was sufficiently well equipped to teach himself the rules of English grammar. Not only that but he published his own complete grammar of the English language called *The pentaglot preceptor*[40] in 1796. The work began with 'A preliminary discourse addressed to the schoolmasters of Ireland', in which he reviewed the best known English grammars of his day. He was critical of the methods of such luminaries as the American lawyer and Quaker, Lindley Murray (1745–1826), who published an English grammar at York in 1795, which became the standard textbook for the use of schools. It ran into one hundred editions and was still in print as late as 1871.[41] He even accused the great classical English writer and lexicographer Dr Johnson 'of several errors in his Saxon etymologies'[42]. Peter Gallegan also had a very professional approach to his work and despite his straitened circumstances, having only sporadic employment over his twelve year teaching career and earning just six pounds per annum,[43] he still considered the teaching of grammar sufficiently important to warrant the transcription of the rules from Murray's grammar. The original book cost between three and five shillings, which his pupils certainly couldn't afford, but Gallegan took great care to transcribe from it in a most ornate and elegant style of handwriting, in a manuscript entitled 'Peter Gallegan – collections in English and Irish, entirely written by himself',[44] dated 16 January

38 D. Kennedy, 'Education and the people' in R.B. McDowell (ed.), *Social life in Dublin 1800–45* (Cork, 1976), p. 58.   39 S. Ua Casaide, 'Patrick Lynch, secretary to the Gaelic Society of Dublin' in *Journal of the Waterford & South-East of Ireland Archaeological Society* 15 (1912), p. 48.   40 P.J. Dowling, 'Patrick Lynch, schoolmaster 1754–1818' in *Studies* 20 (1931), p. 467.   41 J.M. Goldstrom, *The social content of education, 1808–1870* (Shannon, 1972), p. 56.   42 Ua Casaide, 'Patrick Lynch', p. 49.   43 Dowling, *The hedge schools of Ireland*, p. 115.   44 Ms. G. 809.

1824. The manuscript also included the most up-to-date methods on the teaching of reading and grammar, arithmetic and writing.

The foregoing textbooks were barely given a mention by contemporary writers such as Dutton, Wakefield or Shaw Mason. The use of manuscripts seems to have escaped their attention also. Dutton listed a few romantic chapbooks with colourful titles as being representative samples of reading books in general use in hedge schools. This was simply not the case. In a number of hedge schools in counties Donegal, Kildare, Kerry and Galway we have official evidence that the classics of English literature were also read, works such as Milton's *Paradise lost*, Dr Johnson's *Classical essays*, Chesterfield's *Accomplished gentlemen* and *Letters*, Swift's *Gulliver's travels* as well as the poetry of Swift, Cowper and Thomson.

Some hedge schoolmasters developed innovative methods of teaching reading and expanding vocabulary. One such was John Casey of the Banna hedge school in Ardfert, who devised the 'Banna reading' method, which was the practice of synonymous reading in the teaching of English.

> Mr Casey encouraged his pupils to introduce as many synonyms as possible during reading in English by the class in common. As the reading progressed, all the boys – prompted by the teacher – interjected words of identical or similar meaning. In this way they acquired an extended vocabulary and a consequent fluency of expression.[45]

His method was widely used in the many schools in the neighbourhood of Ardfert.

Manson, a Belfast town hedge schoolmaster, liked to experiment in improved methods of teaching. Not only did he compile school textbooks such as *The new spelling primer for beginners*,[46] *Pronouncing dictionary and English expositor adapted to Sheridan's pronounciation*,[47] and *Mason's new primer*[48] but he also invented special learning-playing cards. He believed in the progressive educational theory which specified that learning should be a pleasurable activity, and as card-playing was the favourite form of entertainment among the people, he harnessed this source of interest for educational purposes. He furnished his pupils with:

> packs of cards, like playing cards, on which were printed elementary lessons in reading, spelling, and arithmetic. These lessons the young people of the party were expected to be studying, whilst their seniors

45 M.L. Quane, 'Banna school Ardfert with a prefatory survey of classical education in Kerry in the eighteenth century' in *Journal of the Royal Society of Antiquaries of Ireland* 84 (1954), p. 170.   46 Monaghan, 1798.   47 Belfast, 1816.   48 *Manson's new primer or the child's best guide* (Kilkenny, 1840).

were engaged with cards of a less instructive character 'David Manson's cards' were long well known in Belfast.[49]

He also believed that a happy atmosphere should be maintained in the classroom and he deplored the use of corporal punishment on children. Like many
of his contemporaries he favoured rewarding students' best efforts. He elaborated on the reward system of brass pins by using merit-tickets for successful pupils at morning lessons. The merit-tickets were marked *FRS* for *Fellow
of the Royal Society* and 'the scholars who returned their tickets unsoiled got
a half-guinea medal'. Manson could afford to give generous rewards as his
hedge school was run alongside his brewery business, both of which were successful enterprises.

It can be concluded therefore that in general, the hedge schools met the
requirements of parents. It was they who demanded individual instruction
for their children thus resulting in relaxed classroom management practices.
It was up to the individual masters to ensure that children learned in a happy
homely atmosphere where the needs of each child could be observed and a
suitable academic course drawn up to meet those needs.

The curriculum in the hedge school

> My eyelids red and heavy are
> With bending o'er the smould'ring peat
> I know the Aenid now by heart
> My Virgil read in cold and heat.

> Padraic Colum (1882–1972)

The hedge schools offered an impressive range of subjects which included
religion, history, arithmetic, book-keeping, science, surveying and land measuring, astronomy, geography, Latin, Greek, Hebrew, English, Irish and dancing. The livelihood of a hedge schoolmaster was largely dependent on his
mathematical expertise as 'the ordinary people of Ireland would set no store
by a school in which arithmetic did not figure prominently'.[50]

The most commonly used arithmetics were John Gough's *Arithmetic both
in theory and practice adapted to the commerce of Ireland as well as of Great
Britain*[51] and Elias Voster's *Arithmetick in whole and broken numbers digested
after a new method and chiefly adapted to the trade of Ireland. To which is added
(never before printed) Instructions for book-keeping.*[52] Voster's Arithmetic was

---

49 J. Marshall, 'David Manson, schoolmaster in Belfast' in *Ulster Journal of Archaeology* 12 (1907),
p. 66.   50 Brenan, *Schools of Kildare and Leighlin*, p. 81.   51 Dublin, 1770.   52 Dublin, 1772.

the older of the two and was superseded by Gough's and later by Paul Deighan's *A complete treatise on arithmetic*[53], which also included instructions for book-keeping. It would seem improbable that many of these arithmetics were actually purchased by parents, as they were written more in the style of handbooks of instruction for teachers. Besides, their prohibitive cost would doubtlessly have placed them well outside the reach of most people. The hedge schoolmasters themselves transcribed copiously from Gough and Voster, judging from extant manuscripts.[54] We know from references in contemporary writings that these arithmetics were used extensively in the hedge schools of Roscommon,[55] West Galway[56] and James Baggott's (1771–1806)[57] celebrated mathematical school at Ballingarry, Co. Limerick, together with the hedge schools in the diocese of Kildare and Leighlin.

Hedge schoolmasters tried to ensure that the most modern books were in use in their schools, and three progressive Limerick teachers McElligott, O'Brien and Geoghagan went so far as to publish a 'recommendatory letter' in the *Limerick Gazette* of 2 February 1813 suggesting that parents should purchase the newly published arithmetic by Deighan. They emphasised the utilitarian aspect of the book and recommended it as: 'the only book extant, whereby youth can acquire a knowledge and facility of the most modern and concise methods of counting,' and they concluded that: 'Gough and Voster served well in their day but their methods are now become too tedious and elaborate and are totally exploded in every counting house of eminence'.[58]

Arithmetic was a subject in which hedge schoolmasters excelled. Credit for this was grudgingly given even by their strongest critics, namely Glassford,[59] and Edgeworth. The latter acknowledged the high standards they achieved at all levels in arithmetic. In a letter to Lord Selkirk in 1808, he remarked:

> I rely upon the event of any trials that may be made upon boys of the higher and lower classes in Ireland, in which I am certain it will be found that not only the common but the higher parts of arithmetic are better understood and more expertly practised by boys without shoes and stockings, than by young gentlemen riding home on horseback or in coaches to enjoy their Christmas idleness.[60]

53 Dublin, 1804.   54 Ms. G. 809.   55 See Shaw Mason, *A statistical account*, p. 405 and I. Weld, *Statistical survey of the county of Roscommon* (Dublin, 1832), p. 699.   56 See B. Bean Uí Mhurchadha, *Oideachas in iar-chonnacht sa naoú céad déag* (Dublin, 1954).   57 S. O'C, 'O'Baggott of Ballingarry' in *Irish Book Lover* (March–April, 1930), p. 50.   58 Dowling, *The hedge schools of Ireland*, pp 65–6. McElligott is no doubt R. MacElligott and O'Brien is probably T.M. O'Brien, two Limerick hedge schoolmasters who taught Gerald Griffin, and who were referred to in Herbert's article of 1944 'Four Limerick hedge-schoolmasters', pp 48–55.   59 Glassford, *Notes on three tours*, p. 2. In his capacity as commissioner of education 1825, Glassford undertook two tours of Ireland between the years 1824 and 1826 and concluded at this time that arithmetic was 'the Irishman's hobby'.   60 H.J. Butler and H. Edgeworth Butler, *The black book of Edge-*

Hedge schoolmasters took considerable pride in their mathematical learning, even going so far as to append the epithet 'Philomath' to the end of all correspondence, documents, wills, promissory notes and even love-letters.[61] Brian Merriman (1747–1805) the 'poet of one work' – *Cúirt an mheadhon oídche (The midnight court)*, a poem of 1206 lines, wished to be remembered, not for his famed poetic ability but rather for his mathematical expertise.[62]

Irish people paid special homage to a master who displayed a flair for mathematics or a talent in any other branch of learning by conferring upon him a flattering title such as 'The bright star in mathematical learning'.[63] This was the title which was conferred on Owen Reynolds of Mohill, Co. Leitrim. James Baggott had not only a national but an international reputation as a mathematician, being a personal friend of the eminent physicist Laplace (1794–1827), who was tutor to Napoleon. Because of this distinction he was known as 'The great O'Baggott'.[64] Neither was it unusual for past pupils of hedge schools to compose poems of praise eulogising on the mathematical talents of their much loved teachers. One such poet was Philip O'Connell, from Mountnugent, Co. Cavan, who referred to his hedge schoolmaster euphemistically as 'the great Longinus of my native town', although his pseudonym was 'lame Jack'.

> Where 'midst the simple neighbours who but he
> Could sound the depths of 'Voster's Rule of Three',
> Engrave a Sundial – make a Patrick's Cross,
> And catechise the children after Mass.
> Find the moon's age correct by Doogan's rule,
> And prove each neighbouring pedagogue a fool.[65]

The masters themselves displayed their appreciation of the mathematical expertise of members of their own profession. They did so to Paul Deighan, from Ballina, Co. Mayo, by subscribing to his aritmetic when it was published in 1804. The arithmetic also contained many 'recommendatory letters' from hedge schoolmasters. The following one was written by John Bartley in Drumcondra on 17 May 1804:

worthstown (London, 1927), p. 195. Richard Lovell Edgeworth was a commissioner of education 1806, he also helped to compile the 1791 Report which suggested state control of all hedge schools.   61 Carleton, 'The hedge school', p. 275.   62 Corkery, *The hidden Ireland*, p. 224.   63 O'Connell, *The schools and scholars*, p. 430.   64 Archdeacon J. Begley, *The diocese of Limerick* (Dublin, 1938), pp 411–12. See also S. Ó C., 'O'Baggott of Ballingarry' in *Irish Book Lover* (March-April, 1930), p. 50. Begley attributes the title 'The great O'Baggott' to the master's mathematical talent, whereas S. Ó C. maintains that he earned the title 'great' as a direct result of his planned capture of Limerick Castle in 1803. See also Herbert, 'Four Limerick hedge-schoolmasters', p. 56, who shares the same opinion as Begley.   65 O'Connell, *Schools and scholars*, p. 410.

The muse amaz'd inquires who could contrive,
To make one digit do the work of five,
Lo here a more surprising wonders seen,
One figure does the duty of fifteen.

But Deighan of a more enlightened mind,
More innate genius, talents more refin'd,
... To him a more exalted task is due
To teach the pupil and the master too.[66]

Other masters who made a contribution to the advancement of mathematical pedagogy were Michael Tierney from Limerick and Michael Madden from John Casey's hedge school at Banna, Ardfert, Co. Kerry. Tierney, who probably never heard of Pestalozzi's progressive teaching methods, nonetheless adopted a very similar approach as he too believed in using concrete examples to illustrate solutions to mathematical problems, especially for the teaching of addition and subtraction. His preferred teaching aid was the humble potato and 'in order to explain to a particularly dense pupil the – truth of the Euclidian axiom that the whole is greater than any part, Tierney took a potato, cut a piece off, and convinced his pupil simply and most effectively'.[67] Michael Madden, who taught Edward Day the son of Judge Robert Day in preparation for entry to Trinity College, won acclaim for introducing the compact multiplication table. This was adopted by the schools in the Ardfert area and continued in use up until the 1890s. A year after Madden entered Trinity College as a student, in 1756, he died tragically, in a drowning accident. His death was recorded in a contemporary publication which acknowledged his mathematical genius.

> September 17th – drowned at Rush, Mr Michael Madden of Co. Kerry, a student of our university, of a most promising genius and for his standing greatly advanced in the mathematical sciences.[68]

This strong mathematical tradition which the hedge schools had firmly established in the eighteenth century was reinforced in the early nineteenth century by the publication of almanacs, such as *Lady's and Farmer's Almanack*, the *Lady's Almanack*, the *Belfast Almanack*, *Nugent's Almanack*, the *Telegraphic Almanack*. They appeared annually and provided sufficient reading material for a household for an entire year. They posed mathematical problems, the solutions to which appeared the following year. The main contrib-

---

66 Dowling, *The hedge schools of Ireland*, pp 147–8.   67 Herbert, 'Four Limerick hedge-school-masters', pp 46–7.   68 Quane, 'Banna school Ardfert', pp 167–8.

utors were hedge schoolmasters such as Gallegan and Baggott. It would appear also that the almanacs helped to develop many a mathematical talent that might not otherwise have been developed. A past pupil of the hedge school at Glanellie, Co. Tyrone, named James McCullough became one of the leading mathematicians of the age and went on to become a professor of mathematics at Trinity College, in 1836, at the tender age of twenty-five. He owed much to the hedge schools and the almanacs and it was through the almanacs that 'he first discovered his genius for science by answering these mathematical queries. At the age of ten years, he was able to answer every one of them'.[69]

Science was taught as well as mathematics and was eagerly sought after by the poor, according to the evidence given by the Reverend Dr Hincks before the select committee on foundation schools in 1836.[70] He was well acquainted with the hedge schools of the south of Ireland having taught from 1790 to 1815 in the city of Cork; and, from 1815 to 1821 in Fermoy, when he was appointed principal of the Belfast Academical Institution. He testified to having known:

> instances of very considerable advance in science, especially in mathematics, in the very lowest schools. I have known persons procuring scientific books, and apparently able to make use of those books, who were in very great poverty, in the south of Ireland especially. I think there is much more of such taste for scientific acquirements in the south than in the north.[71]

Book-keeping was also regarded as an important subject. Carleton and his brother John were fortunate enough to have attended the hedge school of Mr O'Brien who was formerly from Connaught but who taught at Findermore, Co. Tyrone. He was such a 'pre-eminent and extraordinary scholar, that he was allowed to append the epithet *Great* to his name, after which the people referred to him as 'the great O'Brien, par excellence'.[72] In his autobiography, Carleton was generous in his praise of O'Brien, whom he regarded as:

> a most excellent teacher, and probably one of the best book-keepers of that day in the north. Several respectable young fellows used to come from long distances to be instructed by him in the art of keeping accounts.

Subjects related to mathematics, such as surveying, land measuring and astronomy were taught to advanced students. Parents in Tyrone and the

69 Kennedy, 'Education and the people', pp 57–8.   70 Reports from the select committees on foundation schools, together with minutes of evidence. Part II, 1836 (12), p. 20.   71 Dowling, *The hedge schools of Ireland*, pp 75–6.   72 Carleton, 'The hedge school', pp 275–6.

northern counties expected a hedge schoolmaster to have a knowledge of surveying and an ability to teach their children land measuring.[73] In Co. Carlow,
John Garrett taught surveying with the aid of no less than three different
books on the subject – *Gibson's surveying, Harding's surveying and Croker's
surveying*. He also taught astronomy from *Brinkley's astronomy*.[74] In the south
of Ireland surveying was taught on a wide scale, judging from the question
put to Dr Hincks, when he was giving evidence before the education committee in 1835. He was asked

> Are you aware that in making an ordnance survey in Ireland great facil-
> ity existed in finding competent persons to assist the surveyors at ordi-
> nary labourers' wages?

This fact didn't surprise him

> I am not at all surprised at the circumstance: there were a great many
> of the hedge schools where there was given a great deal of scientific
> instruction.[75]

Francis McGann (1786–1815), who was described by O'Connell as the
'brilliant county Leitrim mathematical scholar', died tragically in a snowstorm
and was remembered in the popular ballad *The fate of Francis McGann*. He
attended the mathematical schools of Hugh McDonald of Drumlara, Owen
Reynolds, the 'Bright star', of Mohill and the renowned mathematical school
of 'The great O'Baggott' of Ballingarry. Having qualified in higher mathematics he returned home to Drumlara where he earned a considerable reputation for himself as a cartographer and surveyor. He was reputedly offered a
position as a surveyor in India, by the English government of the day, but
rejected it. The legacy he left behind him was 'the art of preparing accurate
large scale maps', which were 'developed later by the ordnance survey'.[76]
    The study of astronomy was aided to a large extent by the publication in
1817 of a textbook on astronomy by the scholarly Patrick Lynch. Like the
titles of most of his textbooks, this one too included the contents of the book.
It was called *An easy introduction to practical astronomy,*[77] *and the use of the
globes; including, in mnemonic verses and rhyming couplets, as the most effectual
means hitherto invented for assisting the memory, the necessary axioms, definitions
and rules of chronology, geometry, algebra and trigonometry, with the prognostics
of the weather etc. etc. for the use of schools, and young ladies.*[78] In it Lynch sup-

73 Carleton. 'The hedge school', p. 284, p. 296.   74 Brenan, *Schools of Kildare and Leighlin*, pp
438–9.   75 Reports from the select committees on foundation schools, p. 20.   76 O'Connell,
Schools and scholars, p. 430–1.   77 Dublin, 1817.   78 S. Ua Casaide, 'List of works projected or
published by Patrick Lynch' in *Journal of the Waterford & South-East of Ireland Archaeological*

plied 'the necessary mathematical foundation for a study of elementary astronomy'. He posed numerous problems on astronomy and supplied the answers.
He also treated the subject from the historical perspective and cited the opinions of forty writers on the subject, of whom twelve lived before Christ.[79]
Lynch was a dedicated researcher as he produced an ambitious work on the
geography of the world and a history of Ireland, that same year. Once again
the textbook bore a lengthy and informative title. It was called *A geographical
& statistical survey of the terraqueous globe, including a comprehensive compend of
the history, antiquities and topography of Ireland. Embellished with a curious map
of ancient Éire. For the use of schools and adult persons.*[80] The book consisted of
340 pages, the first 190 of which were devoted to geography and the remain-
der to history.

The study of Irish history was frowned upon by the government. Edgeworth, in a letter to the board of education, dated 8 November 1808, gave his
explanation as to why history was not a suitable subject for the Irish. He wrote
'to inculcate democracy and a foolish hankering after undefined liberty is not
necessary in Ireland'.[81] Many contemporary writers viewed the hedge schoolmasters as the worst possible choice of teachers for such a sensitive subject as
history. Wakefield feared that Irish children would imbibe from them 'enmi-
ty to England, hatred to the government, and superstitious veneration for old
and absurd customs'.[82] Shaw Mason feared for the security of the state especially when he discovered a 'pernicious little book' called *The articles of Limerick* in the hedge schools of Kilkenny. He considered that it would be
impossible for children to read this book 'without imbibing a spirit of disloyalty to the government, and hatred of the present royal family and the English connection'.[83] These fears continued to be expressed in 1820 by an
anonymous pamphleteer, who doubted very much also, whether, 'the country
schoolmaster' was a loyal subject. He suspected that 'to his little store of learning, he generally adds some traditional tales of his country, of a character to
keep alive discontent'.[84] In 1822 Crofton Croker, when writing about his tour
of the south of Ireland, recorded how he heard the hedge schoolmasters in
the south express their 'disloyalty' quite openly while professing a deep commitment to the broadest republicanism as they deprecated and disclaimed the
Union.[85]

However unsuited to the task, hedge schoolmasters were deemed to be,
one thing is certain, Irish and European history was a subject in great demand

Society 15 (1912), p. 116.   **79** Dowling, 'Patrick Lynch schoolmaster 1754–1818', p. 469.   **80**
Dublin, 1817.   **81** Parliamentary papers 1812–14 Vol. 3rd report, App. No. 10, p. 109, Letter to
the committee of the board of education 8 Nov. 1808. See also Dowling, *The hedge schools of Ireland*, p. 85.   **82** Wakefield, *An account of Ireland*, p. 398.   **83** Shaw Mason (ed.), *Survey of
Tullaroan*, p. 135.   **84** *Thoughts and suggestions*, p. 10.   **85** Crofton Croker, *Researches in the south
of Ireland* (London, 1818), p. 328.

in the hedge schools, where some twenty seven different history books were in use. There was no narrow, provincialism displayed here either as there were texts on the French revolution, Hume's *History of England*, Goldsmith's *Histories of England, Rome and Greece*, together with biographies of emperors of Rome, Empress Catherine of Russia, Frederick [3] of Prussia and Charles XII of Sweden.

Religion was highly prized in Ireland and as a result it was one of the most sought after subjects in the hedge schools. The schoolmasters often worked in close co-operation with the Catholic priests as coadjutors in the teaching of the catechism and the christian doctrine on Sundays.[86] There were twenty-five different religion books in use in the schools of Kildare and Leighlin as well as twenty-six doctrinal and devotional books.[87] The 1825 commissioners of education listed ninety two works under the heading *Religious Works and Tracts*, as well as eleven Roman Catholic catechisms, four of which were in Irish.[88] The first one was bilingual by the Reverend Andrew Dunlevy, prefect of the Irish community in Paris. As the hedge schools offered a non–denominational education the commissioners' list also included four catechisms of the Established Church Stopford's, Mann's, Marriott's and Lewis' together with a Presbyterian catechism by Shorter. Carleton recorded in his autobiography 'that so many Protestants attended a school at which he was a pupil that their withdrawal necessitated its closing down'. Cooke's Presbyterian hedge schoolmaster Joseph Pollock taught 'The Shorter catechism of the Westminster divines, the church catechism, and the christian doctrine of the Roman Catholics ... to the members of the respective sects'.[89] Whereas in the Wexford hedge schools, when there was no suitable teacher to teach the Protestant catechism, 'one of the eldest Catholic boys performed the ceremony'.[90]

Studying the classics – Greek, Latin and Hebrew, formed part of the hedge school curriculum. It was a source of surprise to many that this was so. After all, this was an age which promoted the utilitarian philosophy of Jeremy Bentham (1748–1832), which emphasised 'useful learning as opposed to the decadent and illiberal liberal education'.[91] There was a strongly held con-

86 Brenan, *Schools of Kildare and Leighlin*, pp 65–9.   87 Ibid., pp 67–8.   88 The first one of these catechisms was bilingual by the Reverend A. Dunlevy, prefect of the Irish community in Paris. It was entitled *The catechism of christian doctrine by way of question and answer in the Irish language and character* (Paris, 1742), with the approbation of Louis XV. The Reverend Dr Farrell O'Reilly published his Irish catechism *An teagasc críostaighe* in Dublin in 1750. He was the bishop of Kilmore from 1806–29 and the titular archbishop of Armagh in 1750. A third Irish catechism *Teagusg creesdiú* by Dr J. Butler was published in Cork in 1792 and a fourth one *An teagasc críostaiche, do réir cheiste agus fhreagraidh*, published in Cork in 1831, by the bishop of Cloyne and Ross, William Coppinger. Listed also were the seventeen sermons in Irish published by the titular bishop of Raphoe, J. Gallagher in 1735. An edition in the Roman character was printed in Dublin in 1795 with a second in 1798.   89 J.L. Porter, *The life and times of Henry Cooke* (London, 1871), p. 4.   90 'An Irish hedge school', p. 610.   91 S.J. Curtis and M.E.A.

viction by political leaders, contemporary writers and evangelists that the poor should not be educated above their station in life. Townsend, a clergyman of the Established Church, held fast to this belief. He considered that 'In a country where there is hardly any employment but tilling the ground, it (learning) can eventually be of no use except to such as are bred to trades'.[92]

This was also the principle behind the Lancastrian plan of education submitted to John Foster, chancellor of the exchequer in 1805, and applied by the Kildare Place Society 'to make youth more useful, without elevating them above the situation in life for which they may be designed'.[93] The eighteenth-century historian, Dr Charles Smith, was amazed by the widespread cultivation of the classics in the rugged, isolated areas of Kerry. He wrote:

> Classical reading extends itself even to a fault amongst the lower and poorer kind in this country; many of whom, to the taking them off more useful works, have greater knowledge in this way, than some of the better sort in other places.[94]

The landlords and their agents were far from happy either with this quest for Latin learning by the ragged poor. In a letter to Lord Shelbourne on 2 September 1773, his agent from Kenmare, Joseph Taylor complained bitterly that scholars were being distracted from more practical occupations:

> as to school-masters we have too many, and too many mere schollars, for we abound with schools and schoolboys, and it would be better that our youth should be hammering at the anvil than at bog Latin.[95]

Peel as home secretary (1822–7) expressed the view that such an education was unsuitable for 'young peasants'. He stated as much in the house of commons on 20 March 1826 in response to Spring-Rice, the MP for Limerick. He said that he:

> did not wish to see children educated like the inhabitants of that part of the country, to which the honourable member belongs, where the young peasants of Kerry run about in rags with a Cicero or a Virgil under their arms.[96]

In some instances however, the teaching of Latin, Hebrew and Greek was done to meet the practical needs of students, as Sir James Caldwell, FRS,

Boultwood, *An introductory history of English education since 1800* (London, 1862), p. 51.   92 H. Townsend, *General & statistical survey of the county of Cork*, i (Cork, 1815), p. 97.   93 Corcoran, *Selected texts*, p. 104.   94 G. Holmes, *Sketches of some of the southern counties of Ireland* (London, 1801), p. 151.   95 Marquis of Lansdowne, *Glanerought and the Petty-Fitzmaurices* (London, 1937), p. 90.   96 T. Corcoran, 'Education policy after the Union', in *Irish Monthly* 59, p. 690.

sheriff of Co. Fermanagh, pointed out in a letter to the press in 1764 with regard to the teaching of Latin:

> The papists are not only connected by the general tie of religion that acknowledges the Pope for its common father and head, with the courts of France and Spain, but there is not a family in the island that has not a relation in the church, in the army, or in trade in these countries, and in order to qualify the children for foreign service, they are all taught Latin in schools that are kept in poor huts, in many places in the southern part of the kingdom.[97]

Irish parents had three main ambitions which they held in prospect for their sons, and these were that they would become either a 'priest, a clerk, or a schoolmaster'. The priesthood was the highest accolade they could aspire towards 'The determination once fixed, the boy was set apart from every kind of labour, that he might be at liberty to bestow his undivided time and talents to the object set before him'.[98] However, up until 1793, when the first Irish seminaries were founded at St Kieran's College, Kilkenny and at St Patrick's College, Carlow, Irish students who wished to study for the priesthood on the continent relied exclusively on the native schools for instruction in the classics, in order to meet the entry requirements of these colleges. During the French revolution of 1789 there were seventeen seminaries in France, mostly founded by the Irish 'in which nearly five hundred scholars and masters, were maintained and educated'. Troy, the archbishop of Dublin, in his *Report of the state of the diocese of Dublin to the sacred congregation of the Propaganda*, in 1802, referred to Irish Colleges in Paris, Nantes, Bordeaux, Douai. He mentioned also in Belgium at Louvain and Antwerp and one in Rome which was closed down by the French as Ireland was part of the British Empire.

According to the private report of Dr Curtis, rector of the Irish College at Salamanca, for the year 1789, the academic standard of entrants from Ireland was generally high and the students came from twenty-six different counties. The following progress report on Dr Juan Robinson is representative of the other twenty-eight listed:

> Dr Juan Robinson, student. A native of the D. of Leighlin, of Catholic and noble parents, 24 years of age and two as a student with burse he had learned humanities very well at home, and in this college he has studied a little Hebrew, mathematics and is at present in his second year's philosophy. His progress has been equal to his great talents. He is of fair application and excellent conduct.[99]

97 Lecky, *A history of Ireland* ii, p. 206.   98 Carleton, 'The hedge school', p. 273.   99 Dr P. Curtis, 'Students of the Irish college, Salamanca' in *Archivium Hibernicum* 9 (1915), p. 55.

Practically all of the students mentioned in Curtis' report 'had learned the humanities very well at home', or 'had learned sufficient humanities at home to enter this college'. Considering that the Irish College had been incorporated with the university of Salamanca in 1608, 'the qualifications for entrance must in many cases have been of corresponding university standard'.[100] The Reverend J. Milner, writing in 1808, was of the opinion that 'the Irish students in the foreign universities, down to the very period of the late Revolution, carried off more than a due proportion of prizes and professorships by the sheer merit of superior talents and learning, and a much greater proportion than fell to the lot of all other foreigners put together'.[101]

Kerry was the county which contemporary writers[102] repeatedly singled out as the centre of classical learning in Ireland, especially the famous classical hedge school at Faha. It was here scholars arrived from all over the country, some of whom were intended for the priesthood. They all sought the much coveted 'Munster diploma' for proficiency in Greek, Latin and Hebrew. George Holmes was astonished to meet 'amongst the uncultivated part of the country', 'good Latin scholars' who could 'not speak a word of English'.[103] Milner could testify from his own personal contact with the peasants that a great proportion of them 'some twenty or thirty years back, could even converse fluently in Latin'. He conversed for a considerable time with two of them, 'both being indigent schoolmasters'.[104] One of the indigent masters was none other than Eugene O'Sullivan of Ardfert who earned a reputation for himself as the hedge schoolmaster who conducted his own defence in court in pure Ciceronian Latin. The *Cork Advertiser* of 30 August 1808 reported on his case which took place in the record court of Tralee. It told how a poet and a professor of the learned languages, when arraigned in court, amused those present by refusing:

> to descend to that humble vernacular expression common to the profanum vulgus. No, his glowing mind, stored with the riches of Rome and Athens, was wafted, swift as with the Daedalean wing, to the highest summit of Mount Parnassus.[105]

O'Sullivan won his case as he completely confounded and silenced two learned barristers, who attempted to ridicule him.

Teaching of the classics was greatly assisted by the publication in 1817 of Lynch's *The classical students' metrical mnemonics*, containing in familiar verse, all the necessary definitions and rules of the English, Latin, Greek and

---

100 Dowling, *The hedge schools of Ireland*, p. 67.   101 Reverend J. Milner, *An inquiry into certain vulgar opinions* (London, 1808), p. 14.   102 Carr, *The stranger in Ireland*, p. 380.   103 Holmes, *Sketches*, p. 151.   104 Milner, *An inquiry*, p. 184.   105 S. Ó Casaide, 'Latin in county Kerry' in *Kerry Archaeological Magazine* 3:16 (1916), pp 301–2.

Hebrew languages.[106] Lynch used rhyme as an aid to memory and with the exception of the introduction, he gave the rules of grammar for English, Latin, Greek and Hebrew entirely in rhyming verse. In the teaching of Latin John Casey (*c.*1750) of the Banna hedge school in Ardfert, displayed both flair and imagination. He employed the 'captus' or capping verses method, which worked as follows:

> Two rivals having been pitted against each other, one of them recited a line of Latin poetry usually an hexameter; to which his antagonist replied with a line commencing with the last letter of his antagonist's verse, to which the other rejoined in a similar manner, and thus they continued bandying quotations until the stock of one side began to fail, the other had succeeded in declining the adjective 'captus' before his opponent could furnish the requisite line of poetry in his turn.

Past pupils later acknowledged the merit of this method of intellectual challenge, which resulted in the memory being stored 'with a treasure of classical quotations ready for use and display'.[107]

Eminent past pupils of hedge schools recalled the infectious love of classical learning displayed by their former masters and passed on to them, so that they retained a partiality for the classics, throughout their lives. Edmund Burke claimed to have learned more Latin and Greek from an obscure schoolmaster on the banks of the Nore, than he afterwards acquired at the more celebrated places of education, including the university itself.[108] Gerald Griffin was fortunate enough to have been taught by O'Brien of Limerick in 1814, a teacher who was 'passionately devoted to the ancient poets' and one who 'showed a highly cultivated taste in their study'. The young Griffin quickly acquired a good grasp of the classics which were to become his absorbing interest 'He was exceedingly fond of Virgil, Ovid and Horace, particularly the first, which he read with such an absorbing interest that his lessons lost all the character of a school-boy's task'.[109] O'Brien insisted that his students should speak the Latin language daily, as well as Greek, so that eventually they were as fluent in Latin and Greek as they were in English. In later life they corresponded through Latin and as one contemporary recollected, they even sold pigs at the fair through Latin.

> I recollect when, the scholars made by Kennedy, Cantillon, Buckley and O'Brien used keep up a regular correspondence, meet at the fairs, and buy pigs from each other without ever using a word but Latin.[110]

106 P. Lynch, Dublin, 1817.   107 Quane, 'Banna school Ardfert', p. 170.   108 Milner, *An inquiry*, p. 184.   109 Griffin, *The life of Gerald Griffin*, p. 46.   110 Herbert, 'Four Limerick hedge schoolmasters', p. 54.

One should bear in mind that Latin was the spoken language in general use in western Europe in the post–renaissance period and 'In Ireland there were additional reasons for its study and use in that it was the language of the church and a principal link with Catholic European countries'.[111]

Charles McGoldrick passed on a love of the classics to Carleton, when he attended his school at Tulnavert. In his autobiography he recalled with delight:

> Ovid's Metamorphoses ... charmed me more than any book I had then ever read; in fact I cannot describe the extraordinary delight with which I perused it. The sense of task work was lost, because I did it con amore.[112]

Carleton read the classics as novels and he became totally absorbed in the story:

> If ever a schoolboy was affected almost to tears, I was, by the death of Dido. Even when a schoolboy, I did not read the classics as they are usually read by learners. I read them as novels – I looked to the story – the narrative – not to the grammatical or other difficulties.[113]

Cooke attended the hedge school of Frank Glass at Tobermore (1797–8), where he learned four languages – Latin, Greek, English and Irish, although still practically a child, being under ten years of age. Nonetheless, he acquired from Glass a knowledge of and a taste for the classics. Glass was the model classical teacher:

> a pure Milesian ... a good scholar and a successful teacher. Like many of his countrymen, his love for classic literature, amounted almost to a passion, and he had the rare talent of inspiring favourite pupils with much of his own enthusiasm. Among Latin authors he delighted in Horace ...

Cooke immersed himself in the study of classical literature and poetry:

> While at school, he committed to memory the Odes of Horace, and a great part of the Georgics of Virgil. But the eloquence of Cicero and Demosthenes had greater charms for him than the graces of poetry.[114]

Glass awoke in him an abiding interest in the subject which enriched the remaining years of his life.

---

111 Quane, 'Banna school Ardfert', p. 158.   112 Carleton, *Autobiography*, 53.   113 Ibid., p. 70.
114 Porter, *The life and times*, pp 6–7.

Irish was taught in the hedge schools although demand for it was diminishing. Shaw Mason blamed the decline on 'the hedge schools where English alone is taught', as well as the demands of the English speaking commercial world, which forced the Irish to speak 'English in all their trafficking'.[115] Hedge schoolmasters were meeting the demands of the market place by satisfying the wishes of parents who desired social advancement for their children. Shaw Mason was partially correct in his assessment however, as English was the language of commerce, fair and market. It was the language of the landlord and the tithe proctor, it was the language used in court. English was necessary for the Irish who emigrated to America and it was also the language which came to dominate church service. People were no doubt influenced by the advice offered by Swift when he told them that 'It would be a noble achievement to abolish the Irish language so far as to oblige all the natives to speak only English on every occasion of business in shop, markets, fairs and other places of dealings'.[116] Of greater significance by far was the example given by a native Irish speaker of repute, one described by Charles Greville, the political diarist and clerk to the privy council, as 'the most important and most conspicuous man of his time and country'; this was Daniel O'Connell, one whose name was 'mightier in its appeal in Ireland than any other name',[117] but one who was a declared Benthamite when it came to the use of the Irish language. 'I am sufficiently utilitarian not to regret its abandonment ... a diversity of tongues is of no benefit', he declared, and added dispassionately, 'The superior utility of the English tongue, as the medium of all modern communications, is so great, that I can witness without a sigh the gradual disuse of Irish'.[118]

The Catholic hierarchy too exercised an enormous influence over the Irish people and they conducted mass and church services, mostly through English. In 1796 de Latocnaye attended a mass at Ardfert, where the priest translated the principal part of his sermon into English.[119] William Tighe found a similar situation in Kilkenny in 1801. He wrote 'The priests often preach alternately in Irish and English, but in Irish if they are desired to be well understood'.[120] Another factor which precipitated the decline of the language was the use the proselytising education societies put it too. They issued their religious tracts in Irish as a means of spreading the Protestant religion, all of which 'tended to bring the language into disfavour as a literary medium and thereby hastened its decay'.[121] The Irish language therefore was to have very bad associations in the minds of the people. It was a language which would

115 Shaw Mason (ed.), *Survey of Tullaroan*, p. 133.   116 H. Davis, *Jonathan Swift Irish tracts 1728–1733* (Oxford, 1971), p. 89.   117 M. McDonagh, Daniel O'Connell (Dublin, 1929), pp 15 and 16.   118 D. Corkery, *Imeachtaí na teanga Gaeilge* (Cork, 1956), p. 114.   119 de Latocnaye, 'Promenade d'un Français', p. 111.   120 W. Tighe, *Statistical observations relative to the county of Kilkenny* (Dublin, 1802), p. 515.   121 O'Connell, *The schools and scholars*, p. 381.

retard their progress and keep them backward. The hedge schoolmasters therefore faced a formidable challenge in their efforts to teach Irish as an academic subject. The absence of a wide variety of printed books in the language also made their task much more difficult. Twiss noted this fact back in 1775,[122] an observation later confirmed by Trotter in his *Walks through Ireland*.[123] All the available evidence would in fact suggest that the hedge schoolmasters did what they could to promote and to preserve the language by writing poetry and song, compiling Irish dictionaries, preserving countless Irish legends, medieval tales, songs and Ossianic poems. Croker paid tribute to them in 1822 when he noted that 'modern manuscripts in the Irish character, may be met with in almost every village and they are usually the produce of the leisure hours of the schoolmaster'.[124]

We have ample evidence also to show that the hedge schoolmasters held Irish culture in the highest esteem. They also familiarised their students with Irish folklore from *The royal Hibernian tales*, which 'is the earliest known collection of Irish popular tales or märchen, as well as being one of the rarest books in the field of Irish folklore'. This book met with the approval of the English novelist Thackeray (1811–63) in *The Irish sketch book* (1842), and also some forty years later from W. B. Yeats (1865–1939), who reprinted two stories from it in his *Fairy and folk tales of the Irish peasantry*. It was to be expected that the masters would be discerning in their choice of Irish books as many of them were 'able classical scholars whose only other language was Irish ... men who had mastered the difficulties of old and middle Irish'.[125] Many others were successful Irish poets who must surely have enthused their students with their own love of the language, like the following poet/hedge schoolmasters whose works are familiar to Irish students down to the present day:

122 Twiss, *A tour in Ireland in 1775*, p. 41. This shortfall was met by the scholarly publications of the Louvain Franciscans, most notably Uáitéar Ó Ceallaigh's *Stair an Bhíobla* (1726), the theological writings of Dr Seathrún Céitinn (1570–1650?) as well as his Irish history *Foras Feasa ar Éirinn* (1633) which failed to discriminate between the authentic and the fabulous. In the early nineteenth century, several publications in Irish 'upon Irish ground' appeared – Irish grammars by Dr W. Neilson of Dundalk, Dr P. O'Bryan, Irish professor of Maynooth College, W. Halliday of Dublin, the *Synoptic tables* of Patrick Lynch and the *Irish-English dictionary* of E. O'Reilly. See Anderson, *Historical sketches*, p. 100 and Dowling, 'P. Lynch, schoolmaster, 1754–1818', p. 468.   123 B. Trotter, *Walks through Ireland in the years 1812, 1814 and 1817* (London, 1819), p. 46.   124 C. Croker, *Researches in the south*, p. 331. Philip Fitzgibbon (1711–92), the Kilkenny hedge schoolmaster bequeathed his Irish dictionary which he had compiled, with many other valuable Irish manuscripts to the Reverend Richard O'Donnell, P.P. of St John's, Kilkenny. A remarkable feature of this 400 querto page dictionary was the author's singular omission of the letter 's'. See Séamus Ó Casaide, 'Philip Fitzgibbon' in *Journal of the Waterford and South-East of Ireland Archaeological Society* (January, 1920), p. 50.   125 Dowling, *The hedge schools of Ireland*, p. 71.

Peadar Ó Doirnín	1704–1768
Seán Ó Tuama	1709–1775
Donnchadh Ruadh Mac Conmara	1715–1810
Brian Mac Giolla Meidhre	1747–1805
Amhlaoibh Ó Súilleabháin	1780–1838
Seán Ó Coileáin	1754–1817
Tomás Rua Ó Súilleabháin	1785–1848
Philip Fitzgibbon	1711–1792
Eoghan Rua Ó Suilleabháin	1748–1784
Andrias Mac Craith	1710-1790
Pádraig Denn	1756–1828
Riocárd Báiréad	1739–1819

During the penal days a number of these poet/hedge schoolmasters, under the leadership of Seán Ó Tuama, were so concerned about the threat they perceived to Irish culture, that they assembled in a court of poetry in 1754, at O'Tuama's famous Inn, at Croom. The courts of poetry were originally set up to continue the tradition of the bardic schools, and were normally convened to discuss and recite poetry and to read and exchange manuscripts.[126] But now the warrant or *barántas*, which was the formal summons to the court, indicated the urgency of the situation as 'the poet insisted that what little remained of Irish was sure to vanish utterly unless they took steps towards its revival'.[127] One master who risked his liberty towards this end was Ó Doirnín, who taught Irish in Armagh. He was forced to go into hiding to escape arrest, after he was caught doing so. He took up residence in a cave where he composed an Irish poem *A Ghaeilge mhilis is sáimhe fonn* to mark the event in which he praised the beauty of the Irish language but regretted the hazards involved in teaching it.

O sweet Irish tongue of the beguiling airs;
Swift, bold, strong as the beating waves;
'Twas no crime once to speak you in Fódla,
And your bards went not in peril of their heads.[128]

The hedge schools didn't neglect the liberal arts either. As already mentioned dance teachers were employed to teach the children to dance, for a fee of sixpence a quarter. The dance teachers were accompanied in their travels from cabin to cabin by pipers or a blind fiddler. Young was impressed by this liberal education and he noted also that a fine education was given in reading,

126 Dowling, *A history of Irish education*, p. 18. 127 J.E. Caerwyn Williams and P.K. Ford, *The Irish literary tradition* (Cardiff, 1992), p. 226. 128 A. de Blácam, *Gaelic literature surveyed* (Dublin, 1979), pp, 298–9.

writing and book-keeping, even to the poorest child.[129] The extent of the curriculum depended entirely on the qualifications of the masters. Reading, writing and arithmetic were taught in all schools, according to Brenan's study with only five schools reported teaching less than reading writing and arithmetic. Sixteen of the two hundred and sixty-two teachers upon whom he had information,were conducting schools, with enough Latin taught, to be classified by him as 'classical schools'.[130] The curriculum was more extensive in the hedge schools than in any other school of equal social status and the standard was higher according to the informed opinion of Thomas Wyse (1791–1862), which he expressed in a letter to Doyle in 1830, when he wrote that 'the lower class proportionally to their position, are better educated than the middle and upper classes'.[131]

129 R. Batterberry, *Oideachas in Éirinn* 1500-1946 (Dublin, 1955), p. 119.   130 Brenan, *Schools of Kildare and Leighlin*, p. 79.   131 W.M. Wyse, *The unpublished memoirs of the rt hon. Sir Thomas Wyse, K.C.B.* (Waterford, 1901), p. 16. Wyse was born in the manor of St John, Co Waterford; educated at Stonyhurst and Trinity College, Dublin; historian of the Catholic Association, 1829; MP for Co. Tipperary, 1830-2, and Waterford, 1835-47; a minister under the whigs, 1839-41 and 1846-9; British minister at Athens, 1849; knighted, 1856. An architect of the national education and provincial colleges schemes.

4

'Penny merriments' and 'Penny godlinesses'

The historical development of children's literature, 1671–1851

> Read the histories of the martyrs that dyed for Christ…
> Read also often treatises on death and hell and
> Judgement, and of the love and passion of Christ.[1]

Chapbooks or 'Penny histories' as they were sometimes known, were the most numerous and most important form of English popular literature in the eighteenth century both in England and Ireland.[2] The Irish chapbook market was largely dependent on the English market as most of their books were piracies from that country. The first Irish produced chapbooks appeared at the end of the seventeenth century.[3] There is evidence however, of the appearance of English chapbooks on the Irish market in the early part of the century, from London booksellers' advertisements, which referred to the availability of stock to Irish pedlars, at this time.[4]

In puritan England of the seventeenth century reading for pleasure was considered an abhorrence – a prostitution of the God-given ability to read.[5] From their earliest days, children were warned 'when thou canst read, read no ballads, and foolish books, but the Bible.' They were encouraged to read 'the good godly books', the devotional and theological works which were better suited to the adult mind.[6] There were two chapbooks which were written specifically for children at this period. One was the great classic of puritan literature, the seventeenth-century bestseller, with the chilling title *A token for children being an exact account of the conversion, holy and exemplary lives, and joyful deaths of several children* (1671), and the other was the much more pleasing *Divine songs attempted in easy language for the use of children*,[7] by the

1 G. Avery and J. Briggs, *Children and their books* (Oxford, 1989), p. 97.   2 V.E. Neuburg, *The penny histories: a study of chapbooks for young readers over two centuries* (London, 1968), p. 3   3 E.R. McDix, 'Irish chapbooks, songbooks and ballads' in *Irish Book Lover* 2:3 (Oct. 1910), pp 33–5.   4 M. Spufford, *Small books and pleasant histories* (Cambridge, 1981), p. 111.   5 J.I. Whalley and T.R. Chester, *A history of children's book illustrations* (London, 1988), p. 14.   6 Avery and Briggs, *Children and their books*, p. 97.   7 A. Ellis, *How to find out about children's literature* (London, 1968), p. 118.

non-conformist divine Isaac Watts (1674–1748). *A token for children* was the most quoted book to children, with the exception of the Bible, despite the author's belief that pleasure for children should consist of an awareness of doing right, even if such an awareness could only be achieved through fear of the pains of hell. His book contained detailed accounts of the pious lives and joyful deaths of children as young as two years.[8] The popularity of such a dark and morbid book, preoccupied as it was with death and judgment, can only be explained by the reality of juvenile death for the seventeenth-century reader, as many infants died before they reached their fifth year. This chapbook was available in Ulster in the middle of the eighteenth century along with Watts' *Divine songs* (1715).[9] One can therefore assume that they were read in the hedge schools in the northern counties. We know that *Watts' hymns* were read in the hedge schools of the four provinces of Ireland, as surveyed by the commissioners of education in 1825. Watts had an instinctive understanding of the world of children and his work was firmly based on their everyday childish activities. Little wonder that his verses were an instant success and were to be enjoyed by over two generations of English and Irish children.[10]

An important and innovative development occurred in 1659 with the appearance of illustrations in children's books. Now the written text of the book was accompanied by a series of corresponding pictures. They appeared in Charles Hoole's English translation of Comenius' *Orbis sensualium pictus* (1658).[11] This development scarcely altered the appearance of the chapbooks whose 'woodcut illustrations possessed a vitality which outweighed the undoubted crudity of their execution'.[12] The tendency was either 'through loans or through copying and recutting' to use the 'same cuts' which appeared constantly in different books issued by different printers.[13]

The first in a series of great classics of English literature appeared in 1678 with the publication of the puritan writer John Bunyan's (1628–88) *Pilgrim's*

8 Whalley and Chester, *A history of children's book illustrations*, p. 15.   9 J.R.R. Adams, *The printed word and the common man* (Belfast, 1987), pp 182–4.   10 H. Carpenter and M. Prichard, *The Oxford companion to children's literature* (Oxford, 1984), pp 563–4. Watts was a well educated clergyman who also had considerable experience as a tutor of young children. His 'Divine songs' (1715) was the first children's hymn-book. It was afterwards enlarged and re-named 'Divine and moral songs'. It ran into a hundred editions before the middle of the century. See DNB 20, pp 978–80.   11 Whalley and Chester, *A history of children's books illustrated*. John Amos Komensky or 'Comenius' (1592–1670) was born in a small Moravian village. He was a member of a religious sect known as the Moravian Brethern, in 1616 he was ordained a minister. In 'The great didactic' (1628–32) he set forth 'the whole Art of teaching all things to all men' and dismissed existing schools as 'terrors for boys and shambles for their intellects'. He was one of the first educators to propose that education should be accessible to all. He devised methods of teaching and prepared school books to illustrate how his principles should be applied in practice. His *Orbis pictus* was one of the earliest books to introduce visual aids. See R.R. Rusk and J. Scotland, *Doctrines of the great educators*, 5th ed. (London, 1979), pp 62–79.   12 Neuburg, *The penny histories*, p. 6.   13 Darton, *Children's books*, p. 71.

progress. This was a religious allegory whose style answered the imaginative needs of children so well that they quickly adopted it as their own, even though it was intended for adults. The juvenile reading market was enhanced also by Defoe's *The life and strange surprising adventures of Robinson of York, mariner ... written by himself* (1719) and Swift's great satire *Gulliver's travels* (1726), the abridged versions of which were read by the children of the poor in the hedge schools of Ireland.

Equally popular among the poor of both countries were the truncated accounts of medieval tales of chivalry and romance, which by the sixteenth century had become 'the earliest books for children which provided the qualities of wholesomeness and excitement'.[14] Printers who were often booksellers kept the chapmen supplied with romances such as *Guy of Warwick, Bevis of Southampton, The four sons of Aymon, The seven wise masters, Fortunatus* and *The famous history of Valentine and Orson*.[15] In Ireland they formed a considerable part of the reading material used in the hedge schools. If proof were needed of the important function that these stories played in the imaginative life of the young, one need look no further than the treasured memories of some eminent literary artists of the seventeenth and eighteenth centuries, who owed their love of English literature to this 'degenerate literary form'. Bunyan ignored the puritanical warnings against reading 'vain books, profane ballads ... all fond and amorous romances and fabulous histories of giants, the bombast achievement of knight errantry,'[16] and told how he delighted more in reading about *George on horseback*, or *Beavis of Southampton*, than in reading the scriptures.[17] Johnson read the chivalric romances 'of which he was inordinately fond, while working at his father's bookshop in 1720, and his Scottish biographer James Boswell (1740–95) recalled with fondness his childhood reading which comprised 'Jack and the giants' and 'The seven wise men of Gotham'.[18] Charles Lamb (1775–1834) also grew nostalgic about 'the old classics of the nursery' and William Wordsworth (1770–1850) went so far as to eulogise on them in *The prelude*,

> Oh! Give us once again the wishing-cap
> Of Fortunatus, and the invisible coat
> Of Jack the giant-killer, Robin Hood,
> And Sabra in the forest with St George![19]

Next to the romances, the fairy tales held the strongest appeal for children and not surprisingly 'it was these chapbooks which were printed in the great-

---

14 Neuburg, *The penny histories*, p. 8.   15 Ibid., pp 8–13.   16 Ibid., pp 20–1.   17 Carpenter and Prichard, *The Oxford companion*, p. 106.   18 Spufford, *Small books*, p. 75.   19 Neuburg, *The penny histories*, p. 16.

est numbers'.[20] The fairy tales reached England having 'first being presented at the French court', where they received Louis XIV's royal approval. Subsequently 'the stories which peasants honestly told to their children were furbished up for a pastime of elegant salons'.[21] By 1697 Charles Perrault (1628–1703) had published his book of fairy tales for children entitled *Les fées* and these in turn were translated by Robert Samber in 1729 for the English market, with the title *Histories, or tales of past times told by Mother Goose*. The earliest collection of fairy legends to have been printed in popular chapbook form was by William Dicey, a printer from Bow Churchyard. They appeared at a time when traces of the traditional oral fairy lore still survived among the English peasantry. To Georgian society however, fairy tales merely represented 'the imbecilities of the peasantry'.[22] However, by the end of the eighteenth century when the oral lore had declined, the fairy tales became an important element in children's literature.[23] This was largely due to their survival in chapbook form and they have remained popular with children ever since. In the hedge schools children learned how to read from a primer called *The child's new spelling primer*, to which was added *The stories of Cinderilla*, and *Little Red Riding Hood*.[24] They also read from a book simply called *Fairy tales*, which was probably the popular *History of tales of the fairies*.[25] This was a treat denied to their better off counterparts in the schools of England and Ireland in the eighteenth and nineteenth centuries.

The radical philosophers Locke and his French counterpart Rousseau were to exercise a powerful influence over the writers of children's literature in the eighteenth century. Locke brought the forces of reason and experience to bear on established ideas. His theories on the education of children were quite progressive, considering that he lived in an age unaccustomed to treating children as children. He believed in stimulating children's interests, and in capitalising on the value of play and on the good results that can be achieved by using rewards as incentives. He stressed that 'children may be cozened into a knowledge of their letters ... and play themselves into what others are whipped for'.[26] To Locke, the inculcation of virtue and the moral development of the child were more important than the acquisition of knowledge. It was these two principles – play and the formation of proper habits of morality and conduct, which set the standard for a great deal of eighteenth-century children's literature. Children were to be enticed to read, but not with fairy tales and fairy lore, but rather with

20 Ibid., p. 17.   21 Darton, *Children's books*, p. 85.   22 Neuburg, *The penny histories*, p. 17.   23 Ibid.   24 *The child's new spelling primer* (Dublin, 1799).   25 *History of the tales of the fairies; being a collection of entertaining stories translated from the French. Dedicated to the ladies of Ireland* (Dublin, n.d.).   26 J. Locke, *Some thoughts concerning education* (Dublin, 1728), pp 244–5.

Some easy pleasant book, suited to his capacity ... wherein the entertainment that he finds might draw him on and reward his pains in
reading, and yet not such as should fill his head with perfectly useless
trumpery, or lay the principles of vice and folly.[27]

In addition to the scriptures, Locke approved of *Aesop's fables*, preferably
illustrated, and *Reynard the fox*, as being suitable for the purposes he had in
mind, taking into consideration a child's natural interest in animals. A selection from *Aesop's fables* was included in most school textbooks of the time and
an abridged version of *Reynard the fox* formed part of *The child's new play-
thing*,[28] which was used by the junior classes in the hedge schools. He also
believed in the usefulness and attractiveness of pictures, as an aid to learning,
but he recognised that there was a dearth of suitable reading books for children in the late seventeenth century.[29] His ideas spread slowly and it took
another fifty years before they took root. They eventually found their champion in one John Newbery (1713–67), the philanthropic bookseller and pro-
prietor of the 'Bible and Sun' printing house at 65 St Paul's Churchyard.

While Newbery is generally credited with being the first to produce books
of amusement for children, this isn't strictly accurate. The entertaining children's book probably made its first appearance as early as 1740, with the publication of Thomas Boreman's humorously titled *Gigantic histories* containing
ten volumes of miniature sized books. Boreman displayed considerable style
and possessed an intuitive knowledge of what would appeal to children. Even
though his little books were didactic, they were cheerfully illustrated and ele-
gantly bound in bright colours of Dutch floral or embossed paper. This idea
was in itself, a novel one.[30] Newbery however, can be credited with 'being the
first British publisher to create a permanent and profitable market for children's books, and to establish them as a genre of their own'.[31] His success was
due to his own keen business sense, his friendship with figures of the stature
of Oliver Goldsmith (1730-74) and Johnson, whose talents he called upon
occasionally, coupled with his own genuine affection for children, and his
understanding of their needs. No doubt he was also influenced by Boreman's
success in this lucrative market and by the popularity of Mrs Cooper's *The
child's new play-thing* (1743), which was intended 'to make the learning to read
a diversion instead of a task'[32] and was based on the educational ideas of
Locke. The persistent demand for the ever popular chapbooks would surely
have influenced him also, in his choice of themes.

Newbery's first publication in 1744 of *A little pretty pocket book* reflected
many of these influences, as it was tastefully presented in gilt and embossed

27 Ibid., p. 228. 28 Dublin, 1819. 29 Locke, *Some thoughts*, p. 230. 30 Whalley and Chester,
A history of children's book illustrations, p. 21. 31 Avery, *Children and their books*, p. 114. 32
Dublin, 1819.

paper. He also displayed a shrewd entrepeneurial business sense when he inserted an advertisement in the *Penny Morning Post*, on 13 June 1744, making free offers to Little Master Tommy and Pretty Miss Polly of a ball and pincushion respectively. Even with this, his first children's publication, Newbery explored the possibility of using extra inducements to increase turnover 'the price of the book alone was sixpence, but with a choice of ball or pincushion, only eightpence'.[33] He quoted Locke's advice on the care of children, for the benefit of parental ears and for his juvenile audience, he included two letters from Jack the giant killer. As in most other children's books at this time, he too included the obligatory moral, only Newbery preached in a very gentle manner, 'which stressed the difficulty of avoiding naughtiness, rather than the more intricate philosophy of avoiding sin'.[34]

His next publication which was also designed to amuse children was The *Lilliputian magazine or the young gentleman and lady's golden library. Being an attempt to mend the world … printed for the society*. The 'society' for which it was printed was one invented in the course of the book, supposedly founded on 26 December 1750. The book contained a variety of fascinating stories ranging from an account of the rise of learning in Lilliput, to an anti-cockfighting letter, to jests, songs, riddles and the *Adventures of Tommy Trip and his dog Jouler*. The second volume had the instructive title *A little lottery-book for children: containing a new method of playing them into a knowledge of the letters, figures etc. … published with the approbation of the court of common sense*. The title page was somewhat misleading, and was almost certainly intended to attract customers, but in the book itself, there was nothing concerned with lotteries, except some sentences in the 'Advertisement' which spoke of their evils, and a denunciation of them by Peter Prudence in his capacity as secretary of the court of common sense. *The Lilliputian magazine* was one of the most popular children's books of the eighteenth century, not only in England, but also in the hedge schools, particularly in the north.[35] It was read also in the rest of Ireland.[36] It would have provided great entertainment and stimulation for children, although most of the stories would have required advanced reading skills.

Writers of children's books continued to be influenced by the educational theories of the philosophers 'and in the period immediately after Newbery's death, the works of Rousseau had a very direct effect upon English books for children'.[37] Rousseau's thinking was patterned along the lines of Locke's phi-

33 E. Quayle, *The collector's book of children's books* (London, 1971), p. 23.   34 C. Meigs, A. Thaxter Eaton, E. Nesbitt and R. Hill Viguers, *A critical history of children's literature* (London, 1969), p. 59.   35 Adams, *The printed word*, p. 19. In 1775 a Belfast edition appeared which omitted all illustrations and substituted a hymn for the original preface and added hymns and prayers at the end.   36 *The Lilliputian magazine* (Dublin, 1792). The Dublin publication followed the original more faithfully as there were no additions or deletions made.   37 Darton, *Children's*

losophy and like the English radical thinker, he was firmly opposed to fairy tales and fantasy. He believed that 'man may be taught by fables' whereas 'children require the naked truth'.[38] Rousseau broke with the rationalist outlook, as he did not place all his confidence in reason, but he believed that feeling, sensibilty, and the language of the heart, were the things the child could understand, and were true guides to living. He believed that the child should be removed from the corrupt influences of urban life and brought up in rural seclusion where making and doing should be the basis of the child's progress towards health and virtue. These ideas he experimented with in his epoch-making treatise on education *Émile* (1762).

Chief among Rousseau's followers was the eccentric writer Thomas Day (1748–89), author of the first full-sized narrative for children *Sandford and Merton*. This was practically a juvenile novel. It consisted of three volumes and was heavily influenced by *Émile*. In order to present education along Rousseauite lines, Day employed a favourite technique of the moral school of writers, which was that of contrast. His two principal characters Tommy Merton and Harry Sandford were bad and good respectively. Tommy was the spoilt son of a rich merchant from the West Indies and Harry was the son of a local farmer. Harry's character was based on the Émile prototype as he displayed all the Émilean virtues of self-reliance, courage, kindness and strength. Tommy was sent to be educated with Harry under the excellent tutelage of the worthy Mr Barlow, a clergyman of the neighbourhood. In time, Tommy was transformed into a paragon of virtue, just like his role model, but any resemblance these characters bore to real boys was purely accidental. 'Harry Sandford served as a mere wooden peg on which to hang a deadweight of moralizing, scientific truths and gratuitous information'.[39] No doubt young readers would have passed over much of the extraneous matter, including the episode with the amazing title *History of a surprising cure of the gout*, to read instead of the lively pursuits of the boys and the misfortunes the hapless Tommy encountered on the road to his salvation. Day displayed many weaknesses as a writer, not least being his failure to structure a story. Nonetheless, the original became an eighteenth-century best-seller. A century after its first publication, the editor of a new edition felt justified in claiming that it had 'charmed instructed and ennobled the young hearts and minds of more than half a century with a constant increasing celebrity'.[40] No doubt it charmed

books, p. 140.   38 J.J. Rousseau, *Emilius and Sophia* (Dublin, 1799), pp 166–73. Translated from French by the translator of Eloise.   39 G. Avery, *Childhood's pattern* (London, 1975), p. 40. *Sandford and Merton* was parodied in 1872 by the editor of *Punch*, F.C. Burnand, in a burlesque entitled *The new history of Sandford and Merton*, complete with illustrations by Linley Sambourne. Nonetheless it was translated into several foreign languages before the end of the century. See Quayle, *The collector's book of children's books*, p. 30.   40 Meigs et al., *A critical history of children's literature*, p. 40.

the children in the hedge schools also as it made its first appearance in Belfast in 1787 and was re printed in 1791 and 1797. The complete edition in one volume was printed in Dublin and ran into its tenth edition in 1812.

In his own country Rousseau's ideas influenced Arnaud Berquin in his *L'ami des enfants*, a periodical of pleasant moral tales, later translated into English as *The looking glass for the mind*, by Richard Johnson, under the pseudonym 'The Reverend W.D. Cooper'. The French writer, the Contesse de Genlis, owed much to Rousseau also, and translations of her stories had wide transmission in England.[41] These French writers served as an inspiration to English writers of children's books such as Laetitia Barbauld (1743–1825), Lady Eleanor Fenn and the distinguished Anglo–Irish writer and educator Maria Edgeworth (1767–1849), who 'included in her list of friends and acquaintances ... Mme de Genlis and indeed Mrs Barbauld'. Maria Edgeworth was influenced also by Thomas Day, who was actually a family friend. Her father Richard Lovell Edgeworth was her mentor and he exercised an inordinate influence over Maria. He had educated his large family of eighteen children along strict Rousseauite principles which didn't allow for tales of fantasy or flights of imagination. Maria collaborated with her father in a book of essays entitled *Practical education*, which did much to spread the theories of Rousseau and which was very influential in its day. Unfortunately her father's influence proved to be a limiting factor, which was evident in her children's book *Harry and Lucy*, which had been started by Edgeworth and his wife Honora but later finished by Maria.[42] These were determinedly didactic stories with a utilitarian bias, which clearly derived from Rousseau. In general Maria Edgeworth's stories were 'highly esteemed by most critics'.[43] *The Edgeworth tales*[44] were read in the hedge schools, not for their heavy moralising, but 'because they were really good stories, told in simple delightful English, with frequent humour'.[45]

The Rousseauists weren't allowed to monopolise the world of juvenile fiction. They had to share the market with leading members of the bluestockings. The end of the eighteenth century and the beginning of the nineteenth marked 'the heyday of the bluestockings' as writing children's books began to rank as an occupation for gentlewomen, many of them being commissioned to do so from 1780 onwards.[46] As 'the authorship of children's books was

41 M. Thwaite, *From primer to pleasure* (London, 1963), pp 67–8.   42 Meigs et al., *A Critical history*, p. 94.   43 Darton, *Children's books*, pp 140–1.   44 Dublin, 1804.   45 Op. cit., p. 140. 46 Neuburg, *The penny histories*, p. 64. The bluestocking circle of literary women centred around the major salon hostesses Mrs Mary Wortley Montagu, known as the 'Queen of the blues' and Mrs Vesey. They wished to replace the limited social outlets for women, with intellectual conversation and encouraged them to take up serious writing. Montagu coined the term 'bluestocking' in a letter in which she referred to Benjamin Stillingfleet, scholar and botanist, who had appeared wearing blue worsted wool stockings, the dress of a working man, rather than silk hose,

regarded as a very inferior branch of learning'[47] some of the bluestockings preferred to remain anonymous. The 'mildly pious' Barbauld, and the 'stern-ly moralistic' Trimmer broke with social convention and published under their own names, and both were to suffer from the prevailing prejudices of the time. The attack came from Charles Lamb who criticised the solemn female writers, who made a 'puritanical onslaught on the literate youth of the day'.[48] In a letter penned to his friend, the poet Samuel Taylor Coleridge (1772–1834) in 1802, he complained bitterly that his sister Mary had difficul-ty finding a copy of his favourite childhood book, because

> *Goody two-shoes* is almost out of print, Mrs Barbauld's stuff has ban-ished all the old classics of the nursery and the shopman at Newbery's hardly deigned to reach them off an old exploded corner of the shelf, when Mary asked for them. Mrs Barbauld's and Mrs Trimmer's non-sense lay in piles about.[49]

Lamb's censure of the diffident Barbauld was quite unfair considering her significant contribution to children's reading, especially her *Lessons for chil-dren, from two to three years old*, in three parts. The first part was published in 1778, with parts two and three following in 1794 and 1803. Lindley Murray – who became one of the most popular writers of English textbooks in the nineteenth century, thought so highly of Barbauld's *Lessons* that he included a selection in his books, as did Fenning in his *Universal spelling book*. Three of Murray's textbooks were used in the indigenous schools in the diocese of Kil-dare and Leighlin *Murray's primer, Grammar* and *English reader*. In other schools of native origin, the master had a transcribed copy of *Murray's gram-mar*.[50] Its widespread use was unlikely considering that Murray's *English read-ing book* alone sold at prices ranging from three shillings to five shillings.[51]

Trimmer was probably more deserving of Lamb's malediction, being a belligerent moralist and educationalist of conservative views. She was also a devout evangelical who promoted Sunday schools, and did all in her power to provide instruction and 'proper books' for poor illiterate children in England. She was greatly alarmed by the French revolution and by the introduction of Rousseau's system. Day's books caused her some disquiet also because she believed that they were badly infected with dangerous philosophical principles imported from France. She could take little comfort from Edgeworth's books

the dress of a gentleman. Originally the term referred to learned men, who acted as mentors to women in the salons but by the late eighteenth century it was used as a derogatory term for a group of female intellectuals. See Deirdre Raftery, *Women and learning in English writing 1600-1900* (Dublin, 1997), pp 99–100.   **47** Thwaite, *From primer to pleasure*, p. 72.   **48** Quayle, *The collector's book*, p. 30.   **49** Darton, *Children's books*, p. 129.   **50** Ms. G. 809, pp 272–8.   **51** J.M. Goldstrom, *The social content of education, 1800-1870* (Shannon, 1972), p. 56.

on education either which she considered too secular. But there was one area where she shared common ground with the Rousseauists and that was in her aversion to fairies and works of fantasy. She denounced *Cinderella* as 'a compendium of vice', but unlike Rousseau and his followers, she condemned *Robinson Crusoe* as a dangerous book 'which led to an early taste for a rambling life'.[52] Whatever one might think of Trimmer's strong moralistic views, no one could doubt her sincerity as she attempted to protect society from what she considered dangerous books. She did this by her campaigning efforts in her periodical the *Family Magazine* (1788–9) and later in her *Guardian of education* (1802–6). In the *Guardian* she expressed her complete disenchantment with the *Books of education* and *Children's books*, which she felt would infect the minds of youth and subvert the social order.[53] She abhorred chapbooks as reading material for juveniles and supplied the Sunday schools with her own *Oeconomy of charity*, her *Charity school spelling book* and its related *Teacher's assistant* in an effort to improve the education of the poor in these schools. She also produced a series of prints illustrating sacred and profane history, an accompanying set of lessons, and a volume of scriptural extracts, which were read in the hedge schools of Ireland.

Children could at least find some relief from the heavy piety which characterised many of the children's books during the late eighteenth and early nineteenth centuries in the chapbooks which were still being supplied by several printers in English provincial towns during the 1780s, 1790s and into the first decades of the nineteenth century.[54] It was clear to see however that 'the heyday of the chapbook' was over by this time, as an ever-increasing English reading public rejected them in favour of political books and pamphlets, such as Tom Paine's *Rights of man*. In the wake of the industrial revolution people no longer had any use for the chivalric romances of the past. They were not looking for escapism but rather for guiding principles to help them to adjust to their changed living conditions. It was to the radical writers that they turned for this direction. It was at this stage also that the prolific evangelical writer Hannah More decided to follow in the footsteps of Trimmer and launch her offensive literary campaign against the 'seditious' writings of Paine. She armed herself with over a hundred religious tracts[55] in an effort to

---

52 R.C. Churchill, *The concise Cambridge history of English literature* (Cambridge, 1970), p. 512.
53 Darton, *Children's books*, p. 160. In her *Guardian of education* she published notices and reviews of the many children's books, and works on educational theory, newly published. The public came to regard her as an authority on education. She was infuriated with Joseph Lancaster's non-denominational monitorial schools. She fomented trouble between fellow educationalist Andrew Bell (1753–1832) and Lancaster, whom she called this 'Goliath of schismatics' by informing Bell (Sept. 1805) that Lancaster 'had been building on your foundation'. See D. Salmon, *Lancaster and Bell* (Cambridge, 1932).   54 Neuburg, *Penny histories*, p. 65.   55 Carpenter and Prichard, *The Oxford companion*, p. 361.

counteract the evil influences of the radical writings and the immoral influences of the chapbooks, on whose format she modelled her series. She failed
to replace the chapbooks but she succeeded in achieving a commercial success with her venture.

The last of the female writers of children's books for this period was the
sternly evangelical Martha Sherwood (1775–1851), who was the most formidable of the writers of the moral tale. While in India she came under the influence of the missionary Henry Martyn whose rigid Calvinist views laid a deep
impression on her. This influence would, in time, be reflected in her books, as
she adopted the hell-fire and brimstone morality one associates with the
Calvinists of the seventeenth century, most notably James Janeway. She
believed that:

> All children are by nature evil, and while they have none but the nat-
> ural evil principle to guide them, pious and prudent parents must
> check their naughty passions in any way that they have in their power,
> and force them into decent and proper behaviour and into what are
> called good habits.[56]

This was her guiding philosophy in her most popular children's book *The
Fairchild family*, and she repeated this belief many times throughout the book
and quoted scripture to lend support to it. The first part of the book was published in 1818, the second and third parts followed much later, in 1842 and
1847 respectively, but it was part one which earned Mrs Sherwood most
acclaim. This was primarily a family story, the first of its type designed for
children, in which every chapter had its moral lesson. The Fairchild children,
Lucy, Emily and little Henry delighted their readers by behaving like normal
children and getting into mischief time and time again even though they knew
they would be severely punished if caught. Indiscretions and misdeeds not
only brought immediate retribution but also led to eternal damnation. Purged
of its macabre incidents and pruned of a great deal of theology *The Fairchild
family* became a nineteenth-century bestseller,[57] but it was the less popular
Stories on the church catechism[58] which were read in the native hedge schools.

56 Darton, *Children's books*, p. 168. In 1803 she married her cousin Captain Henry Sherwood
and in 1804 went to India with him. She founded the first orphan asylum in India.   57 Thwaite,
From primer to pleasure, p. 64. Practically every middle class Victorian child was brought up on
The history of the Fairchild family. There were macabre incidents in the book as when the high
spirited Fairchild children were taken on a gruesome visit to examine the gibbeted body of a
man who had murdered his brother in a fit of anger. Mr Fairchild pointed to the fact that the two
brothers had started off by simply quarrelling, just like the children had that morning, but what
resulted was death for one of them and possibly an extended period in hell. See S. J. Kunitz and
H. Haycraft (eds.) *British authors of the nineteenth century* (New York, 1936).   58 App No. 221,
p. 555.

The chapbooks still had a large share of the juvenile market, and they were once again to be used as 'penny godlinesses', following in the wake of More's success with her religious tracts. This time the evangelical writer was George Mogridge (1787–1854), one who 'had been brought up on chapbook literature – *Friar Bacon*, *The seven champions* and *Tom Thumb*'.[59] He wrote a large number of books for children, most of which were published by the Religious tract society, founded in 1799. His favourite pseudonyms were Ephraim Holding, Peter Parley and Old Humphrey, which he used for his 'fifty three little 32mo books',[60] which were produced to resemble chapbooks in appearance, although 'the contents could not have been more unlike those of the penny histories'.[61] There was really very little to distinguish Mogridge from the other early nineteenth-century writers of children's books, like Trimmer. He too condemned the romances which he enjoyed in his youth and resolved never to read them again. In keeping with the trend at the time, he outlawed the fairies and fantasy 'and on at least one occasion he went out of his way to criticize Tom Thumb as being likely to corrupt children'.[62]

Despite the fashion for 'self-improvement' and 'morality' in children's books, there was one printer in England who continued to expand the chapbook market by producing books to amuse and delight the young reader. This was James Catnach, the printer who set up in business in 1813 at Nos. 2–3 Monmouth Court, Seven Dials. Catnach had an instinctive business sense and he displayed a natural flair as he supplied the market with a variety of cheap books designed to appeal to public taste. Because of his entrepeneurial skills, the chapbooks enjoyed a remarkable revival in the nineteenth century, and Catnach amassed quite a fortune as a result. It wasn't that he produced an original series of chapbooks, on the contrary, he simply reprinted the old favourites, and children were once more supplied with *Jack Spratt*, *Cock Robin*, *Mother Goose*, *Tom Hickathrift*, *The tragical death of A apple pie*, *Cinderella*, etc.'.[63]

In the 1880s the final owner of the Catnach Press, W. S. Fortey, went out of business and the chapbooks rolled off the presses for the last time. The 'penny histories', which had brought endless pleasure to both adults and children in Ireland and England and which had proved so durable, finally had to yield to popular taste. The day of the chapbook was over as 'penny dreadfuls' had superseded 'penny histories' and *Fortunatus* was obliged to give way to *Varney the vampire*.[64] However, in the hedge schools of Ireland, it was the chapbooks which held the greatest appeal for children, especially the books of criminal biography and the books of entertainment.

---

59 Darton, *Children's books*, p. 224.   60 Neuburg, *Penny histories*, p. 74.   61 Ibid., p. 66.   62 Ibid., p. 73.   63 Ibid., pp 68–9.   64 Ibid., p. 75.

'Penny merriments' – books of criminal biography

There were two criminal biographies which drew down the wrath of critics namely *The life and adventures of James Freney*[65] and *A genuine history of the lives and actions of the most notorious Irish highwaymen, tories and rapparees*.[66] The Rt Hon John Edward Walsh, master of the rolls, considered that 'The general character of such volumes was loose and immoral'. His concern was that children would emulate the actions of their heroes, in particular the ill-famed James Freney, about whom he wrote 'Among the rapparees was one held in high esteem by the youth of the peasantry, and a representation of his deeds formed part of their play and sports. The person was James Freney.'[67] Likewise Carleton expressed his aversion to criminal biography but he too recognised that 'the youth of the peasantry' took considerable pleasure in what he called, these 'Eulogiums on murder, robbery and theft' which 'were read with delight in the histories of *Freney the robber* and *The Irish rogues and rapparees*'.[68] It wasn't just the children who enjoyed the exploits of Freney and O'Hanlon, according to Crofton Croker (1824) but the parents who purchased the books in the first place:

> A history of rogues and rapparees is at present one of the most popu-
> lar books among the Irish peasantry, and has circulated to an extent
> that seems almost incredible: nor is it unusual to hear the adventures
> and escapes of highwaymen recited by the lower orders with the great-
> est minuteness and dwelt on with the greatest fondness.

Just as the medieval chivalric romances and the French fairy legends enjoyed an elite readership in their early editions, so too did the Irish crimi-nal biographies, according to Niall Ó Ciosáin in *Print and popular culture in Ireland* (1997). The first edition of the *Life and adventures of James Freney, commonly called Captain Freney*, was published by subscription and the list of purchasers included none other than the provost of Trinity College, and a number of the newer landlords of Kilkenny. Ó Ciosáin concluded also that *Irish rogues and rapparees, a genuine history*, had an elite readership because in the early editions buffoon figures, such as William Maguire were included, a feature which would have been offensive to a popular readership with a strong attachment to an oral culture.[69] By the late eighteenth and early nineteenth centuries these texts had an exclusively popular audience.

The principal characters of the two criminal biographies James Freney and Redmond O'Hanlon were real-life highwaymen who were admired by

65 *The life and adventures of James Freney, commonly called captain Freney, written by himself* (Dublin, 1754).   66 J. Cosgrave (Belfast, 1776).   67 J.E. Walsh, *Ireland sixty years ago* (Dublin, 1847), pp 102–3.   68 Carleton, *Traits and stories*, i, p. 313.   69 N. Ó Ciosáin, *Print and popular culture in Ireland 1750-1850* (London, 1997), pp 96–7.

THE

LIFE and ADVENTURES

OF

JAMES FRENEY,

Commonly called

Captain *FRENEY.*

FROM

The Time of his firſt Entering on the HIGHWAY, in *Ireland*, to the Time of his SURRENDER; being a Series of Five Years remarkable Adventures.

Written by HIMSELF.

DUBLIN :

Printed and Sold by S. POWELL, for the AUTHOR, MDCCLIV.

4 Title page from *The life and adventures of James Freney, commonly called Captain Freney* (1754)

the people, because they struck a blow at the establishment, while operating outside the law. Highway robberies were a common feature of travel in eighteenth-century Ireland and it was not unusual for travellers to place notices in the newspapers of the time, requesting 'escorts of dragoons or coaches advertised as bullet proof.'[70] But Freney and O'Hanlon were the folk heroes of the poor people, the romantic highwaymen on horseback, with masks and pistols, who robbed the rich to help the poor, in the time honoured fashion of Robin Hood. On the road between Clonmel and Kilkenny, the scene of many of Freney's robberies, an elm tree was planted in his honour, known as 'Freney's tree'.[71] Freney himself was to come to a rather inglorious end, as he informed on his friend in order to gain a royal pardon.

His counterpart O'Hanlon, achieved equal notoriety in the north of Ireland. O'Hanlon was identified in the minds of the people with those who were driven from their lands by the confiscations of Cromwell and William and Mary. He was the terror of the rich landlords of Armagh and the neighbouring counties for nearly twenty years. The people supported the highwaymen or rogues and rapparees, as they were a dispossessed people themselves, who could empathise with the outlaws and take pride in their exploits. The people rejoiced when the highwaymen managed to strike a blow at the planters or the tory-hunters and yeomanry leaders. The tory-hunters who represented the establishment became one of the most hated groups in local tradition. They were well-known to the people, especially O'Hanlon's chief pursuer, Johnston of the Fews. There were others also 'men like Seaver of the Bog and Batchy Kirk and Lucas of Dromolane, all approximating in villainy to the local demon, Johnston of the Fews'. The people prayed that they might be spared from the wrath of Johnston: 'Jesus of Nazareth, King of the Jews, Save us from Johnston, King of the Fews'.[72] The reasons for the longevity of the appeal of *The life and adventures of James Freney* have been very well documented by Ó Ciosáin. He enumerates its episodic nature which aided oral repetition, the lack of moral reflections or repentance and the attraction of the chivalrous bandit hero who conducted his solo highway robberies, as among the main reasons.[73] One could add to this Freney's ability to tell a good story in simple conversational style, tinged with sardonic humour, which was most likely unintentional. Young readers aged ten and upwards would have readily understood this biography and while there were no illustrations of any kind, the variety of action and the lively pace sustained throughout, would have more than compensated for this shortfall.

70 K. Danaher, 'Highwaymen – they robbed the rich' in *Biatas* (October 1961), p. 487.   71 Walsh, *Ireland sixty years ago*, p. 106.   72 T. Ó Fiaich, 'The political and social background of the Ulster poets' in *Léachtaí Cholm Cille* (1970), p. 51.   73 Ó Ciosáin, *Print and popular culture*, p. 95.

Freney's parents were employed at the 'big house' of Mr George Robbins, and he himself was employed as a pantry boy for Mrs Robbins, who took a special interest in the boy, even to the point of supplying him with a private tutor. Her best efforts failed as he was too partial to pleasure seeking at the expense of his household duties. The list of his misdemeanours appear total- ly innocuous when compared to the leisure pursuits of our modern 'high- waymen'. They included attending 'all the little country dances, diversions and meetings' and worst of all he 'became, what is among them deemed a good dancer'. His big confession came with his admission that he had 'an idle disposition' as he spent his time 'hurling, horse-racing, gaming, dancing'.[74]

More serious flaws developed in his character following the death of his benevolent mistress in 1742. It was then that he branched out on his own, married and set up in business in Waterford on the strength of her dowry. His business failed as he proved unacceptable to the other traders in the city. He moved to Thomastown, Co. Kilkenny but found himself fifty pounds in debt. He was left with little choice but to join up with a former member of the Kel- lymount gang to pursue a life of petty burglary and highway robbery.

As a highwayman Freney wished to exemplify all the gentlemanly virtues. During one such robbery he entreated with a gentleman to part with fifty pounds but having received this amount he immediately returned the sum of £1 30s. 10d., to cover the gentleman's expenses home.[75] As well as that he had a strong desire to portray himself not just as a heroic figure but as one of hon- our and dignity. He related how the son of his former patron known as Coun- sellor Robbins, was now his chief pursuer, and how despite the promptings of his friends and the many opportunities presented to him 'to blow the Coun- sellor's brains out: yet to his immortal honour … he refused that temptation, agreeable as it was, declaring that he had eaten too much of that family's bread ever to take the life of one of them'.[76]

Contrary to expectations, the number of exciting highway robberies were far outnumbered by crude house burglaries, conducted by the gang with blackened faces, sledges and lighted candles. Disappointingly, the booty usu- ally consisted of a few household valuables and purses of gold and silver coins and some moidores. Finally our hero abandoned his friend Bulger 'and left him there in a break of briars … surrounded by the army'.[77] All of Freney's friends were subsequently tried, convicted and hanged, while he himself obtained a pardon, through the influence of Lord Carrick. When Lord Car- rick and Counsellor Robbins sought to raise a subscription to help Freney and his family 'quit the kingdom',[78] the local gentry refused to assist him, and con- sequently he was forced to raise money by writing his autobiography.

74 *The life and adventures of James Freney*, pp 2–4.   75 Ibid., pp 7–8.   76 J. Freney, 'The life and adventures of James Freney' in William Thackeray (ed.) *The Irish sketch book*, i (London, 1887), p. 293.   77 Ibid., p. 307.   78 *The life and adventures of James Freney*, p. 145.

A GENUINE
HISTORY
OF THE
LIVES and ACTIONS
Of the moſt notorious
Iriſh Highwaymen, Tories and Rapparees,
from *Redmond O Hanlon*, the famous Gentleman-
robber, to *Cahier na Gappul*, the great Horſe-
catcher, who was executed at *Maryborough* in
Auguſt, 1735,

To which are Added,

THE GOLD-FINDER;

Or, the Hiſtory of *Manus Maconiel*, who under the
appearance of a ſtupid, ignorant Country Fellow,
(on the Bog of Ailen, by the ,Help of his Man
Andrew) played the moſt notorious Cheats and
remarkable Tricks on the People of Ireland that
were ever known,

ALSO,

the remarkable Life of *Gilder-Roy*, a Murderer,
Raviſher, Incendiary and Highwayman ; with
ſeveral others, not in any former Edition.

The NINTH EDITION, with Additions,

By J. COSGRAVE.

Behold !——here's Truth in ev ry Page expreſs'd ;
O *Darby*'s all a Sham, in Fiction dreſs'd ;
Save what from hence his treach'rous Maſter ſtole
To ſerve a knaviſh Turn, and act the Fool.

BELFAST:
PRINTED AND SOLD BY THE BOOKSELLERS
∞∞∞∞∞∞∞∞∞∞∞∞∞∞
M,DCC LXXVI.

A 3

5 Title page from *A genuine history of the lives and actions of the most notorious Irish
highwaymen, tories and rapparees* (1776)

The authorities eventually decided that his special talents should not be wasted. They therefore gave him a job as a customs officer and water bailiff in New Ross, in which peaceful occupation he ended his days.[79] The history of Freney's life became one of the most popular reading books in the 'rustic universities' as Thackeray called the hedge schools, and his adventures were the favourite themes of school-boys, and the representation of his achievements their favourite amusement.[80]

Robbers' lives formed the basis of large collections of criminal biography in the early eighteenth century, of which the best known were Alexander Smith's *A complete history of the lives and robberies of the most notorious highwaymen* (1713–4) and Charles Johnson's *General history of the lives and adventures of the most famous highwaymen* (1734). According to Ó Ciosáin, *The lives and actions of the most notorious Irish highwaymen, tories and rapparees* was to Irish crime literature what the collections of Smith and Johnson were to that of London, although this is just a single volume containing nine lives, later editions contained thirteen lives. The Irish volume was clearly based on the English ones, even to the point of borrowing 'the few criminals of Irish origin who appeared in those books: Patrick Fleming, William Maguire and Richard Balf'.[81] The book was more familiarly known by the title *Irish rogues and rapparees* and in the Belfast edition of 1776 this wording was used as the running title along the tops of the pages'.

It first appeared some time in the 1730s or 1740s and covers a period from the 1650s to 1735. He describes the life of a bandit hero whose 'gentlemanly' robberies, daring escape and unhappy end were faithfully recorded by John Cosgrave, about whom nothing is recorded. O'Hanlon was a reduced gentleman who looked to his countrymen 'to pay him tribute towards his maintenance'. He operated what is now commonly known as a 'protection racket', only O'Hanlon saw himself more in the light of a philanthropist, who rendered a public service to his friends. His friends and acquaintances paid him to guard them against thieves such as himself and if 'they didn't pay up … they would pay for it'. He carried his pocket book around with him, which contained a list of the names of those who had paid him.[82]

---

79 Danaher, 'Highwaymen – they robbed the rich', p. 487. 80 Freney, 'The life and adventures of James Freney', p. 311. See Ó Ciosáin, *Print and popular culture*, pp 98–9 for references to Freney in ballads, poetry, folklore and newspaper articles in the eighteenth and nineteenth centuries, as he soon became the archetypal highwayman and bandit hero, most likely due to the wide circulation of the chapbook. See also *Proceedings and papers of the Kilkenny and South-East of Ireland Archaeological society* 1:1 (1856), pp 59–61 for the ballad *Bold captain Freney*. The ninth stanza of the ten refers directly to an episode in Freney's *Life and adventures* in which he states that he would never rob a tailor, who was a figure of fun in folklore 'saying I would rob nobody but a man'. The ballad copied this in 'I'll rob no tailor if I can' – / 'I'd rather ten times rob a man a man' / 'and it's oh, bold Captain Freney, etc'. 81 Ó Ciosáin, *Print and popular culture*, p. 88. 82 Cosgrave, *A genuine history*, pp 6–7.

Like Freney, he was a benign highwayman, of the Robin Hood confraternity, who frequently shared 'what he got from the rich to relieve the poor in
their necessities'.[83] He too valued his reputation. This is clear from the incident in which he encountered a distraught pedlar, who protested that O'Hanlon had robbed him of five pounds and his box, and had kicked and abused
him like a dog. O'Hanlon was so enraged by these lies that he 'called him a
rascal and a lying son of a whore'. He then wrote a mittimus and sent the
criminal under a proper guard, to Armagh gaol, thus reducing the entire court
to laughter 'till they were ready to burst'.[84]

Cosgrave told the story well and the daring disguises of O'Hanlon, his near
escapes, capture and subsequent escape, would have enthralled any school
child. The reader's interest was retained by the introduction of the great robber of Munster, Richard Power of Killbolane, whose fame rested on his
'pleasant habit of waiting until the rents were collected and the receipts safely in the hands of tenants' before he 'held up the landlord's agent and halved
the loot with the tenants'.[85] Following a dual in which his opponent revealed
himself to be the great Redmond O'Hanlon, the two highwaymen became
close friends, with both of them agreeing to come to the rescue of the other,
should the need arise. O'Hanlon honoured this pact and when the Munster
tory was confined to Clonmel gaol, he gained entry by posing as a gentleman
and by supplying the officers with liberal quantities of whiskey, thus allowing
Power time to escape.[86]

The hero himself lived in permanent danger of being captured by the infamous Johnston of the Fews. A price of four hundred pounds was placed on
his head as he became one of the most wanted men in the country, and forty
pounds on each of his men. The 'country people knew of his haunts' but
'none of them would touch the blood-money'.[87] Eventually his own wife
betrayed him, as 'Redmond took some occasion to abuse her' and he was
imprisoned in Armagh gaol. Later he was found guilty at the assizes and his
body was 'ordered to be cut into four quarters and to be hung up in different
places, as a terror to others'. This blood-curdling description must surely have
served as a salutary lesson to many young readers. O'Hanlon escaped from
prison only to be betrayed this time by his foster brother Art, who was greedy
for the reward. He shot O'Hanlon and then carried his head on a staff to
Armagh, where it was stuck unceremoniously 'on a spike over the gate of
Downpatrick gaol'.[88] This is the longest story in the collection and it finishes

83 Ibid., p. 4.   84 Ibid., pp 5–6.   85 Danaher, 'Highwaymen – they robbed the rich', p. 487.
86 Cosgrave, *A genuine history*, pp 19–20. Power was betrayed by his sweetheart, who poured
water into his pistols while he was asleep and then sent for the soldiers, and as the song tells us
'he couldn't shoot the water and a prisoner he was taken'. Power was hanged in public in Clonmel in 1685. See Danaher, 'Highwaymen – they robbed the rich', pp 486–7.   87 Op. cit., p.
486.   88 Danaher, 'Highwaymen – they robbed the rich', p. 486.

on an amusing note with Cosgrave bemoaning the fact that many of O'Hanlon's exploits were never recorded for posterity. Had they been Cosgrave
believed that 'they would have made as remarkable a history as most of the
Irish giants'.[89]

Some passages of the life of strong John MacPherson, a notorious robber, was a
short story in the collection which gave an entertaining account of a robber
who was reputed to have been 'the strongest man in the nation'. MacPherson
was partial to the 'company of pert women and gamesters' and like Freney
he had a 'weakness for hurlings, patrons and matches of football'. Reduced
circumstances forced him into a life of burglary and highway robbery,
although he tried to give his occupation an air of respectability by describing
himself as a borrower rather than a thief.

Strong John's naivety knew no bounds. He once decided to rob a country
house, single-handedly and in broad daylight. Not only that but he deposited
each member of the household that he encountered, in the same locked room
without first checking upstairs, where a number of workmen were about their
tasks. The workmen released the family who attacked MacPherson 'with
clubs and other instruments till he was almost overpowered'. He took hold of
the 'woman of the house' to 'skreen himself from the blows' and released her
only on receipt of twenty pieces of gold. Finally he was 'taken up by treachery' and in 1678 he was tried, found guilty and condemned to death by hanging. Whatever about the tawdry deeds of Strong John's life, his exit from the
world was quite spectacular. His fearlessness in the face of death was in sharp
contrast to his former cowardice and reminded one of the last moments in
the life of Shakespeare's treacherous Thane of Cawdor from his play *Mac-
beth*, who 'died/As one that had been studied in his death/To throw away the
dearest thing he owed/As t'were a careless trifle/.' Astonishingly Strong John
heralded his own departure from this world by playing 'a fine tune of his own
composing on the bagpipe' which as Cosgrave informs the reader 'retains the
name of MacPherson's tune to this day'.[90]

No less entertaining was *The history of Sir John Falstaff, a highwayman*,[91]
which was a revised version of Shakespeare's great comic creation – the much
loved corpulent, cowardly rogue Jack Falstaff. Falstaff once described himself in flattering terms in Shakespeare's play *King Henry IV Part I* as 'Sweet
Jack Falstaff, valiant Jack Falstaff, and therefore / More valiant being as he
is, old Jack Falstaff'. 'Sweet Jack Falstaff' would have been well pleased with
this new interpretation, which laid blame on the great master of English literature for misrepresenting him as a very great coward, instead of the 'man of
courage and resolution' which he really was.

89 Op. cit., p. 29.   90 'Some passages', p. 32.   91 'The history of Sir John Falstaff, a highwayman' in *A genuine history*.

As his pension was insufficient to support his gregarious lifestyle, Falstaff was forced to become a highwayman, in which 'profession' he was joined by the three Shakespearean characters – Poins, Bardolph and Peto and the two new Irish creations – Harvey and Rossil.[92] There was a humorous twist to every tale recorded, from the robbery on Gad's Hill when Falstaff ordered his uncooperative victim to join with him in prayer to see if divine intervention might fill his pockets, to an occasion when he dressed in women's apparel and lay prostrate on the road like a damsel in distress to await the arrival of a rich merchant from the fair at Guilford. Falstaff was eventually caught and sent to Maidstone gaol but King Henry pardoned him on condition that he would leave his native land within a month. This proved too much for the patriotic highwayman and sadly it 'broke his heart before the time was expired'.[93]

Writing in 1842, Thackeray expressed his regret that these criminal biographies had been replaced by such books as *Conversations on chemistry*, *The little geologist*, *Peter Parley's tales about the binomial theorem* and the like. Just as Lamb writing in 1802, lamented the replacement of the medieval romances and children's books like *Goody two shoes* with the works of evangelical writers like Trimmer and the wretched 'Barbauld crew'.[94] In any event the criminal biographies would have offered little by way of encouragement to the young reader to join the criminal class. With the exception of James Freney who benefited from a royal pardon, most of the other highwaymen were either murdered or hanged. This would surely have affected impressionable readers. No doubt they admired the daring nature of some of Freney's and O'Hanlon's highway robberies, their chivalrous decorum in respect of their victims and the cunning methods they used to dupe the law officers. It is likely that they viewed the Irish highwaymen in the same light as Robin Hood or Dick Turpin, as supermen and not mere mortals. These books would have provided children with enjoyment and entertainment and would most likely have inculcated in them a love of reading.

In the case of successive commissioners of education from 1806 to 1825, they shared the contemporary writers' suspicions that these chapbooks had a subversive sub-text. It should be remembered that Redmond O'Hanlon was one of the dispossessed landowners who was viewed by the people as one who was simply striking a blow against the new planters. As Adams (1987) observed in his book *The printed word and the common man*, Redmond O'Hanlon was a symbol of defiance and 'one of the main attractions of such figures was the extent to which they stood outside the established order and threatened it'. Under such circumstances, one could readily understand why these

---

92 'The history of Sir John', p. 175. 93 Ibid., pp 176–8. 94 Darton, *Children's books*, pp 128–9.

'little histories were not quite respectable to those in power and why their moral tendency was generally condemned'.[95]

'Penny merriments' – books of entertainment

Among the books of entertainment was *The unfortunate concubines or the history of fair Rosamond, mistress to Henry II, and Jane Shore, concubine to Edward IV, king of England*.[96] Books on 'illustrious prostitutes' could produce nothing 'but the very worst effect' on young readers, according to Dutton (1808),[97] an opinion shared by his fellow writer Shaw Mason (1819). No doubt, these were the same books which the commissioners of education 1806–12 had in mind when they referred to 'the evils arising from the want of proper books adapted to the inferior schools' and to 'the corruption of morals and perversion of principles too often arising from the books actually in use'.[98]

The legend of *Fair Rosamond* was based on the historical Rosamond Clifford, with whom Henry II lived in open adultery, after the great rebellion of 1173–4, having first imprisioned his wife Eleanor.[99] The earliest chapbook version was printed *c.*1640 entitled *The life and death of fair Rosamond, King Henry the second's concubine and how she was poysoned to death by Queen Eleanor* and numerous editions were published.[100] The second royal concubine Jane Shore may well have been a historical figure also, as Edward IV (1442–83) was pleasure-loving and given to amorous intrigues. A separate chapbook on her life was printed in Newcastle in the seventeenth century. As a forerunner to this chapbook there was 'a very lugubrious and classical poem of nearly two hundred verses, or twelve hundred lines, called 'Beawtie dishonoured''written under the title of "Shore's wife",' which was published in London in 1593.

THE HISTORY OF FAIR ROSAMOND
In the histories of fair Rosamond and Jane Shore an adulterous lifestyle was strongly condemned. The reader was warned that this immoral behaviour could only lead to a painful, fatal or humiliating end, just like that suffered by the unfortunate Rosamond and misguided Jane Shore, when they became

95 T. Wall, *The sign of Dr Day's head* (Dublin, 1958), p. 90.   96 Dublin, 177–.   97 Dutton, *Statistical survey of the county of Clare*, pp 236–7.   98 Commissioners of Irish education inquiry 1806–12 Fourteenth report, pp 331–2.   99 The legend was first mentioned in Higden's *Polychronicon* in the mid fourteenth century and was turned into a ballad in the late sixteenth century by the popular versifier Thomas Delaney. See Carpenter and Prichard, *The Oxford companion to children's literature*, p. 175. *Fair Rosamond* was made the subject of drama many times, the most notable was that of John Bancroft, 'A tragedy acted at the Theatre Royal' in 1693.   100 See J. Ashton, *Chapbooks of the eighteenth century* (London, 1882), p. 388.

royal concubines. Both stories, which were contained in the one book, were very moralistic. Unlike other stories of the didactic nature, the moral came at the beginning so that the reader knew in advance how the story would end. The adolescent reader was left in no doubt as to the purpose of the stories – while it was true that both ladies 'sought not the royal favour, but endeavoured to avoid it as much as possible', yet Rosamond 'was willing to taste the pleasures of the court', as she wrongly believed that 'she could have kept herself from the pollutions of it'. Jane Shore, the writer added, should have 'staid with her own husband and then she had done well', and 'if we would be innocent, we must not only avoid doing evil but all the ways that lead to it'. The dire consequences occasioned by sin were exemplified in these histories, as they emphasised that: 'lust is a pleasure bought with pain, a delight hatched with disquiet, a content passed with fear, and a sin finished with lasting sorrow'. The 'awful warning' was then sounded as the reader was reminded that: 'If any are so weak, as to be taken with the gaudy trappings of royalty and glittering pomps of the court, let them read on, and see the dreadful catastrophy of this imaginary greatness.'

The devestating results of such folly were spelt out and the wages of sin were catalogued so effectively, that any female who might have harboured royal aspirations, would have felt obliged to have a re-think about the matter. The writer explained that Queen Eleanor was the lady scorned and that she forced Rosamond, who was the king's paramour to drink a cup of poison, the horrendous outcome of which was then described:

> her late beautiful face is disfigured, and the rose of her cheeks all dead and withering, her eyes distorted, and her whole body quite swelled up and labouring under horrid convulsions.

Jane Shore in turn came to experience extreme humiliation as she was brought to a demeaning end. She was condemned to a life 'doing penance through Cheapside bare foot and bare legged and afterwards gladly picking up the refuse of dogs, upon the dunghill and afterwards dying in a ditch'.

These two romances were intended for an adult readership and were written in difficult, archaic language. There were no illustrations but the accounts had a brisk pace and lively appeal. Both were piracies from English chapbooks. The story of fair Rosamond was regaled over seven short chapters which numbered a mere fifty-two pages in all, but nevertheless the readers' interest was maintained throughout. The writer told how King Henry, though married to Queen Eleanor, had heard of Rosamond's great beauty and 'become enamoured of her'. He couldn't sleep at night from thinking about 'the peerless rose of the world'. He therefore decided to visit her father's house 'and to that end took a progress into Oxfordshire'. The King was destined to fall instantly in love with fair Rosamond 'at the first sight she appeared in his eyes like an angel'. He commanded her to sit down directly opposite to him. Rosamond's 'pretty eyes' affected the royal appetite 'he so long gazed, that he forgot oftentimes to eat, taking in a long draught of love'.

Henry eventually succeeded in winning the love of the fair Rosamond. First he enticed her by bestowing costly jewels upon her. Then he engaged the services and co-operation of her unscrupulous governess Alethea, through bribery. Fair Rosamond realised that she was in an invidious position as Henry was married, but the attraction 'to glitter near a throne, though but in a tinsel splendour' was overwhelming and besides Henry had 'protested that if that vacancy happened, he would raise her to the dignity of the crown'.

The king's intentions towards Rosamond were quite dishonourable as he plotted with Alethea to gain access to her bed, by exchanging places with her. The scheme was one of great simplicity as Alethea explained it to the king:

> may it please your majesty ... the way that I would have you to take is this: that you should come visit my chamber tomorrow night, a little before bed-time: and I will leave you there alone awhile, till I have got my lady Rosamond to bed, whereas I be with her every night, I will delay the time of my going to bed, as I sometimes do, till she is asleep, and I will bring your majesty into the chamber and you shall go to bed to her in my stead.

She was rewarded with a rich diamond ring for coming up with such a daring plan. It was put into operation the following night. It worked exactly as planned by the worldly Alethea, to the amazement of the bemused reader. King Henry took the place of Alethea and when Rosamond made this discovery she simply resigned herself to her fate because:

> since things were gone so far she had better oblige the King, than to deny him that which he would take whether she could or no. And thereupon without resisting any further suffered the King to do what he pleased, which pleased the King so well, that before the morning light appeared, he pleased fair Rosamond also.

King Henry found Rosamond's presence in the palace uplifting but Queen Eleanor found it infuriating, so much so that 'she caused' her son to raise a war against his father in Normandy. The king was then obliged to leave Rosamond to the care of her uncle, while he departed from the country to fight his enemies. The lady scorned took advantage of his absence to plot fair Rosamond's death. Queen Eleanor gained entry into her bower and having found 'Queen Rosamond arrayed like an angel ... compelled her to drink a bowl of poison, of which she died'. Upon his return to court, King Henry put many to death and imprisoned Queen Eleanor for life and 'building a famous sepulchre for fair Rosamond ... soon after died himself'.

THE HISTORY OF JANE SHORE

Jane Shore, the beautiful femme fatale, was no stranger to male admirers. From an early abduction attempt by Lord Hastings, to a forced marriage to Matthew Shore, to the advances of Edward IV, Jane's downfall was predictable.

Mrs Blague, the royal lace-maker conspired with King Edward, just as Alethea had done with King Henry, to bring about the fatal encounter between Jane and Edward. Having lived some time in great splendour at the court, Jane's happiness ended abruptly with the death of the king. Lord Hastings then did her the 'honour' of taking her as his concubine but he failed to protect himself much less the unfortunate Jane Shore, as 'crooked-back' Richard, brother of Edward, arranged his death. Jane was shown no mercy either as she was condemned to do penance through Cheapside and Lombard Street, dressed in a smock and white sheet, holding a lighted taper of wax in one hand and a cross in the other. Once again the moral of the story was driven home lest the reader might have missed the point about the inadvisability of adulterous relationships with kings.

> Sure, it must be extremely surprising that she who was served in plate and treated with the costliest viands ... should ever be reduced to that extraordinary degree of misery as to be forced to sit upon a dunghill, and glad to eat the refuse of dogs.

However, it was Jane Shore's lamentation at her death, which was designed to lay the deepest impression on readers, in order to discourage them from a life of vice. She professed to being 'happier now upon this dunghill than ever, I was in his princely arms, for O it was an adulterous bed indeed, a bed of sorrow it has been to me'. She repented sincerely and hoped others might learn from her mistake:

> O happy dunghill, how do I embrace thee, from thee, my pardoned soul shall soar to heaven, though in this ditch I leave my filthy and polluted carcass. O that the name of Shore may be an antidote to stop the poisonous and foul contagion of raging lust forever.

The fears expressed by concerned contemporary writers on the evils attendant upon reading about the fate of the two royal prostitutes fair Rosamond and Jane Shore were completely unfounded. Children couldn't possibly have understood the content of this crudely printed, miniature sized book. Adolescents would probably have read it for the interesting storyline but would hardly have been encouraged to stray from the path of righteousness as the anonymous writer issued several warnings to them not 'to be taken in with the gaudy trappings of royalty and glittering pomps of the court' and outlined the horrendous consequences of failing to do so.

'Penny Godlinesses' – the moral tales of Hannah More

Contemporary writers never mentioned that the moral tales of Hannah More (1745–1833) formed part of the reading literature in the hedge schools, possibly because they were unaware of this fact but more likely because they were so alarmed by the 'Penny merriments', which they knew were being read. In any event, it would be reasonable to assume that the 'Penny godlinesses' of this formidable evangelical writer would have served as an antidote to the former.

More who was born in Gloucestershire, the fourth of five daughters of a High Church schoolmaster, led a most interesting and self-sacrificing life. Having carved out a very successful literary career in London, where she was favoured with the friendship of the distinguished portrait painter Sir Joshua Reynolds (1723–92), Samuel Johnson and Drury Lane manager David Garrick (1717–79), she decided in 1789, along with her sisters, to set up Sunday schools for the poor in the neighbourhood of Cheddar in Somerset. She met with stiff opposition from the local farmers who objected to her teaching the poor to read, an episode she later recalled in one of her stories *The Sunday school* when farmer Hoskins complained that 'of all the foolish inventions, and new-fangled devices to ruin the country, that of teaching the poor to read is the very worst'.[101] After the outbreak of the French revolution the Sunday schools under non-Anglican control were looked upon as hotbeds of Jacobinism.[102] More was singled out for criticism for producing a literate working class who eagerly read Paine's pamphlet *The rights of man*, which argued, after Rousseau, that it was only by the determination of the people that government could be legitimised.[103] She was rather unfairly charged with 'sedition, dissaffection, and a general aim to corrupt the principles of the community'. In fact, when Paine's 'blasphemy' was being distributed by the chapman there was nobody more horrified than More as she bitterly complained that

> Vulgar and indecent penny books were always common but speculative infidelity, brought down to the pockets and capacities of the poor, forms a new aera [*sic*] in our history.

101 R.D. Altick, *The English common reader* (Chicago, 1957), p. 69.   102 Jones, *The charity school movement*, pp 153–4.   103 H. Blamires, *The age of romantic literature* (London, 1990), p. 13.

She defied her critics and confronted the problem by deciding 'to take over the whole of English popular literature for the greater glory of God and the security of the nation'[104]. She was prompted to do this by the importunate requests of her 'friend' Bishop Porteous, the bishop of London, who urged:

> her acquaintance with the habits and feelings of the lower orders, and her clear and vigorous style, as an irresistible call on her pen for some simple production, calculated to dispel the delusions so assiduously propagated among the vulgar.[105]

What resulted from this was a long series of moral tales and ballads, known collectively as the *Cheap repository tracts*. For her method and manner of publication, she was indebted to her predecessor Sarah Trimmer 'of whose, "Family magazine" the cheap repository' was 'almost a continuation'.[106] Her tracts were designed to look like the pamphlets they were intended to supersede 'decked out with rakish titles and woodcuts', they were 'sent out like sheep in wolves clothing, to be sold by hawkers in competition with their old trash' on 3 March 1795. By March 1796, the total number of tracts sold reached staggering 2,000,000.[107] More's success was unprecedented in the history of English books. The best known of these tracts was *The shepherd of Salisbury plain* (1795), which followed the usual format that readers had come to expect – virtue was always rewarded, usually by a chance encounter with a benevolent and charitable individual while vice was suitably punished by either a term in jail, or, in extreme cases, by transportation or hanging.

The moral tales read in the hedge schools included *Black Giles the poacher*,[108] a story told in two parts about a parasite named Black Giles. This miscreant who was reminiscent of Fagan in Charles Dickens' novel *Oliver Twist*, with his 'bad boys', his slovenly wife Rachel and his youngest son Dick, who incidentally was the only family member with any sense of integrity. Poaching and rat-catching were their specialities. Giles had trained his boys in begging from early childhood but More had her own ideas on how these children might have spent their idle hours – she suggested 'knitting at home', 'working in the field' or 'learning to get their bread in honest ways'. However, More's obvious sense of fun added an amusing dimension to an otherwise didactic story. She told how some fathers, like Old Jim Crib, whose son was transported for sheep stealing, held the Giles boys up as excellent role models for their sons. Old Crib complained to his boys 'that Giles' were worth a hundred of such blockheads'. After all Giles always had 'some little comfort-

104 Altick, *The English common reader*, pp 73–4.   105 H. Thompson, *The life of Hannah More* (Edinburgh, 1838), p. 135.   106 Ibid., p. 151.   107 Altick, *The English common reader*, p. 75. 108 H. More, 'History of Black Giles the poacher' in *Cheap repository tracts* 1 (Dublin, 180–).

able thing for supper, which his boys had pilfered in the day, while his undutiful boys never stole anything worth having'.

Giles reaped his finest harvest when his victims were inside church praying. It was his 'most profitable day of the week'. Rachel wasn't idle on Sunday either. She caught up with her domestic chores as she took a break from doing the work of the devil 'telling fortunes and selling dream books and wicked songs'. She had no moral conscience either as she sold defective, sub-standard products such as peppermint and distilled waters to unsuspecting customers, always ensuring however, not to visit the same house twice.

Black Giles suffered a fatal accident when a wall collapsed on top of him, but the event was to lead to his spiritual awakening. He was touched by the generosity of the victims of his petty crimes, who not only forgave him but brought him some broth, rice milk and apple dumpling. He was in awe of this religion which allowed for such forgiveness and compassion. He 'often cried out, that there must be some truth in religion, since it taught a body to deny himself and to forgive an injury'. Black Giles repented on his death bed, that he might save himself and possibly his sons. The story finished with a Sunday sermon by the minister Mr Wilson who was determined to rid the neighbourhood of poachers like the deceased. His prayers were answered, for, 'This together with the awful death of Giles, produced such an effect, that no poacher has been able to show his head in that parish ever since'.

Sinful Sally told her own sad life's story in a very engaging style in the poem *The story of sinful Sally*. Even though it contained some forty three stanzas of four lines the reader was captivated from the start as Sally pleaded pitifully, 'Come and drop a mournful tear/O'er the tale that I shall tell'.[109] The pathos was maintained as she summed up a battered life, which had once held out such promise. She had lived a life of child-like innocence contentedly knitting, clad in her humble kersey gown, surrounded by adoring parents and affectionate friends in an idyllic rural setting. Her happiness was shattered when she approached her eighteenth year, when 'modest youths' came 'abounding, all to Sally on the Green'. Sir William exploited her innocence by wooing her with presents and colourful ribbons, until soon Sally found herself 'mistress to a rake'.

Her moral decline was now unstoppable. She became the 'child of Hell'. She no longer attended church, neglected her bible reading for 'that impious book so new' and 'that filthy novel too'. She then moved to London 'Powder'd well, and puff'd and painted', where she entered upon a career in prostitution. She became insufferably proud, as she considered herself superior to her rivals. An inner voice told her that her life of pleasure was a life of sin

109 H. More, 'The gamester, to which is added the story of sinful Sally' in *More tracts* 2 (Dublin, n.d.), p. 18.

but she wasn't ready to change. She plunged deeper into sin as she drowned her sorrows in bottles of gin

> Now no more by conscience troubled,
> Deep I plunge in every sin,
> True! my sorrows are redoubled
> But I drown them all in gin.

She became an accomplished criminal, teaching others how to steal and then becoming the receiver of stolen goods herself. It was immaterial to her whether there was a murder involved in the course of the robbery or that her youngest protégé Mark would hang for it. Soon sinful Sally was afflicted with a 'fierce disease' and her physical decay was terrifyingly presented as a stark reminder of the dangers of prostitution

> Here with face so shrunk and spotted
> On the clay-cold ground I lie!
> See how all my flesh is rotted,
> Stop, O stranger, see me die!

She was sick and dying when she turned to the Lord once more for help and begged for forgiveness that He might 'save the vilest harlot'. Sally knew that the Lord's forgiveness was 'all atoning' but because she had transgressed so badly she believed her 'day of grace' was past. In a heartrending plea to her Saviour to come to her assistance in her hour of need, she promised to place her faith in Him forever.

> Saviour! Hear me or I perish:
> None who lives is quite undone:
> Still a ray of hope I'll cherish
> 'Till eternity's begun

Her Saviour listened to her pleas and Sally was at last redeemed.

In *The wonderful advantages of adventuring in the lottery, or, The history of John Doyle,*[110] More set the conscientious John Doyle from the path of right-eousness by putting the temptation of the lottery in his way. One fateful day he received a hand-bill from a man standing in the door-way of a lottery-office which 'invited all who had a mind to be rich in a hurry to seize the lucky hour of adventuring in the wheel of fortune'. John had the temerity to approach

110 H. More, 'The wonderful advantages of adventuring in the lottery, or, The history of John Doyle' in *More tracts* 2.

Molly his wife, about trying 'our fortune in the lottery'. She reminded him that this was hardly God's will and it certainly wasn't hers as 'the child needs clothes'. She reminded him of his responsibility to the child's poor old grandfather 'Sure (said she, while a tear stole down her cheek) you will not forget our dear Johnny.'

John didn't succumb to this emotional blackmail but made the bold decision to ignore his wife's counsel and instead entangled himself in a web of deception. He lost all his money, stole a silver goblet and spoons from his master, and finally got involved in a highway robbery in which an innocent man was shot dead. When he returned home to his wife, with a pistol in his pocket, 'she trembled like an aspen leaf' as she suspected the worst. Her suspicions were soon realised and having accompanied her weakling of a husband to Newgate prison she sank beneath the weight of the ordeal and died. Her dying wish was that John would seek God's mercy and repent.

When the case came before the court the judge passed sentence and condemned him to immediate death. He also warned others against the dangers of gambling on the lottery and advised them 'to abhor the thoughts of adventuring on it – to fly from it as a plague ... to consider it only as the cunning artifice of designing men to enrich themselves'. More hoped that his fate would act as a deterrent to others: John '... was executed according to his sentence: and would to God that his history might prove a warning to all, against trying their fortune in the lottery'.

The More tracts appealed to Irish parents and their children despite the lessons in morality, the reforming advice, and the sparcity of woodcuts or illustrations of any kind. Hannah More could tell an interesting story in simple, colloquial language and with a sense of merriment and good humour one doesn't normally associate with evangelical writers. It is easy to understand how her readers could remain blissfully unaware of the fact that what she was really trying to do was to save their souls from eternal damnation.

'Penny Godlinesses' – The pleasant art of money-catching

An 1825 commissioner of education visited a hedge school in Sligo and was dismayed when he observed

> ... a child holding the *New Testament* and in its hands, sitting between two others, one of whom was supplied with the *Forty Thieves*, and the other with *The Pleasant Art of Money Catching*.[111]

---

111 First report of the commissioners, 1825, pp 43–4.

THE PLEASANT

A   R   T

OF

MONEY-CATCHING.

TREATING,

I. Of the Original and Invention of MONEY.
II. Of the Misery of wanting it, &c.
III. How Persons in Want of MONEY may supply themselves with it.
IV. A new Method for ordering of Expences.

V. How to save MONEY in Diet, Apparel, and Recreations.
VI. How a Man may always keep MONEY in his Pocket.
VII. How a Man may pay his Debts without MONEY.
VIII. How to travel without MONEY.

To which is added,

THE WAY TO TURN A PENNY,

OR, THE ART OF THRIVING.

With several other Things, both Pleasant and Profitable.

The Fourth Edition, Corrected and much Enlarged.

D U B L I N:

Printed by T. M'DONNEL, No. 50, Essex-street, opposite the Old Custom-House.

M,DCC,XCIII.

6 Title page from *The pleasant art of money-catching* (1793)

Like many contemporary writers, the commissioners considered *The pleasant art of money-catching*[112] to be an unsuitable book of entertainment for children to read. A cursory glance at the table of contents would have revealed that far from being a work of fiction of questionable moral value, it was in fact a worthy precursor of the lesson books published by the commissioners of national education in the 1830s. It conveyed useful factual information and upheld similar attitudes and values. For example the writer considered the existing social order or rich and poor to be part of God's plan, an opinion which held currency in the eighteenth and nineteenth centuries.[113] 'We know indeed, that by the Divine Providence, in the body of a commonwealth, there must be as well poor as rich'.[114] This view was shared by the compilers of the national education lesson books. In the *Supplement to the fourth book* of 1850, it was stated that

> It is a general law which God has established throughout the world, that riches and respect should attend prudence and diligence: and as all men are not equal in the faculties of either body or mind, by which riches or respect are acquired, a necessity of superiority and subordination springs from the very nature which God has given us.[115]

The writer of *The pleasant art* believed that when the poor moved up the social ladder to occupy positions of wealth and power, it occurred through a miracle of God: 'Yet God raiseth up as by a miracle, the children and posterity of these, oftentimes to possess the most eminent places, either in church or common-wealth'.[116] Likewise in the *Fourth books of lessons* (1834) readers were warned that riches and success came only to the chosen few among the poor: 'It is, of course, not to be expected that may poor men should become rich, nor ought any man set his heart on being so'.[117]

The conscientious attention to duty and work were considered to be the highest of the religious virtues. Quoting the Apostle Paul, the writer urged the reader to 'Labour night and day, rather than be burdensome'. He condemned the idler as a burden on society, one of 'the drones of a commonwealth who deserves not to live', and while alive deserved to starve: 'He that laboureth not must not eat'. Like Solomon, whose wise words the writer constantly referred to, he wished that 'the sluggard shall a scarcity of bread'.

---

112 *The pleasant art of money-catching* (Dublin, 1793).   113 This was evident in the well known Victorian hymn 'All things bright and beautiful' by Mrs Cecil Frances Alexander (1823–95): The rich man in his castle,/The poor man at his gate,/God made them high or lowly/And ordered their estate./See W.H. Monk (ed.) *Hymns ancient and modern* (London, n.d.), p. 815. 114 *The pleasant art*, p. 36.   115 *Supplement to the fourth book of lessons for the use of schools* (Dublin, 1850), p. 143.   116 Op. cit., pp 36–7.   117 Dublin, 1842, p. 225.

This was also a favourite theme in the lesson books where lessons on the 'busy bee' and the 'thrifty ant' were conveyed in poetry and prose. In the sequel to the *Second books of lessons* (1866), the grasshopper, who wasn't great- ly enamoured by work, sought sustenance from the assiduous ant, only to be refused with the following rebuff:

> Be prudent and mind what I say,
> Do not spend all your leisure
> In riot and pleasure
> But while the sun is shining make hay.[118]

The *Pleasant art* like the lesson books promoted the rationalist principles of the utilitarian philosophy which placed an emphasis on such matters as hard work, prayer, frugality and fidelity. This is evident from the nine pages of proverbs which emphasised a number of duties. The reader was told to

> Do your duty and fear not the consequence.
> Get thy spindle and thy distaff ready, and God will send thee flax

The mother had clearly defined duties which were expected of her

> The foot on the cradle, the hand on the distaff,
> Are certain signs of a good house-wife.

She was also expected to be subservient to her husband

> He who lets his wife go to every feast
> And his horse drink at every water,
> Shall neither have good wife, nor good horse.

Women could take little comfort from the advice offered to young men in this manual. They were warned against the dangers of rejecting the tradi- tional practice of match-making by making a free choice and ending up with

> Proud, foolish and light housewives, or such eternal clacks,
> that one were better to have his diet in hell, than his
> dinner at home, there to be troubled with her never ceasing tongue.

Marrying beneath their class for the sake of 'a little handsomeness and eye- pleasing beauty' was shown to be a ruinous course of action for young gen- tlemen to take. He did allow that women of the 'meanest condition may make good wives' but that their husbands would quickly take 'a surfeit of their

118 Dublin, 1866, pp 32–4. *Fourth book of lessons for the use of schools*, p. 224.

beauties ... and fly abroad'. At no stage did the writer condemn these phi-
landering husbands who 'not only doat upon others, but devise all the ways
they can (being grown desperate) to give away or sell all they have'.

Female fashion didn't meet with his approval either as he viewed it in purely utilitarian terms rather than as a creative art from. He condemned the
extravagant female that 'chaos of depravity' who 'prostituted fashion' by
transgressing the limits of propriety in dress with her 'towering head-dress-
es and flaming lappets,' who displayed 'a propensity of quitting this terres-
trial abode, in the pursuit of aerial castles, constructed by female imagination'.
He was no less critical when it came to what he considered female excess in the
use of cosmetics

> When apothecaries shops are ransacked and stripped,
> in order to make the luxury of art gloss over the
> imperfection of nature.

He reserved his most vitriolic lines however, for the dramatic concluding
homily entitled 'An essay on morality'. One might reasonably assume after
reading this that the writer of *The pleasant art* was a clergyman. He commenced by warning that intoxication and bad company led one into temptation but that the real causes were 'private meetings with women'. 'wanton
books', 'lewd pictures', and 'gazing into beauteous faces'. He considered prostitution an odious vice and the prostitute as one who would sell herself to the
devil. He alleged that:

> Having prostituted herself to one, becomes a common sewer, and
> receives the filth of all; baser than a beast, voluntarily hiring out her
> body, to those whose faces are more frightful than a dead man's skull;
> and was the devil to assume a human shape, and proffer a purse of
> gold, she would be his prostitute.

He warned the reader against the prostitute's flamboyant exterior and corrupt interior, and her potential to physically infect those she managed to gull:

> Be not deceived, the fine gay flirt is a meer cheat in everything; not only
> her dress, but face is borrowed, and what is enough to electrify you with
> horror the hollow wrinkles in it are patched and daubed over it with
> paint like a decayed sign-post. Like a stately tomb she is showy with-
> out, but she is all rotte[n]ness and stench within ... this land syren sal-
> lies forth, as the extender of Satan's empire to gull mankind; and by
> spreading her fiery infection; she maims as many as would fill an hospi-
> tal, and communicates all the distempers that are to be found in one.

He gave the examples of New Prison and Kilmainham Jail, where many young men in the bloom of their youth owed 'all their misfortunes to debauchery', and to 'abandoned females' who 'proved their destruction'. He was evidently intent on instilling fear into his prospective sinners as he asked them to look inside their hospitals to see the appalling physical ravages and pain that could result from a promiscuous lifestyle.

> Look into you hospitals and you will see the shocking examples of licentious lust, wretches dying with excessive sickness, their heads swelled to an enormous size, their eyes ready to start out of them, their tongues hanging from their mouths, and filthy spittle drivelling down their deformed lips; their corrupted bodies and ulcerated limbs causing a most intolerable stench; add to this, the unhappy creatures scream when the red-hot caustics are applied to their sad sores; Good God; what a complicated scene of misery, agony and horror; Ah, it is not to be equalled on earth, and it can only be exceeded in Hell.

The pleasant art was never intended for a juvenile audience. It was a vademecum for the self-employed and those who wished to economise, or to lead useful and frugal lives of self-denial and piety. This grave book was written in archaic language, interspersed with Latin quotations, biblical references and classical aphorisms. There were no illustrations to make it more appealing to its reader and the level of complexity of the vocabulary employed demanded a comprehensive knowledge of the English language from the reader.

It is indeed ironic that a book which promoted the utilitarian philosophy and which upheld so many of the values and attitudes later conveyed in the national education lesson books should have been offensive to the visiting commissioner of 1825 to the Sligo hedge school, especially in light of the fact that this book couldn't possibly have been read by children.

5

'Penny histories' – chivalric and neo-chivalric medieval romances

Chivalric and neo-chivalric romances were by far the most popular of the chapbook literature in the indigenous schools. This is evident from the print-ers' lists and advertisements for the eighteenth and nineteenth centuries. In Ireland they consisted of re prints of English texts which were imported to the country by Irish publishers and printers engaged in piracy.[1]

Medieval romances originated in France during the latter half of the twelfth century. Within a little over a century they went into a decline in France but flourished in Germany and England. The English romances were different however from the French *chanson de geste* – whose central theme was the establishment and defence of Christian nations, whereas the chivalric romances, like *Guy, earl of Warwick* emphasised the search for individual iden-tity within an already established society. Now jousts and single combats took the place of battles in defence of christendom.[2]

By the late sixteenth century the genuine chivalric romances were rein-forced, firstly by a whole wave of translations, mainly from Spanish and then by imitations, whose literary worth was negligible. According to Schlauch in *Antecedents of the English novel* (1963) they were 'Jejeune romantic concoc-tions ... belated representatives of the medieval school. The translated romances of this period are, briefly speaking, of the type that drove the good knight of La Mancha mad.'[3] She was referring to Anthony Munday's (1553–

1 Ó Ciosáin, *Print and popular culture*, p. 72. 2 L.C. Ramsey, *Chivalric romances* (Indiana, 1983), p. 3. By the late fourteenth century there was a discernible change in the romance audience. It was no longer the preserve of the nobility. It broadened out to include the common reader and the middle classes who had aspirations of dignity and courtliness. It was the nobility themselves, the dukes of Burgundy who gave the symbolisms of chivalry vitality in the fifteenth century. It was in the court of Duke Philip of Burgundy and his wife the Duchess Margaret, sister of the English king Edward IV, that William Caxton, was encouraged to begin his series of transla-tions from French into English. See Robert W. Hanning, *The individual in twelfth-century romance* (London, 1977). 3 M. Schlauch, *Antecedents of the English novel* (London, 1963), p. 165. Apart from his plays, Munday did many translations of romances, particularly those of the Palmerin cycle from French, once described as the 'Grub Street Patriarch's worst piece of work'. It contained the work of many writers, not just Munday's. Ford was a romance writer, and at the end of *Parismus* there was a recommendatory letter from his friend Munday, using the pseudo-

1633) output as translator, which was quite considerable and comprised the *Palmerin de Olivia, Palmerin of England* (1581–94) and also *Don Belianis of Greece* (1598). The old fashioned romance now emerged in very crude form with new editions and re-written truncated versions keeping printers busy as they catered for a completely different and vastly bigger market, than the original aristocratic one.

Richard Johnson, a writer of the late sixteenth-century recognised a lucrative chapbook market just waiting to be served. He published *The seven champions of Christendom* (1596–7), which was to enjoy an avid readership for the next three centuries. Emmanuel Ford followed in his footsteps and produced a series of chivalric romances such as *Parismus, prince of Behemia* (1598) and the sequel *Parismenus; Ornatus and Artesia* (1607); and *The famous history of Montelyon knight of the oracle* (1633), which proved to be just as popular.

The Irish chapbook market reflected a similar trend as the chivalric romances remained perennially popular in the hedge schools. Among the favourites were *The renowned history of Valentine and Orson; Guy, earl of Warwick; Fortunatus;* and the much maligned favourite *The seven champions of Christendom;* as well as the classic pre-medieval romances of *The story of Reynard the fox; The seven wise masters of Rome* and its female variant *The history of the seven wise mistresses of Rome.*

Valentine and Orson belonged to the Charlemagne cycle and was one of the few romances of chivalry to have survived the middle ages. The main reason for this was a political one, and it concerned the fall of Constantinople in 1453 and the consequent expansion of Turkish power in the Balkans and the eastern mediterranean. This resulted in a belated revival of literary interest in the early feudal epics about wars previously waged against saracens both in Spain and Palestine.[4] *Valentine and Orson* was typical of the more romanticized prose tales of the crusading cycle and much space was devoted to accounts of fictitious wars against the saracens, centred about Constantinople. To the modern reader it can only remain a source of amazement that such a long, complicated story, one hundred and forty-four pages in length, unrelieved by illustrations could attract so wide an appeal. Its readers would have required

---

nym (LP) Lazarus Piot. The book imitated the Spanish romances. Its style was euphuistic, but its story was for the most part original, and was very well received. See DNB, pp 1187–94. **4** Ibid., p. 50. *Don Belianus of Greece* is listed in App. No. 221, p. 556, *Parismenes*, p. 557, *The famous history of Montelyon knight of the oracle*, p. 555. Charlemagne (*c*.742–814) also known as Charles the great, king of the Franks and Lombards, founder of the new Roman empire in the west, and one of the great rulers in history. By the end of his reign he dominated all of central Europe. In the popular mind he became the supreme legislator of Europe, the conqueror of the barbarians, the defender of Christendom. A vast body of legend was condensed into the Charlemagne cycle of romances. The holy Roman empire of the German nation, which took its origin from the imperial coronation of Charlemagne, survived for a thousand years until it was shattered by another great conqueror, Napoleon.

remarkable powers of concentration, a vivid imagination and advanced reading skills. Its appeal can only be explained by the many fantastic elements it contained not least being the fact that Valentine's brother had been nursed by a bear, hence the reason he was called Orson,[5] and the fact that Valentine killed his father mistakenly as he wore the disguise of a saracen. Readers possibly valued *Valentine and Orson* because it provided an escape route to a magical place above the clouds where horses could fly. This world of sheer fantasy contained an awesome Green Knight, benign and malign giants, a hostile enchanter named Adrimain and an affable dwarf enchanter called Pacolet. It had bloodletting and heroics, a talking Brazen Head encased within four pillars of jasper in a chamber studded with rubies, diamonds and a multitude of precious stones. This must have been quite an enthralling and an enchanting place, an ideal place for the young and the imaginative to escape to. This romance appealed to English and Irish readers alike, having survived up to the twentieth century in England, and the mid-nineteenth century in Ireland.[6]

By far the most popular of the chivalric romances was *The story of Guy, earl of Warwick*. Guy was an English hero of romance and legend, whose great exploits were first written down by an Anglo-Norman poet. The Anglo-Norman original *Gui de Warewic* was believed to have been composed between 1232 and 1246.[7] By the fourteenth century fiction was confused with fact and Guy was regarded as an historical figure.[8] Spufford in *Small books and pleasant histories* (1981) drew copiously from the chapbook collection of the famous English diarist Samuel Pepys (1633–1703). She referred to two versions of this story, one which was a lengthy account giving Guy a noble lineage, and targeted at the gentry class, and the other a shorter version of twenty four pages, presenting Guy as the son of the earl of Warwick's steward, targeted at the common reader.[9]

To many readers both in the middle ages and since, Guy of Warwick has seemed the prototype of chivalric romances. The adventures of Guy, originally conceived as entertainment for an adult feudal aristocracy, became by the eighteenth century and early nineteenth centuries the reading matter for unsophisticated persons of a quite different sort, including children.[10] The

---

5 *The renowned history of Valentine and Orson. The two sons of the emperor of Greece* (Dublin, n.d.), p. 1.   6 M. Pollard, *Dublin's trade in books 1550–1800* (Oxford, 1989), p. 223.   7 Ramsey, *Chivalric romances*, p. 48.   8 I.H. Evans, *Brewer's dictionary of phrase and fable* (London, 1970), p. 497. Centenary edition.   9 Spufford, *Small books*, p. 225. In the lengthy edition the writer claimed that Guy was remotely descended from Cassivellaunus, king of the Belgae, and the immediate heir of a nobleman, from Northumberland. The first printed version of the medieval manuscript has been variously ascribed. Carpenter and Prichard in *The Oxford companion* (p. 233) credited Wynkyn de Worde with having done so *c.*1500, while John Ashton in *Chap-books* (p. 138) and Victor E. Neuburg in *The penny histories* (London, 1968), pp 8–9, attributed it to Richard Pynson. Neuburg believed that numerous printed editions followed Pynson's by Wynkyn de Worde, William Copland and John Cawood.   10 Schlauch, *Antecedents of the Eng-*

Irish chapbook story of Guy which was added to *The child's new play-thing*
was a miniature edition, drastically reduced to a mere four pages. This was a
simplified account in large print. The story was embellished with a woodcut
which showed Guy with an axe in his hand, stoutly confronting a wild cow, of
mean demeanour and unnatural dimensions. This unsophisticated rendering
of the famous romance did have the satisfying happy ending, and it would
certainly have entertained its very young readers.

The story told how Guy fell in love with Phyllis, the beautiful daughter of
the earl of Warwick. To win her love he had to prove his valour by noble deeds
of arms. His first adventure involved the aforementioned monstrous wild cow.
Even though Guy found her a challenging opponent, she proved no match
for our hero, who inflicted such deadly blows that the beasts of the forest were
frightened by her terrible roars. The wild cow then collapsed and 'with a hor-
rid groan expired.' To immortalise the achievement 'one of her ribs was hung
up in Warwick castle, and is to be seen there to this day.'[11]

Guy's next series of encounters took place in a French forest where he laid
low a giant called Rumbo, a lion and a dragon. After many such victories he
returned to England where he married his beloved Phyllis, and found himself promoted to earl of Warwick, following the death of her father. The Irish
reader was then allowed to believe that the happy couple lived out the rest of
their days in matrimonial bliss. In the English chapbook, which was true to the
original, Guy's marriage had no sooner taken place than the hero decided to
embark on a pilgrimage to the Holy Land. He behaved heroically, like a true
chivalric knight, until the end of his life, which he devoted to one of prayer.
He lived as a hermit in a cave 'very pensive and solitary'. In the end as he lay
dying, he sent a messenger to his long abandoned wife who had spent her life
giving alms to the poor and building a large hospital for the elderly. She
arrived just in time and 'with sweeping joy they embraced each other' and the
much loved hero 'departed this life in her tender arms.' Phyllis died just fifteen days after him.

Truncated forms of *Guy, earl of Warwick*, *Reynard the fox* and *The history
of Fortunatus* formed part of the hedge school textbook *A child's new play-
thing*. The purpose of these stories was to amuse the child and all three were
illustrated however crudely and written coherently to facilitate his ready
understanding. As in the case of *Guy, earl of Warwick*, the Irish abridgement
of *The history of Fortunatus* told a somewhat different story from its English
original. It did however retain the two important motifs of the magical purse
that never emptied and the wishing hat which, when worn, transported a person wherever he wished to be. It told how a lady called Fortune gave Fortunatus a present of a 'purse which will never be empty'. He mishandled his

lish novel, p. 82. 11 *The child's new play-thing* 'The story of Guy, earl of Warwick', pp 116–17.

new found wealth and as a result of his spending spree found himself in the court of a grand seignior in Constantinople. It was here he was shown a wishing cap, which when worn would grant your every wish. Fortunatus pretended to test the weight of the hat and wished to be transported to his own country. The reader could then take some pleasure when the cunning daughter of the king of England managed to dupe Fortunatus and rob him of his hat and purse. He could taken even more delight when the beautiful but greedy princess was outwitted by a reformed Fortunatus. The moral of the story was that 'great riches are a great burthen and that having our wishes, often leads us to miseries and misfortunes'. Fortunatus, threw his old magical hat and overflowing purse in the fire, thus disposing of temptation for all time. In the preface of Pepys seventeenth-century abbreviated version of the medieval story *The seven wise masters*, it was claimed that the work was so highly regarded in Ireland, that it was used in schools as an English reader:

> of all histories of this nature, this exceeds, being held in such esteem in Ireland that it is of the chiefest use in all the English schools for introducing children to the understanding of good letters.[12]

This view was reinforced by Francis Kirkman (1632–74), who translated it from French in the sixteenth century. He stated that it 'was held in such estimation in Ireland, that it was always put into the hands of young children after the hornbook'.[13] Pepys had collected *The seven wise masters* in the 1680s together with a seventeenth-century imitation – *The seven wise mistresses*.[14] The latter was included in the second part of the Dublin chapbook version published in 1814. Senior students with advanced reading skills would have understood these two long protracted stories. There were no illustrations to relieve the tedium but readers knew that they could easily skip the many short stories within the main story itself, without losing out on the dramatic ending in each case.

In the preface to this late seventeenth-century version of *The seven wise masters*, the 'courteous reader' was told that the aim of the story was to teach the reader a lesson through the 'allurement of tales and fables'.[15] The writer

12 Spufford, *Small books*, p. 74.   13 Barry, *A century of children's books*, p. 11. Kirkman was a bookseller and author, he also had a circulating library. By dint of private study he acquired some knowledge of French and Spanish. He wrote *The famous and delectable history of Don Bellianus of Greece, or the honour of chivalry* which was founded on the Spanish romance of T. Fernandez. In the preface he gave an account of most of the romances which had been published in England. He translated from French *The famous and renowned history of Amadis de Gaule* (1652) and *The seven wise masters of Rome* (1674). See *DNB*, pp 219–20.   14 Spufford, *Small books*, p. 225.   15 *The seven wise masters and mistresses of Rome* (Dublin, 1814), Preface. App. No. 221, p. 555. The seven wise masters didn't represent the seven liberal sciences but were in fact astrologers, diviners and magicians.

fulfilled his promise as he told how the second wife of Emperor Pontianus, attempted through treacherous means, to get her stepson Diocletian executed for having rejected her amorous advances. Each night the inventive empress related a story for Pontianus about an imperious son who dispossessed his father, and each day, in order to counteract her propaganda, the seven wise masters, who were the boy's tutors, recited stories about the treachery of women. The objective was to buy time, in order to stay his execution.

The second empress was the daughter of the king of Castille, and there were many references in the story to sons and heirs to the kings of Egypt, France and Spain. The story itself was rich in symbolism as outlined in the chapbook preface:

> To give the meaning of this moral, it is thus. The Emperor may signify the world, who but having one only son – who is Man – him to bring well up is all his case. But man losing his own mother – who is Reason and Divine Grace – falling into the hand of the step-mother – signifying Sin – who is an Empress of great bewitching: and one that commands the world: she works by all possible means the confusion of man and would prevail against his weakness, but that a star from heaven – by which is meant Goodness from above – instructs man how to avoid the allurement of sin, by not opening his mouth to bid her welcome and the better to prevent her mischief, he hath sent Seven Wise Masters which are seven liberal sciences, to give him wholesome instructions.

The climax, which the reader had been anticipating for so long, occurred at the end of seven days, a period after which the planetary forces considered it safe for Prince Dioclesian to speak. He did so to startling effect by proving that the empress' favourite chambermaid was in fact a man, her paramour Ribauld. Both were condemned to die a cruel death. She was to 'be bound to a horse's tail, and drawn through the streets of the city, to the place of execution and there to be burned to death', and Ribauld was to be 'quartered and smitten to pieces' and his flesh 'cast to the hounds' so 'that the beasts and birds of the air', should devour him.

The story of *The history of the seven wise mistresses of Rome* was the female variant of the foregoing. The seven wise mistresses served a similar function to their male counterparts only the villain of the piece this time was Radamentus, Empress Lucretia's consul, a gentleman who tried to discredit her daughter Sabrina for rejecting his advances. Radamentus' villainy was exposed by Sabrina when it transpired that he had a liaison 'with a pretended gentleman of his bedchamber'. The empress then resigned and handed over power to Sabrina who ordered Radamentus and his concubine 'to be drawn at the horses tails, thro' the city to the place of execution and there under the common gallows be consumed to ashes'. The lesson common to both stories was that evil and wrongdoing lead to harsh retribution while goodness and integrity merit their own reward.

The story of *Reynard the fox*, the beast epic which used animals to satirise society and the follies of mankind, was famous for many centuries and rivalled *The seven wise masters* in antiquity. A poem in Latin by Paulus Diaconus was known as early as the nineth century but the earliest prose edition was dated 1479 and was printed at Gouda, near Rotterdam. William Caxton based his translation on this work and it was published in 1481.[16] It reached the English chapbook market in 1780, pirated copies of which found their way into Irish hedge schools. One such copy was printed in Belfast in 1814 entitled *The most pleasing and delightful history of Reynard the fox*. It consisted of nine pages and eight short chapters, each with a crude illustration, and title heading.

Despite these limitations a lively, simple account was presented, which was well within the understanding of children and it was written in a humorous and entertaining style. The humour was often of the bawdy, earthy variety as the wily Reynard, the trickster hero would stoop to any level to achieve his ends. From the opening chapter complaints came from the many animals he had duped and mistreated, particularly from Isegrim the wolf, who alleged that Reynard entered his house violently and then 'befouled' his children in such a rank manner that they became instantly blind'.[17] The other animals were easy prey for the cunning fox. Children would have appreciated the clever manner in which he outwitted his opponents by playing on their weak-

16 *Reynard the fox* (1489) (London, 1976), p. 1. In Diaconus' Latin poem the bear is substituted for the wolf. A poem in Flemish, called *'der Reinart'* was known in the eleventh century and in two verses of the Troubadors, attributed to Richard I, the names of Isegrim the wolf and Reinhart the fox were to be found. See Ashton, *Chap-books*, p. 95. Master Nivardus of Ghent, otherwise unknown, wrote what is probably the finest of all beast epics *c.*1150, called the *Ysengrimus*. This poem was known in Low German, French and Latin in the twelfth century. See Carpenter and Prichard, *The Oxford companion*, p. 449. One of the most artistic productions of the poem appeared in 1860 by T. J. Arnold after the German version by J. Goethe (1749–1832), German poet and playwright of repute, who ennobled the subject by his poem in 1794. See T. J. Arnold *Reynard the fox* (London, 1860), Preface, p. 3. *The story of Reynard the fox* had been current in western Europe for well over three hundred years, continually throwing out new branches. One branch of it at least would have been familiar to some of Caxton's readers from Chaucer's (1343–1400) 'Nun's priest's tale', which he had printed among the *Canterbury tales* in 1478. See G. Chaucer, *Canterbury tales* (London, 1966) pp 457–94, A.C. Cawley (ed). See also N. Coghill and C. Tolkien, *Chaucer the nun's priest's tale* (London, 1970). Caxton's translation was so successful that he re-printed it in 1489. A further edition by Wynkyn de Worde appeared about 1515. See N.F. Blake, *William Caxton and English literary culture* (London, 1991) pp 259–60. Finally, there was an edition printed by Thomas Gaultier in 1550. See E.G. Duff, *Fifteenth century English books* (London, 1917), pp 99–100.   17 *The history of Reynard the fox* (London, 1870), p. 97.

nesses, especially their greed. The ending would hardly have surprised the bemused young reader. It took the form of animal to animal combat, which was of course a burlesque on chivalric jousts. All the formalities of medieval chivalry were observed even down to the lion as king of the beasts, presiding over the event. Reynard's jousting techniques couldn't have been further removed from the dignified world of chivalry. Having overcharged his bladder beforehand, he saturated his tail with his own urine and used it to devestating effect during the combat to blind his opponent. The reader was informed that 'when they began to fight, he whisked it two or three times in the eyes of the wolf and quite blinded him'.

A purified version by Goethe (1749–1832) the universally acclaimed German poet and playwright, appeared in poetical form in 1793, and was translated by T.F. Arnold in 1860. *Reynard the fox* served for Goethe as a useful and amusing means of expressing satirical ideas on the diverse passions of men and on the peculiarities of society. He did this under safe animal disguises.[18] The royal lion, the voracious wolf, the sly fox, the timorous hare also represented human types and served as a basis for a satirical attack on human weaknesses. The coward, the flatterer, the deceiver, the seducible wife, the dull ursine male relying on his physical strength, all these were 'simple exaggerations of human types seen under a feral guise'.[19]

A copy printed in Dublin in 1749 entitled *The most pleasing and delightful history of Reynard the fox and Reynardine his son*, also outlines the allegorical nature of the story, when the reader was told that:

> Here, as in a mirror, the politick statesman may see his counterfeit: the flattering parasite how to carry himself even, and sail with all winds; the powerful and mighty, how weak it is to rely wholly on strength, when they have a subtil enemy, to deal with. And those that trust fawning friendship, are here convinc'd, that in adversity, but few will stand by them.

Just as *The seven wise masters of Rome* was rich in symbolism so too was *Reynard the fox*, although it is highly unlikely in either case, that children concerned themselves with their subtleties of meaning, but rather read them as very interesting and entertaining stories.

Of all the controversial chapbooks read in the hedge schools, few were mentioned as frequently or caused as much outrage as Johnson's *The seven champions of Christendom*.[20] It was an unusually long, convoluted story some four hundred pages in length, unrelieved by any illustrations of any sort, a

---

18 T.J. Arnold (tr.), Goethe, *Reynard the fox*, pp 4–5. 19 Schlauch, *Antecedents of the English novel*, p. 79. 20 R. Johnson, London, n.d., App. No. 221, p. 555.

mere pocket-sized book of the smallest print size imaginable. It had a loose plot structure interwoven in a complex maze of sub-plots, tenuously connected. Much of Johnson's work reflected his own unique style of writing but it was clear from certain themes that he drew some of his inspiration 'from fragments of old English romances, eked out with his own fantasies'.[21] The book was clearly intended for adults if one is to judge from the vocabulary employed. Adolescents would have relished this book. It had many compelling features which included adventure, enchantment, blood and gore mixed with chivalric romance to hold the young imagination captive. This would account for its impressive longevity over three hundred years. In England it 'went into at least ten editions in the century following its publication', and rivalled *The history of Valentine and Orson* in popularity. In Ireland its twenty-second edition was published in Limerick in 1806, and a copy was published in Dublin as late as 1840.

The seven champions were St George of England, St Denis of France, St James of Spain, St Anthony of Italy, St Andrew of Scotland, St Patrick of Ireland and St David of Wales. The heroes bore little resemblance to the saints whose names they were assigned. Although Johnson seemed to base some of his story of St George on medieval legends, he created the rest from his own stock of knowledge of popular romances. His patriotic bias was evident from his choice of St George, the patron saint of England, as the greatest hero among the seven champions of christendom. His life and adventures were elaborated on at far greater length. He was the saint who offered leadership when a crisis occurred. He was the only one of the seven who was never defeated in combat or lured by the seductive charms of female spirits. Every aspect of his life was described in heroic terms from his unnatural birth – 'the infant was taken alive from the bed of its creation' by use of 'the proper instruments of incision', – to the imprint on his chest of the lively image of a dragon', and 'upon his right hand a blood-red cross, and a gold garter on his left leg' to his extraordinary upbringing in a cave by the fell enchantress Kalyb.[22]

St George's daring deeds were the first ones recounted. The Irish chap-book version of these events entitled *The story of St George and the dragon*[23] would appear to have been drawn from this source.[24] His most memorable encounter was against a dragon who had been terrorising the country of Egypt for twenty-four years. His appetite could only be appeased by the 'body of a real virgin, whom he swalloweth down his envenomed throat'. Only one virgin remained in Egypt, and this was the King of Egypt's only daughter

21 Adams, *The printed word*, p. 57.   22 Johnson, *The seven champions*, p. 4.   23 *The child's new play-thing*, 'The story of St George and the dragon', pp 111–14.   24 Spufford, *Small books*, p. 253.

Sabra. Her father, King Ptolemy, promised any knight who could slay the dragon, his daughter's hand in marriage and the throne of Egypt after his death. The microscopic details of this encounter between St George and the dragon laid a lasting impression on the young John Bunyan along with may other blood-thirsty readers as it was particularly vividly portrayed. Johnson wrote:

> He smote the dragon under the wing, where it was tender and without scale … From thence whence there issued such an abundance of reek-ing gore, as turned all the grass in the valley to a crimson hue, and the ground, which was before parched up by the burning breath of the dragon, was now drenched in the moisture that proceeded from the venomous bowels.[25]

The individual adventures of the other six champions were not quite so spectacular but they all had one thing in common, the inclusion of virgins in the story line. Virgins would appear to have been Johnson's obsession. Take for example, the experiences of St James of Spain in Jerusalem, when he attempted to gain the reward offered by King Nebuzaradan, for the warrior who would slay the first wild beast in the forest. With typical Johnsonian extremism he described how St James performed the feat by killing a deformed loathsome looking boar who 'drank the blood of human creatures, and devoured their flesh'. He dutifully presented the trophy to the king, and expected to be given the king's beautiful daughter Celestine as a reward. Instead he discovered that the law of Judah dictated that 'he should be sub-jected either to an untimely death or instant banishment as he was an uncir-cumcised man'. For his final request before he died St James asked 'to be shot by a true virgin'. Fortunately for him the love struck Celestine interceded with her tyrannous father and secured instead his banishment from the kingdom.

St Denis of France had his own bizarre experience in Thessaly when hunger reduced him to eating berries from what turned out to be an enchant-ed mulberry tree, after which he turned into the likeness of a hart. Seven years later he regained his human shape and having struck the root of the enchant-ed tree he beheld what must surely have been a rare sight for a saint as 'there ascended from the hollow tree a naked virgin" the king of Thessaly's daugh-ter, the proud Eglantine. One would have expected lengthy accounts of how the champions fought heroically in defence of Christendom but in fact John-son did not concentrate his energies on this aspect of the story. He was much more at home when describing grotesque creations like the 'mighty and ter-rible giant' who 'ravished seven of the queen's maidens and afterwards

25 Johnson, *The seven champions*, pp 12–13.

devoured them alive into his loathsome bowels', or the Two-Headed Knight 'who was a ravisher of virgins, an oppressor of infants', who was decapitated by the Christian knights.

Beautiful virgins and evil knights featured strongly in part two also. The champions came to the assistance of an elderly shepherd grieving for the death of his daughter, who had been strangled by Loeger, the merciless Knight of the Black Castle. When news of the brutal killing reached the ears of her older sister, Loeger's wife, she entered her murderous husband's chamber and in a fit of uncontrollable anger: 'she called him traitor, and like a fierce tigress with the dagger that she brought in her hand, before his face she cut the throat of the innocent babe, and threw it to him on the bed'. She had intended killing her unfaithful husband as she threw the dagger at him 'but it rebounded back into her hands', so that she thrust it into her heart and killed herself. In the meantime the champions determined to fulfil the promises they made to the honour of knighthood, proceeded towards the island where the Knight of the Black Castle had his residence. They were the first to arrive at Loeger's castle, where they observed the owner walking along the top of it with his necromancer and seven sturdy giants. A long and bloody battle ensued between the giants and the champions and Johnson didn't neglect to mention the gruesome details:

> the giants were quite discomfited and slain: some lay with their hands dismembered from their bodies, weltering in purple gore; some had their brains sprinkled against the walls: some lay in channels with their entrails trailing down in streams of blood: and some jointless with bodies cut in pieces, so that there was not one left alive to withstand the Christian champions.

Defeat was staring Loeger in the face when Rosana met up with him and regaled some family history to him. Her mother, his estranged wife, the queen of Armenia, had been dishonoured by him and banished in disgrace from her country and Rosana was looking for answers from her father: 'Is it thou are that forgetful and disloyal knight which left the unfortunate queen of Armenia with so great pain and sorrow, big with child, among those unmerciful tyrants, her countrymen, which banished her out of her country, in revenge of thy committed crime'. He was so overcome with grief that he committed suicide and Rosana was so impressed by his sincerity that she arranged with the necromancer to transport her with Loeger's body to her mother's grave. Towards the end of this sombre episode Johnson introduced a magical flight in an iron chariot, with flying dragons, to take the reader into fantasy land as 'they feld through the air more swift than a whirlwind, or a ship sailing on the seas in a stormy tempest to Armenia'. The grim tale continued as they opened the queen's sepulchre and laid Loeger's body upon the lady's exhumed carcass. This macabre scene was followed by a double suicide, to complete the tragedy. Firstly, Rosana 'took forth a naked sword … and putting the pummel to the ground, cast her breast upon the point', then the necromancer, having buried Rosana in her parents' grave, enclosed himself within the walls of the monument of the stately tomb 'where he consorted chiefly with furies and walking spirits, that continually fed upon his blood'.

Part two ended as the story had begun, with a heroic picture of England's patron saint. St George's death resembled the pattern of his life, being both daring and self-sacrificing. He was mortally wounded as a result of a dragon's sting sustained during a gallant fight against the infectious dragon on Dunsmore Heath. He returned home triumphantly to the city of Coventry, where he presented the assembled gathering with the dragon's head, which up until then had terrified the neighbourhood. Now sadly his own life was quickly ebbing away until finally he died. All England mourned St George's death for a full month and the king declared 23 April St George's Day. He ordered 'a solemn procession about the king's court, by all the princes and chief nobility of the country,' on that day. He then paid the highest tribute of all to St George when he decreed that the patron saint of England 'should be named St George, our Christian champion'.

6

Advanced reading books of the hedge schools

The hedge schools of Ireland served as preparatory schools for students intended for the priesthood, for service in the foreign armies, for trading on the continent or for employment at home. Consequently English reading books at a
more advanced level than the chivalric romances were therefore essential. Once
again it was Irish parents who supplied books to their sons and daughters,
books, which reflected the interests of the people and the concerns of the time.

A contemporary account of the reading material in use in the hedge
schools of Co. Wexford,[1] illustrates the diversity of the reading material read.
It ranged from *The academy of compliments* (1770-1850), and the pious polem-
ical romance fiction of Penelope Aubin, namely *The noble slaves* (1722) and
Adventures of Lady Lucy (1726) to the novels, *Clarissa* (1747–48) by Richardson and *Castle Rackrent* (1800) by Edgeworth. It would appear also from the
list of thirty seven chapbooks which had been purchased by the Kildare Place
book subcommittee that the books of Aubin were widely appreciated, as well
as the two commercially successful novels of Smollett, *Roderick Random*
(1748) and *Adventures of Peregrine Pickle* (1751).[2]

But the most comprehensive list of advanced readers however is contained
in the appendix to the report of the education commissioners of 1825.[3] The
list was an eclectic mix of both the major and minor literary genres which
formed part of the popular reading taste of the time. Up until the 1730s there
was a reading audience for short stories of romance and intrigue by female
writers. These were works such as Aphra Behn's (1640-89), *The amours of Philander & Sylvia*, and Eliza Haywood's (1719–50) translation of Madeleine
Poisson de Gomez's *La belle assemblée – The adventures of six days* (1726).
There was also a demand for Defoe's novel *Moll Flanders* (1720) which was
written as a factual account in order to satisfy the taste of those who regarded fiction as little more than gilded lies. Utilitarian works, such as conduct
books like *The new academy of compliments* which told people how to behave on
social occasions and books of familiar letters like *The complete letter writer*
which instructed the unlettered on how 'to indite' were also sought after.

1 'An Irish hedge school' in *Dublin University Magazine* (Nov. 1862), pp 600-16   2 KPS
11/23/31. List of the Burton's purchased by the Kildare Place Society, 15 April 1819.

One could argue that parents who purchased these books of self-improvement did so to equip them to take their place in society and to familiarise themselves with formal letter writing. When they had done so they passed on their books to the more mature members of their families who attended hedge schools. Another strong indication that parents were engaged in self-education is the appearance on the list of the hugely successful essay periodical *The Spectator* (1711), by the classical English writers Richard Steele and Joseph Addison. *The Spectator* had two hundred imitators in the eighteenth century and according to Addison's calculations some 3000 copies were distributed daily. Literary historians such as Leavis contended that the assistance of *The Spectator* to the self-educated in England was incalculable – the same must surely have held true for the people of Ireland. Leavis wrote:

> In the history of the self-educated in the eighteenth and early nineteenth centuries ... volumes of the Tatler and Spectator were observed to turn up in the homes of the respectable poor as their early reading, so numerous were the editions.[4]

After 1730 the production of novels in England, the country of origin for the majority of the advanced reading books of the hedge schools, declined, and public taste changed. People in that country now looked for fiction which was more moralistic and decorous than before. Haywood adapted her work to suit the new fashion by producing a monthly periodical, the *Female Spectator* (1744–6), in which she inveighed against her own short romances of passion of the 1720s and 1730s. But Irish parents did not follow the trends of the English book market slavishly and even when these romances peaked in the 1720s only a couple of them, written by Behn and Haywood, were read in Ireland. Likewise in the 1730s when a second group of lady writers supplied a ready market with pious and decorous romance, only one writer, Aubin, found a reading audience for her works in Ireland. It is interesting to note also that the romance novel of the French writer Marivaux *Adventures of Marianne*, which bore such a strong resemblance to Richardson's *Pamela*, was also read in Ireland. It was in fact from a synthesis of many of these literary genres that Richardson produced the first novel.

'Lady novelists' emerged in England following the publication of *Pamela* (1742) and their novels were well received in Ireland. These were the anti-romance novel *The female Quixote*[5] (1752) by Charlotte Lennox (1720-1804),

3 First report of the commissioners, 1825. App. No. 221, pp 553–9.   4 Q.D. Leavis, *Fiction and the reading public* (London, 1965), p. 123.   5 Ibid., p. 559. Her first publisher Samuel Paterson introduced her to Johnson, who gave her favourable mention in his dictionary, and he introduced her to Richardson. Her novel *The female Quixote or the adventures of Arabella* (1752) appeared without her name but earned her the admiration of Fielding and Johnson. See *DNB*,

and the novels of Fanny Burney (1752–1840), a member of the bluestockings, dubbed by Johnson as that great 'character monger'[6] – *Cecilia, or the memoirs of an heiress* (1782) and her third novel *Camilla: old wife and young husband* (1786). In the late eighteenth century in particular the profile of the 'lady novelist' was enhanced by the success of the evangelical writers, most notably More and Trimmer.

Women writers now dominated the genre, due in large measure to their change in image. Literary historians like Turner (1994) have assigned a major role in their ascendancy to Richardson[7] who emphasised female virtues and also to the ideology of the Enlightenment philosophers Locke and Rousseau. The latter singled out unique feminine attributes such as emotion, spontaneity and intuition for idealization. Raftery (1997) drew attention to another factor which influenced the rise in the number of women writers, namely the launch of the bluestocking circle of literary women in the mid-eighteenth century. This circle led to a widening of women's intellectual interests and acted as a spur to many women to take up the pen.[8]

However, if one is to judge the popularity of novels by references to them in contemporary writers' accounts then the four major novelists of the eighteenth century – Richardson, Smollett, Sterne and Fielding would have to be rated among the most popular. In Wexford the 'Constant visitor' observed a young student reading aloud *Clarissa Harlowe's escape with Lovelace*, which was an extract from Samuel Richardson's second novel *Clarissa* (1747–8) while Glassford expressed his dismay at the fact that these novels were being read in the hedge schools of Ireland. In a letter to the earl of Roden in 1829 he stated:

> It is not unusual to find the children in these schools reading promiscuously some portions of scripture, along with the Romances of Fielding or Smollett, or the works of authors still more objectionable.[9]

The commissioners' list bears adequate testimony to the appeal of these novels which included Richardson's *Pamela, Clarissa,* and *Sir Charles Grandison,* Smollett's *Peregrine Pickle* and *Launcelot Greaves;* Fielding's *Joseph Andrews* and Sterne's *Tristam Shandy* and *Sentimental journey.* The Irish market had ready access to them due to an oversight in the Copyright Act of 1709, which allowed Irish printers to reprint English originals and sell them at a considerably reduced cost.

Cole gave an interesting account of the reprint industry in Ireland in *Irish booksellers and English writers, 1740-1800* (1986). He referred to a considerable number of Dublin booksellers who were engaged in piracy. Some of

pp 929–30.   6 E.A. Baker, *The history of the English novel. The later romances and the establishment of realism* (London, 1929) 'Fanny Burney', p. 157.   7 C. Turner, *Living by the pen* (London, 1994), p. 10.   8 D. Raftery, *Women and learning*, p. 99.   9 Glassford, *Letter*, p. 39.

them were well known among London printers for their diligence in obtaining sheets from their printing houses, a practice Richardson found objectionable. Cole reported that 'The Dublin pirates were so successful that the pirated edition of *Sir Charles Grandison* was published before the London edition and Richardson reported his fear that the Dublin pirates would charge him with piracy'. To add to his disquiet the Dublin reprints sold for two shillings less than the London originals. Consequently the novels of Richardson, Fielding, Smollett and Sterne dominated the sixth decade of the eighteenth century[10] in Ireland. Parents could also rent novels from the circulating libraries, which were first introduced in Dublin in 1737. They spread rapidly throughout Dublin, Cork and Belfast, during the last two decades of the century, thus putting the expensive novel within reach of the ordinary people. At this time also there were numerous lending libraries open to the public, which stocked re-prints of the novels, which the poor could avail of freely.[11]

In the third quarter of the eighteenth century a startling change took place in literary taste with the arrival of the novels of terror or gothic novels. They were written in the anti-realist mode, and offered a challenge to the rationalist philosophy of the age of the Enlightenment, which insisted on rules and emphasised reason. All of these were now being rejected by the Gothic writer of fiction who deconstructed the very realities of life itself.[12] Irish readers welcomed the rebellious Gothic literature, which peaked as Ireland was making preparations for the revolution of 1798. During this turbulent period people read Clara Reeve's (1727 1807) *Old English baron*, the Lee sisters Harriot and Sophie's translation of *Warbeck*, Radcliffe's *Mysteries of Udolpho*, and Matthew Gregory Lewis' *The monk*.

An eclectic mix of popular literature in the eighteenth-century hedge school

> There is no better proof of the greatness of a household, a country or a period than its readiness to laugh at itself and to concede to the young complete liberty of reading.[13]

There was a dearth of Irish books printed in this country especially from the seventeenth to the nineteenth century. The Catholic church looked to their religious orders on the continent to meet the shortfall but their contributions were mainly scholarly theological publications in Irish. Sometimes priests who trained in seminaries abroad also wrote for the home market, priests such as

---

10 R.C. Cole (London, 1986), p. 70. 11 Pollard, *Dublin's trade in books*, p. 31. 12 D. Punter, *The literature of terror* (London, 1996), pp 27–8. 13 R.C. Churchill, *The concise Cambridge history of English literature* (Cambridge, 1970), p. 513.

Geoffrey Keating (1570-1650) from Co. Tipperary, who was educated at Bordeaux and Spain. However, neither source of supply could have been expected to meet the needs of the entire reading population in the early eighteenth century.[14]

It should be remembered also that during the first half of the century people were afraid to be found with Irish books or manuscripts in their possession. Sometimes they even went so far as to bury them in the earth, as Ó Súilleabháin recounted in *Manners and customs of the ancient Irish*

> During the first half of the eighteenth century if you were found with an Irish book in your possession, you were immediately under suspicion, or perhaps raided. The fear of being found in possession of Irish books or manuscripts lasted for many years. I saw Irish manuscripts that were so long buried underground, that the print was practically faded and the edges destroyed. They were buried lest the Yeos should discover them when they visited the house.[15]

In the 1790s when the Catholic church was undergoing reform, there was a surge in demand for devotional literature and bilingual catechisms were available. But Irish books of entertainment were not being printed and writers were still committing the old stories to manuscripts. Even though there were fifty printers in Dublin at this time, and thirty four provincial presses, original English books of fiction by indigenous writers, were a rarity.[16] Only in this context is it possible to understand why so much diverse material was read in the hedge schools and why most of it had been imported from England.

At the end of the seventeenth century, the industrial revolution in England resulted in the capitalisation of the domestic home industry of spinning and weaving. Ireland, being an agricultural country was affected to a far lesser extent. In England it rendered middle class women an idle class. The increase in wealth which resulted for the upper classes brought about a change of outlook among women from this class. They now withdrew from their role of responsibility in household management and affairs of business to lead lives of leisure. It was for these middle and upper class ladies that booksellers catered. Even as early as 1691 the enterprising bookseller John Dunton (1659–1733) recognised the importance of the feminine reading public and devoted monthly numbers of his *Athenian Mercury* (1691) and his *Ladies Mercury* (1692) to matters of special interest to women. Some of the published matter took the form of long confessional letters concerning love affairs. As Day in *Told in letters* (1966) observed 'Dunton was only one of many who discerned

14 R.A. Breatnach, 'The end of a tradition: A survey of eighteenth century Gaelic literature' in *Studia Hibernica* 1 (1961), pp 128–50, p. 238.   15 R. Batterberry, *Oideachas in Éirinn, 1500-1946* (Dublin, 1955), pp 123–4.   16 Whelan, *The tree of liberty*, p. 63.

the profitable connection between women and sentimental epistolary fiction'.[17] In fact a whole new industry grew up as a result, with all of the best selling hack writers from Grub Street, a place synonymous with literary drudgery, engaged in writing letters. Booksellers like Dunton and Edmund Curll (1675–1747) employed the needy female writers Behn, De la Riviere Manley (1663–1724) and Haywood, all of whom transcribed works from French, to supply the market. Between 1660 and 1740 there was a large influx of French translations, which peaked in the 1680s,[18] and English original fiction had difficulty competing with these importations.

Behn remained among the few writers who managed to do so. Her broad literary experience as a playwright[19] and translator of French textbooks,[20] enabled her to draw on theatrical themes and to pattern her work on the fashionable French nouvelle or short romances of intrigue. The most frequently translated nouvelle were stories in letter form – epistolary fiction. They were either letters telling a story of love, relating a journey, or similar adventure, spy letters or scandal chronicles largely or wholly in letters.[21] Behn's preference was for scandal chronicle or nouvelle historique. Her most influential work in this genre was *Love-letters between a nobleman and his sister*[22] (1694), which was on the commissioners' list as *The amours of Philander & Sylvia*. It bore strong resemblances to the French model *Lettres portugaises* (1678) and became a bestseller in the eighteenth century, running into sixteen editions and producing a host of imitations.[23]

Her *Love-letters* took the form of an exchange of letters between a young French nobleman during the period of the Huguenot rebellion in Paris and his wife's sister. The incestuous and adulterous relationship was discussed at length in these letters before finally being consummated at the end of the story. The hero Philander wrote about what was natural and what was artificially imposed upon man by misguided social codes:

> Here is no troublesome honour, amongst the pretty inhabitants of the woods and streams, fondly to give laws to nature, but uncontroul'd they play, and sing and love; no parents checking their dear delights, no slavish matrimonial ties, to restrain their nobler flame. No spies to interrupt their blest appointments.[24]

17 R. Adams Day, *Told in letters* (Michigan, 1966), p. 76.   18 P. Salzman, *English prose fiction 1558–1700.* (Oxford, 1985), p. 308.   19 P. Salzman, *An anthology of Elizabethan prose fiction* (Oxford, 1987), p. 34.   20 Raftery, *Women and learning*, p. 47.   21 Day, *Told in letters*, p. 32. 22 A. Behn, 'Love-letters between a nobleman and his sister' in Natascha Wurzbach (ed.), *The novel in letters: epistolary fiction in the early English novel 1678–1740* (London and Coral Gables, 1969).   23 Turner, *Living by the pen*, p. 29.   24 Behn, 'Love-letters', p. 221.

Philander protested his right to 'incestuous love', although Sylvia wasn't in fact his sister but his wife's younger sister. His wife had also been cuckolding him with somebody else but Sylvia proclaimed 'False as she is, you are still married to her'. When the affair was discovered it caused deep offence to her family and considerable public outrage. Sylvia wrote to Philander: 'Philander, all that I dreaded, all that I fear'd is fallen upon me: I have been arraign'd and convicted: three judges, severe as the three infernal ones, sate in condemnation on me, a father, a mother and a sister'. Philander was pursued by lawsuits for rape and incest. The problem was eventually resolved by Sylvia marrying one of Philander's lackeys, who agreed to be married in name only, acting as a front for Philander himself. Behn introduced a note of authentic passion into English fiction by exploiting a famous contemporary scandal involving Lord Grey and his sister-in-law Lady Henrietta Berkeley.[25] Part two of the book consisted of a series of intrigues which reflected the influence of the Spanish novella or short story, then in vogue.[26]

Manley satisfied the public taste for sentiment and scandal in England and used her books as a medium to attack prominent members of the whig party. She was imprisoned after the publication of her successful scandal history *Secret memoirs and manners of several persons of quality* (1709). However the Irish rejected her scandal chronicles, as they did those of her successor Haywood. This prolific writer of amatory novellas reached the height of her popularity between 1724 and 1726 when in order to meet public demand, she produced on average, one novel every month, penning some twenty-eight novels in all during this period.[27] Her favourite themes were reminiscent of popular restoration plays, some of which she would have written before turning to prose fiction. These were the possibilities of sexual conflict, predatory male lust in pursuit of female innocence, thwarted and successful sexual assault which she first described and then condemned just as Richardson was to do some twenty years later in his novels *Pamela* and *Clarissa*.[28] The only works of Haywood to find favour here were her English translation of *La belle assemblée* and her tasteful periodical entitled the *Female Spectator*[29] (1744-6) published in emulation of Richardson who rejected fanciful romance for reality.

In England the epistolary novels of Haywood rivalled Defoe's in popularity. But in Ireland Defoe enjoyed a much more extensive readership, as some

---

25 S.D. Neill, *A short history of the English novel* (London, 1951), p. 40.   26 Salzman, *English prose fiction*, p. 311. Several collections of novella had been translated including the French playwright Paul Scarron's (1610-60) translation of Miguel de Cervantes (1547-1616) *Exemplary novels* from Spanish to French, which were re-translated into English by John Davies in 1665. 27 Neill, *A short history*, p. 80.   28 Leavis, *Fiction and the reading public*, pp 105.   29 Ibid., p. 557. Mrs Haywood figures prominently in the *Dunciad* by Alexander Pope (1688-1744) when he satirized her under the name of 'Eliza' and represented her 'with cow-like udders and with ox-like eyes'. See Forsyth, *The novels and novelists*, p. 203.

of his works held an enduring appeal for adults and children alike, especially that well known classic of children's literature *Robinson Crusoe* (1719). His next best known work was *Moll Flanders*, which appeared in 1722 (dated 1721). It was an instant success. This was due in some measure to its supposed scandalous character and to Defoe's sensational advertising of its contents. The full title reveals the marketing strategy applied. It read:

> The fortunes and misfortunes of the famous Moll Flanders etc. who was born in Newgate, and during a life of continu'd variety for three score years besides her childhood, was twelve years a whore (whereof once to her own brother) twelve years a thief, eight years a transported felon in Virginia, at last grew rich, liv'd honest, and died a penitent, written from her own memories.[30]

No doubt Defoe, who had been imprisoned himself in Newgate for political offences (1703) brought his experiences to bear when writing *Moll Flanders*. He depicted Moll as a victim of the society she lived in. She had no control over her circumstances. She never wished to engage in criminal activity and while she had leanings towards honesty and loyalty she believed she couldn't afford to indulge such impulses. Moll's moral message was similar to that of Defoe's in the author's preface, when he advised the reader to make 'virtuous and religious uses' of the story. He also warned parents who decked their children in finery and allowed them to go to dancing school alone, of what might ensue. Just as when Moll robbed a child and practically murdered the infant, she rationalised the event as follows: ' ... as I did the poor child no harm, I only thought I had given the parents a just reproof for their negligence, in leaving the poor lamb to come home by itself, and it would teach them to take more care another time'.[31] McKillop in *The early masters of English fiction* was of the opinion that 'Defoe proved himself to be the archetypal novelist in his characterisation of Moll Flanders and he was the first writer to do so'[32]. This type of picaresque or rogue literature appealed to the Irish and it remained popular with a wide section of the reading public. There were three editions of *Moll Flanders* in 1722 and another abridged edition in 1723, besides innumerable chapbook versions.[33]

Contrasting styles of writing had popular audiences in the eighteenth century and the classical writers Swift, Addison and Steele enjoyed as much acclaim as Haywood or Defoe even though the former despised the latter because they believed that members of the Augustan literary movement like

---

30 A.D. McKillop, *The early masters of English fiction* (Westport, Conn., 1979), pp 31–2. 31 D. Defoe, *Moll Flanders* (Oxford, 1991), pp 4–5. 32 Op. cit., pp 30–1. 33 I.Watt, *The rise of the novel* (London, 1979), p. 122.

themselves, were superior. This movement insisted on rigorous literary standards being upheld as they believed that 'classical literature contained the
highest cultural authority'[34]. They regarded the new trend in the literary market for epistolary romances and puritan realism as reprehensible. They saw
that literature was in danger of being turned into a mere market commodity
and writing converted into a mechanical trade.

This superior tone was implicit in Swift's reference to Defoe, as '... the
fellow that was pilloried I have forgot his name'.[35] Nonetheless Swift earned
a well-deserved reputation for himself as a formidable prose satirist, arguably
the greatest in English literature. But the very qualities which made him a
great satirist also precluded him from becoming a novelist. Swift had little
tolerance of human weakness and frailty, which he attacked with stinging
irony. In Swift's works satire was everything, but satire can only be part of the
novelist's make-up. His masterpiece was *Gulliver's travels or travels into several remote nations of the world* by Lemuel Gulliver (1726). It was superficially a
children's story but in actuality it was a profound satire on the irrationality of
human behaviour, and a subtle commentary on political and social conditions
in eighteenth-century England. Swift added little to the development of the
novel, but he created a flawless prose and he showed how irony could be
employed in fiction, to maximum effect.

An elegant, ornate style of writing was promoted by those two great exponents of the Augustan movement Steele and Addison, both of whom had
attended Oxford College. Addison started to write for *The Spectator* in 1711
and his contribution to the history of the essay periodical marked a turning
point. He endowed it with the lofty style of cultured writing, a style Fielding
was to adopt in the preface to the eighteen books of his novel *Tom Jones*. He
also named the characters in his essays, so that they were not mere generic
beings. He was also responsible for a literary innovation still in use today, that
of the *Letters to the editor*, only his editor was the venerable moralist Mr Isaac
Bickerstaff, a character he borrowed from his fellow Augustan, Jonathan
Swift. But probably the most significant contribution Addison and Steele
made to the substance of the novel was the creation of a group of vivid, life-
like characters, who became household names. There was Steele's fictitious
creation Sir Roger de Coverley the affable original thinker, who was loved so
much by his readers that when Steele finally put him to sleep, they mourned
him as a friend. Addison's equally winning character Will Honeycomb was
also a favourite with readers in the eighteenth century because of his engaging charm and optimism in the face of life's tribulations. Addison and Steele

34 E.A. Baker, *The history of the English novel: the Elizabethan age and after*, p. 253. The Augustans took their name from the Augustan period of the Roman empire (63 BC – 14 AD) when
Greek forms were adapted to Roman themes in literature and art. English Augustans 'saw their
period of national history as analogous to this past age in that it too, seemed to them a silver age:

had provided what Baker (1930) described as 'brilliant examples of prose fiction' which proved invaluable to those involved in self-education.

A further indication that people were keen to improve themselves was the appeal of such books as *The complete letter writer*. This was a letter manual, containing not only *Miscellaneous letters on the most useful and common occasions* such as *A son's letter at school to his father, From a young woman just gone to service, to her mother at home, From a young apprentice to his father, to let him know how he likes his place and goes on*, but also *Letters of courtship and marriage*. In this section the social etiquette in such matters was evident from letters like the one *From a young person in business to a gentleman, desiring leave to wait on his daughter*, or *From a young lady to her father, acquainting him with a proposal of marriage made to her*. Another letter which reflected the social mores of the time was one from a daughter who objected to her interfering father's match-making efforts for her, entitled *From a daughter to her father, whereon she dutifully expostulates against a match he had proposed to her, with a gentleman much older than herself*, as well as a letter from a compliant daughter on the same topic *From a young lady, to a gentleman that courted her, whom she could not like, but was forced by her parents to receive his visits, and think of none else for her Husband*.

Part three contained *Familiar letters of advice and instruction etc. in many concerns in life*. From the contents it would appear that the author was catering for a female readership. It contained such letters as one *From a sensible lady, with a never failing receipt for a beauty wash*, to *Domestic rule, the province of the wife*, or *From a lady to her acquaintance on growing old*, and finally *To a lady who had lost her beauty by the small pox*.

Part four was monopolised by the Augustan writers, and in particular by the poet Alexander Pope's (1688–1744) *Elegant letters on various subjects, to improve the style and entertain the mind*, to his fellow Augustans Steele, Addison and Swift. The earl of Chesterfield's *Of letter-writing* was also included in this section. The manual also contained *A plain and compendious grammar of the English tongue* to which was added *Directions how to address persons of all ranks, either in writing or discourse*.[36]

Compared to the letter manuals, the books of compliments were somewhat artificial, with the content resembling the dramatic situations later encountered in Richardson's novels. Many of the problematic situations depicted in these manuals were hardly selected for being typical. In *The new academy of compliments* for instance, among the examples of types of letters readers should emulate was one headed *A lover to his false mistress*, signed 'Base wretch, Thine once but now his Own'.[37] There was another titled *A crackt*

that is, it seemed poised between golden achievements in the past and possible future collapse into a barbarous age of bronze'. See Punter, *The literature of terror*, pp 27–8. **35** Allen, *The English novel*, p. 37. **36** *The complete letter writer or polite English secretary* (Cork, 1800), preface. App. No. 221, p. 556. **37** London, 1713, p. 33.

THE

UNFORTUNATE CONCUBINES,

OR, THE

HISTORY

OF

FAIR ROSAMOND,

MISTRESS TO HENRY II.

AND

JANE SHORE,

CONCUBINE TO EDWARD IV.
KINGS OF ENGLAND.

Shewing, how they came to be so, with their
Lives, remarkable actions, and unhappy ends
Extracted from eminent Records.

The whole illustrated with a new set of CUTS,
engraved by J. Hanvey, suitable to each subject.

DUBLIN: PRINTED
BY R. CROSS, 28, BRIDGE-STREET

7   Title page from *The history of fair Rosamond* [177-].

virgin, to her deceitful friend who hath forsook her for the love of a strumpet which
finished with the wounded words 'Wicked wretch, your Friend, till you
abused her'. One letter in particular was worthy of a place in an epistolary
novel. It was written by *A husband to his lascivious wife* as follows:

Wicked and wretched Woman,
    Hadst thou forgot all goodness, that you darest lift up thy adulter-
ous eyes to behold the crystal light? Hast thou no sense of thy own

filthy deformity? Dost thou know the world brands thee for a whore, a notorious strumpet? Art thou not sensible how thou hath made me become a scorn and by-word to all that know me?

Not that the credit of an honest man can de dashed by the infidelity of a strumpet! But so it is, that the corruption of the times, have created a custom to set the wives' sins upon the husband's forehead! Thy children are either hated or pitied by all, and I myself dare not look upon them, lest I permit my fears to whisper to me thy whoredoms, and their bastardy ...

The sad and much injured Husband.

The manual contained letters dealing with the usual assortment of personal problems as well as letters on social etiquite such as *A brother, on the occasion of his brothers not writing*, or *Civil compliments from one friend to another*, or *Comfortable advice to a friend on the death of a son, or other near relation*. It is difficult to ascertain whether the aphorisms offered as *Complemental expressions towards men leading to the art of courtship* were intended to amuse or instruct. The following breath-taking compliments were recommended:

Sir, such is the excess of my Affection that all my passions do but wait upon your good fortunes.
Sir, such is your deserts and my necessity that I want both words and services to express how unfeignedly I honour you.

To the much more pithy:

Sir, you are the rising sun, which I adore.
Sir, I wear you in my heart.

Assistance was also provided for gentlemen seeking to woo the ladies, in a section headed *Complements towards ladies, gentlewomen, maids &c.* These ranged from convoluted expressions like the following:

Madam, It was not thro' a conceit of my own deserts, that I have shot at so fair a mark as your vertuous and innocent fair self, my presumption hath only this excuse, and it was, directed by love, and I may well stray, when my guide is blind.

To the more succinct 'Madam in those smiling dimples, Cupid hath pitched his tents', and the somewhat dubious 'Madam, your heart is like a pebble, smooth but stony'.

In the early eighteenth century a counter tradition of the moral lady novelist was established when Jane Barker, Elizabeth Townsend Rowe (1673–1737) and Aubin wrote pious polemic and didactic love fiction in reaction to their disreputable counterparts Behn, Manley and Haywood. The Irish reader rejected the works of Barker and Rowe, which isn't too surprising. Barker's superior heroines always responded heroically by asserting themselves in a male dominated world of lust and avarice.[38] Rowe's tendency was to employ an inflated prose style to moralise about the pains of a life of sin and the comforts that can come from living virtuously.

Aubin's approach was much more acceptable. She presented her novels to the public as an undisguised attempt 'to seduce them, into virtue through the familiar diversions of popular narrative'. She hoped to 'reform by pleasing' and by 'encouraging virtue in her readers'.[39] She believed in giving her readers what they found so exciting in the love novellas – the bizarre complications, exotic dangers, disasters and coincidences. As variety was an essential ingredient, travel featured largely in her novels. She took the reader to Mexico, South America and North Africa in *The noble slaves* (1722) and to Germany in *Life and adventures of Lady Lucy* (1726). Her novels generally ended on a triumphant note with virtue reigning supreme, as in *The noble slaves* when she urged 'since our heroes and heroines have done nothing but what is possible, let us resolve to act like them, make virtue the rule of all our actions, and eternal happiness our only aim'.[40] Even though Aubin could have made more money if she took the advice of her publisher to write 'more modishly … less like a Christian and in a style careless and loose, as the custom of the present age is to live', she rejected the advice with her decision to 'Leave that to the other female authors, my contemporaries, whose lives and writings have, I fear, too great a resemblance'.[41]

It was the moral lady novelists who were in the ascendancy from the 1730s onwards. When women writers such as the 'reformed' Haywood and Charlotte Lennox appeared in the novel market after 1744, they did so 'as the inheritors of Rowe'.[42] The late eighteenth-century saw the arrival of the learned lady novelists, writers such as Burney, the toast of the bluestockings, who broke new ground with her novel *Cecilia; or memoirs of an heiress* (1782), when she abandoned the epistolary form in favour of a detached narrative voice. Burney's reputation rested on her satirical portrayal of the mannerisms and idiosyncrasies of the affected fops and eccentrics of her time.[43] Her third novel *Camilla, or a picture of youth* (1796) gave her ample scope to portray such human foibles and absurdities. There were several character types ranging from the good-hearted but foolish old baronet, the learned but absent-minded tutor, the self-satisfied bumpkin who was over-attentive to the ladies and the coxcomb. However, the most striking feature of these novels was the sheer complexity of the plots, and the elaborate and exaggerated use of lan-

38 J.J. Richetti, *Popular fiction before Richardson* (Oxford, 1992), pp 236–7. 39 Ibid., p. 219.
40 Richetti, *Popular fiction*, p. 229. 41 R. Ballaster, *Seductive forms. Women's amatory fiction from 1684 to 1740* (Oxford, 1992), p. 33. 42 Turner, *Living by the pen*, p. 52. 43 Baker, *The later romances*, pp 164–7. Burney came into contact with a large number of different personali-

guage which surely must have posed difficulties for Irish readers. Take for example the following speech by the coxcomb, Sir Sedley Clarendel:

> Why should it be so vastly horrid an incongruity that a man who, by chance, is rich, should do something for a woman who, by chance, is poor? How immensely important is the prejudice that forbids so natural a use of money? Why should the better half of a man's actions be always under the dominion of some prescriptive slavery?[44]

Eighteenth-century novelists – Richardson, Fielding, Smollett and Sterne

By 1740 all the diverse literary elements of the novel were to hand. They took on a mature form as a distinct literary genre when *Pamela, or Virtue rewarded* appeared in two volumes in November 1740. It was written in the form of 'a series of familiar letters from a beautiful young damsel to her parents, in order to cultivate the principles of virtue and religion in the minds of the youth of both sexes'. This significant development was the work of Richardson, an introverted middle-class printer, who left school at sixteen. The course of his uneventful career can be followed from his long autobiographical letter written in 1753 to one of his admirers and translators in Holland, the Reverend Johannes Stinstra of Harlingen. Richardson was born in Derbyshire in 1689, the son of a joiner who couldn't afford to educate his son for the ministry but had him apprenticed to a printer instead.[45]

From and early age, in his writing career, he displayed a tendency towards moral didacticism. According to Richardson he was only 'eleven years old' when he assumed the persona of an adult and 'wrote spontaneously a letter to a widow of near fifty, who pretending to a zeal for religion and who was a constant frequenter of church ordnances, was continually fomenting quarrels and disturbances, by backbiting and scandal, among all her acquaintance' he 'exhorted her' and 'expostulated with her' to mend her ways. When he was thirteen years old 'all the young women of taste and reading in the neigh-

ties, many of them prominent in literary and artistic circles and in refined society, because she was the daughter of a distinguished master and historian of music Dr Charles Burney, who invited them to his home.   44 Ibid., pp 171–3. Johnson called her a 'character-monger', meaning that her chief effects were obtained in the portraying of character. She is a worthy predecessor of Jane Austen. See Raftery, *Women and learning*, pp 108–11.   45 McKillop, *The early masters*, pp 51–2. Richardson spent seven years of unmitigated drudgery apprenticed to John Wilde but he married his master's daughter and succeeded to the business, which he built up to become one of the most prosperous printing businesses in London. While his work brought Richardson into contact with literary artists such as Aaron Hill, James Thomson and Edward Young, he remained an introvert and there was therefore nothing to suggest or anticipate the creation of *Pamela*.

BLACK GILES,
THE POACHER;
With some Account of
A FAMILY WHO HAD RATHER LIVE BY THEIR WITS THAN THEIR WORK.
IN TWO PARTS.
PART I
TO WHICH IS ADDED,
The Hampshire Tragedy, a true Story.

DUBLIN·
PRINTED FOR WILLIAM WATSON,
NO. 7, CAPEL-STREET,
Printer to the Cheap Repository for Religious and Moral Tracts
And by the Booksellers, Chapmen and HAWKERS
in Town and Country.

PRICE ONE PENNY.

8   Title page from *Black Giles*

bourhood' requested him to read to them when they did their needlework. Three of the group engaged the young Richardson to compose their love-let-ters for them. This experience may well have influenced Richardson's later writing, as the books he read were probably translations of French romances which were popular among women at this time. We know he was acquainted with contemporary plays from his censorious comment on Restoration com-edy in his first published work, *The apprentices vade mecum* (1733). This was a handbook for printers' apprentices which closely resembled the conduct books for servants. In it he complained about 'the popular pantomimes of the day'. Of greater significance was the talent he revealed for caricature in his humorous passages and satiric descriptions which were interspersed with the sober advice. This would later blossom in his delineation of Jackey in *Pamela* or the fops and beaux which appear in his later novels *Clarissa* and *Sir Charles Grandison*. His next published work was also to have a big influence on his creative writing. This was his adaptation of *Aesop's fables* (1739). He freely admitted that it was merely a revision of Sir Roger L'Estrange's edition of 1692. Nonetheless, he learned the value of colloquialisms and the art of nar-ration from l'Estrange and the merit of a lively free-flowing style.[46]

Richardson was just finishing the *Fables* when he received a request from two bookseller friends Charles Rivington and John Osborne in 1739 to write a type of manual which would provide models of business and personal let-ters to assist the semi-literate. The 'letter writer' had been a minor genre of popular literature for over a century at this stage and Richardson simply fol-lowed the tendencies already shown in Henry Care's *Female secretary* (1671) and John Mills' *Secretary's guide* (1687). Literary critics have often seen in *Familiar letters* the 'future Richardsonian characters in embryo'[47] as Richard-son 'was pre-occupied with showing his readers how they should think and act as well as indite'.[48] He became absorbed in his new project especially a section which was to consist of letters from a daughter in service, asking her father's advice when she was threatened by her master's advances – this of course became the germ of *Pamela*. As one critic noted 'The new literature center-ing upon the encounter between a sexually aggressive male and the innocent superior female was the traditional conduct book fictionalised'.[49] But accord-ing to Richardson the plot for *Pamela* was something he elaborated on from an anecdote which had been told to him by a deceased friend. The epistolary method, which the general reader in the 1740s was habituated to, suggested itself to Richardson, as he worked on his book of *Familiar letters*, a task he was obliged to put aside in order to write his novel.

46 M.A.Doody, *A natural passion* (Oxford, 1974), p. 25.   47 Doody, *A natural passion*, p. 29. 48 Day, *Told in letters*, p. 54.   49 M. Le Gates, 'The cult of womanhood in eighteenth-century thought' in *Eighteenth-Century Studies* 10 (1976), pp 21–39. Cited in Turner, *Living by the pen*.

In England *Pamela* was an immediate success and became a bestseller in its first year of publication 'Everybody read it; there was a *Pamela* rage, and *Pamela* motifs appeared on teacups and fans'.[50] It was even recommended from the pulpit in Dr Slocock's famous sermon.[51] Alexander Pope predicted that it would 'do more good than many volumes of sermons'.[52] In less than six months it had gone into a fourth edition, with a fraudulent sequel being published a year later, entitled *Pamela's conduct in high life* by John Kelly.[53] Among the often under-estimated factors in its success was the advertising and promotion that Richardson, as a printer was able to give it, and 'the verbal puffing it received from Aaron Hill and other literary friends of the author'. The books impressive bulk together with its combination of 'warm scenes' and moral preaching would also have added to its popularity.[54] Although it should be added that not all Richardson's contemporaries were happy with the morality of his novel. As Skelton (1977) reminds us 'For some it was disgustingly prurient in its concentration on a young virgin's sexual charms, while some scenes in it were distinctly 'warm''. It is notable that the French translation of the first volume of *Pamela* remained on the index of prohibited books until 1900, when it was replaced by the English original.[55]

The story Richardson told in *Pamela*, or *virtue rewarded* was based on a true story which he had heard from an acquaintance of his youth, about a Mr B. the owner of a great house who married a beautiful and virtuous young girl, one of his mother's maids. After his mother died he tried to seduce the girl. She had recourse to many innocent stratagems to save herself and in the end the squire was so impressed by her virtue that he married her. After she was married, she conducted herself with such humility and charm that she softened the hearts of her husband's disapproving relations. Richardson achieved much in this novel. He created a real life-like character in *Pamela* and he was the first novelist to give an insight into the workings of the female mind, by his innovative method of writing to the moment. He made the novel

50 P. Sabor (ed.), *Pamela* (London, 1987). Margaret A. Doody, 'Introduction', p. 7. 51 Day, *Told in letters*, p. 207. 52 E.A. Baker, *The History of the English novel, Intellectual realism from Richardson to Sterne* (London, 1930), p. 31. 53 App No. 221, p. 558. 54 Day, *Told in letters*, p. 207. 55 D. Skelton, *The English novel* (Devon, 1977), p. 21. Richardson had his detractors among the literati. Samuel Taylor Coleridge (1722–1834) allowed that Richardson had admirable artistic ability but he believed that he was a pedantic, small-minded person, who felt himself to be inferior to his arch-rival Henry Fielding, a superior writer with classical learning. There was some substance to William Hazlett's (1778–1830) criticism that Richardson wrote like an introvert, as he did in fact suffer from anxiety neurosis and rarely socialized. Johnson endorsed Richardson's novels enthusiastically in preference to Fielding's, possibly, as some critics have suggested, because Richardson had once saved him from being arrested for debt, although modern critics reject this suggestion. James Boswell (1740–95) Johnson's Scottish biographer and admirer, disagreed with his mentor and showed a distinct preference for Fielding's work. See Baker, *Intellectual realism*, pp 45–72. See also Watt, *The rise of the novel*, pp 207–97.

respectable by his emphasis on serious morality, contrary to Fielding's assertion in his pamphlet *An apology for the life of Mrs Shamela Andrews* that *Pamela* possessed very little virtue and a great deal of hypocrisy. He banished the overt author by using the epistolary technique. By making a common servant the heroine and writer, he raised the ordinary person, the colloquial and the familiar to significance.[56]

Richardson's masterpiece *Clarissa* (1747–8) appeared first in seven volumes, and then in an edition of eight volumes, with letters and passages restored from the original manuscript (1749–51). This was the longest of Richardson's works, written in the epistolary form. It consisted of more than five hundred letters, and contained an estimated million words. The interest rested mainly on the psychological insights received rather than on the development of the theme, which was so slow that Johnson quipped 'if you were to read Richardson for the story, your patience would be so much fretted that you would hang yourself'.[57] In *Clarissa* there were four chief correspondents, two young ladies of honour Miss Clarissa Harlowe and Miss Howe and two gentlemen of free lives, Mr Lovelace and Mr Belford. Clarissa was the beautiful daughter of a wealthy but avaricious gentleman who had ambitions to raise his family to the rank of the nobility. Lovelace, on the advice of his uncle, paid court to the younger daughter of Mr Harlowe, who had just inherited a fortune. When he addressed himself to the wrong sister, he transferred his attention to Clarissa but she wasn't responsive to his advances, due to his notorious reputation. Her brother James and the family urged Clarissa to marry Roger Solmes, a suitor she despised, solely because his estate lay contiguous to the one James stood to inherit. Richardson was merely depicting social life as it was in eighteenth-century England, when financial marriages were commonplace as the land poor nobility became reliant on middle class cash. In desperation, Clarissa rather unwisely sought the assistance of Richard Lovelace who abused her trust and decoyed her from the house, after she had refused to elope with him. As soon as Clarissa was in his power, he looked for revenge by seducing her, drugging her and then raping her. She escaped from confinement, during the temporary absence of Lovelace and placed herself under the protection of Belford.[58] *Clarissa* was so real to Richardson's readers that he received many requests to contrive a happy ending, a temptation he resisted. In the end Clarissa's cousin and guardian Col Morden sought summary justice and avenged her death in a duel in which Lovelace was fatally wounded.[59]

56 Neill, *A short history*, pp 52–4.   57 W. Forsyth, *The novels and novelists of the eighteenth century* (London, 1970), p. 219.   58 Baker, *Intellectual realism*, pp 37–44.   59 Ibid., p. 54. The appeal of *Clarissa* was wide-ranging from Lady Wortley Montagu, Fielding's cousin, to Lord Chesterfield (1694–1773) and Lord Macauley (1700–59) historian and statesman. Richardson was unrivalled as a novelist until the publication of Fielding's masterpiece *Tom Jones* (1749).

In 1754 Richardson produced his third novel *Sir Charles Grandison* which came in seven volumes and told the story of a flawless, colourless hero. It was Richardson's most ambitious undertaking as he introduced over fifty characters. The heroine who rivalled the hero in human perfection, was Miss Harriet Byron. The third major character was the misguided Italian girl Clementina, who loved Sir Charles, but who left him as she was drawn towards the religious life. Harriet had a moderate fortune and many suitors, one of whom was Sir Hargrave Pollexfen, baronet, who decided to abduct her after a ball only to be apprehended by Sir Charles who arrived just in time to rescue her. Much later Sir Charles revealed to Harriet that he was conscious of her regard for him but that he was already committed in honour to Clementina della Poretta. Clementina was so distraught after his departure from Italy, that her family requested him to return. They informed him that even though he was a foreigner and a heretic, they would accept him as a son-in-law, on condition that he converted to Catholicism and resided in Italy. These conditions were unacceptable to Sir Charles but now Clementina had a relapse into melancholia and the hero received an invitation to Italy to discuss new settlement terms. During the complex negotiations Harriet was pining for Sir Charles in London when Clementina finally realised that she couldn't possibly marry a non-Catholic, preferring instead to take the veil. Sir Charles was now free to marry Harriet but it took Richardson almost two volumes to relate the event. Sir Charles eventually married her. But Greville, a former suitor of the bride, decided he would like to fight Sir Charles, but happily he was disarmed. Sir Hargreave Pollexfen died and left most of his property to the happy couple. The story might well have ended there but it didn't. Clementina arrived in England in a very distracted state, followed by her parents, who managed to persuade her to look favourably on the suit of the count of Belvedere, now that she had abandoned the religious life.

The novel *Sir Charles Grandison* was quite an achievement for its time. Johnson acknowledged as much after he had read it, with these words: 'You, Sir, have beyond all other men the art of improving on yourself'.[60] Few critics have complimentary comments to make about Richardson's skill at characterisation. Baker called Grandison the 'faultless monster that the world ne'er saw', and Forsyth saw him as 'too much of a paragon – too much praised by everybody'. The problem lay with the superhuman task that Richardson had set himself of creating the ideal gentleman, an anti-type to Lovelace and Fielding's *Tom Jones*. Not alone that but Grandison was expected to demonstrate exactly how a good life was to be led and this necessitated much preaching and moralising by the hero.[61] Richardson did however, display great

60 J. Harris (ed), *The history of Sir Charles Grandison* (Oxford, 1972), p. 22.   61 Forsyth, *The novels and novelists*, pp 244–5. The novelist who followed closely in his path, Jane Austen

narrative skill and command of fluent dialogue. His familiarity with the romance genre would appear to have been due to his French predecessor Madame de la Fayette. He mentioned her in *Sir Charles Grandison* – her novel *La princesse de Cléves* (1678) was one which Harriet's grandmother, Mrs Shirley, read when she was young. Richardson's singular achievement in his novels was not so much an innovation as an adaptation of popular feminine and domestic fiction and the development of the romance and fable from 'low' fiction to a more elevated plane so that it became part of the tradition of the novel, not only in England but also in Europe.[62]

Richardson's antagonist Henry Fielding, made a more significant contribution to the development of the novel genre. He was very different from his rival in his ancestry and in his intellectual capacity. His father Edmund Fielding, served as an officer under Marlborough and was the grandson of the earl of Desmond, and great-grandson of the earl of Denbigh. His father was a gambler and when his mother died, Henry, aged eleven, was sent to Eton where he remained until he was eighteen or nineteen, where he became a proficient Latin scholar. In 1728 he made his way to London where he published a satirical poem, *The masquerade* and a comedy, *Love in seven masques*. After this he went to the university of Leyden where he studied classical literature but he had to leave after only eighteen months, due to financial difficulties. He was then obliged to return to London to take up his career as a playwright. Between 1729 and 1737 Fielding wrote some twenty five dramatic pieces of great variety. He had a strong antipathy to hypocrisy and the double standard, sentiments reflected in his two satires against the corrupt administration of Robert Walpole (1676–1745) – *Pasquin* (1736) and *The historical register* (1737). His satirical arrows were too well pointed because they led Walpole to introduce the Theatrical Licensing Act (1737), which brought Fielding's career as a playwright and theatre manager to an abrupt end. Now he was forced to support himself by incidental writing.

In April 1740, following the third edition of *Pamela*, Fielding published his sixty page pamphlet *An apology for the life of Mrs Shamela Andrews ... by Mr Conny Keyber*, the authorship of which he consistently denied.[63] Fielding took exception to what he considered the dubious moral values promoted in

(1775–1817) testified to his remarkable achievement with her comment that 'Every circumstance narrated in *Sir Charles Grandison*, all that was ever said or done in the cedar parlour, was familiar to her'. It is likely that she was influenced by the scene where Sir Hargreave Pollexfen proposed to Miss Byron, when she came to write her own celebrated declaration of Mr Collin's proposal in *Pride and prejudice* (1797). See Harris, *The history of Sir Charles*, p. 23.   62 Baker, *Intellectual realism*, p. 69. His novel *Pamela* ushered in the romantic era (1790s, 1800s) and was to influence Russeau, Diderot, Goethe and Pushkin. See Doody, 'Introduction', p. 8. See also Baker, *Intellectual realism*, p. 76.   63 Op. cit., pp 86–7. He imputed it to Colley Cibber (1651–1757) English dramatist and actor of limited ability, the butt of satirists jokes, among

Pamela, which were clear from the sub-title *virtue rewarded*. Throughout the novel, Pamela's 'virtue' was equated with the defence of her chastity. Her stalwart defence was finally rewarded by her marriage to a landed gentleman. Fielding suggested that Pamela had taken one step beyond prostitution.[64] He argued that this was the message in *Shamela's* much quoted line: 'I thought once of making a little fortune by my person, I now intend to make a great one by my virtue'.[65] What Fielding failed to see was that Pamela was in fact behaving according to the feminine code of her time, as Richardson explained in Johnson's periodical *The Rambler* (1751) 'the feminine role in courtship made it immoral as well as impolite for a girl to allow herself to feel love for a suitor until he had actually asked for her hand in marriage'.[66] In *Shamela* Fielding parodied not only the morality of the fable of *Pamela* but also the technical means by which Richardson attempted to persuade the reader of the realism of his fiction.[67]

Ten months later *Joseph Andrews* (1742),[68] his first novel appeared in two volumes, which according to the title page, was *written in imitation of the manner of Cervantes*, author of *Don Quixote*. The novel contained many satirical references to Pamela but the novel was much more than a caricaturing of *Pamela*. The plot of *Joseph Andrews* was a burlesque on romantic plots in general but the novel was pure comedy, not burlesque. His narrative contained repeated ironic assurances that the book was a 'true history', these assurances occurring at the most unlikely points in the plot. Unlike Richardson, he introduced himself in the novel as the author even though he recounted a plot which was by no means realistically convincing. He declared that his story was fictitious and his characters invented. He often matched characters in contrasting pairs such as Adams and Trulliber, the good and bad parsons. He displayed no interest whatsoever in psychological realism, but he created something entirely new in fiction – a wide range of characters, well observed and drawn from all classes of society, from effeminate fops to cheating lawyers and brutal squires. This was a comic novel in which Fielding displayed a tolerance of human weakness and an acceptance of both the good and the bad in humanity.

In his preface to *Joseph Andrews* Fielding announced that he proposed to give the English reader an example of a new kind of writing. He wanted to create a comic romance, which was to be a 'comic epic poem in prose, differing from comedy, as the serious epic from tragedy'. This comedy was to have its source in affectation because he believed that affectation was caused by one of the two weaknesses of vanity and hypocrisy. The biggest influence on

them Fielding.   **64** S. Copley (ed.), *Joseph Andrews* (London, 1987), p. 5.   **65** A.J. Smallwood, *Fielding and the woman question* (London, 1989), p. 59.   **66** Watt, *The rise of the novel*, p. 189. **67** Copley, *Joseph Andrews*, p. 5.   **68** H. Fielding, *The history of the adventures of Joseph Andrews* (Dublin, 1767), App. No. 221, p. 558.

Fielding's writing was the picaresque style popularised by Cervantes, Le Sage (1688–1747), and Scarron. He was also acquainted with the works of the French dramatist and novelist Pierre Marivaux (1688–1763), who was celebrated for his comedies. His novel was not quite as successful as Richardson's *Pamela* even though it went into three editions, it still only sold half the number of copies which were sold of *Pamela* at the same time. This was probably due to the fact that Fielding made many enemies because of the unrestrained political and social satire of his plays and by his outspoken journalism. Fielding's biggest contribution to this genre was that he freed the novel from its slavery to fact and to realistic detail. It became as a result, a much more flexible genre for the novelist to work in, and with the reading public, an immensely popular one as well. They had been given the novel of sensibility by Richardson and the novel of character and humour by Fielding and to these Smollett now added satiric caricature.

Smollett came from an eminent Scottish family, being the grandson of Sir James Smollett, the laird of Bonhill. Sir James strongly disapproved of his son's match and therefore furnished Smollett's parents with just enough money to live on. After his father died Smollett was well educated but he had no personal fortune at his disposal. He attended Glasgow university for some years but never graduated. Next he became apprenticed to two local surgeons and it was at this stage he wrote a play, a tragedy called *The regicide*. He left the apprenticeship in 1739 and headed for London in an effort to have his play staged but he was to be bitterly disappointed, as every theatre manager he approached rejected it. Smollett, who was irascible of temper, allowed his resentment to smoulder for years afterwards.[69] This prompted him to leave London, abandon his writing and pursue his medical career. He took the unconventional route to do so however, by going to sea in March 1740 as a surgeon's mate, on board H.M.S. *Chichester*. This was a naval expedition under Admiral Vernon, which took part in the unsuccessful war against Spain at Carthagena. Smollett found the whole experience most unpleasant but it provided him with the inspiration for a new vein of naval fiction which would have far-fetching effects on the English novel of the future. Smollett married a Jamaican Nancy Lascalles and on the strength of her dowry returned to England in 1742 and set up in practice as a surgeon in the exclusive Downing Street quarter of London. He entertained lavishly and lived beyond his means and soon financial problems forced him to leave medicine and turn to literature to earn a living.

This was a fortuitous move because at twenty six years of age Smollett was to become a best-selling author. His first novel *Roderick Random* was published anonymously on 21 January 1748 and as the authorship was disclosed

69 P.-G. Boucé (ed.), *The adventures of Roderick Random* (Oxford, 1979), p. 19.

he soon became one of the most popular novelists in the eighteenth century. By November 1749 *Roderick Random* was in its third edition and it was translated into German (1754), French (1761) and Russian (1788). By 1750 the novel was so well known that one racehorse owner took the unusual step of calling one of his horses *Roderick Random*.[70] The popularity of the novel cannot be attributed to its lighthearted or uplifting nature. It was written by an angry young man of the 1740s with a bleak, pessimistic outlook on life. Very few characters were set in a pleasing light except at someone else's expense. Many readers were offended by his blatant vulgarity and Rabelaisian humour and his vicious personal attacks against the people who had rejected or criticised his play in 1739, and against his rival Fielding whom he suspected of plagiarism. The novel appeared to be autobiographical, although Smollett strongly denied this. However, the comparisons between the life of the selfish and unprincipled hero and that of his creator were striking. Roderick was a Scotsman, the grandson of a wealthy gentleman who disapproved of his father's marriage. Tom Bowling was Roderick's maternal uncle who rescued him from an indifferent grandfather and a horde of acquisitive cousins. His uncle was obliged to go to sea again and Roderick was left to fend for himself. He set out on his journey to London to seek his fortune with his old school friend Strap. Sensational incidents followed in rapid succession very much in the style made famous by Scarron. Like Smollett, Roderick was eventually given the post of surgeon's mate on a man-of-war, which sailed with the Carthagena squadron. Smollett displayed remarkable literary talent in this novel, especially in his discovery of the seafaring tribe, who were all individual creations. This was something unique in English literature. They consisted of Lieutenant Bowling and Jack Rattlin with Commodore Trunnion, Jack Hathway and Tom Pipes, who gave such a display of sparkling wit and imagination, even though Fielding dismissed Smollett's mariners as 'monsters, not men'.[71]

In 1751 Smollett produced his second picaresque novel *The adventures of Peregrine Pickle*.[72] In it he rendered a most entertaining account of the bizarre behaviour of the nautical trio, Trunnion, Hatchway, and Pipes, now living on land. Smollett told the story of Peregrine who was an object of scorn even to his own mother so that his father Gamaliel secured a foster parent for him in Commodore Hauser Trunnion. This was an eccentric seafaring man, who lived in a neighbouring garrison, defended by walls and a moat. He and his old comrade, Hatchway, and the boatswain, Pipes, maintained the same sort of life on land that they used to lead on shipboard. Women were not allowed entry after dark. Evenso Trunnion, who was a confirmed misogynist was

70 D. Blewett (ed.), *Roderick Random* (London, 1995), p. 11.   71 Baker, *Intellectual realism*, pp 203–6.   72 Dublin, 1751; App. No. 221, p. 556.

helpless against the extreme seductive methods applied by Gamaliel Pickle's sister Grizzle, one of Smollett's more grotesque creations. She had 'a very wan, not to say sallow complexion, a cast in her eye, and an enormous mouth and was slightly addicted to brandy'. She was assisted by Hatchway, who persuaded Pipes to lower a bunch of rotten and phosphorescent whitings down Trunnion's chimney, with the aid of a rope. This he did while Hatchway used a speaking trumpet to challenge the terrified sailor to yield to the lady's advances, which he felt compelled to do 'against the current of my inclination'.[73] One of the most memorable scenes in the novel was Trunnion's death-bed scene, in which Smollett wrought pathos out of the seaman's speech, in a performance reminiscent of the death of Shakespeare's rogue character Jack Falstaff in *King Henry IV. Part I.*

> Swab the spray from your bousprit, my good lad, and coil up your spirits. Many a better man has foundered before he has made half my way; tho I trust, by the mercy of God, I shall be sure in port in a very few glasses, and fast moored in a most blessed riding, for my good friend Jolter has overhauled the journal of my sins; and by the observation he hath taken of the state of my soul, I hope I shall happily conclude my voyage and he brought up in the latitude of heaven.[74]

Smollett used a well-known marketing strategy when writing this novel. He included a sensational episode in the tradition of the interpolated history or chronique scandaleuse, favoured by the notorious triumvirate of Behn, Manley and Haywood. He called it *Memoirs of a lady of quality*. These were the scandalous recollections of a well-known lady of fashion called Lady Vane, who was more noted for her amours than her probity.[75] The novel finished in a similar mode to that of *Roderick Random*. Peregrine was arrested for debt and lodged in the Fleet, just as Random was at the Marshalsea. Then in a final reversal, he secured a fortune when his father died intestate, and a bride when Emilia forgave him for his past misdeeds. Near the end of 1757 Smollett expurgated the original to remove or soften the bitter personal attacks on his erstwhile enemies. Revisions were also made in the *Memoirs* of Lady Vane, at her request. No doubt Smollett's change of heart was precipitated by the rebukes of his critics. It wasn't until the turn of the century that he finally got the credit he deserved for his remarkable skill at creating vivid eccentric

73 Forsyth, *The novels and novelists*, p. 281. 74 J.L. Clifford (ed.), *The adventures of Perigrine Pickle* (Oxford, 1964), p. 392. 75 Ibid., p. 16. Samuel Richardson called it 'the very bad story of a wicked woman'. Surprisingly the 'Queen of the blues' Elizabeth Montagu recommended it in a letter to her sister Lady Mary Wortley Montagu. See Clifford, *The adventures of Peregrine Pickle*, p. 17. Mary Delany (1700-88) friend of Swift's and once referred to by George III as his 'dearest Mrs Delany', regarded it as 'wretched stuff'.

types with their picturesque nautical lingo. *Peregrine Pickle* was eventually acknowledged 'as a masterpiece even if a scandalous one'.[76] It even had curative powers if one is to believe the reported story of a London physician who had a 'pleasant habit of writing on his prescription ... recipe, every day for a few hours, several pages of *Peregrine Pickle*'.[77]

For Smollett's third novel *The adventures of Ferdinand Count Fathom* (1753) he borrowed the idea of a scoundrel-hero from Fielding, only the tone Smollett used was not one of ironical admiration. He also borrowed from Shakespeare. As a result his work was derivative, and read as if it had been translated from another language. This would lend some weight to Thackeray's suggestion that 'Smollett didn't invent much'.[78] He used a curious mixture of styles in this novel, as Baker observed 'First, he confounds the tale of picaresque adventure with the criminal biography: then he changes over to crude romance'. The most noteworthy feature of this novel was the atmosphere of terror and suspense which Smollett successfully created, which gave a foretaste of the gothic novel of terror. His account of Ferdinand's night in the forest was in this vein, with 'the emotional diction as well as the landscape-painting of the Radcliffe school, but a generation earlier'.[79]

Smollett had a far from endearing personality and tended to attract more enemies than friends because of his outspokenness. Admiral Knowles took his displeasure with Smollett's written disapproval of his conduct during the Carthagena expedition, to the courts. Smollett was fined and imprisoned for three months in the King's Bench (1759) for libelling Admiral Knowles in the May 1758 edition of the *Critical Review*. While in prison he spent his time writing chapters of his next novel *The adventures of Sir Launcelot Greaves*. The novel appeared as a serial in a new periodical the *British Magazine*, which Smollett himself edited, assisted by Goldsmith.[80] It was, however, hastily and carelessly written, with resultant repetitiveness and occasional inconsistencies.

Smollett had completed his translation of *Don Quixote* in 1755 and he incorporated some of its elements into his novel. *Launcelot Greaves* had only a few scenes specifically imitated from *Don Quixote* but what Smollett owed to Cervantes was the basic metaphor of the hero as both satirist and knight errant. One of the most attractive features of the novel was the idea of a group

76 Clifford, *The adventures of Peregrine Pickle*, pp 18–19. A second edition was not called for until 1758, at which stage Smollett's animosity towards Fielding, and David Garrick (1717–1779) and George Lyttleton (1709–73) first baron and liberal patron of literature, had mellowed. Many of the great romantic poets and writers of the nineteenth century such as Wordsworth, Coleridge, Lamb, Dickens and Hazlett were youthful admirers of Smollett.   77 Ibid., p. 29.   78 D. Grant (ed), *The adventures of Ferdinand Count Fathom* (Oxford, 1971), p. 11. 79 Baker, *Intellectual realism*, pp 217–8.   80 Ibid., pp 220–1. This novel was listed in App No. 221, p. 557. According to Sir Walter Scott, Smollett wrote some of the chapters hurriedly and haphazardly during a visit to a Scottish friend in 1760. In order to meet the 'post time' he neglected to correct or even proof read his script.

of varied caricatures, who formed around Sir Launcelot.[81] There was the obligatory seafaring member Captain Crowe who spoke in rich nautical metaphors and nurtured a deep distrust of lawyers. There was the fashionable sentimental character Clarke, who responded emotionally to scenes of distress. Smollett produced not one but two Quixotes as Sir Launcelot had his Sancho Panza in Timothy Crabshaw and a double in Captain Crowe. Among the corrupt public servants that the group encountered, those most sharply delineated were the election candidates and the justice of the peace. Smollett used broad irony in the scene at the hustings when he parodied the political speeches of both candidates to expose their selfish motives. Sir Launcelot's role in the novel was that of redressor of grievances and spokesman for the values he represented. Here he outlined the ideal qualifications of a candidate for parliament as well as the considerations that should occupy the mind of the ideal voter.[82] Smollett's novel got a disappointing reception when it was first published in 1762. It was acknowledged in a single line in the *Critical Review*.[83] Nonetheless he introduced an innovative feature into the novel form when instead of the conventional methodical introduction he painted 'a little tableau in the Scarron style'. The scene opened with a group of travellers, the landlady and her two daughters, immersed in natural conversation, in the kitchen of the Black Lion hostelry. Regular narrative was dispensed with and the story proceeded by means of dialogue and word-play. What Smollett produced was a conversation novel, but one which also included incidents.

Just when it seemed that the novel form and structure had been established, along came Laurence Sterne who produced a novel without a plot, a heroine or any action whatsoever. He didn't adhere to any novelistic parameters, but he did succeed in demonstrating just how flexible a form the novel was when new styles and techniques were applied to it. He showed that action wasn't essential when ideas or verbal banter could be substituted for it. Two elderly gentlemen with a passion for talking could engross the reader just as much as the exploits of the heroes and heroines of romance. There was nothing in Sterne's upbringing or education to indicate that he would be the originator of a masterly work like *Tristram Shandy* (1759–67). Born in Clonmel, Co. Tipperary, in 1713, the son of an ensign in an infantry regiment, the family followed the regiment about until his father died when Laurence was aged eighteen. It was from these many wanderings about with the regiment that

81 David Evans (ed.), *The life and adventures of Sir Launcelot Greaves* (Oxford, 1973), pp 11–13.
82 Ibid., p. 17. It is possible that the idea for this scene received its impetus from W. Hogarth's (1697–1764) *Four prints of an election* (1755–8) based on an Oxfordshire contest of 1754, as Smollett was an admirer of the satirical painter and he alluded to Hogarth in all his novels with the exception of *Ferdinand Count Fathom*. Both Smollett and Hogarth viewed the social life of eighteenth-century England with critical eyes, but used different artistic mediums to convey their displeasure.   83 Ibid., p. 10.

Sterne gained familiarity with military life, a knowledge he brought to bear on *Tristram Shandy*. In 1733 he was admitted to a sizarship at Jesus College, Cambridge. Having graduated, he was ordained in January 1736, and through the influence of his clergyman uncle, Jacques, received the benefice of Sutton-in-the-Forest. He remained there until 1759, the year he started his novel.[84]

In 1759 Sterne published the first part of his great anti-novel, the full title of which was *The life and opinions of Tristram Shandy, gentleman*, in which he parodied the characteristics and problems of the new genre. He started with Fielding's literary method of writing a comic epic in prose by suggesting that *Tristram Shandy* was not following any classical authorities such as Horace. He also parodied the idea of Richardson's characters 'writing to the moment'. *Tristram Shandy* seemed to start out in the tone of an autobiography, but then it suddenly changed course and strayed into a description of the hero's birth. Tristram wasn't in fact born until the end of the fourth volume. Although the reader was assured, even from the title of the book, that his life and opinions would be set out, his life was hardly mentioned. The only opinions expressed came from his father, the 'great motive monger'[85] who possessed a theory on most issues. But like Sir Roger de Coverley's ideas, Mr Shandy's were loosely based in the world of reality. He was a quixotic figure and Toby acted as his Sancho Panza. They were figures of the purest comedy who dovetailed perfectly. The same could not be said of the comical partnership of Mr and Mrs Shandy, who were quite incompatible. Mr Shandy, who was 'master of one of the finest chains of reasoning in nature' was married to a woman 'with such a head-piece that he cannot hang up a single influence within side of it, to save his soul from destruction'.[86]

Sterne's method of narration had no precedent but he claimed to have based it on Locke's theory of the association of ideas, which he applied to the 'individual and eccentric mental behaviour'[87] of Mr Shandy. He used Locke's principles in the portrayal of character and sentiment and as a connecting thread between them. Underlying the movement of the whole book was another philosophical conception derived from Locke, which was to do with the time-shift in the novel and Locke's theory of duration. Sterne was interested in the discrepancy between duration in terms of chronological and psy-

---

84 Baker, *Intellectual realism*, pp 245–6. Sterne had access to Hall-Stevenson's library and also to the library at York. He borrowed from both without restraint. Baker described Sterne as 'a genius among plagiarists who robbed unrestrainedly and unashamedly from his predecessors', a charge Sterne openly admitted to. When his library was sold in 1768 his sources were apparent. The main sources of his literary inspiration were Burton's *Anatomy of melancholy*, Cervantes' *Don Quixote*, the *Histories of Gargantua* by F. Rabelais (1494–1553) and the philosophical treatises of John Locke.   85 Skelton, *The English novel*, pp 46–8.   86 Neill, *A short history*, p. 74.   87 Op. cit., p. 47.

chological time. His main interest lay in the states of mind and the character of the protagonists rather than their actions. The true duration was therefore subjective, measured by values, not by the clock. It consequently varied in length with each individual, having regard to the circumstances and frame of mind in which he happened to be.[88] This concept of a background of duration, distinct from the physic time, perceived in the passage of ideas through the mind was vital in Sterne's narrative method. He was the first novelist to apply it deliberately to fiction.

Perhaps the greatest curiosity of this novel was its actual form. In the book everything was displaced and transposed. The dedication turned up after the first two chapters, in violation of the conventions of content, form and place. Likewise the preface was misplaced. It occurred in chapter twenty of volume three, rather than at the beginning of volume one. Sterne confided in the reader: 'all my heroes are off my hands: 'tis the first time I have had a moment to spare – and I'll make use of it, and write my preface'. The confusion was added to by the displacement of chapters eighteen and nineteen of volume nine so that they followed chapter twenty five. Sterne's motivation was to teach a lesson to all future novelists that they might adopt an individualistic approach to story telling. 'All I wish is, that it may be a lesson to the world, to let people tell their stories their own way'.[89] His novel had an extraordinary international vogue with streams of translations, imitations, and spurious continuations still appearing in the nineteenth century, but it shocked the literati of the day. Walpole and Goldsmith were critical of it on moral and literary grounds. Richardson saw little in it but 'unaccountable wildness, whimsical incoherence, uncommon indecencies'. Johnson, made an erroneous judgement regarding the future of *Tristram Shandy* when he predicted that 'nothing odd will do long. *Tristram Shandy* did not last'.[90]

In October 1765 Sterne set out on a seven months tour through France and Italy and later wrote about it in his travel novel *A sentimental journey* (1768). In ways this account was typical of the many other travel books of the period, in that it too conveyed sympathy for the living conditions of men and of all living creatures. Sterne stated as much when he said it was designed 'to teach us to love the world and our fellow-creatures better than we do' only he emphasised 'those gentler passions and affections which aid so much to general goodwill'. Sentimentalism was an integral part of Sterne's philosophy. He preached a gospel of obedience to the feelings alone because he believed that 'When the heart flies out before the understanding, it saves the judgement a world of pains'. He contended that man upset his equilibrium by con-

88 A.A. Mendilow, 'The revolt of Sterne' in John Traugott (ed.), *Laurence Sterne. A collection of critical essays* (Englewood Cliffs, NJ, 1968).   89 V. Shklovsky, 'A parodying novel. Sterne's Tristram Shandy' in *Laurence Sterne. A collection of critical essays*, p. 67.   90 Traugott, 'Laurence Sterne', p. 2.

sulting his reason alone. He wrote: 'I was never able to conquer any one single bad sensation in my heart so decisively as by beating up as fast as I could
for some kindly and gentle sensation to fight it upon its own ground'.[91] It was
a happy coincidence that Sterne's refined sentimental style suited the new
fashion for sensibility in the 1760s. In fact this trend owed much to his first
novel *Tristram Shandy* and to scenes like Le Fever's death, or Uncle Toby
sparing the life of a fly.

Baker attributed the artistic style of writing employed by Sterne in this
novel, to his exceptional artistic ability. During his years as vicar of Sutton, he
displayed talent as an artist and a keen appreciation of music, so that it was
hardly surprising that he should produce a 'masterpiece of a new style of art
impressionism', namely *A sentimental journey*, which was a series of such
impressions. There is much merit in Baker's analysis of Sterne's technique
and in his rejection of the influence of Locke's theory of sensation on the
novel. Sterne prided himself on his familiarity with Locke's philosophy. He
quoted copiously from his *Essay concerning human understanding*, and he would
have justified his method 'by appealing to the great empiricist's theory of sensation', but as Baker pointed out, Sterne's work owed little to philosophy and
everything to impressionism, because his very reasoning was 'a stringing
together of impressions'[92]. Yet it is to Sterne that English fiction is indebted
for the novel of sentimentality and stream of consciousness.

Literature of terror or Gothic literature

The Augustan writers of the eighteenth century had been superseded by the
four major novelists, whose works contained antithetical elements to Augus-
tanism. The novels of Richardson, Fielding and Smollett also contained elements which preshadowed the Gothic novels. According to Watt in *The rise of
the novel* (1979) *Tom Jones* contained 'the first Gothic mansion in the history
of the novel', and the death scene at the end of Richardson's *Clarissa* could be
regarded as graveyard literature comparable to the death–gloom of the graveyard poetry of Edward Young (1683–1765), Thomas Gray (1716–71) and
Thomas Parnell (1679–1718).[93] With Fielding and Richardson we see the
gathering together of Gothic props, but 'the first important eighteenth-century work to propose terror as a subject for novelistic writing was Smollett's
Ferdinand Count Fathom'.[94] In it Smollett furnished something of a link
between realism and Gothic.

91 Baker, *Intellectual realism*, pp 260–1.   92 op. cit., p. 263.   93 F. R. Karl, *A reader's guide to the
development of the English novel in the eighteenth century* (London, 1975), p. 237.   94 Punter, *The
literature of terror*, p. 40.

The Gothic novels challenged the novel internally within twenty years of the firm establishment of the genre. They were written not as a form of escapism but as a form of revolt against the constraints which the philosophy of the Enlightenment, with its emphasis on reason, placed on the English reading habits of the people. The Gothic writer reflected the self-confidence of an age, which rejected hypocrisy, the denial of the emotions and the emphasis on empirical facts, by writing in an anti-realist mode.[95] Bayer-Berenbaum in *The Gothic imagination* (1982) drew attention to the fact that Gothic literature was an outcome of the revolutionary upheavals in Europe. She supported her argument by citing Bréton, a spokesman for surrealism, who considered 'Gothicism a revolutionary art form produced by revolutionary sentiments'. Varma spoke of these same revolutionary tendencies in *The Gothic flame* (1957), and related the Gothic novel directly to the French revolution, as did Sadlier in his essay *The Northanger novels: a footnote to Jane Austen* (1927). He wrote: 'The Gothic romance and the French symbolist movement were in their small way as much an expression of a deep subversive impulse as were the French revolution itself and the grim gathering of forces for industrial war'.[96]

Gothic writers were revolutionary insofar as they spurned the common restrictive bounds by providing literature which gave scope for the portrayal of violent emotion, even in the most improbable settings and implausible circumstances. A striking feature of this new romantic period was the strong interest shown in the past. In the 1790s 'the literary market was flooded with a mass of fiction which rejected direct engagement with the activities of contemporary life in favour of geographically remote action and settings'.[97] The main criterion was that the past should differ from the present, so the Gothic writers revived the middle ages in the literary and artistic sense, and their revived existence was then interwoven into the life of the present. The new era of Gothic romanticism emphasised passion, emotion, fear and mystery. The setting for most Gothic novels was an ancient, lonely, ruinous castle or abbey, with dark corridors and forbidden chambers to convey a special atmosphere of awe and horror to stimulate the emotion of fear in the reader. Gothicism answered the need for the release of strong emotions following great social upheavals. Bayer-Berenbaum observed that the 'Romantic qualities of yearning, aspiration, mystery and wonder nourished the roots of the Gothic movement' and that 'Sensualism, sensationalism, and then sadism were nurtured in an orgy of emotion'.

The conventions of the Gothic novel were established by Walpole, son of the famous whig minister Sir Robert Walpole, Radcliffe and Lewis. But Goth-

---

95 Punter, *The literature of terror*, p. 85. **96** Linda Bayer-Berenbaum, *The Gothic imagination* (New Jersey, 1982), pp 42–3. **97** op. cit., p. 54.

ic was neither uniform nor constant as Karl (1975) pointed out, 'there were vast differences between Radcliffe's 'romantic' Gothic and the psychologically harrowing Gothic of Matthew Lewis'.[98] Varma outlined the development of Gothic from the main stream of Gothic romance which issued from Walpole's *The castle of Otranto* (1764), and which diverged into three parallel channels; the Gothic-historical type developed by Clara Reeve and the Lee sisters, Sophia and Harriet, especially Sophia Lee's *The recess* (1783–5); secondly the school of terror initiated by Radcliffe: and lastly the works of the Schauer-Romantiks or the school of horror followed by Lewis.[99]

While Walpole wasn't the sole founder of Gothic, it was he who brought together the various elements we now identify as typical of the genre: 'The Gothic machinery, the atmosphere of gloom and terror, and stock romantic characters'. In his preface to the second edition of *The castle of Otranto* Walpole said that his book was an attempt to unite the 'imagination and improbability' of romance with 'nature', because in contemporary fiction 'the great resources of fancy [had] been damned up by strict adherence to common life'.[100] As Punter noted, this novel was in fact 'the earliest and most important manifestation of the late eighteenth-century revival of romance, that is of the older traditions of prose literature', which had been supplanted by the rise of the novel.[101] *The castle of Otranto* was set around the twelfth century and it took place in a fantastic version of the writer's own house at Strawberry Hall, fictionally expanded from a decorated villa into an ancient Italian castle. It had many of the ingredients of romance – a tyrannical feudal baron, complicated revelations about paternity and a host of supernatural portents such as an armoury of magical helmets, speaking pictures and ghostly giants. Punter drew attention to the fact that in *The castle of Otranto* Walpole gave the eighteenth century perspective and viewpoint on feudalism and the aristocracy by using what was to become a favourite theme in Gothic fiction – the revisiting of the sins of the fathers upon their children. In this, Walpole clearly appealed to the keenness of the middle classes to read about the aristocracy. His book proved very popular and quickly ran into more than a hundred and fifteen editions since it first appeared and was published anonymously.

Walpole consistently associated his work with the drama and claimed that his method was a combination of low-comedy and high-tragedy, based on no less an authority than Shakespeare's practice in *Hamlet* (1601) and *Julius Caesar* (1599).[102] He effected this Shakespearean contrast by juxtaposing the 'sublime' experiences of the principal characters with the comic naivety of the domestic ancillaries in order to set 'the former in a stronger light'.[103] Walpole

98 Karl, *A reader's guide*, p. 238.   99 D. Prasad Varma, *The Gothic flame: being a history of the Gothic novel in England: its origins, efflorescences, disintegration, and residuary influences* (London, 1957), p. 206.   100 Skelton, *The English novel*, p. 60.   101 Punter, *The literature of terror*, p. 43. 102 Karl, *A reader's guide*, p. 242.   103 Skelton, *The English novel*, p. 60.

tried to make the supernatural appear natural by asking the reader to excuse 'the air of the miraculous' and to 'allow the possibility of the facts'. He tried to turn the unusual into realistic detail by informing the reader that he was no more than a translator of a manuscript found in the library of 'an ancient Catholic family in the north of England'.[104] Walpole's familiarity with oriental fairy tales was evident from the style adopted in the beginning of *The castle of Otranto*. Manfred, prince of Otranto, had one son and one daughter. The motifs of cruel parenthood and of one lovely and one unlovely child are originally oriental.

Walpole originated the Gothic genre but it was another thirteen years before a successor appeared in Clara Reeve, whose novel *The old English baron* was published in 1777. Despite the long gap, there was specific continuity between Walpole and Reeve as both produced 'framed' narratives or texts purporting to be manuscripts which they discovered and of which they were, supposedly, the 'editors'. But there were also marked differences in theme and style between the two writers. Reeve tried to combine the supernatural features of *The castle of Otranto* with the historical settings of such novels as Thomas Leland's *Longsword* (1762) and William Hutchinson's *The hermitage: a British story* (1772), to give narrative interest to a tale with a didactic purpose. To Reeve the past was not a source of fear and wonder, but a source of comfort. The supernatural was not terrifying and ghosts were dealt with in a very matter-of-fact way. By adopting this fundamentally rationalist ideology Reeve's novels were brought closer to the mainstream of eighteenth-century literature.

The historical realism in the novel of her successor, Sophia Lee (1750–1824), entitled *The recess* (1783–5), was much more impressive. Lee owed a great deal to the French historical romance, in particular to the Abbé Prévost (1697–1763) who translated Richardson's novels into French.[105] This was also a framed narrative that derived its form from the epistolary novel, and interspersed letters and portions of manuscript with considerable abandon. *The recess* was set in the reign of Elizabeth, and Lee recounted the adventures of two imaginary sisters, the illegitimate daughters of Mary queen of Scots. In the process she managed to bring in almost every major event and personage of Elizabeth's reign but she connected them to the narrative with considerable skill. The whole plot was based on persecution and on the danger which the existence of Mary's daughters presented to the state and on the attempts made to suppress that danger. Lee originated a trend in treating Elizabeth as a persecutor and in *The recess* she depicted her as 'unnatural'. The theme of persecution was going to become 'peculiarly the property of Gothics' in the years that followed.[106]

---

104 Op. cit.,   105 Punter, *The literature of terror*, pp 49–50. Reeve's *The old English baron* was in App No. 221, p. 556.   106 Ibid., p. 52.

Radcliffe who followed Reeve as a writer of Gothic 'thrillers', exercised a more important influence on literature. She wrote five novels under the influence of *The recess* but her finest work was *The mysteries of Udolpho* (1794), which was widely acclaimed and followed by scores of imitations. The story, which was set in the sixteenth century, opened with a pleasing account of the idyllic peace at the chateau of La Vallée, the home of the St Auberts in Gascony. This was where the orphaned Emily St Aubert lost her heart to Valancourt, a young man from a good family of moderate means. Having been placed at the mercy of her aunt at Tholouse, their courtship was encouraged for purely economic reasons. Her guardian was married to a sinister Italian, Signor Montoni. Emily was whisked away first to Venice, where she was almost married against her wishes to one Count Morano, and then to Montoni's Gothic castle at Udolpho, where she was effectively imprisoned. Here, with all the apparatus of sliding panels, secret passages, abductions and suggestions of the supernatural, dark dealings were carried on, because Montoni was the head of a band of robbers and the castle was his lair.

Many dangers threatened Emily at Udolpho – at one moment it appeared to be forced marriage, at another rape, at another the theft of her remaining estates, at another supernatural terrors. The latter never materialized as Radcliffe disclosed that her apparently supernatural machinery was no more than mere trickery. The mysterious intimations that had terrorized the persons in the novel were shown to be entirely natural in origin.[107] This did not take away from the power which her ghosts had over Emily or indeed the reader.

Like *The castle of Otranto, The old English baron* and *The recess*, Radcliffe's next novel *The Italian, or the confessional of the black penitent* (1797) was 'framed' as a book read by later English visitors to Naples. She even included tales which turned out to be totally irrelevant to the main plot. Written under the influence of *The monk* (1795) Radcliffe created more fear and suspense in order to feed the growing demand for horror stories. In *The Italian* the orphan Ellena di Rosalba was loved by Vivaldi, the only son of a marquess. His aristocratic mother conspired with her confessor, a monk named Schedoni to remove Ellena to the appalling convent of San Stefano. The choice of a Catholic monk as the satanic villain was deliberate because anti-Catholic feelings had been stirred up in England during the French revolution. Radcliffe borrowed from Lewis' scenes on the Inquisition, which she described largely in dialogue form. These were almost impressionistic with mysterious voices in the gloom, flitting figures and unknown instruments of torture, all designed to create an atmosphere of fear. Punter described it as a 'virtuoso demonstration of the imaginative power of the half-seen and half explained', which allowed the reader to release the springs of his imagination and fantasy.[108]

107 Ibid., pp 55–9. *The mysteries of Udolpho* was in App No. 221, p. 558.   108 Ibid., p. 63. *The*

Literary historians tend to the belief that Radcliffe designed her novels in accordance with the principles of Edmund Burke's *Philosophical enquiry into the origin of our ideas of the sublime and the beautiful*. Scenes of danger, fear, imprisonment or torture took place in sublime settings such as mountains with rocky crags and deep gorges, or dark underground places calculated to stimulate the emotion of terror, while normal social life continued in beautiful villas, gardens and vineyards. Each condition was heightened by a contrast with its opposite, as Burke advocated. But by far the biggest influences on Radcliffe were Shakespeare, from whom she quoted at length, and the puritan poet John Milton (1608–74). The character of Schedoni, Radcliffe's villainous hero owed a debt to Milton's portrayal of Satan in *Paradise lost* (1667). She was influenced too by the eighteenth-century writers – Richardson in England, d'Arnaud in France and Schiller in Germany. Radcliffe's style owed much to the dark morbid poetry of the 'graveyard poets' the 'poets of the landscape and the night' particularly Young and James Thomson (1700–48).[109] The romantic novelists and poets of the nineteenth century were inspired by Radcliffe's depiction of Schedoni, the 'fatal man' who was half angel, half devil, perpetually torn by the conflicting emotions of passion and remorse. The complex monk was probably the prototype of the poet Lord Byron's (1788–1824) satanic heroes.

Radcliffe attempted to 'wed tragedy to melodrama' but her successor Lewis, tried to move Gothic towards the mainstream of the novel through a psychological orientation. Probing the subconscious was Lewis' forte but in the process he exploited nearly every aspect of Gothic suggested by Walpole and developed by Radcliffe.[110] He did so under the influence of the German romantic movement and the wave of terror fiction which flourished in Germany in the 1790s. The youthful Lewis became a prominent literary figure as a result of eighteen plays which he had either written or translated from German. He was well versed in the works of Goethe, Schiller and Wieland   and had translated from the works of the German terror-writer Heinrich Zschokke. No doubt some of the extremism and sensationalism to be found

---

monk was in App No. 221, p. 558.   **109** Skelton, *The English novel*, p. 62. The poetry of Young and Thomson appear on App No. 221, p. 556. Johann Christoph Friedrich Von Schiller, German poet, dramatist and aesthetic philosopher, was influenced by the literary movement known as *Sturm und Drang* (storm and stress) which absorbed something of the doctrine of human rights, stemming in part from Rousseau. The movement reacted against the rigid constraints of classic formalism. It was as a student that Schiller wrote *Die Räuber* (The robbers), a story of two brothers one principled, the other a scoundrel. The principled brother having been dishonoured became the head of a band of robbers and in defiance of the laws attempted to defend individual rights in a degenerate age. Finally acknowledging the error of his ways, he gave himself up to justice. Schiller became close friends with Goethe after 1789 when he appealed to Goethe for contributions to his periodical *Die Horen*.   **110** Karl, *A reader's guide*, pp 252–6.

in *The monk* can be attributed to the German influence because 'most of the German material was extraordinarily crude, even by comparison with the worst of Lewis'.

The monk concerned the saintly monk Ambrosio, the superior of the Capuchins of Madrid, who was corrupted by a demon woman, a vampire called Matilda, who entered the monastery disguised as a novice, and won the affections of Ambrosio. In reality she was an agent of Satan, sent to destroy the monk physically and spiritually. Matilda seduced Ambrosio, a deed which released his pent-up passions and set him on a self-destructive course. He became depraved by the desires she aroused in him. He then grew dissatisfied with Matilda and seduced one of his penitents, the naive Antonia. Matilda offered him supernatural assistance which he reluctantly accepted. The scheme went wrong when Ambrosio murdered the girl's mother to prevent her from publicly revealing his true character. With further demonic help, Ambrosio was enabled to carry Antonia off, apparently dead, to a crypt where, on her awakening, he savagely raped her. Discovered at last, he was captured and brought before the Inquisition. Matilda, who had been captured with him, succeeded in tempting him to complete his transactions with the devil by selling his soul in exchange for freedom. However, he failed to bargain for more than release from prison. Satan cheated him and the fiend carried him to the top of a high mountain and 'darting his talons in the monk's shaven crown, he sprang with him from the rock'. Lewis utilised elements of existing legends favoured by the romantics, the *Wandering Jew, Faustus, the pact with the devil*, and lesser known legends popularised by German writers, like that of the *Bleeding nun*. He also copied from Radcliffe's *The mysteries of Udolpho* (1794). There was one major difference between Radcliffe and Lewis, however; with Mrs Radcliffe the reader was filled with terror at potential horrors but with Lewis the reader felt revulsion at their realisation.[111]

The monk was completed by Lewis in ten weeks[112] and became very popular. It was censored continuously since the time it was written and was more noted for its diabolical elements, being possibly written under the influence of the French writer Marquis de Sade (1740-1814), who was famous for his perverse novels. Lewis was known to have purchased a copy of de Sade's book *Justine* in 1792[113] and he seemed to follow in his steps as he toyed with the Sadean notion of man's almost infinite potential for evil. His principal character Ambrosio was, after all 'a voyeur, a rapist, a sadist, a masochist, a

111 Punter, *The literature of terror*, pp 56–61. Christoph Martin Wieland grew up in a strongly pietistic environment. One of his main literary influences was Samuel Richardson. Gradually he withdrew from pietism and turned to ancient Greek thought. Wieland's natural inclination was to hedonism. His *Agathon* (1766–7), a novel with a Greek background, is a story of his own conversion to hedonism and marks the beginning of the psychologicial novel in Germany. 112 Neill, *A short history*, p. 102. 113 Op.cit., pp 80–81.

necrophiliac, a matricide, as well as incestuous'.[114] To Punter *The monk* was 'a disturbing book', 'a piece of deliberate extremism' by a writer who was an avid seeker of publicity. He tried to 'challenge his audience, to upset its security, to give the reader a moment of doubt about whether he may not himself be guilty of the complicated faults attributed to Ambrosio'.[115] Like Karl, Skelton (1977) gave Lewis credit for his talent at probing the subconscious, taking as his example the dream-basis of *The monk*. Lorenzo had a nightmare about his bride Antonia being snatched from him at the altar by a monster that plunged with her into a flaming gulf, as the cathedral crumbled around them, and she escaped upwards, leaving only her pure white robe in the fiend's possession. According to Skelton the nightmare pre-figured the story-pattern of the novel as a whole and demonstrated how Gothic fiction, dismembered the psyche and personified its different aspects, and set them in dramatic conflict with each other. Skelton concluded that 'this least "true to life" of English fiction' had 'more immediate access to the subconscious than many great realistic masterpieces of literature'.[116]

114 Karl, *A reader's guide*, p. 253.   115 Punter, *The literature of terror*, pp 79–81.   116 Skelton, *The English novel*, p. 65.

7

The Kildare Place Society – reforming the habits of the Irish

'There were fairy tales enough, and histories of noted robbers'

> *Go, visit her cottage, though humble and poor,*
> *'Tis so clean and so neat you might eat off the floor*
> *No rubbish, no cobwebs, no dirt can be found,*
> *Though you hunt every corner and search all around.*

'The tidy wife' (1825)[1]

The Kildare Place library readers were arguably one of the finest achievements of the Society. This was mainly due to the professional work done by their literary assistant, the Reverend Charles Bardin. From the very outset the book subcommittee set themselves the challenge of entering into what Kingsmill Moore, their historian called 'a life and death competition with the dissolute publications which held the market'.[2] By 1825 fifty-two titles had appeared covering a vast range of information under such category headings as *Religious, moral or illustrative of Scripture*; *Instructive in arts or economy*; *Natural history*; *Voyages, travels etc.* and *Miscellaneous*.[3]

Bardin had a keen business sense and recognised a potentially lucrative market for books on voyages and travels, especially now that travel was safe, in the wake of the Napoleonic wars. Bardin who was widely travelled, prided himself on being able to say in some cases, that he had 'gone over' every spot which he described,[4] produced at least twenty-four books on travel over an eleven-year period (1821–32).[5] Initially however, the Society concentrated on

1 *The history of Tim Higgins. The cottage visiter (sic)* (Dublin, 1825), p. 78.   2 H. Kingsmill Moore, *An unwritten chapter in the history of education* (London, 1904), p. 248.   3 Ibid., pp 248–51.   4 Ibid., p. 257.   5 Hislop, 'The Kildare Place Society 1811–31', p. 223. The popular books were *Wonderful escapes* (Dublin, 1819); *The discovery of America* (Dublin, 1820); *The life of Captain James Cook* (Dublin, 1820); *Dangerous voyage. Containing an account of the wonderful and truly providential escape of Captain Bligh* (Dublin, 1817); Richard Walter, *A voyage round the world in the years 1740–44 by George Anson, now Lord Anson* (London, 1748); *Byron's narrative* (Dublin, 1817); *The life and most surprising adventures of Robinson Crusoe of York, mariner* (London, n.d.); *The history of little Jack a foundling* (Dublin, 1819); *The history of Prince Lee Boo* (Dublin, 1822).

publishing books which already formed part of the popular market, but later produced books which would have stimulated and fascinated the young reader. Invariably these books had attractive eye-catching illustrations and were printed in a clear legible style. In *Prince Lee Boo* for example, there were intriguing pictures entitled *Black Pelew islanders, canoe with natives*, and *A view of a landing place*. In *Travels in Sweden, Denmark and Norway*[6] there were imaginative illustrations of *The great geyser, Mt Vesuvius* and *The pyramids of Egypt*. Another well-illustrated book called *Amusing stories: a collection of histories, adventures and anecdotes*[7] introduced the reader to exotic adventures in mysterious parts of the world, such as those of *Madam Godin in the country of the Amazons* or *A tiger hunt in India*. Other interesting titles included *The cataract of Niagara in Canada; An account of the salt mines in Wielitska; Short account of the plague in London in 1665; Wonderful escape of a hunter from the Blackfeet Indians* and an *Account of the earthquake in Calabria in 1638*.

Several of the Society's readers contained a great deal of self-improving advice for the poor of Ireland, so much so that it is difficult to escape the conclusion that the overriding consideration of the Society, was to change the habits of the Irish people. Firstly, the weaknesses of the Irish character were referred to in various stories. In *Travels in Sweden, Denmark and Norway* the reader was reminded of 'the common fault of the Irish, of never looking beyond the present'. A salutary lesson was taught, that the 'appearance of a single swallow', shouldn't be taken 'as the proof that summer was at hand' and that one would be wise 'to think of the future as well as the present'. In *The history of Tim Higgins* excessive drinking was condemned and its consequences clearly spelt out. The reader was asked 'How often do we see what might be harmless mirth and amusement, turned into the most shameful scenes of vice and mischief, by the one sin, drunkenness'. In a dialogue between Jenny and her grandmother in *The cottage fireside* the latter concluded, with all the wisdom of her years, that 'we may well talk of hard-times: the times will never be good till poor men leave off whiskey and poor women tea. I'll tell you one fault more I have with tea-drinking: I think it prevents charity; sometimes at least I should not wonder if it did'.[8] When Isaac Jenkins in *The history of Isaac Jenkins* abandoned 'the heinous practice of drunkenness' major improvements took place in his domestic life, 'The house smelled sweet and fresh', 'The clothes of the children were all patched indeed, but no longer ragged or full of holes'.[9]

The main emphasis in the readers was on the virtues of order, regularity, tidiness and cleanliness, themes which would be repeated many times in the

6 *Travels in Sweden, Denmark and Norway* (Dublin, 1826). 7 *Amusing stories. A collection of histories, adventures and anecdotes* (Dublin, 1819). 8 *The cottage fireside* (Dublin, 1822), p. 85. 9 *The history of Isaac Jenkins* (Dublin, 1817), pp 56–8.

lesson books of the commissioners of national education. In *The history of Richard MacReady* home improvements were described down to the most minute detail, while at the same time the reader was reminded of the slovenly habits of Irish women 'the cabin was whitewashed; shelves were put up, on which Susan could lay her few plates and delft articles, instead of leaving them on the window stool, or on a chair, as, before ... nails and pegs were also placed along the walls, on which she could hang a cloak or great coat, instead of throwing them down'. But Susan 'was still slovenly; and sometimes she would let the basket on the turf-kish lie on the floor, to be stumbled over by James, notwithstanding all that Dickey used to say, about a place for every thing, and every thing in its place'.[10] These sentiments were repeated in *The schoolmistress* as the writer engaged in some publicising of the Society's books. 'All round the schoolroom there were racks, for hanging the spelling and reading tablets sold by the Education Society, and in short, there was a place for every thing, and every thing in its place. Indeed the sentence was written over the door as you entered', and, the writer added 'it would be well that every school had the same'.[11] It would only be a matter of time before this message would be taken to every national school in Ireland.

That self-improvement was the goal of some readers is obvious from the list of contents of *The schoolmistress* in which there were lessons *Against Idleness;* on *The fair; On good management; On cottage cookery; On drunkenness* and on *Going to service.* Utilitarian values were to the fore also in *The cottage fireside* with lessons on *Potatoes; The pig; Dress – A single life; Sickness; Vaccination; The garden; Butter; Cleanliness; Tea-drinking,* and *Whiskey-drinking at fairs.* On occasions the readers were used as a medium for discrediting the chapbooks they were intended to supplant and also to discredit the indigenous schools. This was most noticeable in *The pedlars*, a book commissioned by the Society from the Irish Quaker Mary Leadbeater, who was well known for her 'improving' school in Co. Kildare. In Leadbeater's story Darby Brady's parents objected to hedge schools because they feared 'the associates to whom it might introduce him', besides they didn't 'approve of that mode of teaching'.[12] The Society's readers were then promoted in a dialogue between Darby and Pat the book pedlar:

> In my young days, there was a great dearth of good books for young persons. There were fairy tales enough, and histories of noted robbers; but what profit could be derived from nonsense concerning things which never had existence, or from accounts of people, who were a terror to their neighbours and at last met the punishment which their crimes deserved. I often think, what great advantage the young now

10 *The history of Richard MacReady the farmer lad* (Dublin, 1824), pp 28–9. 11 *The schoolmistress* (Dublin, 1824), p. 15. 12 *The pedlars* (Dublin, 1826), p. 13.

enjoy, who have such books as these prepared expressly for them, and suited to their capacity.

In *The history of Tim Higgins* a dialogue, along the same lines, took place between Tim and a book pedlar as follows:

Tim: I like those books of yours very much: will you let me know where you buy them?

Pedlar: I bought them in Dublin, at the Society for Promoting the Education of the Poor of Ireland, in Kildare Street: but I believe they may also be in most of the principal towns in Ireland.

The contents of the pedlar's bag were then revealed in order to advertise the society's books on natural history, travels and voyages. The pedlar reassured Tim that these were all factual accounts to which Tim replied:

Tim: I recollect the time when such as you had a different kind of book in your basket – the History of Noted Thieves, and fairy tales and song books; why don't you sell them still?

The pedlar then claimed victory for the readers over the chapbooks

Pedlar: The reason is very plain, because the people won't buy them; they find it a great deal more useful, and certainly not less entertaining, to read accounts of what really happened, than of such things as were only in the brain of those who wrote those fairy tales; and to tell you the truth, over and above this, the books I now sell are much cheaper: they have nicer cuts in them; and as I heard once from a gentleman who bought them for his children, and appeared to know them very well, they have nothing in them which can do harm to the youngest child that reads them.[13]

Here the pedlar was expressing the optimistic assessment of their historian, based on a report from the book subcommittee in 1823. The report claimed that, with the exception of Belfast 'the cheap books were everywhere supplanting the pernicious literature'. Moore's assessment was also based on the evidence of the findings of the general committee in 1824, which stated that:

13 *The history of Tom Higgins*, pp 87–9.

printing presses in Dublin which formerly teemed with immoral and mischevious publications were now idle, those productions being quite unequal to any successful competition with the publications of the Society.[14]

But this wasn't in fact the case. The demand for chapbooks had been so great at this time that four Dublin booksellers were engaged in printing them exclusively in 1825 – one of whom had four presses in operation and published 50,000 annually. Other presses were located in Cork, Limerick, Belfast and Galway. From all these sources, it was estimated that circulation of chapbooks grew to about 300,000 per annum.[15] This pattern was set to continue into the 1830s, and on 6 July 1837, Robert Sullivan, one of the board of national education professors in the Central training establishment, gave evidence to this effect before the select committee for that year, with Thomas Wyse questioning him. He gave a list of the chapbooks in general use in schools 'never connected with any society or Board' and then proceeded to say:

> It will appear from these titles that they are still published by different booksellers in various parts of Ireland, Dublin, Belfast, Limerick etc. ... Books of this nature are not only in print, but as appears by the titles I have given, in course of publication in every part of Ireland, for the use of schools.[16]

Adams suggested in *The printed word* that Bardin 'probably had a greater effect on Irish reading habits, and was more widely read, than many a famous mainstream literary author'[17]. But this view would not accord with the research findings of Hislop, which placed a question mark over whether the Kildare Place books reached the Society's target audience in any significant number. While, as Hislop stated 'the Society had produced works of a high standard' the problem lay in the fact that they 'could not control the price or destination of the works which the book dealers purchased'. It transpired that books which were sold unbound in sheets, were being purchased by unscrupulous booksellers, who printed their own title pages, showing an inflated price, which was sometimes as high as double the original price. This automatically put the books out of the reach of the poorer classes for whom they were intended.[18]

There is further evidence available that the books didn't reach their target audience, which arises from an examination of the parochial returns for 1824

14 Moore, *An unwritten chapter*, p. 255.   15 Warburton, et al., *History of the city of Dublin*, ii, p. 875.   16 Report of the select committee of the house of lords on the plan of education in Ireland 1837, pp 574–5.   17 Adams, *The printed word and the common man*, p. 101.   18 Hislop, 'The Kildare Place Society 1811–31', p. 249.

for the diocese of Kildare and Leighlin. It reveals that the number of Kildare Place books listed for hedge schools is negligible. This is confirmed also by the commissioners of education in 1825 who reported that chapbooks were still being read in the hedge schools. They supplied a list of the books with the comment 'We have nevertheless found the traces of their former abundance in the following catalogue of books'.[19]

As the library readers didn't reach the social class they were targetting, to any significant degree, we can only speculate as to whether they would have supplanted the chapbooks, had they managed to do so. Hislop's research showed that the books which 'sold well' for the Society were 'The classics such as *Robinson Crusoe, Aesop* and *Voyage of Captain Cook* ... together with a number of the works on travel and all the volumes on natural history.' The didactic books of advice such as *Cottage fireside* and *Tim Higgins* 'sold only moderately'.[20]

From the very start the book subcommittee set out to dominate the book market by undercutting the price of the chapbooks, as they mistakenly believed, according to Ó Cíosáin (1997) 'that the principal reason for the popularity of 'vile-trash' was its cheapness, rather than any attractions in the subject matter'.[21] Crofton Croker, who was in a good position to comment on the popular literary tastes of the period, recognised why the Society's publication of *Elizabeth or The exiles of Siberia*, met with such a high rate of approval. He conjectured:

> As further proof of the natural good taste (of the Irish peasantry) it may be mentioned that of all the books printed and circulated by the Kildare Street Society, none is found to equal in sale Elizabeth ... Much may be said respecting educating the lower orders according to their taste and through the medium of their superstitions as the most attractive and effectual mode of instruction.[22]

Elizabeth had many of the traditional fairy tale qualities which appealed to the Irish. The library readers may well have supplanted the chapbooks had they appealed more to the imagination and had they taken on board the love of story telling and fairy lore which was so much a part of the culture of the poor.

However, the Kildare Place can be credited with pioneering the principle of graded textbooks in this country. As Moore admitted, they may have been 'doctrinally colourless'[23] but like the library readers, they avoided all traces of sectarianism and showed a genuine concern for the moral, social and economic

19 First report of the commissioners, 1825, p. 43.   20 Hislop, 'The Kildare Place Society 1811–31', p. 251.   21 Ó Cíosáin, *Print and popular culture*, p. 141.   22 T. Crofton Croker, *Fairy legends and traditions of the south of Ireland* (London, n.d.), p. 336.   23 Moore, *An unwritten chapter*, p. 219.

welfare of the poor. The library readers were of a high standard and the wide range of topics covered showed the extent of the Society's commitment and dedication to the cause of supplying good reading material, in a country where heretofore there was a dearth. They were of such a high quality that their influence spread much further afield than Ireland. The British museum requested a specimen set and the Society for promoting Christian knowledge in England reprinted several of them.[24] The Coast Guards also placed an initial order for some 12,964 volumes, and they were also exported in large quantities to India via the regimental libraries.[25]

National education and 'the great rule of regularity and order – a time and a place for every thing, and every thing in its proper time and place'

By 1831 the Kildare Place had lost the confidence and support of the Catholic population, due mainly to its rule that the bible should be read without note or comment. The government withdrew financial support from it and other voluntary education societies, in order to create a national system of education, under its own control. The state-sponsored system was founded not by statute, but under the terms of what became known as the Stanley letter. This was a letter from Stanley, the chief secretary, to the duke of Leinster, inviting him to take up the position as president of the new board of education, and outlining the terms under which the non-denominational system of national education would be based. Stanley directed the commissioners, on behalf of the government to exercise 'complete control' over the schools connected to the system, 'absolute control' over parliamentary funding, and 'the most entire control over all books to be used in the schools'.[26] Consequently the first priority the commissioners set themselves was to rid the schools, which had joined the new system of 'books calculated to incite to lawless and profligate adventure, to cherish superstition, or to lead to dissension and disloyalty'.[27]

Daly's (1979) research revealed that few genuinely new schools came into existence. She concluded that 'The national schools did not mark a sudden discontinuity, in many instances existing schools and teachers continued with a new source of finance'.[28] It therefore took a concerted effort by the commissioners and their inspectors, over a period of at least six years before Sullivan could testify before the select committee on 6 July 1837, that they had successfully managed to remove the chapbooks from their schools. In answer to Wyse's questions, Sullivan replied as follows:

24 Ibid., p. 253.   25 P. O'Farrell, *England and Ireland since 1808* (London, 1975), p. 143.   26 Thirteenth report of the commissioners of national education in Ireland for the year 1846. H.C. 1847 (832) 17, pp 14–15.   27 First report of the commissioners, 1825, p. 38.   28 Daly, 'The development of the national school system, 1831–40', p. 163.

Are those books now in use in any school?
They are to be found in hedge schools very often.
Are those books still to be found among the pupils educated in the national schools?
I have not found any of them: it is possible that there may, but it would be in gross violation of the rules.
They are gradually disappearing in the country?
Yes, they are fast disappearing.[29]

Some forty years on, when the Powis commission was set up to investigate the progress of the national education system, the assistant commissioners recalled the days when 'every child brought to school the book furnished by the domestic library'. They explained how they succeeded in removing the objectionable books from schools when the Kildare Place and the Catholic book society had failed to do so. It was due to the fact that they had

> at command resources practically unlimited, the commissioners edited and printed their own school-books, distributed them gratis to schools, promoted their use by a general system of inspection and examination, taught the masters to employ them, and finally succeeded in introducing them everywhere into primary schools.

The Kildare Place and the Catholic book society by comparison 'did not possess strength or scope enough to banish objectionable books'.[30]
Just as the Kildare Place ensured that the various religious denominations were represented on its committees, so too did the chief secretary when he appointed the seven commissioners of national education. There were two Presbyterians – the resident commissioner Dr James Carlile, a Scottish Presbyterian minister, and Robert Holmes, queens counsellor, three anglicans, Dr Whateley, the Protestant archbishop of Dublin, the duke of Leinster and Dr Sadleir, provost of Trinity College; and two Catholics, Dr Murray, the archbishop of Dublin and Anthony Blake, the former treasury remembrancer and education commissioner for the year 1825. Both the Kildare Place sub-committee and the commissioners tried to ensure that their books would be free from religious bias or sectarianism and went to great lengths to satisfy all denominations in this respect. James Kavanagh who had been a head inspector of the board of education recorded in *Mixed education: the Catholic case*

29 Report on the new plan 1837, p. 575.   30 Report from the commissioners of primary education (Irl) 1870, Powis, p. 119. In 1831 the commissioners of national education sought and received permission to use the books from the Kildare Place society and from the Catholic book society – the latter was a society established by Catholic clergy to distribute Catholic books, until such time as they could provide their own books.

stated, the difficulties Carlile had to surmount in order to appease his fellow clergymen commissioners with regard to the religious content of the books. On one occasion, no book could be found to meet the stipulations of Murray and a new compilation was called for.[31]

The Kildare Place book subcommittee, like their successors had to function during a period of religious tension and had to contend with what James Godkin in *A handbook of the education question* called 'the evils which the baneful spirit of sectarianism has inflicted upon this country'.[32] Both bodies succeeded in upholding the principle of religious neutrality in their books, while in no way shirking their acknowledged responsibility for the moral and social development of students. Once again, it was mainly clergymen who wrote the lesson books. Carlile was responsible for the compilation of *Lesson books one, two, four and five* and the *Girls' book of reading.* Whateley and his friends compiled *Sequels nos. 1 and 2 to the second book of lessons,* as well as the *Supplement to the fourth book of lessons.* One Irishman William McDermott (a future inspector of the board), was employed as literary assistant from 1832 to 1834, and he compiled the first edition of the *Third book of lessons* (1835–46), which was revised by Whateley in 1846.[33]

To judge from the contents of the lesson books, the commissioners were clearly influenced by the recommendations of the 1825 commissioners who recommended 'Books in which moral principles should be inculcated in such a manner as is likely to make deep and lasting impressions on the youthful mind' as well as 'ample extracts from the Sacred Scriptures themselves'. It was considered that they would prove 'indispensible, in forming the mind to just notions of duty and sound principles of conduct'.[34] The commissioners claimed that 'a sound moral was conveyed in almost every lesson'[35] in their books. The elementary books concentrated on teaching the simple virtues such as honesty, truthfulness, diligence, humility, kindness to animals and generosity. These were conveyed by jingles or mottoes.

We must not be idle.[36]

He gives twice who gives with a good will
You must not vaunt or boast of your skill
None but those who are bad will beat a poor horse
   or use him ill.
A good boy will not tell a lie.[37]

31 J.W. Kavanagh, *Mixed education. The Catholic case stated* (Dublin, 1859), p. 38.   32 J. Godkin, *A handbook of the education question* (Dublin, 1862), p. 84.   33 Akenson, *The Irish education experiment,* p. 231.   34 First report of the commissioners, 1825, p. 39.   35 An analysis of school books published by the authority of the commissioners of national education, 1853, p. 3.   36 *Second book of lessons for the use of schools* (Dublin, 1866), p. 73.   37 *First book of lessons* (Dublin,

Respect for parents and obedience to their wishes was encouraged in the readers. This was the theme of *The basket of eggs* in *Sequel no. 1 to the second book of lessons*. Ruth who was eight years old was sent on an errand for the very first time, by her trusting mother. A basket of eggs had been entrusted to her, to be delivered to Mrs Simpson at the shop. Unfortunately Ruth was tempted by the sight of a wild strawberry on the bank and stopped to gather it. Tragedy struck when a large dog overturned her basket thus destroying over half the eggs. The reader was taught a lesson by the warning 'How much did she now repent of her disobedience'. She then encountered her irresponsible friend Sarah who advised her to lie to her mother by pretending she had an accident, to which suggestion, Ruth replied indignantly 'But, Sarah, that would not be true, and I cannot tell a lie'. Sarah had no such qualms of conscience but urged Ruth to re-consider her decision, only to be reminded that 'God would know and he would be displeased with me if I were to tell a lie, – no I shall tell mother the truth though I think she will punish me'.[38]

In a lesson entitled *The drop of rain* children were advised that they should be content with whatever God saw fit to grant them in life 'Let us not grieve at our lot though low it be cast for we know not what God may have in store for us'. The theme was expanded in *Martin the errand boy*, to show that sometimes the rich had to endure great hardships that the poor knew nothing of. It followed that the poor should not be envious of the rich but should rather count their blessings. The story told how poor Martin the errand boy was envious of a young gentleman he saw in a coach with his tutor, who was being served wine and chicken. But when the coach door was opened he discovered that the young gentleman was in fact disabled. He told Martin

And I ... would gladly be poor if I had only the use of my limbs. But as it is God's will that I should be lame and sickly, I try to be patient and cheerful ... Remember that if you have poor clothes and hard fare, you have health and strength, and that money cannot buy.[39]

A favourite theme in the lesson books, as in *The pleasant art* was the merit of hard work. This was conveyed in either prose or verse, while the more advanced lesson books were used to convey similar morals, but they were given a more indepth treatment. Lessons on morality were given under such headings as *The miseries of indolence; Strict honesty; Integrity,* and *The vice of lying*. The work ethic was emphasised consistently and examples were given of 'rags to riches' stories in biographical sketches, such as that of the budding tycoon William Hutton. William was so poor he was forced to leave school at

1887), p. 44; p. 23; p. 32; p. 26. 38 *Sequel no. 1 to the second book of lessons* (Dublin, 1866), pp 13–17. 39 *Sequel no. 1 to the second book of lessons*, pp 22–5.

the age of seven to work in a silk mill. He worked relentlessly so that eventually he became 'by his own economy, one of the richest men in Birmingham'.[40] Similarly, the story was told of Martha Dunne, who despite suffering a serious accident 'took great pains to improve herself so that she became the village schoolmistress'.[41] Just as Bardin was careful to remind the readers of his voyages that while Christopher Columbus and Captain Cook exemplified the principle that men of humble birth could rise to prominence through hard work, it was not to be expected that all the poor would achieve a similar elevation to the higher strata of society.[42] Whateley in the *Fourth book of lessons* also subscribed to this view,[43] as did the writer of *The pleasant art*. The importance of preserving the social order of rich and poor was demonstrated by means of a 'fairy tale' told by Mrs Marcet in the *Supplement to the fourth book of lessons*. In a story reminiscent of George Orwell's *Animal farm*, a fairy made everyone equal but the consequences were so devestating that soon everyone pressed for a return to the status quo.[44]

Among the unstated aims of the commissioners' lesson books would appear to have been an attempt to win favour for the English 'connection'. Now that Ireland was united in government with England, greater loyalty must surely have been expected from its young citizens. Even in the elementary lesson books children were obliged to learn the national anthem 'To the tune of "God save the queen". Peace was its central theme:

> God bless our native land,
> May Heaven's protecting hand
> Still guard our shore:
> May peace her powers extend
> Foe be transformed to friend,
> And may her power depend
> On war no more.
>
> Through ev'ry changing scene,
> Oh Lord: preserve the Queen ...[45]

In the *Fourth book of lessons* Whateley showed that he too was interested in maintaining peace and stability in the country. He expressed the view that 'it was a mistake to suppose that religion and morals alone would be sufficient to save a people from revolution ... if a proper idea of political economy were not cultivated by that people'. He included lessons on topics such as *Value,*

40 *Supplement to the fourth book of lessons* (Dublin, 1850).   41 *Second book of lessons*, p. 158.   42 Hislop, 'The Kildare Place Society 1811–31', pp 221–2.   43 *Fourth book of lessons for the use of schools* (Dublin, 1842), p. 225.   44 *Supplement to the fourth book of lessons*, p. 301.   45 *Sequel no. 2 to the second book of lessons for the use of schools* (Dublin, 1882), pp 20–1.

Wages, Rich and poor, Capital, Taxes, Letting and hiring, which were directed towards maintaining a system of law and order in society. The main functions of the government were clearly stated and those were the protection of the people and their property. Whateley was careful to ensure that readers should not think badly of the British government so he reminded them that 'Even the worst government that ever was, is both much better and much cheaper than no government at all'.[46] He emphasised the unity between the two countries, the geographical ties and the common bond of language and nationhood 'many people who live in Ireland were born in England and we speak the same language and are called one nation'.[47] In *Sequel no. 2 to the second book of lessons* the Christian ideal of living in peace as brothers and as members of one race, was put forward:

> We are, then, brethern, – whether of one nation
> and language or another – whether black or white,
> bond or free – we are of 'the Sons of God'.
> Christ has encouraged us as such in dying for us
> and I trust the time will come through the sole
> influence of his name, wars and violence, and mutual
> injustice will cease among us, and that all the great
> families of the earth, will be brought to acknowledge their
> brotherhood and to dwell together in peace.

Bardin's travel books were also used as a medium to convey support and loyalty to the British government. Putting recent Irish history to one side and ignoring the effects of the penal laws on the Irish psyche, Bardin maintained 'Tis only in England or Ireland, of all the places I ever was in, that the laws are made equally for both rich and poor'.[48]

There was sharp criticism levied against the board's lesson books, on the grounds that they studiously avoided references to Irish history and culture. Nationalist parties such as the Young Irelanders expressed their displeasure in their newspaper *The Nation,* on the grounds that the books were 'very useful and respectable in their proper place ... but that place is not Ireland'.[49] Nor were they the only ones to take offence at this omission, a witness before the Powis commission of 1868 complained bitterly that there was:

---

46 *Fourth book of lessons,* 1847, p. 56. See J.M. Goldstrom, *The social content of education, 1808–70* (Shannon, 1972), pp 52–90. See also Sr Eileen Whelan, 'Primary school readers in the nineteenth century' in *Oideas* 19 (1978), pp 38–50.   47 *Second book of lessons,* p. 135.   48 *Travels in Africa* (Dublin, 1824), pp 107–8.   49 L. Walsh, 'The social, political and economic content of nineteenth century schoolbooks' in *Oideas* 33 (1988), p. 46.

scarcely anything in their books about the history of Ireland. There was in the third book a description of the lakes of Killarney and the Giant's Causeway, but I don't know for what reason, unless perhaps that it was too 'national'. These extracts have been expunged from the last edition and their place has been inserted a description of some lake in Hindostan.[50]

A contemporary writer, Barry O'Brien, felt that Whateley had a case to answer in this respect. In *Fifty years of concessions to Ireland 1831–1881*, he drew attention to the *Third book of lessons* (1835) which contained patriotic verses by Mrs Balfour. In them she made references to 'the harp' and her 'native land'. There was also a poem by Campbell, called 'The harper', which contained dangerous references to 'shamrocks', 'patriot smiles' and the 'green banks of the Shannon'. Whateley was so concerned by these references that he expunged all of them from his revised edition in 1846. He also censored two further poems which he excluded from the second edition – Campbell's *The downfall of Poland* which contained the offending line 'and Freedom shriek'd as Kosciusko fell', and Sir Walter Scott's *Love of country*, which asked:

> Breathes there a man with soul so dead,
> Who never to himself hath said,
> This is my own my native land?[51]

A hymn of praise was retained however, which must surely have caused some confusion in the minds of Irish children as to what their true cultural identity really was. It said:

> I thank the goodness and the grace
> That on my birth have smiled,
> And made me in these Christian days
> A happy English child etc.

Nationalists' reservations regarding the books were summed up accurately by the witness before the Powis commission who complained that:

> up to the present moment, until the last edition of the books of board, you might have introduced them into a school in Canada, or into a school in Africa just as appropriately as into a school in Ireland.[52]

50 Report from the commissioners of primary education (Irl) 1870, Powis, p. 679.   51 R. Barry O'Brien, *Fifty years of concessions to Ireland, 1831–81* (London, n.d.), pp 193–4.   52 Report from the commissioners of primary education (Irl) 1870, Powis, p. 679.

In fact it was this lack of national orientation, together with their cheapness and their literary merit which ensured that the books of the national board were a huge commercial success, not only in England, but also in Scotland, Australia, Wales, Newfoundland, India, British Guiana and Canada.[53] The success was such that in one year alone, 1851, the commissioners claimed that sales of their books exceeded one million copies.[54]

Geography was one of the more appealing subjects covered in the lesson books. It owed its world-wide vision to a large extent to the interesting travel books of Bardin. The debt is clear from lessons with such interesting titles as *The Laplanders are a harmless, inefficient people,* or *Boiling fountains in Ireland.* In the various lesson books each country was classified according to its religion, national characteristics, type of government and occasionally its level of education. A sympathetic attitude was conveyed towards most countries, but their inhabitants tended to be stereotyped in a less than flattering way. The English, one must assume, were above censure, because a critical account of that country didn't feature in any of the books. Diplomacy was to the fore, in the description offered of the Irish race. The reader was told that they were

> a clever, lively people: formerly very much given to drink and very ignorant: but now, it is believed that they are one of the soberest nations of Europe, and it will be their own fault, if they are not also one of the most educated.[55]

The commissioners were also aware of the weaknesses of the Irish and were in full agreement with Bardin, that these were lack of foresight, intemperance and improvidence. In the *Fourth book of lessons* compiled by Carlile he reminded the Irish of their national weaknesses

> But labourers often suffer great hardships from which they might save themselves by looking beyond the present day. They are apt to complain of others, when they ought rather to blame their own imprudence. If when a man is earning good wages he spends all as fast as he gets it in thoughtless intemperance, instead of laying up something against hard times, he may afterwards have to suffer great want when he is out of work, or when wages are lower: but then he must not blame others for this, but his own improvidence.

Like the Kildare Place book subcommittee, the commissioners of national education shared the ideal of reforming the habits of the Irish poor. This was

53 Walsh, 'The social, political and economic content', p. 40.   54 Eighteenth report of the commissioners of national education in Ireland for the year 1851, H.C. 1852-3, pp 21-2.   55 *Second book of lessons*, 1847, p. 135.

apparent not only from the contents of their books, but also from the course of training in the national education Central training establishment. Prospective teachers were told to give priority to order, tidiness and hygiene in their classrooms, and to lead by example in order to break down the prejudices of the people. These views were implicit also in the *Twelve practical rules for the teachers of national schools* laid down by the board of education, especially the sixth rule which obliged teachers 'To observe themselves and to impress upon the minds of their pupils, the great rule of regularity and order – a time and a place for every thing, and every thing in its proper time and place'. The seventh rule expected them 'To promote, both by precept and example cleanliness, neatness and decency'.[56]

In *Sequel no. 2 to the second book of lessons* children were reminded of the important lessons they had learned in these areas of social behaviour, since starting school.

> First, then, you were taught to come to school, with clean hands, face and hair ... Next, you were taught order, to put away your things, your hats or cloaks or bonnets, in their proper places; to be civil and respectful in your behaviour towards your teachers, and gentle to each other; to be silent during lessons; and to conform to all the other rules of your school.

One lesson in particular merited repetition in the advanced readers, and this was *On tidiness*. In the *Supplement to the fourth book of lessons* Whateley reprimanded Irish women for being 'slatterns from laziness'. He wrote in angry tones 'If it is disgraceful to a farmer that his fields should be overrun with weeds, how much more disgraceful is it for a woman to wear, day after day, gowns, or other clothes full of holes'. It was his belief that 'few things would add more to the comfort of the poor than tidiness'. He went on to advise 'a stitch in time ... saves nine. No poor man or woman needs to be ashamed of patched clothes. Every patch is, on the contrary, creditable, for it bespeaks industry'. In the *Agricultural class book* which included *Hints on domestic economy* Irish girls were told that 'there is no tax on water. Why then, not be cleanly in person or dress?' Their sense of national pride and dignity was then appealed to by a reminder of the low opinion visitors had of the slovenly, beggarly appearance of the Irish. Even when compared to the poorest in Russia, the Irish fared badly. In Russia 'the poorest will not allow his nakedness to be seen, as one frequently does in Ireland among those far above the class of beggars! ... to go about in rags is nowhere allowed but in Ireland'.[57]

56 Report from the commissioners of primary education (Irl) 1870, Powis, pp 119–20.   57 *Agricultural class book or how best to cultivate a small farm and garden together with hints on domestic economy* (Dublin, 1853), p. 175.

Even though the Stanley letter made no reference to plans for agricultural education, in 1838 the commissioners opened their model farm at Glasnevin in order to give an agricultural training to national teachers. By 1858 thirty-six model agricultural schools were operating as well as about sixty of the national schools with school farms attached.[58] By 1850 the *Agricultural class book* was ready for publication. In it the commissioners showed their determination to dispense practical as well as theoretical instruction, for boys in agriculture and for girls in domestic science. The agricultural section was written in the form of a story in which a gentleman met an Irish peasant who was just about to emigrate to America because he couldn't survive on his farm. The gentleman informed him that he had no one to blame for his squalid existence but himself. He proceeded to offer him 'improving' advice which he took, and consequently became a successful farmer. In the girls lessons on domestic economy the story was told of Mrs Doran, an inept housewife, lacking in foresight. She was over-reliant on potatoes and didn't take into account how often the crop failed due to blight, nor did she consider the expense involved. She should have considered a mixed diet of coarse bread, oatmeal, milk, cheap cuts of meat and grease soup (a mixture of beef suet and hog's lard to which are added left-overs). Like her counterpart, Mrs Doran adopted changes in her domestic habits, having learned a variety of useful skills from keeping a vegetable garden to cooking economically, down to purchasing sensible, hard-working clothes, so that she too finally shed her slovenly, inefficient ways.[59]

The commissioner's policy with regard to female education was clearly stated in their comment on the *Reading book for the use of female schools* (1838), when they said that it contained 'information pecularly adapted to the character and pursuits of females in the middle and humble ranks of life'. The contents of the *Girls' reading book* (1860) revealed the 'character and pursuits' the commissioners had envisaged for Irish girls in the nineteenth century. They consisted of lessons under such headings as Amusements of children; Bread; Dairy management; Breakfast cookery; Soups; Household hints; Duties of female servants and The laundry. As Walsh in *Images of women in nineteenth century schoolbooks* (1984) rightly observed 'The largest source of female labour in nineteenth century Ireland was domestic service'. The number employed in domestic service in Ireland in 1891 was as high as 394,000,[60] so the commissioners' books catered for the future needs of their female students by ensuring that lessons were both practical and utilitarian. In the *Reading book for the use of female schools* not only were girls instructed on cookery and baking but they were also advised about the care of food and their cook-

58 Coolahan, *Irish education*, pp 23–4.   59 *Agricultural class book*, p. 113.   60 Lorcan Walsh, 'Images of women in nineteenth century schoolbooks' in *Irish Educational Studies* 4:1 (1984), p. 75.

ing utensils, the uses of salt, the baking of mushrooms and finally they were instructed on how to furnish a house.[61]

The duties of the laundry maid were set out. It was felt that much responsibility rested with her 'independently of her having to care for the family linen ... she will probably be required to take charge of the several materials used in washing: such as soap, starch, blue soda, and a variety of other little things which it is necessary always to have at hand'[62]. The care of children was given the same extensive treatment in the readers, as the hints on domestic economy, particularly in the *Supplement to the fourth book of lessons*. In a lesson called simply *A nursery maid* the reader was advised that 'proper food, cleanliness, good air, and gentle nursing' were essential in the care of children. It was essential that 'the room in which children sleep and live should be kept pure and wholesome' and that draughts should be avoided at all costs.[63] In a lesson on the *Management of the sick* girls were informed that females displayed higher levels of expertise, stamina and selflessness in the care of sick children when compared to males:

> It has often been remarked, that in sickness, there is no hand like a woman's hand, no heart like a woman's heart: and there is not. A man's breast may swell with unutterable sorrow ... yet place him by the sick couch ...

and

> his eye will close and his spirit grow impatient of the dreary task.[64]

Readers of the lesson books in general were left in no doubt as to the important role mothers played in the Irish society by virtue of being loving mothers who cared for their children. According to one poem in the *Reading book for the use of female schools*; a mother's love knew no bounds. A dramatic effect was achieved by a series of rhetorical questions to the reader:

> Hast thou sounded the depths of yonder sea
> And counted the sands that under it be?
> Hast thou measured the height of heaven above?
> Then may'st thou speak of a Mother's love.

The female readers provided girls with a thorough preparation for their future lives as domestic servants, housewives and mothers, and took every precaution to ensure that they would carry out their duties with efficiency and

61 Dublin, 1854, p. 127.   62 *Girls' reading book for the use of schools* (Dublin, 1873), p. 123.   63 *Supplement to the fourth book of lessons*, pp 419–20.   64 *Girls' reading book*, p. 59.

integrity. Walsh argued 'that the schoolbooks ... were very limited in preparing girls for life ... that the books not only failed to open avenues but in fact
closed off, in an attitudinal manner, possible roads to future development'.[65]
But Whateley and Carlile never set out to break the mould of Irish society,
their ambitions were much more modest. They wished to change the domestic habits of the poorest in the land and in order to do so they took every possible step they could to provide girls with all the practical information they
needed in the reading books to bring this situation about.

The Kildare Place and the national education commissioners envisaged a
utilitarian education for the poor in Ireland, so too did More in England. But
the type of instruction More had in mind was of a limited nature. She wrote:

> My plan for instructing the poor is very limited and strict.
> They learn ... such coarse work as may fit them for servants ...
> My object has not been to teach dogmas and opinions, but
> to inform the lower class of habits of industry and virtue ...
> To make good members of society has been my aim.[66]

Education policy makers in Ireland also wanted to train the poor in habits of
industry and piety. They too wanted 'to make good members of society'.
They used library readers and lesson books full of well meaning improving
advice and useful information to teach the children of the poor, in the belief
that they would return home and teach their parents. This was the view
expressed by Kavanagh, at one time a head inspector of the board. He had

> no doubt, that from a good school, a child goes home in fact, as a mis-
> sionary to his parents: thus to some degree, reversing the order of
> nature ... There is no doubt that the instincts which are so developed
> in childhood, will remain and are sure to be noticed by and will influ-
> ence the parents and thus gradually influence the family and the
> home.[67]

But More and the evangelical movement she represented, wished to maintain
the status quo in society. They had no desire to educate the poor above their
station in life. It was enough to provide instruction for the poor 'as may fit
them for servants'. By comparison the Kildare Place and the national education commissioners gave the poor an opportunity to raise their expectations in
life and to climb the social ladder. They did so by providing books on a broad
range of topics, to a very high standard, and by providing a series of graded
textbooks, which were reputedly the best available at that time.

65 Walsh, 'Images of women', p. 81.   66 J. and M.Collingwood, *Hannah More* (Oxford, 1990),
p. 77.   67 Godkin *A handbook of the education question*, p. 89.

The main flaw in the books which modern observers such as Akenson (1970), Whelan (1978) and Walsh (1988) referred to, was their lack of an historical or cultural context, for the students for which they were intended. This omission was no doubt due to the compilers' anxiety to ensure that all controversial issues were avoided in their readers and that a spirit of loyalty and good will was fostered in the young Irish citizen for the sovereign parliament. It wasn't until 1873, when a major revision of the board's lesson books took place that the cultural orientation of the children was taken into account and that nationalist sensitivities were respected. As Walsh noted in *The social, political and economic content of nineteenth century schoolbooks* 'The compilers demonstrated that they were not immune to criticism and published in the 1870s a set of books which answered all the negative comments so loudly expressed since their initial publication in the early 1830s', so that 'By the end of the century the national board books would be easily identified as being Irish'.[68]

68 Walsh, 'The social, political and economic content', p. 48.

Conclusion

An uneasy relationship existed between the government at Westminster and her Irish colony. De Montbret understood well the weaknesses of both countries when he wrote:

> I picture England and Ireland as two sisters, the elder steady, thrifty, attentive to her business, thoughtful but over exacting and a little jealous, and so treating her younger sister rather badly at times. The younger less poised, a little giddy and inconsistent, fickle, scarcely perturbed about the morrow ...[1]

The government's attempts at reforming the weaknesses of 'The younger less poised' sister were conducted mainly through a network of sponsored schools – parish, diocesan, royal and charter. Tudor and Stuart legislation had conversion to the Protestant religion at its core as well as a desire to spread the English language. Georgian Ireland saw the creation of the charter schools which provided a practical education and aimed to 'rescue the souls of thousands of popish children from the miseries of idleness and begging.'[2] Predictably all of these bids at rescuing the Irish from being Irish failed. Catholics and Presbyterians rejected these schools and supported instead the non-denominational fee-paying hedge schools. But, the belief still persisted in government circles that it was through education that the Irish would be socialized and politicized along loyal, law abiding lines.

Thomas Orde, the chief secretary of Ireland, stated as much when he introduced his plan of education to parliament on 12 April 1787. On that occasion he attributed 'all the violent and atrocious acts which had too often disgraced this nation' to a 'want of education'. He saw education as a means of infusing 'the balm of information into the wound of ignorance'. He argued also, that Catholic participation in his proposed plan for a Protestant education system, would surely disperse 'the mists of ignorance' and encourage Catholic appreciation 'of the superiority of our own (Protestant) doctrines'.[3]

---

1 Ní Chinnéide, 'A Frenchman's impressions of County Cork', p. 24. 2 Jones, *The charity school movement*, pp 232–5. 3 Akenson, *The Irish education experiment*, p. 59.

Twenty years of agrarian violence and a rebellion in which hedge school-masters were known to have been involved, meant that control of Irish education would have to change hands. Add to this, the inability of Church of Ireland clergymen to meet their educational responsibilities and you have a situation which necessitated far greater state control of Irish education. Consequently, four consecutive commission of education inquiries for 1791, 1799, 1806 and 1825 recommended greater state involvement in education supply. They recommended teacher training and the monitoring of book supply in any new system. In other words, the official recommendation was, that education should be taken out of the hands of hedge schoolmasters and that chapbooks should be replaced by those which met with official approval.

Politically the hedge schoolmasters were considered persona non grata by the authorities but the same could not be said of that one time illegal body – the Catholic church, to which most masters were affiliated. Throughout the eighteenth century in particular, the bishops displayed their loyalty to the government not only through addresses of loyalty but by excommunicating Whiteboys and United Irishmen. By the end of the century Catholic bishops were in constant contact with Dublin Castle and in 1795 they were rewarded for their loyalty when Camden, the lord lieutenant, granted them their own domestic seminary at Maynooth, Co. Kildare.

In the eighteenth century it was a symbiotic relationship which existed between the Catholic church and the hedge schoolmasters. This relationship operated on a quid pro quo basis. The priests granted their approval of the masters and the masters co-operated in the teaching of religion or served in the honorary position of parish clerk, to assist the priests. However, by the 1820s when the struggle for the control of Irish education got underway and the Catholic church under the leadership of Doyle fought tenaciously for a share of state aid for Catholic education, this relationship became strained. If the masters wished to stay in business they had no choice but to remain silent when Doyle sacrificed their reputations in a bid to challenge the monopoly enjoyed by the Kildare Place with regard to state funding. As if to add salt to the wound Doyle consistently overstated the contribution of his clergymen to Irish education despite admitting in a letter to the *Carlow Morning Post* that priests were 'overwhelmed with other duties of their calling'.[4] Priests were in fact in the worst possible position to engage in teaching duties due to a lack of manpower in the church. There was only one priest to every 1587 Catholics in 1731, compared to 2627 Catholics per priest at the end of the century.[5] Doyle also undermined the professional ability of the masters although he knew from the parochial returns for his diocese for 1824, that 64% of them were competent to give further instruction beyond the basic numeracy and literacy skills.[6] The

4 McGrath, *Politics*, p. 158.

unkindest cut of all came in 1821 with his assertion that the main reason why the peasantry were induced to take rash oaths and join illegal societies, was due to a lack of an early religious education.[7] But hedge schoolmasters were the main providers of this education and nothing could have been further from the truth as the plethora of catechisms, meditations and religious tracts used in their schools bear adequate testimony to.[8]

Doyle himself testified before the 1825 commissioners of education that Sunday schools were thriving in his own diocese,[9] although he neglected to add that the hedge schoolmasters were the main instructors in these schools. Now it served his purpose to ignore once again the masters' contribution in this regard. The stakes were high for Doyle, He was putting his case as forcibly as he could for state aid as the church simply couldn't afford to educate the poor themselves. Under such circumstances and bearing in mind the questionable loyalty of some masters, it is easy to understand why the government dismissed their contribution to education out of hand.

This was to be their biggest mistake. They completely disregarded what was being taught in hedge schools and remained unaware of the professional expertise of many of the masters. The reports of the commissioners of education for 1806 and 1825 would certainly bear this out. Yet proof of high standards of literacy abound for the eighteenth century. In the 1790s there were fifty printers in Dublin alone, thirty four provincial presses and at least forty newspapers.[10] Besides the 1861 census revealed that 54% of Catholics could read and that 35% could read and write.[11] It could be argued also that Catholic emancipation might never have been achieved had the people not been sufficiently educated to read the vast quantity of propaganda newspaper articles and pamphlets produced during this period.

There can be little doubt that Irish parents set a high value on a hedge school education and made enormous sacrifices to secure it for their children. This is all the more remarkable when one considers the difficult social conditions which prevailed with the poor overburdened with various taxes. Yet they took extreme steps on occasions to ensure that this education was available in their area by kidnapping hedge schoolmasters from other parishes.[12] The masters for their part tried to meet the demand by holding night classes in their hedge schools, from 6 o'clock in the evening to 11 o'clock at night.[13]

Teaching was by no means a lucrative profession and few masters survived solely on the fees they received from the poor. In fact one hedge schoolmaster complained that 'schoolmastering is an empty trade'.[14] Despite these lim-

5 Connolly, *Priests and people*, pp 32–3.   6 Brenan, *Schools of Kildare and Leighlin*, p. 79.   7 McGrath, *Politics*, pp 164–6.   8 Op. cit., pp 65–8.   9 First report of the commissioners, 1825, App., p. 792. 14 April 1825 Examination of Dr Doyle.   10 Smyth, *The men of no property*, p. 162.   11 Connolly, *Priests and people*, p. 28; p. 77.   12 Carleton, 'The hedge school', pp 257–8.   13 Commissioners of Irish education inquiry 1806–12. Fourteenth report, p. 331.   14 Mac Conmara, *Eachtra ghiolla*, p. 36.

itations the profession did have its attractions, not least being the status the masters enjoyed in their local communities. The people regarded the master as 'one of their own'. They even recognised their scholarly achievements by conferring honorary titles on the most deserving, for instance the classical scholar Donnchadh an Chorráin O'Mahony was known as 'The star of Ennistymon', and Carleton's book-keeping teacher as 'The great O'Brien par excellence'. The hedge schoolmasters had much in common with the poor. They shared the same reverence for culture, music, song and poetry. They did much to preserve the manuscripts, sometimes at considerable sacrifice to themselves. This is evident from an entry made by Gallegan on one of his manuscripts when he informed the reader 'what a vast quantity of ink and pens have been used in the work, together with the price of candles in the winter season'.[15] They also shared the same political ideals as the people, judging from the enormous support for O'Connell's emancipation campaign. The priests also shared the same cultural and political aspirations as the people, but they were obliged by a church undergoing reform in the nineteenth century to distance themselves from the people on the social level. This occurred as a result of a church ruling forbidding them from attending a variety of festive gatherings and places of amusement. The situation deteriorated further when they were obliged to adopt a distinctive clerical dress. This marked a 'new social distance between the pastor and his flock'[16] a situation which was not helped by their repeated threats of excommunication for attendance at patterns, and their condemnation of irreverent practices at wakes. In contrast the hedge schoolmasters remained close to the people and far from criticising the practices and customs of the 'merry wake', they were in fact leading participants in it as it was they who provided the wake house for many a poor family who lacked suitable accommodation of their own.[17]

It follows then that the parent/teacher relationship would be a close one, based on the mutual respect. It took the form of a strong partnership in which the master allowed parents to select the curriculum for their children. He accepted the reading books they supplied and agreed to give three classes of individual instruction to their children before lunch.[18] What comes as a surprise to to-day's reader is the fact that the choice of some of the poorest in the land was for a classical education for their children and also that many of the masters had the expertise to provide such an education. It is true that a small number of them had studied for the priesthood abroad, such as Mac Conmara and Ó Coileáin but the majority of them had not. It should of course be stated that the curriculum wasn't uniform throughout the country

15 Dawson, *Peadar Ó Gealacáin: scríobhaí*, p. 36.   16 Connolly, *Priests and people*, pp 58–74.   17 Carleton, 'The hedge school', p. 322.   18 Atkinson, *Irish education*, p. 47. 'An Irish hedge school', p. 602.

and depended on the qualifications of the master but what can be stated with certainty is that the hedge schools were the only preparatory schools available to young men intended for the priesthood, who wished to enter the Irish Colleges in Salamanca and Louvain up until the year 1793, that students from all over Ireland attended these colleges and that the entry requirement was at university level.[19]

The genuine fears and concerns expressed by conservative members of Irish society and the education commissioners throughout the nineteenth century with regard to the fairy tales, chivalric romances, criminal biographies and works of entertainment read in the hedge schools were unfounded. It would be fair to state that the poor children who read these books in the indigenous schools had the edge over their Protestant and Catholic counterparts in the state sponsored schools who were deprived of the pleasure derived from reading them. Works of the imagination were eagerly sought after by the Irish and the *Life of Freney, the robber,* far from leading to a life 'of lawless and profligate adventure'[20] was far more likely to have given young readers a taste for literature and a desire to read many more books of adventure. The medieval romances were read by Shakespeare, the greatest playwright in the English language and Bunyan sought pleasure and escapism by reading *The seven champions of Christendom.* The chivalric romances enjoyed by the poor in the hedge schools of Ireland also formed part of the juvenile reading material of the best writers of their time, namely Johnson, Boswell, Lamb and Wordsworth in England, and Griffin and Carleton in Ireland, upon whom, one could argue, they had only the very best effect.

Books such as Defoe's *Moll Flanders* or *The history of fair Rosamond and Jane Shore* or *The pleasant art* were wrongly ascribed by Dutton (1808) and Shaw Mason (1814) to a juvenile readership. Only advanced students of English could possibly have understood them. But what must surely come as a surprise to the modern reader is the eclectic mix of titles which made up the advanced reading books in the hedge schools. The popularity of imaginative works such as the decorous romances of Aubin, or the polished prose essays of Swift, Addison and Steele or the realistic novels of Defoe will surprise few. What is noteworthy however, is that the best available literature of the time found a place in Ireland's hedge schools, namely the novels of Richardson, Fielding, Smollett and Sterne, and the intellectually challenging Gothic novels of Radcliffe and Lewis. We know from the many references to the eighteenth-century novelists in contemporary writers' accounts and from official records, that they had a wide readership but what comes as something of a surprise is the fact that Irish parents and their adult sons and daughters could read and comprehend such complex works.

19 Dowling, *The hedge schools of Ireland*, p. 67.   20 First report of the commissioners, 1825, p. 38.

Previous writers on the topic of hedge schools regarded contemporary writers' criticism of chapbooks as merely vindictive assaults on the integrity of the successful hedge schoolmasters and as a deliberate bid to discredit them in the eyes of the authorities. Their argument doesn't bear up in the light of the philosophical thinking of the age, of both liberal and conservative groups in society. Locke, the radical philosopher, viewed fairy tales as 'perfectly useless trumpery',[21] and Rousseau believed that 'children required the naked truth',[22] while Trimmer denounced *Cinderella* as 'a compendium of vice' and condemned *Robinson Crusoe* as a dangerous book which led to an early taste for a rambling life.[23] It is in this context that one should view their concern.

All attempts to replace or suppress the chapbooks in Ireland failed. The Kildare Place Society's book subcommittee made a very concentrated attempt to supplant the chapbooks and few would doubt the sincerity of the motivation behind their actions. The aim of the library readers was clearly to improve the habits of the Irish but Irish readers did not want didactic works of improving advice. This would account for the fact that the only readers which appealed to them were ones on travel, voyages, natural history and a story with a fairy tale quality called *Elizabeth, or The exiles of Siberia*.[24] The national commissioners of education of 1831 only succeeded in replacing the chapbooks with their own lesson books by making them compulsory reading in all but name. In fact it took the commissioners six years before they savoured success and they only achieved this by providing their own lesson books free of charge to schools and by making teachers' promotion conditional on their passing an examination on their contents.[25]

By 1831 the death knell was sounding for the hedge schools of Ireland. They had served well in their time as Dowling rightly pointed out, but their day was over. Now a better financed and structured system of education was required to cater for a growing population. But it was a natural disaster – the great famine of 1845 which put the final nail in the coffin of the hedge schools, although they lingered on in dwindling numbers until the passing of the Intermediate Act of 1878.

On 9 September 1831 Stanley revealed his proposals for a national education system and Doyle was well pleased with it. It was clear for all to see that he had won an impressive victory over the Kildare Place Society because for the first time ever there was going to be power sharing in Irish education. The Catholic priest would now share managerial power and the right to catechise in Irish schools on equal terms with his Protestant counterpart. It also meant that the Catholic church would have complete insulation from the threat

21 Locke, *Some thoughts concerning education*, p. 228.   22 J.J. Rousseau, *Emilius and Sophia*, pp 166–173.   23 Churchill, *The concise Cambridge history of English literature*, p. 512.   24 Crofton Croker, *Fairy legends and traditions*, p. 336.   25 Report from the commissioners of primary education (Irl) 1870, Powis, p. 119.

posed by proselytizing schools, as well as being released from carrying the financial burden for Catholic education. Gratifying as this must surely have been for Doyle, he made no secret of the pleasure he took in the fate of the independent hedge schoolmaster. Perhaps it would be stretching the bounds of credulity too far to have expected him to pay tribute to the masters for their unique contribution to Irish education in providing non-denominational education for the majority of school-going children in this country for over one hundred and thirty six years. He never paid such a tribute but rather, with barely concealed delight he said he looked forward to the displacement of the hedge schoolmasters by fully trained national schoolteachers, who 'will aid us in a work of great difficulty, to wit that of suppressing hedge schools'.[26]

26 Dowling, *A history of Irish education*, p. 118.

Appendices

Appendix 1: First Report of the Commissioners of Education Inquiry, 1825 (400), xii, 1

Appendix No. 221

A LIST of books used in the various Schools situated in the four following counties in Ireland; abstracted from the sworn Returns made to the Commissioners; *viz.*

County Donegal	—	—	—	Province Ulster
County Kildare	—	—	—	Province Leinster
County Galway	—	—	—	Province Connaught
County Kerry	—	—	—	Province Munster

Distinguishing, Catechisms, Religious Works, and Works of Entertainment.

Catechisms

Stopford's	—	—	—	—	⎫
Mann's	—	—	—	—	⎬ Established Church
Marriott's	—	—	—	—	
Lewis's	—	—	—	—	⎭
Shorter's	—	—	—	—	Presbyterian
Butler's	—	—	—	—	⎫
Fleury's	—	—	—	—	
The Poor Man's	—	—	—	—	
Historical Catechism	—	—	—	—	
General	d'	—	—	—	⎬ Roman Catholic
Reilly's (Irish)	d'	—	—	—	
Devereaux's	d'	—	—	—	
Donlevy's	d'	—	—	—	
McMahon's	d'	—	—	—	
Coppinger's	d'	—	—	—	
Philosophical	d'	—	—	—	⎭

Religious Works

Testament.
Dr Troy's Scripture Lessons.
Dr Gallagher's Irish Sermons.
Think Well on it.
Imitation of Christ.
Parables, Miracles, Sermon on the Mount, from New Testament.
Allen's Alarm to Unconverted Sinners.
Gahan's Extracts from Old and New Testament.
Crossman's Introduction to the Knowledge of the Christian Religion.
Questions on the Gospel of St Luke, by Rev. Thomas P. Magee.
The Christian Atonement.
Preparation for Death; or, the Churchman on a Sick Bed.
Moore's Monitor.
Roman Catholic Manual.
Last Hours of the Rev. J. Cowper ⎫
Work of the Holy Spirit   ⎬ Tracts
Parental Duties   ⎪
Hopes of Eternity   ⎭
Trimmer's Scripture Lessons.
Watt's Hymns.
Sellon's Scripture History.
History of the Jewish Nation.
Footstep to Mrs Trimmer.
An Answer to the Excuses about the Sacrament.
Spouse of Christ – the best Marriage.
Christian Morals, selected from some of the Epistles of the New Testament.
Christian Covenant.
History of our Saviour.
The Path of Paradise, by Gahan.
The Key of Paradise, by Gahan.
The Poor Man's Manual.
The Christian Directory.
Abridgement of Christian Doctrine by Butler.
Defence of Catholic Principles, in a Letter to a Protestant Minister, with recom-
    mendatory Preface by Rev. R. Hayes.
Travels of St Paul.
Ward's Errata to the Protestant Bible.
An Essay for Catholic Communion.
Challoner's Reflections on the Truth of the Christian Religion.
Gobinet's Instructions for Youth.
Dorelle's Moral Reflections.
Economy of Human Life.
Life of God in the Soul of Man.
Elevation of the Soul to God.
Thomas à Kempis.
Life of St Benedict.
Portrait of a true and perfect Christian; translated from the French by the Rev. Mr.
    Ruyter.
History of the Saints.
St Augustine's Confessions and Meditations.

Spiritual Combat.

Fifty Reasons why the Catholic Apostolic Religion ought to be preferred to all the Sects in Christendom.

A Treatise on the Difference between Temporal and Eternal.

The Stations and Devotions of the Passion of our Lord Jesus Christ, as they are made in Jerusalem.

St Francis de Sales.

Jeremy Taylor's Contemplations.

Treatise of the Scapular.

Dupin's History of the Church.

The Exclamations of the Soul to God, or the Meditations of Saint Theresa after Communion, by Dr Milner.

Life of St Mary of Egypt.

Life of St Joseph.

Maxims of Christian Philosophy, drawn from Considerations of Eternity.

The Holy Law explained.

The Spiritual Combat: to which are added, the Peace of the Soul; Pious Reflections on Death, and some Reflections upon the Prerogatives, Powers and Protection of St Joseph, Spouse of the blessed and ever immaculate Virgin Mary, Mother of God.

A Treatise by the Bishop of Barcelona.

Grounds of Catholic Doctrine.

Paley's Principles of Religion.

Reeves' History of the New Testament.

Prince Hohenlohe's Prayer Book.

Fleming's Meditations and Prayers, adapted to the Cross.

Life of the Blessed Virgin.

St Joseph and St Anne, mother of the Virgin.

A Dissertation on Indulgencies.

Reflections on the Prerogative of St John.

Life of a Catholic Christian.

Hell opened to Sinners.

An Epistle to an Unconverted Reader.

The nature of Conversion, and the Burning Lamp.

Timothy O'Sullivan's Pious Miscellany, in Irish.

Secker's Lectures.

Heaven taken by Storm.

Hervey's Meditations.

The Duties that relate to Man, considered as an Individual.

Parson's Christian Directory.

Pastorini's Prophecies.

Moylan's Devotions to Jesus Christ.

Fenton's Reflections and Instructions for the Sacraments of Penance, Confirmation and the Eucharist.

Bishop Wilson's Sermons on the Death and Sufferings of Christ.

The Saint's Everlasting Rest.

The Virgin's Nosegay.

The Litany of Saints.

Plain Directions for spending one Day well.

Life of Father Thomas in Jesus.

The shortest Way to end Disputes in Religion.

The Protestant Trial by the written Word.

Life of St Cyprian.

Life of St Augustin.
The Victory of Grace over Sin and Death.
Funiculus Triplex; or, Cord of St Francis.

Works of Entertainment, Histories, Tales &c.

Don Quixote.
History of Troy.
Modern Story Teller.
Life of Baron Trenck.
Jack and his Eleven Brothers.
Hibernian Tales.
Guy, Earl of Warwick.
History of the Seven Wise Masters and Mistresses of Rome.
Death of Abel.
Vicar of Wakefield.
Dean Swift's Letters.
The Battle of Aughrim.
The Siege of Londonderry.
Polite Preceptor.
Tristram Shandy.
Sandford and Merton.
American Magazine.
Bruce's Travels.
Seven Champions of Christendom.
Milton's Paradise Lost.
John Doyle's Account of his Losses by the Lottery.
Hume's History of England.
Goldsmith's History of England.
        Ditto - - - Rome.
        Ditto - - - Greece.
Life of Lord Chief Justice Hale.
Siege of Chester, and History of the Cathedral of Chester.
Dusseldorf on Fratricide.
Grandmother and Jenny.
Life of Lady Lucy, daughter of an Irish Lord, who married a general officer and was by
        him carried into Flanders, where he became jealous of her and a young nobleman,
        his kinsman, whom he killed, and afterwards left her wounded and big with child
        in a forest.
Arabian Nights.
Drake's Voyages.
Guicciardini's History of Italy.
Gentleman's and Ladies' Monitor.
Monthly Magazine.
Dr Faustus and the Devil.
School of Delights.
Life of St Patrick.
Paddy from Cork.
Robin Hood.
Mrs Sherwood's Stories on the Church Catechism.

Fairy Tales.
Father and Daughter, by Mrs Opie.
History of Tom Simpkins.
Travels to the North Seas.
History of Jack the Bachelor.
Cecilia.
Manning's Moral Entertainment.
The Blind Child.
The Miscellany.
The History of Tythes; their influence on Agriculture and Population.
Lady Mary Wortley Montague's Letters.
Chapter of Accidents.
La Belle Assemblée.
History of Harriet Stuart.
Life of Buonoparte.
Select Story Teller.
Miscellanea Curiosa.
Madame de Sevigné's letters.
Montelion; a Romance.
History of the Persians and Grecians.
Artless Tales.
Gil Blas.
Conquest of Mexico by Cortez.
Noble Slaves.
Dialogues between Lady Louisa and Mentoria.
Mary Leadebater's Tales.
Montague's Essays.
An Act of Parliament for Encouragement of Planting of Trees.
Newspapers.
The Truant reclaimed.
Don Belianis of Greece.
The virtuous Scholar.
Life of a Student in the University of Paris.
Virtue rewarded and Vice punished.
Complete Letter Writer.
Swift's Poems.
Cowper's Poems.
Dr Johnson's Classical Essays.
The Idler.
Expedition against the Ohio Indians.
The Mendicant, or the lost Child.
Warbeck.
Female Adventurers.
Old English Baron.
Life of Colonel Gardiner.
Chesterfield's Accomplished Gentleman.
Entertainment for Lent.
The Beggar Girl.
The discarded Son.
History of Fanny Meadows.
Henry and Isabella.
Dodsley's Preceptor.

Young's Night Thoughts.
Thompson's Seasons.
Spectator.
Jack Brown in Prison.
A Hackney Coachman on the way to get a good fare.
The wonderful Advantages of venturing in the Lottery.
The Gamester.
Sinful Sally.
History of the French Revolution.
Gulliver's Travels.
Fair Rosamond.
Tales of the Castle.
Juliana Ormston.
Voltaire's Universal History.
Life of Frederick III of Prussia.
Irish Rogues and Rapparees.
Captain Freney, the Robber.
Moll Flanders,
Principles of Politeness.
Seven Wonders of the World.
History of Charles XII of Sweden, by Voltaire.
Hermione.
Sturm's Tracts.
Secrecy; or the Ruin on the Rock.
The Victim of Intolerance; or the Hermit of Killarney. A Catholic Tale.
Life of Oliver Cromwell.
The obliging Husband and Imperious Wife.
The honest London Spy, exhibiting the base and subtle Intrigues of the Town.
Peregrine Pickle.
The Chevalier de Faublas.
Adventures of Marianne.
The pleasant Art of Money-catching.
History of Philander Flashaway.
Frederick Latimer.
History of Reynard the Fox.
Sorrows of the Heart.
Adventures of John of Gaunt.
Jane Shore.
Essays on Shakespeare and Misrepresentations of Voltaire.
The Fortunate Country Maid.
The Virtuous Widow.
Sir Charles Grandison.
Transition of a Moment.
Genuine History of Ireland.
The Military Articles of Limerick.
Bishop Plunkett's Speech in 1681.
Parismos and Parismenos.
Reflections on Ridicule.
Garden of Love; Feast of Love.
Memoirs of George Farquhar, containing "Love and a Bottle".
Sir Harry Wildair; or the Constant Couple.
Olivia; or the Deserted Bride.

Life of Redmond O'Hanlon, the Robber.
The Feats of Astrologers.
Rousseau's Eloisa.
The Post-chaise Companion.
Warner's History of Ireland.
History of the English Rebellion.
History of the Emperors of Rome.
Female Policy detected.
Letters of Pope Clement XIV.
Errors of Innocence.
Dialogues of the Dead.
Life of Dean Swift.
Chesterfield's Letters.
Hero and Leander.
Sully's Memoirs.
Dorastus and Favora.
Camilla; Old Wife and Young Husband.
Paul and Virginia.
Lydia (a loose Novel).
The Adventurer.
Launcelot Greaves, Adventures of.
Memoirs of a Man of Fashion.
The Discarded Son.
The Gypsey Countess.
Apology for the Life of George Anne Bellamy.
History of Limerick.
Battle of Ventry Harbour.
Aunt Mary's Tales.
Pantheon.
Female Spectator.
Journey to Paris.
Peruvian Tales.
An Enquiry touching Happiness.
Uncle Thomas; a Novel.
Alvin; a Novel.
Memoirs of Catherine Jemmett.
History of England, by a Nun.
Life of Lord George Sackville.
Plain Sense.
Life of Lord Elmwood.
Life of William the Third.
Dr O'Leary's Letters.
The Vanity of Human Wishes; a Novel.
The Child of Chance.
History of Black Giles.
Clarissa Harlowe.
History of Tate Wilkinson.
John de Lancaster.
The Academy of Compliments.
Good and bad Ministers; a political work.
The Labyrinth of Life.
History of Julia and Cecilia de Valmont.

Private Life of Louis XVI.
History of the Irish Rebellion of 1798.
The Garden of Fidelity.
Leland's History of Ireland.
Comerford's ditto.
Keating's dittoo.
Moore's Views of France.
Pamela.
The Noble Slave.
The Chamber of Death.
Ann of St Ives.
Irish Excursion.
The Reverie.
Women as they are.
History of Louis XIV.
Almoran and Hamet.
Dangerous Connections.
Sublime Friendship delineated.
The Complete Attorney and Solicitor.
First Impressions.
Flowers of Modern History.
History of the Prince of Wales.
The Monk.
History of Donna Rosina, a notorious Cheat.
Life of Captain Grant, a gentleman Robber.
Turkish Tales.
Stern's Sentimental Journey.
Rousseau's Letters.
The Enchanted Castle.
Letters of Theodosius and Constantia.
Cambrian Legends.
History of Paul Plaintive.
The Chances.
Fashionable Involvements.
The Soldier of Pennaflor.
Life of Lord Nelson.
Historical Beauties for Young Ladies.
History of Dorothea.
The Trance of Thomas Delany.
The Three Spaniards.
Life of the Empress Catherine of Russia.
History of the Nine Worthies.
The Mysteries of Udolpho.
The Memoirs of the Duchess de la Valliere.
The Effects of Love.
The Posthumous Daughter and the Brothers (a story that happens every day).
An Old Friend with a New Face.
Novel Memoirs of Amoranda.
Macintosh's Defence of French Revolution.
Life of Mahomet.
Life of Garrick.
Life of George II.
Bouverie; a Novel.

The Knights of Malta.
Delicate Distress.
The English Hermit.
Memoirs of Captain John Creighton.
The Old-fashioned Farmer's Motives.
The Farmer's Daughter of Essex, an Account of her Seduction, &c., &c.
Joseph Andrews.
Philanda Sylvia.
History of Waterford.
Belsham's History of England.
Haunted Cavern.
Lucilla.
David, or the Reprobate reformed.
Life of Coningsmark, the Robber.
Nocturnal Visit.
Honoria, or the Infatuated Child.
The Munster Farmer's Magazine.
History of the Garden of Love, and the Flower of Fidelity.
The supposed Daughter, or Innocent Imposter.
The Child of Nature.
Economy of Beauty.
The Night Cap.
The Jewish Spy.
Sydney Biddulph.
Fatal Follies.
Eliza Loveless.
Caleb Williams.
Locke's Essays.
Feelings of the Heart.
Pamela in High Life.
Fool of Quality.
La Vaillant's Travels.
Poor Man's Manual.
Travels through the English Shires.
History of Crowned Heads.
Solitary Wanderer.
Embarrassed Attachment.
Life of Don Carlos.
History of the Commonwealth of Rome.
L'Histoire de deux Familles de Norwich.
Chinese Tales.
Debates on Catholic Question.
Nocturnal Revels.
Literary Amusements.
Delineation of the Heart.
Friendly Hints for Servants and Apprentices.
Travels of St Leon.
Memoirs of Charles Fox.
Julia Manderville.
Female Quixote.
Memoirs of the Marquis Bretange.
The Invisible Spy.

Appendix 2: English textbooks in the hedge schools of the diocese of Kildare and Leighlin from the parochial returns of the hedge schools of the diocese of Kildare and Leighlin, 1775–1835

Reading Made Easy	*Fenning's Universal Spelling Book*	*Murray's Books*
Martinstown	Abbeyleix	Dublin St
Graveyard, Ballynakill	Park Bawn	Water Lane
Church St., Ballynakill	Dysart	Carlow
Chapel Lane, Ballynakill	Ballontrain	Gore's Bridge
Dysart	Ballontrain	Course, Tullow
Ballontrain	Castlemore	
Boly	Rossbran	
Cashel	Boly	
Raheen	Raheen	
Tornduff	Tornduff	
Knockroe	Knockroe	
Newtown	Newtown	
Corroughlane	Pollerton Rd.	
Ballycabis	Burn St	
Bortle	Potato Market	
Bortle	Bortle, Co. Wicklow	
Ballinguile	Bortle, Co. Wicklow	
Carricknamiel	Ballinguile, Co. Wicklow	
Moyne, Co. Wicklow	Carricknamiel, Co. Wicklow	
Ratheaden, Co. Carlow	Moyne, Co. Wicklow	
Ballytarsna	Ratheaden	
Corries	Ballytarsna, Co. Carlow	
Sliguf	Corries	
Sliguf	Sliguf	
Ballyellen	Sliguf	
Knockmanus	Ballyellen	
Courleigh	Knockmanus	
Cross Roads, Bornafea	Courleigh	
Whitehall, Paulstown	Whitehall	
Castlekelly	Castlekelly	
Gore's Bridge	Gore's Bridge	
Gore's Bridge, Lowgrange	Gore's Bridge, Baramount	
Drumquin, Co. Carlow	Gore's Bridge, Lowgrange	
Paulville or Tankerstown	Gore's Bridge, Lowgrange	
Ardoyne	Drumquin	
	Rathdaniel	
	Ballyhacket	
	Course, Tullow	
	Ardristan	
	Ardoyne	

Appendix 3: Mathematical textbooks in the hedge schools of the diocese of Kildare and Leighlin

GOUGH	VOSTER
A treatise or arithmetic in theory and practice	*Arithmetic in whole or broken numbers*
Martinstown	Martinstown
Newtown	Newtown
Ballontrain	Newtown
Castlemore	Clonegall
Carlow	Coolrow
Thommahan	Corroughlane
Ballycabis	Thommahan
Graig	Ballycabis
Moneybeg, Bagenalstown	Graig
Moneybeg, Bagenalstown	Copenagh
Drumquin, Co. Carlow	Moneybeg, Bagenalstown
Course, Tullow	Moneybeg, Bagenalstown
Copenagh	Curracrut
	Ratheaden
	Ballytarsna, Parish of Nurney
	Whitehall, Paulstown
	Goresbridge, Lowgrange
	Drumquin, Co. Carlow
	Ballyhacket
	Course, Tullow
	Copenagh

Appendix 4: List of 'Burton' chapbooks purchased by the Kildare Place Society Book Subcommittee, 18 April 1819

The Destruction of Troy	Reading Made Easy
Montelion	Reynard the Fox
Tales of the Fairies	Noble Slaves
Fair Rosamond	James Freney
Seven Champions	Irish Rogues
Parismus	Narrative Pieces
Don Bellianis	Peregrine Pickle
Fairy Tales	Seven Wise Masters
Lady Lucy	Roderick Random
Holy Bible Abridged	Art of Money Catching
Historical Catechism	Battle of Aughrim
Think Well On't	Moral Story Teller
Life of God in the Soul Of Man	Cooke's Voyages
Arabian Nights	Jack And His 11 Brothers
Robinson Crusoe	Death of Abel
Valentine & Orson	Aesop's Fables
Royal Primer	Fortunate Lovers
Life of St Mary of Egypt	History of The Old Testament
St Joseph	

Appendix 5: Kildare Place Society library readers in the hedge schools of the diocese of Kildare and Leighlin

From the parochial returns of the hedge schools in the diocese of Kildare and Leighlin (1775-1835)

Dublin spelling book
Clubbin
Ballycon
Mountmelick (sic)
Derrycloney
Seskin Ryan
Corries
Sliguf

Elizabeth or the exiles in Siberia
Ballycon
Corries
Gore's Bridge
Gore's Bridge

Voyage of Christopher Columbus
Corbally
Mulloughanard
Church St Ballynackill
Curracrut

Travels in Africa
Ballybrittas
Church St Ballynakill
Newtown
Courleigh

Mongo, the little travelller
Goresbridge

Cottage fireside
Moneybeg

The brothers
Kilcarig

Picture of the seasons
Ballytarsna

Dublin reading book
Whitefield
Curracrut
Corries
Sliguf

Cooke's voyages
Feighcullen
Brackina
Clubbin
Newtown

Anson's voyages
Ballyellen
Castlekelly
Drumquin

Moral lessons
Mountmelick (sic)
Seskin Ryan
Ballytarsna

Entertaining medley
Seskin Ryan
Gore's Bridge

Isaac Jenkins
Ratheadon

Select story teller
Corbally
Moyne

Miscellanies
Clubbin
Drunquin

Natural history
Whitefield
Town of Edenderry
Moneybeg
Mountmelick (sic)
Grange
Clonoughado
Gurten
Gore's Bridge

Bligh's voyages
Ballycon
Corries

Byrons narrative
Ballycon
Corries

Useful arts and manu-
factures
Corbally
Moneybeg

Animal sagacity
Clonaslee
Corries

History of Little Jack
Corries

New Robinson Crusoe
Ballyellen

Travels through Swe-
den and Germany
Gore's Bridge

Bibliography

CONTEMPORARY MANUSCRIPTS

National Library of Ireland
Ms G 809. Gallegan, Peter. 'Collections in English and Irish. Entirely written by himself'. 16 January 1824.
Ms G 200 Peter Gallegan, 1837–39.
Ms G 1152 Peter Gallegan, 1844–51.
Ms G 199 Peter Gallegan, 1851.
Ms 8146–8147. Mason, William Shaw (ed.), 'Statistical survey of the county of Tipperary'. *c*.1833.

Royal Irish Academy
Betham Collection. Mícheál Óg Ó Longáin (1766–1837) 23 N 14 O'Longan's Irish Ms. Vol. xvii, 1795–1802.
23 G 24 O'Longan's Irish Ms. Vol. V, 1803–5.
23 G 21 O'Longan's Irish Ms. Vol. II, 1802
Ashburnham Collection. Stowe Mss Ó Longáin. Written for Mr James Roche, Cork.
F III 3   Mícheál Óg Ó Longáin, 1820.
F III 4   Mícheál Ó Longáin, 1820.
F III 1   Mícheál and Peadar Ó Longáin, 1820.
F IV 1   Mícheál Ó Longáin, 1819.
F IV 2   Mícheál Óg Ó Longáin, 1816.
F IV 3   Mícheál Óg Ó Longáin, 1809–1811.
24 P 20 Peadar Ó Gealacáin, 1824–26.
3 B 39 Peadar Ó Gealacáin, 1827.

University of Dublin, Trinity College
Ms H. 6 32. No. 1396. 2 Vols.
O'Connell, Peter. 'An Irish-English Dictionary', 1826.

National University of Ireland, Maynooth
Murphy Collection
M 57 Vol. 57 Michael Longan Esq.
M 101 Mícheál Óg Ó Longáin, 1814

M 100 Vol. 1 Michael Longan, 1815
M 94 Michéal Óg Ó Longáin, 1820
M 97 Michéal Óg Ó Longáin, Cornelius Mahony, Denis O'Mahony, 1834
C 73 (j), 65 Tadhg Gaedhlach Ó Súilleabháin
DR 2 (e) Eoghan Ruadh Ó Suilleabháin
M 85 / M 86 Donnchadh Ruadh Mac Con-Mara, September 1779.
O'Curry Collection
3 A 16 Andrias Mac Craith
C 47 Filíocht na Maighe.

Church of Ireland College of Education, Dublin

KPS 1/MS/101 *The humble petition of the Society for Promoting the Education of the*
Poor of Ireland. Memorial to the House of Commons, 30 November 1815.
KPS 1/MS/100-106 *Committee minutes and resolutions, 1811–1841.*
KPS 1/MS/109 *General committee minutes, 1832–1834.*
KPS 1/MS/119 *Minutes of the cheap book committee, 1814–1816.*
KPS 1/MS/120 *Letters re: sale of cheap books, 1814–1815.*
KPS 1/MS/123–138 *Petitions of the Society to Parliament.*

PARLIAMENTARY PAPERS

Fourteenth Report of the Commissioners of the Board of Education in Ireland, H.C.
    1812–1813 (21) V, 221.
Fourteenth Report of the Commissioners of the Board of Education in Ireland, H.C.
    1813–1814 (47) V, 331.
First Report of the Commissioners of Irish Education Inquiry, 1825 (400), xii, 1.
First Report of the Commissioners of Irish Education Inquiry, 1825 (400), xii, 1. Appen-
    dix No. 221, 553–60.
Second Report of the Commissioners of Inquiry. (Abstract of Returns in 1824, from the
    Protestant and Roman Catholic Clergy in Ireland, of the State of Education in
    their respective Parishes); 1826–27 (12), xii, 1.
Report of the Select Committee of the House of Lords on the plan of education in Ireland;
    with minutes of evidence, H.C. 1837 (543–1), viii, pt. i, 1.
Minutes of evidence taken before the Select Committee of the House of Lords on the plan of
    education in Ireland, H.C. 1837 (543–11), viii, pt. ii, 1.
Report of the Select Committee appointed to inquire into the progress and operation of the
    new plan of education in Ireland, H.C. 1837 (485), ix.
Royal Commission of Inquiry into primary education (Ireland), Vol. 1, pt. 1;
Report of the Commissioners, H.C. 1870 (c6), xxviii, pt. 1,1.
Report of the General Meeting for Promoting the Education of the Poor in Ireland, Dublin,
    1820.
Second Report of the Society for Promoting the Education of the Poor of Ireland. Dublin:
    John Jones, 40 Sth. Great Georges St., 1814.
Report on the Distribution of Books, 1815. KPS/11/13/1.

CONTEMPORARY NEWSPAPERS AND JOURNALS

Belfast Newsletter
An Claidheamh Solais
Dublin Evening Post
Dublin Review
Dublin University Magazine
Dublin Weekly Register

Ennis Chronicle
Finn's Leinster Journal
Freeman's Journal
General Advertiser, or, Limerick Gazette
Irish Ecclesiastical Record

CONTEMPORARY PAMPHLETS

Hints on the Formation of Lending Libraries in Ireland. Dublin, 1824.
Thoughts and Suggestions on the Education of the Peasantry of Ireland. London, 1820.
Doyle, James (J.K.L.). *Thoughts on the Education of the Irish Poor, as contained in the letters of the Right Reverend Dr Doyle, R.C.B.* Carlow, 1820.
——*A letter from the Right Reverend Dr Doyle, Bishop of Kildare and Leighlin to the Catholic Association, in reply to the mis-statements reported to the House of Commons by Mr. North on the Education of the Poor in Ireland.* Dublin, 1824.
——*Letters on the State of Education in Ireland, and on Bible Societies, addressed to a Friend in England.* Dublin, 1824.
——*Letters on the State of Ireland addressed by J.K.L. to a friend in England.* Dublin, 1825.

CONTEMPORARY PRINTED WORKS

Travellers' accounts
Anderson, Christopher. *The native Irish and their descendants.* Dublin, 1846.
Bicheno, J.E. *Ireland and its Economy ... In a Tour Through the Country in the Autumn of 1829.* London, 1830.
Bowden, Charles Topham. *A tour through Ireland.* Dublin, 1791.
Bush, John. *Hibernia curiosa.* London, 1769.
Carr, John. *The stranger in Ireland.* Blackfriars, 1806.
Chatterton, Lady. *Rambles in the south of Ireland.* London, 1839.
Cooper, George. *Letters on the Irish nation.* London, 1800.
Croker, T. Crofton. *Researches in the south of Ireland.* London, 1824.
Curwen, S.C. *Observations on the state of Ireland.* London, 1818.
de Beaumont, Gustave. *Ireland social, political & religious.* London, 1839.
de Montbret, Coquebert. 'A Frenchman's impression of Limerick'. In *North Munster Antiquarian Journal*, 1948.
——'A new view of eighteenth century life in Kerry'. In *Journal of the Kerry Archaeological and Historical Society*, 1973.
——'A journey from Cork to Limerick in December, 1790'. In *Kerry Archaeological and Historical Society*, 1971.

——'A new view of Cork city in 1790'. In *Journal of the Cork Historical & Archaeological Society*, 1973.

——'Coquebert de Montbret's impression of Galway city and county in the year 1791'. In *Journal of the Galway Archaeological and Historical Society*, 1952.

——'Coquebert de Montbret in search of the hidden Ireland'. In *Journal of the Royal Society of Antiquaries of Ireland*, 1952.

——'A Frenchman's impression of County Cork in 1790'. In *Journal of the Cork Historical & Archaeological Society*, 1974.

Glassford, James. *Notes on three tours in Ireland in 1824 and 1826.* London, 1832.

Hall, Reverend James. *Tour through Ireland.* London, 1813.

Hall, S.C. Mr & Mrs. *Ireland. Its scenery, character etc.* London, 1841.

Holmes, George. *Sketches of some of the southern counties of Ireland.* London, 1801.

Inglis, Henry D. *Ireland in 1834. A journey throughout Ireland.* London, 1834.

Kohl, J.G. *Travels in Ireland.* London, 1844.

Luckombe, Philip. *A tour through Ireland.* London, 1780.

Newenham, Thomas. *A view of the natural, political and commercial circumstances of Ireland.* London, 1809.

Otway, Reverend Caesar. *Sketches in Erris and Tyrawly.* Dublin, 1841.

——*Sketches in Ireland.* Dublin, 1827.

——*A tour in Connaught.* Dublin, 1839.

Pococke, Richard. *Tour in Ireland in 1752.* Dublin, 1891.

Reed, William. *Rambles in Ireland.* London, 1815.

Reid, Thomas. *Travels in Ireland in the Year 1822.* London, 1823.

Trotter, Bernard. *Walks through Ireland in the years 1812, 1814 and 1817.* London, 1819.

Twiss, Richard. *A tour in Ireland in 1775.* London, 1776.

Wakefield, Edward. *An account of Ireland, statistical and political.* London, 1812.

Young, Arthur. *A tour in Ireland: with general observations on the present state of that kingdom; made in ... 1776, 1777 and 1778 ... and brought down to the end of 1779,* Dublin, 1780.

Statistical surveys

Archer, Lieutenant Joseph. *Statistical survey of the County of Dublin, with observations on the means of improvement; drawn up for the consideration and by the direction of the Dublin Society.* Dublin, 1801.

Coote, Sir Charles. *General view of the agriculture and manufacturers of the King's County and observations of the means of improvement drawn up in the year 1801 for the consideration and under the direction of the Dublin Society.* Dublin, 1801.

——*General view of the agriculture and manufacturers of the Queen's County. Drawn up in ... 1801 ... under the direction of the Dublin Society.* Dublin, 1801.

——*Statistical survey of the county of Cavan.* Dublin, 1801.

——*Statistical survey of the county of Monaghan.* Dublin, 1802.

——*Statistical survey of the county of Armagh.* Dublin, 1804.

Dubourdieu, Reverend John. *Statistical survey of the county of Antrim.* Dublin, 1812.

——*Statistical survey of the county of Down.* Dublin, 1802.

Dutton, Hely. *A statistical survey of the county of Clare*. Dublin, 1808.

——*A statistical survey of the county of Galway*. Dublin, 1824.

Fraser, Robert. *Statistical survey of the county of Wicklow*. Dublin, 1801.

——*Statistical survey of the county of Wexford*. Dublin, 1807.

Mason, Reverend William Shaw. *A Statistical Account or Parochial Survey of Ireland*. Dublin, 1816.

——*Survey of Tullaroan*. Dublin, 1819.

McEvoy, John. *Statistical survey of the county of Tyrone*. Dublin, 1802.

McParlan, Dr James. *Statistical survey of the county of Leitrim*. Dublin, 1802.

——*Statistical survey of the county of Sligo*. Dublin, 1802.

——*Statistical survey of the county of Donegal*. Dublin, 1802.

——*Statistical survey of the county of Mayo*. Dublin, 1802.

Rawson, Thomas James. *Statistical survey of the county of Kildare*. Dublin, 1807.

Thompson, Robert. *Statistical survey of the county of Meath*. Dublin, 1802.

Tighe, William. *Statistical observations relative to the county of Kilkenny made in the years 1800 and 1801*. Dublin, 1802.

Weld, Isaac. *Statistical survey of the county of Roscommon*. Dublin 1832.

PRINTED WORKS PUBLISHED BEFORE 1900

Ashton, John. *Chap books of the eighteenth century*. London, 1882.

Barrington, Sir Jonah. *Personal sketches of his own times*. London, 1830.

Bell, Robert. *A description of the condition and manners of the peasantry of Ireland between the years 1870 and 1790*. London, 1804.

Carleton, William. *Traits and stories of the Irish peasantry*. Dublin, 1843.

Croker, T. Crofton. *Fairy legends and traditions of the south of Ireland, 1825–1828*. London, n.d.

Ellis, George. *Specimens of early English metrical romances*. London, 1848.

Fitzgibbon, Gerald. *Ireland in 1868. the battlefield for English party strife*. London, 1868.

Fitzpatrick, W.J. *The life, times and correspondence of the Rt. Reverend Dr Doyle*. Dublin, 1861.

——*Unpublished essay by Dr Doyle*. An essay on education and the state of Ireland. Dublin, 1880.

Froude, James A. *The English in Ireland in the eighteenth century. In 2 volumes*. London, 1872–74.

Glassford, James. *Letter to Rt. Hon. Earl of Roden on the present state of Irish education, 1829*. London, 1829.

Godkin, James. *A handbook of the education question*. Dublin, 1862.

Griffin, Dr *The life of Gerald Griffin*. Dublin, 1857.

Hayes, S. (ed.). *A slave of adversity by Donnchadh Ruadh Mac Con-Mara*. Dublin, 1853.

Kavanagh, James W. *Mixed education: the Catholic case stated*. Dublin, 1859.

Milner, Reverend J. *An inquiry into certain vulgar opinions*. London, 1808.

O'Brien, R. Barry. *Fifty years of concessions to Ireland, 1831–1881*. London, n.d.
Porter, J.L. *The life and times of Henry Cooke*. London, 1871.
Sullivan, Robert. *Lectures and letters on popular education*. Dublin, 1842.
Thackeray, William. *The Irish sketch book*. London, 1887.
Thompson, Reverend Henry. *The life of Hannah More*. Edinburgh, 1838.
Walsh, John Edward. *Ireland sixty years ago*. Dublin, 1847.
Warburton, J.; Whitelaw, Reverend J. and Walsh, Reverend Robert. *History of the City of Dublin*. London, 1818.

PRINTED WORKS PUBLISHED AFTER 1900

Adams, J.R.R. *The printed word and the common man*. Belfast, 1987.
Akenson, D.H. *The Irish education experiment*. Toronto, 1970.
Altick, Richard D. *The English common reader*. Chicago, 1957.
——*Victorian people and ideas*. London, 1974.
Atkinson, Norman. *Irish education*. Dublin, 1969.
Avery, Gillian and Briggs, Julia. *Children and their books*. Oxford, 1989.
——*Childhood's pattern*. London 1975.
Balfour, Graham. *The educational systems of Great Britain and Ireland*. Oxford, 1903.
Ballaster, Ros. *Seductive forms. Women's amatory fiction from 1684 to 1740*. Oxford, 1992.
Barry, Florence Valentine. *A century of children's books*. London, 1922.
Bartlett, Thomas. *The fall and rise of the Irish nation*. Dublin, 1992.
Beckett, J.C. *The making of modern Ireland 1603–1923*. Norfolk, 1981.
Bowen, Desmond. *The Protestant crusade in Ireland, 1800-70*. Dublin and Montreal, 1978.
Brenan, Reverend Martin. *Schools of Kildare and Leighlin A.D. 1775–1835*. Dublin, 1935.
Carleton, William. *The autobiography of William Carleton*. London, 1968.
Connolly, S.J. *Priests and people in pre-famine Ireland, 1780-1845*. Dublin, 1982. New edition, Dublin 2001.
Coolahan, John. *Irish education: its history and structure*. Dublin, 1991. 1st edition 1981.
Corcoran, Timothy. *Selected texts on education systems in Ireland from the close of the middle ages*. Dublin, 1928.
Corkery, Daniel. *The hidden Ireland*. Dublin, 1984. 1st edition 1924.
——*Imeachtaí na teanga Gaeilge*.
Crane, S. Ronald. *The vogue of medieval chivalric romance during the English renaissance*. Menasha, Wis. 1919.
Daly, Mary and Dickson, David. *The origins of popular literacy in Ireland: Language change and educational development 1700-1920*. Dublin, 1990.
Darton, F.J. Harvey. *Children's books in England*. Cambridge, 1982. 3rd edition.
Dowling, Patrick J. *The hedge schools of Ireland*. Dublin, 1932.
Elliott, Marianne. *Partners in revolution*. New Haven & London, 1982.

Ellis, Alec. *How to find out about children's literature.* Oxford, 1968.

Hyland, Áine and Milne, Kenneth. *Irish educational documents, Vol. 1.* Dublin, 1987.

Kiely, Benedict. *Poor Scholar. A study of William Carleton.* Dublin, 1972.

Lawson, John and Silver, Harold. *A social history of education in England.* London, 1973.

McGrath, Thomas. *Politics, Interdenominational relations and education in the public ministry of Bishop James Doyle of Kildare and Leighlin, 1786-1834.* Dublin, 1999.

Milne, Kenneth. *The Irish Charter schools, 1730-1830.* Dublin, 1997.

Murphy, John A. (ed.). *The French are in the bay: The expedition to Bantry Bay 1796.* Mercier Press, 1997.

Neuburg, Victor E. *The penny histories.* London, 1968.

Ó Ciosáin, Niall. *Print and popular culture in Ireland, 1750-1850.* Basingstoke, 1997.

O'Connell, Philip. *The schools and scholars of Breiffne.* Dublin, 1942.

Ó Fiannachta, Pádraig. *Léas ar ár litríocht.* Má Nuad, 1974.

Ó Tuama, Seán. *Caoineadh Airt Uí Laoghaire.* Baile Átha Cliath, 1979.

Ó Tuathaigh, Gearóid. *Ireland before the famine 1798–1848.* Dublin, 1972.

Parkes, S.M. *Kildare Place: the history of the Church of Ireland training college 1811–1969.* Dublin, 1984.

Paulin, Tom. *Ireland and the English crisis.* Newcastle-upon-Tyne, 1984.

Philipin, C.H.E. *Nationalism and popular protest in Ireland.* Cambridge, 1987.

Pollard, M. *Dublin's Trade in books 1500-1800.* Oxford, 1989.

Punter, David. *The literature of terror.* Harlow, Essex, 1996.

Raftery, Deirdre. *Women and learning in English writing 1600-1900.* Dublin, 1997.

Senior, Hereward. *Orangeism in Ireland and Britain 1795–1836.* London, 1966.

Schlauch, Margaret. *Antecedents of the English novel.* London, 1963.

Smith, Anthony D. *National identity.* Penguin Books, 1991.

Smyth, Jim. *The men of no property.* London, 1998.

Spufford, Margaret. *Small books and pleasant histories.* London, 1981.

Townsend, John Rowe. *Written for children.* London, 1990.

Turner, Cheryl. *Living By the pen.* London, 1994.

Vance, Norman. *Irish literature a social history.* Oxford, 1990.

Whalley, Joyce Irene. *Cobwebs to catch flies: illustrated books for the nursery and school-room, 1700-1900.* London, 1974.

Williams, J.E. Caerwyn and Ford, Patrick K. *The Irish literary tradition.* Cardiff, 1992.

WORKS OF REFERENCE

Baker, Ernest A. The history of the English novel, in 8 volumes. London, 1929.

Catalogue of Irish manuscripts in the Royal Irish Academy. Fasciculi VI-X. Dublin, 1931–1933.

Dictionary of National Biography in 22 Volumes. Sir Leslie Stephen and Sir Sidney Lee (eds.) London, 1917.

Lewis, Samuel. *A Topographical Dictionary of Ireland.* London, 1837.

Manuscript Sources for the History of Irish Civilisation in 11 volumes. London, 1965.

O'Fiannachta, Pádraig. *Lámhscribhinní Gaeilge. Fascúil VIII*. Má Nuad, 1973.

Parkes, Susan M. *Irish Education in the British Parliamentary Papers in the nineteenth century and after, 1801–1920*. Cork.

Periodical Sources for the History of Irish Civilisation in 9 volumes. London 1970.

Index